FINLAND'S WAR OF CHOICE

FINLAND'S WAR OF CHOICE

THE TROUBLED GERMAN-FINNISH COALITION IN WWII

HENRIK O. LUNDE

CASEMATE

Philadelphia & Newbury

Published in the United States of America and Great Britain in 2011 by
CASEMATE PUBLISHERS
908 Darby Road, Havertown, PA 19083
and
17 Cheap Street, Newbury RG14 5DD

ISBN 978-1-935149-48-4
Digital Edition: ISBN 978-1-61200-037-4

Cataloging-in-publication data is available from the Library of Congress
and the British Library.

10 9 8 7 6 5 4 3 2

Printed and bound in the United States of America.

For a complete list of Casemate titles please contact:

CASEMATE PUBLISHERS (US)
Telephone (610) 853-9131, Fax (610) 853-9146
E-mail: casemate@casematepublishing.com

CASEMATE PUBLISHERS (UK)
Telephone (01635) 231091, Fax (01635) 41619
E-mail: casemate-uk@casematepublishing.co.uk

CONTENTS

MAPS

PREFACE AND
ACKNOWLEDGMENTS

In the Winter War (November 1939–March 1940), Finland was left alone to face Soviet aggression with only a modicum of assistance from Western countries. Many books and studies have been written about this conflict. The extensive coverage in English of this three-and-a-half month struggle should not be surprising—for it represented the gallant fight of a democratic "David" against a totalitarian "Goliath." The bravery and determination of the Finns against insurmountable odds captured the imagination of the whole world.

The same is not true for the much longer and bloodier war that Finland fought against the Soviet Union at the side of Germany from 1941 to 1944—and their subsequent campaign to drive the Germans out of Finland in 1944–45. It might be true, as Olli Vehviläinen writes, that the war in North Europe was "buried under the avalanche of more newsworthy events in the greater war," but this was not the only reason.[1]

Professor John H. Wuorinen writes the following in the foreword to his book, based on an anonymous Finnish manuscript, which he edited and published in 1948:

> A document which tries to give an objective account therefore cannot be published without unpleasant consequences for author and publisher alike. If this were not so, this book would no doubt have been published in Finland months ago, and the name of the Finnish author would occupy the customary place on the title page.[2]

While it is difficult to pinpoint how long after the war the condition described by Wuorinen persisted, it is worth noting that that the official

1

history of Finland's involvement in World War II was not finished until 1994, more than thirty years after a similar multi-volume history about the war in Norway was completed.

The war at the side of Germany was not viewed in the same manner in the West as was the Winter War—it was not seen as a courageous and gallant fight to preserve democracy and freedom against a giant totalitarian neighbor. While numerous works on the war have been published in Finland, it is to be deplored that virtually none have been translated into English. The war at the side of Hitler was not one that brought pride to the nation and was a period many Finns would rather forget. Due to the lack of impartial and balanced treatment, large segments of the public in the US and Europe continue to believe that Finland found itself at the side of Germany in 1941 because it was attacked by the Soviet Union.

The Finns also refer to the war at the side of Germany as the "Continuation War," an attempt to depict it as a continuance of the Winter War in order, perhaps, to obtain a more favorable reception both domestically and internationally. Both this attempt and the insistence that it was an independent war waged against the Soviet Union fail to stand up to close scrutiny. It has proven hard to overcome the fact that Finland was the only democratic country at Hitler's side.

The Finns' own views about the war at the side of Germany have changed over the years. In the earlier period there was a tendency to emphasize the error of their decision to align themselves with Germany. Later, they appear to have come to the conclusion that the war was a struggle for survival and that the government made what it thought to be the least harmful choice among bad alternatives. While validating the fact that Finland found itself in an isolated and dangerous position after the Winter War and the German conquests in the West, this book will also demonstrate to the reader that there were other alternatives, which were not seriously pursued.

A defensive alliance between Finland, Norway, and Sweden after the Winter War as proposed by Finland and supported by the other two was not specifically prohibited by the Peace of Moscow or its protocols and should have been pressed harder by all countries. It was a serious policy mistake by the Soviet Union to oppose the formation of such a defensive alliance. It may well have spared the whole of Scandinavia from involvement in World War II. Similarly, the military political union proposed by Sweden and accepted by Finland later in 1940 would have benefited the Soviet Union as it specifically ruled out a Finnish war of revenge.

While examining these issues, the main purpose of the book is to deal with the unique problems that arose from an ill-prepared coalition between a democracy and a dictatorship. This book addresses the problems caused by differing war aims and the failure to make plans much past the initial assaults. Following Germany's victories in France and the Low Countries in 1940, it became axiomatic in both Finland and Germany that bringing about the military collapse of the Soviet Union would be easy and take a short time. Likewise, both appear to have harbored the view that Great Britain and the Dominions were defeated. These views are understandable in view of the spectacular victories Germany had racked up in less than two years. An underestimation of British determination—backed by the vast arsenal of the United States— as well as the resilience of the Soviet Union, undoubtedly contributed to a number of unwise decisions by both Germans and Finns.

The harsh and unforgiving climate and terrain in northern Scandinavia and the problems these posed for men and machines in military operations are considered throughout the book. The roads and railroads in this area were marginal and that, together with the great distances involved, posed severe problems for the logistical support of operations.

It became necessary to deviate from a strict chronological approach in this book. Some subjects recur in different time periods and must therefore be discussed in more than one chapter. For the convenience of the reader, complete dates are often provided to avoid confusion.

The Finns were sensitive to what happened on other fronts in World War II, particularly in the area south of Leningrad. Events in these areas influenced Finnish views on the war and consequently impacted on their political/military decision-making. I have therefore woven summaries of events on other fronts into the various chapters thereby hoping to make it easier for readers to understand events in Finland and the relations between Finland and Germany in context.

The best and most comprehensive accounts in English of the German-Finnish coalition war are those written by Earl F. Ziemke and General der Infanterie Waldemar Erfurth, the Chief of the German liaison staff at the Finnish headquarters.[3] Ziemke's work, *The German Northern Theater of Operations* was written in 1959 for the US Department of the Army while Erfurth's book (based on a book he had published in German in 1950) was written under the auspices of the Foreign Military Studies Branch of the Historical Division, European Command, more than twenty years later. Another work of historical research that deserves mention is Major James F. Gebhardt's book, written for the Combat Studies Institute of the US Army in 1989. This excellent study deals in detail with the Soviet breakthrough and pursuit in the Arctic region in late 1944.

There are a number of books by German participants written from the 1950s to the 1980s that have not been translated into English. Some are unit histories. There are also a number of books in Swedish and Norwegian, but again they have not been translated.

Two books by Finnish-Americans, John H. Wuorinen, and Leonard C. Lundin, deserve mention. They were written in 1948 and 1957 respectively.

The memoirs of Marshal Carl Gustaf Mannerheim, the Finnish commander in chief, were published in Swedish after his death in 1952, and in English in 1954. There are numerous discrepancies between what is contained in Mannerheim's memories, noted throughout this book, and what appear in other sources. Marshal Mannerheim did not begin writing his memoirs until illness forced him to move to Switzerland for medical treatment—to the Valmont Sanatorium in Montreaux. His memoirs were written with the help of a number of generals and colonels headed by General Erik Heinrichs, his former chief of staff. Since his book was not finished when the marshal died in January 1951, Colonel Aladar Paasonen, chief of Finnish Intelligence, was given the task of completing the manuscript. The reader should keep this fact in mind as we encounter the discrepancies.

The most recent work translated into English of which I am aware is that written by the Finnish historian Olli Vehviläinen in 2002. However, this excellent book of 199 pages is only partially devoted to Finland's war at the side of Germany. Furthermore the part dedicated to military operations deals primarily with Finnish operations while little space is given to German operations in Finland. Finally, it is weighted toward the political and foreign policy aspects of the war.

Military operations in Finland had profound strategic consequences for the outcome of the war on the Eastern Front. It is hoped that this book, by building on the research and writings of others, will provide useful information in English for the student of military history on an aspect of World War II that is virtually unknown in the West. This book analyzes military operations and military decisions and tries to put them in context of what was happening on other fronts and in the international political arena. In addition, the study of past military operations in the Arctic region with its increasing strategic importance because of the abundance of oil and other natural resources is a worthwhile endeavor.

This book does not address social, economic, and political affairs in Finland during the war unless they are viewed as impacting on military operations or decisions. Additionally, the book does not address air and naval operations to the same extent as land operations. This is not to slight those two services but is primarily due to the scarcity of sources available to me. My own difficulty in reading Finnish has served as a limitation on the use of Finnish sources. The archives of the former Soviet Union have been partially opened and these will undoubtedly throw some new light on the events of the war in the future. My use of Russian sources has basically been limited to works that have been translated to English.

Concerning the names of locations in Finland I have not followed a set pattern. Many names of geographic locations in the territories that are now under Russian control differ from one map to another and some of the places are so small that they do not appear on maps available to me, not even on the excellent maps in Ari Raunio's war atlas. When I use Finnish names in these areas I place the Russian names in parentheses if they are known. Likewise when I use Russian names I place the Finnish exonyms in parentheses—again if they are known to me.

I owe a special debt to all who have written about the various aspects of the war in Finland. They are frequently referenced in text and notes.

I am grateful to a number of libraries and archives, including Mr. Janne Hallikainen at the Photographic Center of the Finnish Defense Forces. The friendly and helpful staff of the Coyle Free Library in Chambersburg, Pennsylvania has been of great assistance. Glennis Garnes, in charge of the Inter-Library Loan Program, worked tirelessly to locate references from across the US, some of them rather obscure.

The Finnish Embassy in Washington, D.C., has helped address the

problem of name changes of locations in former Finnish areas that are
now part of Russia. Specifically, I want to mention the excellent assistance by Nina Pihlman and Ulla Ahola.

Jukka Juutinen, a Finnish national, has helped with the translation
of passages from Finnish sources and answered numerous questions that
I had over the past year. By making available Finnish views on various
aspects of the war he has made a valuable contribution.

My friend, Dr. Enoch Haga of Folsom, California has read and
proofed every draft. He has provided helpful suggestions on various
aspects of the project from its inception. Dr. Loislane Lowe in California
has also assisted in the proofing and editorial process.

Finally, it is obvious that I could not have completed this work without the understanding and support of my family. My debt to them is
immense.

Despite the diligence of those who provided assistance, comments
and advice, I must stress that I take full responsibility for all conclusions
and such errors as this book may inadvertently contain.

NOTES

1. Olli Vehviläinen, *Finland in the Second World War. Between Germany and
Russia.* Translated by Gerard McAlester (New York: Palgrave, 202), p.ix.

2. John H. Wuorinen, editor, *Finland and World War II, 1939–1940* (New York:
The Ronald Press Co, 1948), p.4. The actual author of the book was Professor Arvi
Korhonen who wrote the manuscript in 1945. Due to the political situation it was
not considered possible to publish the manuscript under the real author's name as
the tone was clearly anti-Soviet. Professor Korhonen later became known as the
father of the "drifting log theory." This information, provided by Jukka Juutinen, is
from Jari Leskinen and Antti Juutilainen (editors), *Talvisodan pikkujättiläinen*
(WSOY, 2009), p.29 and Ohto Manninen, *Molotovin cocktail-Hitlerin sateenvarjo*
(Painatuskeskus Oy, 1994), pp.144–145.

3. Waldemar Erfurth was also a doctor of philosophy and authored several books
on military history and strategy. He also served as the official Wehrmacht historian.

PROLOGUE

Turbulent Start

From the 13th century until the reshuffling of borders during the Napoleonic wars, Finland was an integral part of Sweden. Swedish rule brought Western culture and law as well as the Lutheran religion to the country. While most continued to speak Finnish, the official language for administrative purposes and use by the upper classes was Swedish. The Swedish empire in the Baltic began to disintegrate after losing its great-power status in the 18th century. However, it was not until 1809 that Finland was separated from Sweden and became a grand duchy of Russia with considerable local autonomy.

The Finns continued their semi-independence and Western orientation but after 1894 both became increasingly threatened by the drive to centralize the administration of the far-flung Russian empire. Finns were conscripted into the Russian military, new taxes were introduced, and a large number of Russian troops were stationed in the country. The Finns felt their way of life threatened by this centralization.

There was a respite in the centralization process after the unrest in Russia following the Russo-Japanese war. In 1906 Russia allowed the formation of a Finnish parliament based on universal suffrage and Finland became the first country in Europe to give women the vote. The independence movement that began with centralization continued but did not mature until the Bolshevik takeover in Russia in November 1917. The Bolsheviks' professed doctrine of self-determination for non-Russian nationalities gave encouragement to those who wanted nothing short of total independence.

Events appeared to go smoothly after Finland's declaration of independence on December 6, 1917. At the urging of Germany, then engaged in

peace negotiations with Russia, Finland presented a petition for independence to the new Bolshevik leadership. This petition was granted by the Council of People's Commissars on December 31 and sealed by a handshake between Vladimir Lenin and the Finnish representative, Pehr Edvind Svinhufund.

Finland's independence ushered in a turbulent period for the country. In twenty-four years Finland became embroiled in three wars with its large eastern neighbor.

The revolution in Russia also spread to Finland where opposition to the principles of the Bolsheviks was far from universal. A civil war broke out between those on the left (Reds) and landowners and nationalists (Whites). While the Reds were supported by Bolshevik troops, the Whites, under the command of an aristocrat and former general in the Russian Army, Carl Gustaf Mannerheim, gained the upper hand by the spring of 1918. The Whites received both troop and matériel support from the Germans who were interested in weakening Russia through the creation of independent states on its borders. In the end, after toying with the idea of a constitutional monarchy, Finland became a democratic republic with a unicameral parliament and a strong presidency.

In their negotiations with the Soviets the Finns tried to acquire the strategically important East Karelia, arguing for an eastern border running from the White Sea to Lake Ladoga (Laatokka). The Soviets were adamantly opposed and without the support of either Germany or the Western Allies in World War I, Finland had to settle for the boundaries of the former Grand Duchy. Finland's independence and borders were formally recognized by the Peace of Tartu in 1920.

Finland had a difficult time settling on a consistent foreign and security policy after independence. Most of these difficulties were caused by external events. The earlier pro-German orientation ended with Germany's defeat in World War I.

There followed a period of Western orientation along with enthusiastic support for the League of Nations. Even as late as August 2, 1937 Joseph E. Davies, the United States ambassador to the Soviet Union, reported from Helsinki that in European politics Finland followed England's signals because England was Finland's best customer.[1]

The Finns were dismayed by the inability of the League to do anything to hinder the conflicts that broke out in the 1930s and this resulted in a security policy based on neutrality. At the end of 1935 Finland joined the Scandinavian neutrality block. This was a natural move because of the close historical, cultural, and economic ties between the Scandinavian countries.[2] However, this association proved unworkable since these countries could not agree on a common policy when faced with a crisis.

Relations between Finland and Germany cooled in the 1930s. In Finland, as in the other Scandinavian countries, the Nazi regime was sharply criticized. In 1939, Finland caused considerable resentment in

Germany by joining Sweden and Norway in rejecting a proposed non-aggression pact.

Finland signed a non-aggression pact with the Soviet Union in 1932 at the latter's invitation, and this pact was renewed in 1934 for a period of ten years. Tensions with the Soviet Union began to grow in 1938 when the Soviets initiated secret discussions with Finland. The reason for the discussion, according to the Soviet emissary, Boris Yartsev, was the possibility that in the event of a Soviet conflict with Germany, the latter might use Finland as a launch pad for an attack against the Soviet right flank. In such an eventuality, the Soviets would not wait for the attacker to advance to their border, but would strike the enemy in Finland. With this possibility in mind, the Soviets now demanded the right to aid Finland.

The confidential talks with Yartsev continued throughout the spring and summer. On August 11, 1938, the Finns presented Yartsev a draft treaty in which Finland formally declared that it would not permit any foreign power to obtain a foothold on its territory for an attack on the Soviet Union. The Soviets were requested to reiterate their assurance that they would respect Finland's territorial integrity. The Soviet Union was also asked to give its approval to the joint Finnish-Swedish remilitarization of the Åland (Ahvenanmaa) Islands.[3]

The Åland Islands, between Sweden and Finland in the northern Baltic, were demilitarized in accordance with an international treaty in 1921. However, there were growing fears that Germany or the Soviet Union would rush to occupy them in case of a European war.

The Swedish and Finnish governments had agreed that Finland should, with Swedish assistance, embark on a partial remilitarization of the islands. This was approved by the signers of the 1921 agreement and by the League of Nations. The Soviet Union—to which this proposal was also presented although it had not signed the 1921 agreement—delayed its answer and implied that permission would be granted only on condition that the Soviet Union was given the same status as Sweden in defending the neutrality of the islands.[4]

On August 18, 1938 the Soviets demanded a written pledge that Finland would repel a German attack and agree to accept Soviet armed assistance. They also demanded facilities on the Finnish island of Suursaari (Gogland) in the Gulf of Finland for the purpose of building an air and naval base. In return, the Soviets offered to guarantee Finland's independence and territory and to conclude a favorable trade treaty. The Finnish government rejected the proposals.

Soviet Foreign Minister Maxim Litvinov initiated fresh proposals in March 1939. He asked the Finns for the lease of five small islands in the Gulf of Finland so that the Soviet Union could defend the Leningrad passage.[5] Mannerheim, who was now Chairman of Finland's Council of Defense, advised the government not to reject these new proposals without trying to reach a compromise. The government did not heed his advice and rejected the Soviet proposal on March 8. Litvinov sent a special emissary, Boris Stein, to Helsinki to discuss the matter. He offered Finland 183 square kilometers of land on the eastern frontier in exchange for the islands.[6] Mannerheim again advised meeting Stein halfway but again the government did not agree.[7] The discussions broke down on April 6. It was not the failure of these negotiations that changed the situation between Finland and the Soviet Union radically in 1939 but rather the new relationship between Germany and the Soviet Union.

The Ribbentrop–Molotov Pact

On August 23, 1939 the German Foreign Minister, Joachim von Ribbentrop, flew to Moscow where he and the Soviet Foreign Minister, Vyacheslav Molotov, signed the now famous non-aggression pact. The two countries had already concluded an economic agreement on August 19.

The Soviet Union agreed on the economic accord to provide food products and raw materials to Germany in exchange for finished products. In the non-aggression pact, both countries agreed not to take aggressive action against each other if either became involved in war.

A secret protocol to the non-aggression pact (its existence was denied by the Soviets until 1989) spelled out the respective spheres of influence of the two countries in the Baltic area. It reads in part:

> In the event of a territorial and political rearrangement in the areas belonging to the Baltic states [Finland, Estonia, Latvia, and Lithuania], the northern boundary of Lithuania shall represent the boundary of the spheres of influence of Germany and the U.S.S.R.[8]

This shows that Germany left Finland within the Soviet sphere of influence.

This non-aggression pact gave the Soviets the buffer they desired as protection against an attack from the west, something they had been unable to secure from France and Britain in earlier negotiations that summer. For three centuries, the creation of a buffer zone had been—and continues to be—a central goal of Russian security policy.

Russia's concern for its security is understandable when viewed in historical context. For 300 years Russia had faced devastating attacks from the west, beginning with the Swedish invasion in the Great Nordic War (1699–1720) and continuing with the invasions of Napoleon and later Germany, Austria, and Turkey in World War I. It is regrettable that Russian fears led to occupation and repression of neighbors with common borders. The non-aggression pact also secured for Joseph Stalin time to modernize and increase the strength of the Soviet military forces. These forces had been badly weakened by earlier purges, as was soon to be demonstrated by their less than stellar performance in the Winter War.

For Germany, the pacts (economic and non-aggression) were viewed by Adolf Hitler as a temporary detour on the road to the ultimate military destruction of the Soviet Union. They removed the immediate threat of a two-front war. If the Western Allies couldn't count on cooperation from the Soviet Union, Hitler speculated that they would not react militarily to his planned invasion of Poland since there was no way for them to influence the fate of that country without Soviet assistance. In addition, the pacts secured for Germany important economic resources needed for its war industries, thus minimizing the effects of any possible economic blockade.

The Soviet Union acted quickly to take advantage of the free hand given by the Germans in the Baltic region. Each of the Baltic states—Estonia, Latvia, and Lithuania—individually received an *invitation* for their foreign ministers to come to Moscow to negotiate. These negotiations ended in the Baltic states being forced to accept demands granting the Soviet Union bases and mutual aid pacts. Thereafter, these countries were independent in name only. Eventually, during the summer of 1940, they were absorbed into the Soviet Union.

Soviet–Finnish Negotiations

The announcement of the pact between the Soviet Union and Germany did not worry the Finns initially. They even felt safer since their two powerful neighbors had come to an understanding, thus lessening the chance of a war in the Baltic. This view was further strengthened by announcements by German officials. The German ambassador to Moscow, Count Friedrich Werner von Schulenburg, announced on August 30, 1939 that there had been no discussion of any spheres of influence to which Finland might belong at the Moscow meeting in August between Ribbentrop and Molotov.[9] This blatant misstatement of facts was made possible because spheres of influence were spelled out only in the secret protocol mentioned above.

The Soviet Union significantly strengthened its defensive position in the west through the acquisition of air and naval bases in the Baltic states. However, Soviet leaders felt that the security of Leningrad would be menaced as long as they did not fully control sea and land approaches—Leningrad's suburbs were located only around 30 kilometers from the Finnish border.[10]

The Soviet government initiated negotiations with Finland on October 5, 1939, apparently expecting the latter to make concessions similar to those made by the Baltic states. It was suggested that Foreign Minister Väinö Tanner or his representative come to Moscow as soon as possible because the Soviets desired an exchange of ideas with Finland concerning certain political questions caused by the outbreak of World War II. Finland agreed on October 8 to send a representative to Moscow.[11]

The Finns became alarmed over the Soviet request for *negotiations*. To prevent any surprises, several classes of reserves were called to the colors on October 10.

The Finnish foreign minister, Väinö Tanner, asked the German ambassador to Finland, Wipert von Blücher, to see him on October 6. Tanner stated that he did not know what the Soviets had in mind. He pointed out that while Finland was willing to make compromises, any demands involving the Åland Islands or Viipuri (Vyborg) would be rejected. The foreign minister also asked what the position of Germany would be if Finland found Soviet demands unacceptable.[12]

Blücher forwarded a report of the conversation to Berlin. The answer from the director of the Political Department of the German Foreign Ministry arrived the following day. It stated that a conflict between the Soviet Union and Finland was unlikely but that Germany would remain neutral in any such conflict.[13]

Juho Kusti Paasikivi—a former prime minister and ambassador to the Soviet Union—was selected to go to Moscow. He was instructed to make no commitments with respect to military bases on Finnish territory and adjustments of the border on the Karelian Isthmus. On the other hand, the exchange of certain islands in the Gulf of Finland for other territorial compensation was possible.[14]

Sweden now became involved in the diplomatic maneuvering. The Swedish ambassador to Germany, Arvid Richert, called on German State Secretary Ernst von Weizsäcker on October 9, 1939 to enquire about Germany's position on the current problems in Finnish–Soviet relations. Weizsäcker answered that he was unaware of any Soviet demands and that Finland had not been discussed during the visit to Moscow by the German Foreign Minister.[15]

It was obvious to the political and military leaders in Finland that Germany would not provide armed assistance as she had in 1918, but they continued to hope for support in their Moscow negotiations. In his report from Helsinki on October 10, Blücher requested that the possibility of support be considered in one way or another without departing from their basic policy towards the Soviet Union.[16] This request was turned down because it would imperil Germany's relationship with the Soviet Union at a very critical time.[17]

The question about Germany's response should any or all of the Scandinavian nations come to Finland's aid in case of a Soviet attack became more and more pressing as negotiations proceeded in Moscow. Blücher put the following question to the German Foreign Ministry at the request of the Finnish foreign minister on October 10: "Will Germany refrain from disturbing Sweden if Sweden should come to the aid of Finland militarily?"[18] This and the following document (Document No 228) are the first indications that there was anxiety in Germany about possible Scandinavian intervention in a war between Finland and the Soviet Union. The answer came the same day and it stated that any promise to refrain from interference if Sweden sided with Finland militarily would be based on the condition that Sweden guarantee the continued deliveries of iron ore and refrain from giving France and Britain access to the Baltic.[19]

In mid-October the Finns took a step to influence German public opinion, already strongly pro-Finnish, by proposing to send the popular former President Pehr Evind Svinhufund to Germany. The German foreign minister at once ordered Blücher to take appropriate steps to prevent his trip since it would endanger Russo-German relations.[20]

The Soviets presented their demands on October 14. They included: (1) a readjustment of the border on the Karelian Isthmus; (2) a thirty-year lease of the port of Hanko for the purpose of establishing a naval base; (3) Suursaari and other islands at the eastern end of the Gulf of Finland; (4) an island commanding the entrance to the Bay of Viipuri; and (5) the Finnish part of the Rybachiy Peninsula, which would enable Russia to dominate the approach to Pechenga (Petsamo), Finland's outlet on the Arctic Ocean.[21] In exchange the Soviet government offered to surrender some 5,527 square kilometers of territory in Soviet Karelia along the eastern frontier of Finland, north of Lake Ladoga.[22]

The proposed frontier changes on the Karelian Isthmus involved the resettlement of a considerable Finnish population, some valuable industrial areas, and Finland's main defense works. The territory offered in exchange did not compensate for the Karelian territory in value, and Finland viewed it as a future bone of contention between the two countries since the area offered had a relatively large Russian population.

The Soviets insisted that their demands were minimal for the security of Leningrad. The negotiations were in limbo for the next two weeks until the Soviets made them public on October 31, 1939. The Finns felt that the announcement amounted to an ultimatum since the prestige of the Soviet Union as a great power would not permit a retreat from a stated public position.[23]

Negotiations resumed on November 3, 1939 and a climax was reached on November 4. The Finns presented a memorandum in which the lease of Hanko was ruled out. Furthermore, Finland would not agree to the demolition of fortifications on the Karelian Isthmus since they were vital for security.[24] The Finnish delegation left Moscow on November 13.

England, France, the Scandinavian countries, and the US presented notes to the Soviet Union expressing their hopes that the Soviets would not make demands on Finland which would lead to conflict. However, it appears that the Western powers as well as Germany believed that the Soviet Union would not resort to war.

When Dino Alfieri, the Italian ambassador to Germany, called on Weizsäcker on November 30 to clarify Germany's position on the conflict that had just begun between Finland and the Soviet Union, Weizsäcker said that he could not tell him much since his information on the outbreak of hostilities and previous negotiations between Finland and the Soviet Union was scant.[25] From this and other German Foreign Office documents, it appears that Germany believed that a war would not break out in the Baltic involving the Soviet Union and Finland. The embarrassment to Germany was increased by the fact that Italy, Germany's closest ally, openly favored the Finnish cause. Italy had already begun to support Finland with arms and volunteers. However, German action in the evacuation of its citizens from Finland on a voluntary basis in late November indicated that they were not taken completely by surprise when hostilities broke out.[26]

The Winter War

The Soviet Union attacked Finland on November 30, 1939, hoping for a quick victory. However, the attack bogged down with the Soviets suffering heavy losses. After regrouping and bringing up reinforcements, the Soviets resumed their offensive on February 1, 1940. It was to last for forty-two days. The Soviet attack on the Karelian Isthmus was backed by thirty infantry divisions reinforced by strong artillery and armored forces.[27] After two weeks of ferocious fighting resulting in enormous Soviet casualties, the Mannerheim Line was breached on February 13 and by March 1 the Finnish right flank had been pushed back to the city of Viipuri. The situation for the Finns had become desperate. They were short of supplies and their troops were exhausted. The hoped-for—and promised—assistance from the West had not materialized. The total number of foreign volunteers in Finland numbered only 11,500 and 8,275 of these were from Scandinavia—mostly from Sweden. The volunteers also included 300 men in the Finnish-American Legion who received their baptism of fire in the last days of the war.[28]

Blücher suggested to Berlin that under the circumstances that had developed since the outbreak of the Soviet-Finnish War, as well as the exhibition of Soviet military weakness, that it might be possible to adopt an entirely different tone toward Moscow (compared to that of August and September). Furthermore, he pointed out that a Soviet alignment with the Western powers was out of the question since she had seriously compromised herself in these countries through her actions in Finland.[29]

The policy advocated by Blücher in his letter was exactly that which was followed unofficially by the German government in the months that followed. This unofficial attitude came in the form of hints through official and unofficial German channels that the Soviet Union should come to an agreement with Finland.

The consequences of the Soviet-Finnish War for Germany began to be felt increasingly in January 1940. The drawbacks were outlined on January 25 by an official of the German Embassy in the Soviet Union.[30] He emphasized the dwindling supply of raw materials from the Soviet Union to Germany and the danger that the rest of Scandinavia might be drawn into the conflict on the side of Britain and France. Much weight was placed on the fact that the inherent weakness of the Red Army had been revealed in Finland.

The French and British governments offered to send an expeditionary force if the Finns formally asked for it and if Norway and Sweden provided transit facilities. But it was not until March 7, one week before the end of the war, that General Sir Edmund Ironside, chief of the British Imperial General Staff, was able to inform Finland that a force of 57,000 men was ready and that the first division of 15,000 men could be at the Finnish front before the end of the month.[31] Actually, five days previously, both Sweden and Norway had denied transit for troops on their way to Finland. Finland was undoubtedly aware of this and, like the other Scandinavian countries, harbored strong suspicion that the actual objective of the Allies was to seize the iron ore fields in north Sweden from where Germany received so much of her high-grade iron ore.

In general, the Western powers welcomed the possibility of a continuation of the Soviet-Finnish War. They hoped that by helping Finland, Norway and Sweden might be brought into the anti-German block, and even if this did not materialize, the iron ore that Germany received from Sweden could be cut off. A continuation of the war would disrupt the Soviet economy and economic aid to Germany from the Soviet Union would suffer. This, on top of possible British control of the Baltic, could be disastrous for Germany.

The actions taken by the Allies were of course known to the Germans and made them increase their indirect efforts to get the Soviet Union to reach a settlement with Finland. The Swedish Embassy in Moscow was the main channel used by the Germans.[32]

Increasing pressure for German intervention in the negotiations was also placed on the German Foreign Office by German officials in Moscow. Ribbentrop told Blücher on February 13 that it was possible that Germany might mediate in the Soviet-Finnish conflict in the future but he did not state when or how.[33] Blücher suggested to Foreign Minister Tanner on February 1940 that a person respected by the Soviets should meet secretly with some Russians in a third country, preferably Germany, to iron out their differences and arrive at an agreement.[34] This proposal was presented to Ribbentrop, who was requested to feel out Moscow's attitude. These negotiations never materialized, apparently because the Soviets scored their first military victories a few days later.

In a telegram on March 12, Schulenburg stated that it appeared that negotiations arranged by Vilhelm Assarsson, the Swedish ambassador in Moscow, would come to a standstill because of renewed Soviet demands. He asked for permission to hint to Molotov that Germany would welcome a positive conclusion to the negotiations.[35]

Before an agreement was reached between Finland and the Soviet Union through Swedish mediation, the Soviets tried to use Great Britain as an intermediary. The Soviet ambassador to Britain, Ivan Maiski, asked Lord Halifax, the British foreign secretary, on February 26 to transmit the terms that had already been handed to Finland through Sweden but had been rejected because they were too harsh.[36] Lord Halifax answered that he considered the terms unreasonable and refused to transmit them. Maiski then threatened that this British attitude might lead to unexpected developments between Britain and the Soviet Union. Lord Halifax answered that it was hard to prevent conflict between the two nations if the Soviet Union continued its present policy.

Lord Halifax's statement may have convinced the Soviets that they needed to come to terms with Finland or run the risk of war with England and France. At the beginning of March 1940, the Soviets apparently felt that their recent military successes allowed them to soften their terms without a loss of prestige and thus avert Allied intervention.

The Soviets extended an invitation for a Finnish delegation to come to Moscow to discuss armistice terms. The delegation arrived in Moscow on March 7. The Finns, having committed all their trained manpower, and with no hopes of help, agreed to the Soviet demands which were incorporated in the Peace of Moscow on March 12, 1940. The terms—while harsh—were nevertheless not as severe as some had expected, probably because Stalin wanted to terminate the conflict before the Allies could intervene. The cool attitude displayed by Germany was also seen by the Soviets as a warning sign.

While the Soviet losses in the Winter War have never been published, most observers believe that more than 200,000 were killed and a much larger number wounded. The Finns lost 24,923 killed and 43,557 wounded.[37] This was an enormous loss for a nation with a population of only 3.75 million.

Aftermath of the Winter War

The territorial losses resulting from the Winter War amounted to about 64,750 square kilometers or about 10 per cent of Finland's total prewar area, containing about 12 per cent of the population. The Karelian Isthmus, including the province and city of Viipuri, and a large piece of territory north of Lake Ladoga were lost. The loss in resources and manufacturing capacity was devastating. The losses in agricultural lands, forestry, and production of forestry products were almost as severe.

Also lost were several islands in the Gulf of Finland, part of the Rybachiy Peninsula in the far north, and large segments in the Salla-Kuusamo area in the central part of the country. Finland was forced to lease Hanko and the surrounding area at the entrance to the Gulf of Finland to the Soviets for a period of 30 years. Hanko, along with Viipuri, had handled about a quarter of all Finnish exports.

Finland also had to agree to extend the railway from Kemijärvi (southwest of Salla) to the new frontier at Salla within a year. The Pechenga area which had been occupied by the Russians was returned to Finland, probably because of the foreign interests in the nickel mines.

The war left Finland with a monumental problem of having to move almost the entire population—between 400,000 and 500,000 people—of the lost territories to other parts of the country. While these included skilled and semi-skilled workers, a large portion consisted of independent farmers. The resettlement operation, which created new homesteads for the displaced farmers, also produced internal tensions. Much of the land on which these refugees were resettled was in the Swedish-speaking area of the country and this caused some difficult situations.

Finally, the ceded territories represented a crushing strategic blow as they "left the country" in the words of Mannerheim "open to attack and the Hanko base was like a pistol aimed at the heart of the country and its most important communications."[38] The border on the Karelian Isthmus and in the Lake Ladoga area was pushed back and had no fortifications. The war had demonstrated that the Finns did not have the manpower to adequately defend the central and northern area of the country. Acquisition of the Salla area and the demand that the Finns construct a railway from Kemijärvi to Salla where it would connect with a line being constructed by the Soviets was alarming. It created an opportunity for the Soviets to quickly penetrate the waist of Finland to the Swedish border.

There is little doubt that the difficulties the Russians encountered in the Winter War had a profound effect on Hitler and his advisers. Earlier respect for the Soviet juggernaut underwent a radical change in some German circles. This is well demonstrated by an interesting letter from Blücher to Weizsäcker on January 11. It illustrates the changed attitude of Germany with respect to Soviet military strength as well as to the Ribbentrop–Molotov Pact:

> "... the experience gained in Finland shows that Russia has not for some time past constituted a threat to the great power, Germany, and that Germany already had a safe flank in the east and did not need to make any sacrifices for it."[39]

Hitler and many in the German military seriously underestimated the Soviet Army in the period 1940–41 and their views were surely influenced by that army's poor performance in the Winter War. "The Russian mass is no match for an army with modern equipment and superior leadership" was the tone of a German General Staff view on December 31, 1939.[40] Such views had a major influence on later decisions.

Finland's Isolation

The German conquest of Norway and Denmark in the spring of 1940 served to further isolate Finland from the rest of the world. The inability of the Western Allies to come to Finland's aid and their embarrassing performance in Norway seriously eroded their standing as military powers both with the Finnish government and the Finnish people.[41] The German defeat of France completed this process and left Germany as the dominant power on the continent. No future assistance would be likely from the British who were expected to court favor with the Soviet Union at the expense of Finland.

Finland's one remaining port by which it could carry out normal trade with the West was located in Petsamo (Pechenga) and it was separated from the nearest railroad by over 300 kilometers. Importation of food supplies became very difficult and a two-year drought exacerbated this situation.

Another result of the German conquest of Norway was as important as Finland's virtual isolation from the rest of the world. This was the fact that as of late summer of 1940, German troops had arrived on Finland's northern border. This did not occur immediately after the capitulation of Norwegian forces in north Norway on June 10, 1940. The status of Norwegian security forces along the border in the eastern part of the Finnmark Province was part of the negotiations leading up to the capitulation. General Otto Ruge, the commander in chief of the Norwegian armed forces, stressed the importance of a continuous military presence along the border (over 600 kilometers from the nearest German units) in order to insure that there were no violations by foreign powers exploiting a vacuum. The Germans accepted Ruge's suggestion that Norwegian troops continue to secure the border until relieved by German forces.[42]

Norwegian troops in Finnmark were slowly relieved by arriving German units over the next five weeks. The transfer of responsibility and the demobilization of Norwegian forces were completed on July 17, 1940.

The changed military situation allowed Germany to put pressure on both Sweden and Finland. If the Norwegians and the Allies had managed to thwart the German occupation of Norway, that fact would probably have kept Finland from joining Germany in its attack on the Soviet Union.

Hitler's Decision to Deal with the Soviet Union
We have seen that the Soviets took advantage of Germany's preoccupation in the west to quickly consolidate their sphere of influence in the

Baltic region accorded to it in the non-aggression pact with Germany on August 23, 1939. However, the notion that Hitler's decision to attack the Soviet Union had anything to do with Soviet actions in this region is misleading. Hitler's attack on the Soviet Union had deep roots in his ideology going back to the early 1920s. His entry into a closer relationship with the Soviet Union in 1939 was a temporary adjustment to his long-range policy. The timing of his attack was based on strategic considerations.

Hitler concluded that Britain's intransigence was based on their hope of Soviet support and the eventual US entry into the war. He viewed a cross-Channel invasion as too hazardous without having a secure backyard and believed that the British might be more reasonable and come to terms if the Soviet Union could be eliminated from their calculations.

The Soviet Union continued to deliver the food and raw materials arranged for in the economic agreement of August 1939, and Stalin may have increased deliveries if it had been requested by Germany. However, Hitler did not like to depend on something outside his control and in a long war he saw the need for raw materials on a far greater scale than that agreed upon. He felt that it was important to strike while the German armed forces were at peak strength and before his opponents had a chance to strengthen their positions.

Hitler had already decided in July 1940 that he needed to deal with the Soviet Union. His decision was probably influenced by the quick British rejection of the peace feelers floated in his speech to the Reichstag on July 19. Hitler appeared puzzled by British intransigence based on an entry in the diary of General Franz Halder, Chief of the Army High Command (Oberkommando des Heeres—OKH) on July 13. Halder writes that Hitler believed that the British refusal to negotiate must be based on their hope for Soviet assistance and notes that he agreed with Hitler's conclusion that the Soviet Union had to be dealt with before Britain would become reasonable. However, it is equally likely that Hitler had already concluded that the British would reject a negotiated settlement and that his puzzlement was disingenuous.

It is with these facts in mind that we must view Hitler's announcement to his military commanders on July 21, 1940 that he planned to attack the Soviet Union that fall. He claimed that Great Britain was inciting the Soviets to take action against Germany by cutting her off from resources such as oil. He anticipated that the forces required to crush the Soviet army could be assembled in four to six weeks.[43]

Hitler's decision raised the specter of a two-front war. Major General Alfred Jodl, Chief of Operations at the Armed Forces High Command (Oberkommando der Wehrmacht—OKW), briefed his subordinates on July 29, 1940, on the intention to attack the Soviet Union. The prospect of a two-front war led to a protracted argument. Jodl reasoned that a settlement with the Soviet Union was inevitable and it was better to make that settlement while Germany's military prestige and power were as high as they were after a string of spectacular military successes.[44] It is difficult to tell if these were Jodl's own thoughts or whether he was merely a conveyor of Hitler's views.

Hitler, despite his earlier views that the two-front war in World War I had contributed to Germany's defeat and that a similar situation should be avoided in the future, now appeared to have changed his views or overestimated British helplessness. In the wake of the French capitulation he is reported to have told his military advisers that a campaign against the Soviet Union would be child's play.[45]

Despite Hitler's views that the forces required to defeat the Soviet Union could be assembled within four to six weeks, this rosy scenario was quickly ruled out by the German military as impractical.[46] In a meeting with Jodl on July 29, Hitler set May 1941 as the time for the attack and this was communicated to the other military leaders two days later.

The decision to attack the Soviet Union was not translated into a directive until December 18, 1940.[47] Nevertheless, war was not inevitable and Hitler had acknowledged on July 21 that the Soviets did not want a war with Germany. This feeling was even stronger among some of the senior military commanders. As of July 30 the commander in chief of the Army, Field Marshal Werner von Brauchitsch, and the chief of the General Staff, General Franz Halder, favored remaining on friendly terms with the Soviet Union. These two senior officers preferred concentrating on attacking the British in the Mediterranean and at Gibraltar.[48]

Despite these views, the German military did not overtly oppose Hitler's decision announced the following day. The General Staff had, in fact, started preparing feasibility studies for a war against the Soviet Union several weeks earlier.

NOTES

1. Wuorinen, *op. cit.*, p.43.

2. Carl Gustaf von Mannerheim, *The Memoirs of Marshal Mannerheim*. Translated by Count Eric Lewenhaupt (New York: E. P. Dutton & Company, Inc., 1954), pp.285–286.

3. Väinö Tanner, *Finlands Vag 1939–1940* (Stockholm: Albert Bonniers Forlag, 1950), p.13 and William L. Shirer, *The Challenge of Scandinavia* (Boston: Little, Brown and Company, 1955), pp.324–325.

4. Foreign Ministry Document as cited in Tanner, *op. cit.*, p.15.

5. Tanner, *op. cit.*, pp.24–25.

6. *Ibid*, p.25.

7. Mannerheim, *Memoirs*, p.301.

8. Sontag, Raymond James and Beddie, James Stuart, editors. *Nazi-Soviet Relations 1939–1941* (hereinafter *NSR*) (German Foreign Office Documents released by the US Department of State. New York: Didier, 1948), p.78.

9. Wuorinen, *op. cit.*, p.50.

10. It is worth noting that Winston Churchill showed considerable sympathy for the Soviet claims and advised that it would be a mistake to encourage the Finns not to make concessions. See David Reynolds, *In Command of History* (New York: Random House, 2005), p.121.

11. Finland, Ministry of Foreign Affairs. *The Development of Finnish–Soviet Relations During the Autumn of 1939 in the Light of Official Documents* (hereinafter *Documents Concerning Finnish–Soviet Relations*) (Helsinki: FMU, 1940), pp.42–45.

12. Germany. Auswärtiges Amt. *Documents on German foreign policy, 1918–1945* (hereinafter *DGFP*) (Washington: US Government Printing Office, 1954), volume 8, p.240, Document No 206.

13. *Ibid,* volume 8, p.240, Document No 215.

14. Tanner, *op. cit.*, pp.39–41.

15. *DGFP*, volume 8, p.248, Document No 223.

16. *Ibid,* volume 8, p.251, Document No 226.

17. *Ibid,* volume 8, p.267, Document No 240.

18. *Ibid,* volume 8, p.252, Document No 227.

19. *Ibid,* volume 8, p.252, Document No 228.

20. *Ibid,* volume 8, p.255, Document No 232.

21. *Documents Concerning Finnish–Soviet Relations*, p.49.

22. Mannerheim, *Memoirs*, p.311 lists the size of territory the Soviets were willing to give up in East Karelia as 3,455 square miles (8,948 square kilometers).

23. Wuorinen, *op. cit.*, p.58.

24. Hugh Shearman, *Finland. The Adventures of a Small Power* (London: Stevens and Sons Limited, 1950), p.89.

25. *DGFP*, volume 8, p.469, Document No 404.

26. *Ibid,* volume 8, p.268, Document No 241.

27. Wuorinen, *op. cit.*, p.69.

28. Mannerheim, *Memoirs*, p.359.

29. *DGFP*, volume 8, p.651, Document No 526.

30. *Ibid,* volume 8, p.706, Document No 574.

31. Churchill, Winston S. *The Second World War. The Gathering Storm* (Boston: Houghton Mifflin Company, 1948), pp.538–548.

32. Tanner, *op. cit.*, p.271.

33. *DGFP*, volume 8, p.774, Document No 612.

34. *Ibid,* volume 8, p.778, Document No 617.

35. *Ibid,* volume 8, p.869, Document No 661.

36. Wuorinen, *op. cit.*, p.76.

37. Mannerheim, *Memoirs*, p.370 and Richard W. Condon, *The Winter War. Russia against Finland* (New York, Ballantine Books, 1972), p.153.

38. Mannerheim, *Memoirs,* p.388.

39. *DGFP*, volume 8, p.650, Document No 526.

40. Harold C. Deutsch. Presidential address presented on December 27, 1946, at the 25th Anniversary meeting of Phi Alpha Theta, held in New York jointly with the meeting of the American Historical Association.

41. General Otto Ruge, the commander in chief of the Norwegian Armed Forces, sent a courier to Marshal Mannerheim at the end of the conflict in Norway. This courier, Captain Tage Ellinger, was asked about the military situation in Norway. After Captain Ellinger completed his briefing, Marshal Mannerheim remarked caustically that it was lucky for Finland that English troops had not come to help during the Winter War. Tage Ellinger, *Den Forunderlige Krig* (Oslo: Gyldendal Norsk Forlag, 1960), p.116.

42. Trygve Sandvik, *Operasjonene til lands i Nord-Norge 1940* (Oslo: Forsvarets Krigshistoriske Avdeling, 1965), volume 2, p.334 and Birger Gotaas, *Fra 9. april til 7. juni. Episoder og opplevelser fra krigen i Norge* (Oslo: J. Dybwand, 1945), p.229.

43. *Halder War Diary,* entry for July 21, 1940.

44. Walter Warlimont, *Inside Hitler's Headquarters 1939–45.* Translated by R. H. Barry (Novato, California: Presidio Press, 1964), pp.112–114. Warlimont notes that Hitler had already hinted at the necessity of dealing with the Soviet Union earlier in 1940, even before the campaign in the west was concluded.

45. Albert Speer, *Erinnerungen* (Frankfurt am Main, 1969), p.188.

46. Warlimont, *op. cit.*, p.112.

47. The preparations continued based on Hitler's verbal order on July 29 and 31. This order was confirmed in September 1940.

48. *Halder War Diary*, entries for July 21 and 30, 1940.

ONE

FROM FLIRTATION TO COALITION

Careful Approaches

Leonard Lundin writes that the period between the Winter War and Finland's involvement on the side of Germany in its war against the Soviet Union in 1941 presents difficult questions for historians.[1] The most important of these for our purposes was the responsibility of the Finnish political and military leaders for Finland's unfortunate involvement in World War II.

Despite the lack of support from Germany in the Winter War, there was a rapid shift in both Finnish governmental policy and public opinion in favor of Germany soon afterward.[2] The primary reason was Finland's isolation from the world following Germany's victories in Scandinavia and the West. To the Finns Germany looked like a rising star and the only country that could offer Finland some protection against the Soviet Union.[3]

In June 1940, as Germany was preoccupied in the west, the Soviet Union moved to occupy the Baltic states. Simultaneously, the Soviets began to exert renewed pressure on the Finns. The pressure took the form of several demands:

1. Return all properties removed from Hanko.
2. Soviet or joint operation of the nickel mines at Kolosjoki (Nikel).
3. Demilitarization of the Åland Islands.
4. Right to send trains across Finnish territory to Hanko.

The Finns agreed to demands 1 and 3 while the others were made subjects for negotiation. At the end of July the Soviets charged that the

Finns were trying to suppress the activities of Soviet supporters in the country. To the Finns these Soviet activities were ominous and could signal that military moves against the country were in the making. German intelligence shared this view and concluded that the Soviet Union could begin military operations against Finland in mid-August.[4]

Conservative circles in Finland had argued for closer cooperation with Germany, and urged the government in that direction, as the Western Allies were going down to defeat in France and as the Soviets occupying the Baltic states had begun to exert pressure on Finland.[5] The Finnish government needed little persuasion and its foreign minister, Rolf Witting, told the German ambassador in Helsinki, Wipert von Blücher, on July 4, 1940 that all efforts were directed at having a government oriented towards Germany. He also told Blücher that Finnish public opinion believed that the country would be able to reconquer its lost territories in the near future with the help of Germany. A month later Witting told Blücher that he wished to travel to Germany and meet with Hitler.[6]

Blücher told the Finnish foreign minister that it would be objectionable to have a Finnish government which overtly favored Germany. He suggested that a government that continued a neutral posture but cooperated secretly with Germany would be more acceptable. This statement was too strong for the German government. Blücher was admonished by his superiors and told to refrain from expressions that could raise false hopes among the Finns.[7]

However, the Germans soon began to show signs of reciprocity to the friendship expressed by the Finns. While this was no doubt tied to Hitler's decision to attack the Soviet Union, it began before the July 31, 1940 conference at which Hitler announced his decision.[8]

Another factor that influenced the change in German attitude involved the nickel mine concessions that were part of the Soviet demands on Finland. I. G. Farben, the German industrial concern, had contracted for delivery of 60 percent of the nickel ore production in July 1940. Finish nickel was of considerable importance to the German war industry, as was the supply of Swedish iron ore. The availability of these raw materials was an important factor in Hitler's decision-making.

German belief that the Soviet Union might attack Finland in August 1940 caused Hitler to reinforce north Norway with units from all three services. Mountain Corps Norway, formed in June 1940, consisted of the 2nd and 3rd Mountain Divisions under General der Gebirgstruppe

Eduard Dietl. The 2nd Mountain Division, located in the Trondheim area in August 1940, was sent to the Kirkenes area in the far north. Dietl was directed to prepare plans for a speedy occupation of Pechenga and the nickel mines at Kolosjoki in case of a Soviet attack on Finland. The planned operation was code-named *Renntier* (Reindeer).

The Soviets were well aware of the turn in Finnish foreign policy toward Germany. The Soviet ambassador to Finland, Ivan Zotov, warned Moscow of this new trend and opined that the Finns, feverishly engaged in building fortifications, might invite the Germans into their country.[9]

The Transit Agreements

A German lieutenant colonel, Joseph Veltjens, appeared in Helsinki on August 18. He came ostensibly as a personal representative from Hermann Göring to Marshal Mannerheim.[10] Veltjens' task was to seek Mannerheim's approval of a German proposal for the transit of supplies to German forces in north Norway and for the transit of German soldiers who were sick or on home leave. Göring was the director of Germany's Four Year Economic Plan and one of Veltjens' tasks was to firm up the option on the nickel mine concessions in Pechenga.[11] For their part, the Germans proposed to provide Finland with military equipment and supplies. According to Mannerheim, he told Veltjens that he was not authorized to enter into any agreements of this nature and suggested that the proper person was the Finnish foreign minister. Veltjens replied that he was only authorized to deal with the marshal and that he was expressly forbidden to discuss the questions with the government or politicians.[12]

Mannerheim raised the issue with President Ryti.[13] We don't know what recommendation Mannerheim made but he had expressed an interest to Veltjens in obtaining matériel for the armed forces. Mannerheim was told to give an affirmative reply to Veltjens and it therefore appears that the ultimate responsibility for this action lies with Ryti. Finnish civilian leaders who later claimed ignorance of this exceedingly important issue for Finland's future are less than sincere.

The German ambassador to Finland was very surprised when Veltjens told him that Hitler had made this decisive policy change[14] and "that he [Veltjens] had come to explain to the Finns that all their weapon needs would be met."[15] Blücher sent his military attaché, Colonel (later Major General) Horst Rössing, to Berlin to verify the information given by Veltjens. Colonel Rössing called the ambassador from Germany and stated "The things that were reported on the day of my departure are confirmed with minor deviation."[16]

General Rudolf Walden, the Finnish minister of defense, also sent officers to Berlin to clarify the German position. Further negotiations continued in Helsinki and a secret informal military agreement was reached in early September 1940. It provided for the transit of Luftwaffe personnel and equipment through Finland to Kirkenes in Norway. Notes on the subject were exchanged between the two governments two months later.

The stated purpose of these agreements sounded innocent enough but we are entitled to ask why Germany felt it necessary to make this arrangement with Finland. Sweden had allowed transit of German supplies and personnel since April 1940 and continuation of that transit would not have aroused the ire of the Soviets. The unstated purposes become obvious in Blücher's writings about what the transit agreements actually involved:

> During these weeks [April and first half of May 1941], the German military in Finland were very active. German military transports arrived in increasing numbers. Lines of communications were built throughout the country, food and ammunition depots established, and west–east roads and bridges improved. It was not possible to conceal these actions and they became the subject of discussion among the Finnish people. It was generally viewed within the framework of a German-Russian war.[17]

While Hjalmar J. Procopé observes that it remains a mystery which military officials supported the decision to let the Germans into the country, I believe we can draw some rather logical conclusions after we review the various known contacts between the military in the two countries. Procope's observation that the democratic institutions in Finland were not functioning as they should is not accurate.[18] The president/prime minister and probably other cabinet members were involved. Based on the fact that he immediately sent a team to Germany, we know that the minister of defense was informed. It would have been inconceivable to keep Foreign Minister Witting in the dark.

The implementation of some parts of the agreement not pertaining to the movement of military personnel had already begun as negotiations were taking place and this indicates that Veltjens' visit may not have been much of a surprise. We have already noted that I. G. Farben obtained a concession for the nickel ore in late July and shipments of military equipment and supplies for the Finnish armed forces began in August.[19]

All this must be viewed in relation to the position in which Finland found itself after the Winter War and particularly after the German victories in Norway and the west. The country was isolated and threatened by its powerful neighbor and no help could be expected from the Western democracies. For the Finns, the transit agreements and the delivery of weapons and supplies for their armed forces essentially broke the isolation in which they had found themselves. These agreements may have put a brake on Soviet plans. Marshal Mannerheim writes that Finland would have fallen victim to the Soviet Union in late 1940 had it not been for the agreements reached with Germany.[20] Nevertheless, it was a high-stakes gamble for the Finns to invite German forces into their country, irrevocably tying their future to that of Germany. Closer relations with Germany also damaged their relations with Great Britain and the US. The improvement in relations from the German side must also be viewed in relation to the events of the summer of 1940. These included the Soviet moves into the Baltic States and their demands on Finland, particularly as related to raw materials in the far north. Finally, Hitler's decision in late July 1940 to mount an attack on the Soviet Union gave the final impetus and urgency to improving relations with Finland. Reports from the German military attaché in Helsinki gave the Finnish armed forces high praise.[21]

Soviet Reactions to the Transit Agreements

There were many spies in Finland, and the Germans realized that they needed to inform the Soviets about some of the arrangements they had made with the Finns. Schulenburg, the German ambassador in Moscow, was told to bring the matter up with the Soviets in a casual manner, but not before the afternoon of September 21.[22] The Finns were also informed about German explanations to the Soviets through Ambassador Blücher in a separate message.[23] The explanation the Soviets were given focused on antiaircraft reinforcements (one battalion) for north

Norway to counter British air attacks. Schulenburg was instructed to tell the Soviets the following:

> Investigation of the transport facilities revealed that for this purpose the route by way of Finland would present the least difficulty. This antiaircraft battery will presumably be landed near Haparanda on September 22 and transported to Norway, part way by rail, and the rest by road. The Finnish Government appreciating the special circumstances has granted the German request to permit this transport to take place.

It appears that Schulenburg left for Berlin on September 21 without carrying out his instructions. In Schulenburg's absence the Soviet foreign minister queried the German chargé Werner von Tippelskirch about reports, including in the Finnish press, of German troops landing in a number of Finnish ports. Molotov requested a copy of the German–Finnish agreement, including any secret protocols. The chargé, who may not have been privy to Schulenburg's instructions, answered that he would communicate Molotov's request to the German government.[24]

Ribbentrop delayed his answer until October 2.[25] He instructed the Embassy in Moscow to inform the Soviets that the German–Finnish agreement involved a purely technical matter without political implications, similar to that reached with Sweden about transport through Swedish territory to Oslo, Trondheim, and Narvik. The one with Finland involved only the area of Kirkenes, which could be best reached through Finnish territory. Because of the technical nature of the agreement the Germans had seen no need to notify the Soviets. The agreement resulted from an exchange of notes between the Finns and Germans and the embassy was instructed to give the Soviets, in the form of a memorandum, verbatim the four points in the agreement. These four points were spelled out in Ribbentrop's message.

While the Soviets requested additional and more detailed information (number of troops involved, whether it involved only a single operation or a series, and whether the destination only involved Kirkenes) they did not press the matter. However, their suspicions lingered and it was only a matter of time before it surfaced at the highest levels.

Molotov's Visit to Berlin

The Soviet foreign minister, Molotov, made his much-written-about visit to Berlin in the middle of November 1940. The discussions are fully reported by participants and in documents.[26] Molotov was a survivor of the many purges in the Soviet Union and the Germans found him to be the toughest negotiator they had encountered. He was known for his no-nonsense approach and an unyielding preference for directness and explicit details that sometimes surprised and dismayed the people with whom he negotiated. They were used to politeness, subtlety, and vagueness—qualities completely missing from Molotov's lexicon.

Hitler had never faced a foreign visitor like Molotov, who brushed aside Hitler's broad generalities and demanded detailed answers to very specific questions.[27] First and foremost on his agenda was Finland and what Germany was up to in that country. The direct, detailed, and uncompromising approach by his visitor apparently caught Hitler off-guard and the meeting was adjourned to the next day when full answers to Molotov's questions were promised.

The Soviet negotiator was equally persistent when the meeting reconvened. Again, Molotov's focus was on Finland and he and Hitler, in the words of William Shirer, "soon became involved in a bitter and caustic dispute."[28] Molotov came right to the point on the issue of Finland, which he had raised on the previous day. He noted that Finland was the only area where the Soviet-German pact had not been fulfilled and he asked if the agreement between the two countries with respect to Finland was still valid. Molotov insisted that the presence of German troops in Finland was unacceptable as were Finnish political agitations against the Soviet Union. He was very blunt in classifying visits by prominent Finns to Germany as part of the agitation that the Soviets wanted to end.

Hitler disavowed any interests in Finland except for the uninterrupted delivery of nickel and lumber. He told Molotov that the transit of troops would end in a very short time. He stressed the importance of avoiding a war in the Baltic that could strain German-Soviet relations since it could lead to British and Swedish intervention. He labeled the whole Finnish issue as theoretical since Germany had agreed in 1939 that the country belonged in the Soviet sphere of influence.

Hitler's statement must have sounded disingenuous to his visitor since the subject of Finland was anything but *theoretical* to the Soviets.

Furthermore, Sweden, which was basically surrounded by German forces, showed no signs of altering its policy of neutrality, and the Germans were claiming that the war in the west had been won except for British refusal to recognize that fact. Molotov stated that he was perplexed about who would start a war in the Baltic since there was no danger of a conflict if Germany adhered to the position it had taken the previous year. Molotov wanted German acquiescence in a Soviet settlement—without war—of the Finnish issue in accordance with the Soviet-German treaty. When asked by Hitler what this meant Molotov stated bluntly that they wanted a settlement along the same lines as the one with Bessarabia—occupation—and he asked Hitler for his opinion, apparently in an effort to soften this exceedingly blunt statement. Hitler avoided a direct answer and only repeated his earlier statement that there must be no war in the Baltic.

The talks between Hitler and Molotov became very heated and Ribbentrop attempted to alter the subject by trying to entice the Soviets with a share in the breakup of the British Empire. Molotov did not take the bait and switched the conversation back to Europe. The Soviets were more interested in northern and southern Europe than in some illusive promise of possible outlets to the sea in India. Hitler apparently grew tired and weary of negotiating with the Soviet Foreign Minister and the session broke up early.

That night the Soviets hosted a party for the Germans at their embassy but Hitler did not attend. The party was interrupted by a British bombing raid and everyone hurried to the nearest air raid shelters. Churchill claims that the raid was timed for the occasion: "We had heard of the conference beforehand and though not invited to join in the discussions did not wish to be entirely left out of the proceedings."[29]

Ribbentrop and Molotov shared the same air raid shelter and Ribbentrop presented Molotov with a draft treaty, which would make the Soviet Union a member of the Tripartite Pact between Germany, Italy, and Japan. He proposed that the extension of the pact, minus the secret protocols, be made public. The secret protocol spelled out spheres of influence and the Soviet Union's was referenced vaguely as territories south of that country towards the Indian Ocean. This did not satisfy Molotov who pressed for an expansion in the southern part of East Europe towards the Mediterranean and outlets from the Black and Baltic seas by firm agreements that would guarantee his country's security. He raised a whole series of questions and issues that Ribbentrop was not prepared to answer. Ribbentrop therefore tried to steer the conversation back to the division of the British Empire since that country was defeated. This allegedly resulted in a rather caustic reply by Molotov, "If that is so, why are we in this shelter, and whose are these bombs which fall?"[30]

Molotov carried the proposed treaty back to Moscow and he promised an answer. There is no reason to believe that the Soviet Union would have rejected joining the Tripartite Pact if the membership conditions spelled out in their November 26 reply were met. However, these demands were so extensive that the Soviets must have known that Germany and the other triple alliance members would not accept them. Among these conditions was a demand for the immediate withdrawal of German troops from Finland. The Soviets, in turn, would guarantee peaceful relations with Finland and insure that German economic interests in that country were protected.[31]

The visit of Molotov to Berlin and the Soviet demands for joining the triple alliance spelled the beginning of the end to any meaningful German-Soviet collaboration. The idea of the Soviet Union joining the Tripartite Pact died a natural death. In the months that followed Germany avoided replying to the Soviets. Ribbentrop told the Japanese foreign minister in March 1941 that Germany would not attempt to bring the Soviet Union into the alliance at this time since the Soviets had set unacceptable conditions, particularly with regard to Finland and Turkey.[32]

An apparently angry and resentful Hitler proceeded to expedite the planning for the onslaught on the Soviet Union and the directive for that operation (*Barbarossa*) was issued on December 18. The Soviets came away from the conference with the distinct feeling that they had been warned by the Germans to stay out of Finland and they heeded this warning.

Finnish Reactions to Molotov's Berlin Visit

Molotov's visit to Berlin raised Finnish anxieties. They considered it possible that the Germans and Soviets had agreed to another division of spheres in East Europe and that their own future could have been part of such an agreement. Finnish worries were exacerbated when they considered the German decision to opt out of negotiations over the nickel mining concessions in October in the context of what may have happened in Berlin the following month.[33]

The Germans were aware of Finnish unease and Veltjens was sent on another mission to Helsinki to reassure them. He arrived in the Finnish capital on November 23 and was instructed to make three main points known to the Finns. The German ambassador to Finland made a similar representation a few days later:

1. That nothing had transpired in recent German-Soviet talks that made it necessary for Finland to adopt a yielding attitude in their negotiations with the Soviets.
2. That Germany had opted out of the mining concession talks since the matter of awarding concessions was viewed as a purely Finnish decision and that Germany would understand if Finland decided to keep the concessions for itself.
3. That the Soviets were fully aware that Germany viewed any complications in the north as undesirable and that they would keep this in mind when dealing with the Finns.[34]

The next sticking point in Finnish–Soviet relations was the presidential election in Finland in December 1940. The Finns wanted to elect an individual fully acceptable to the Germans and Ribbentrop threw his support behind Toivo Mikael Kivimäki, the Finnish ambassador to Germany. The Germans changed their minds after the Soviets informed the Finns that the election of a number of individuals, including Kivimäki, would not be in the best interest of Soviet-Finnish relations. The Germans decided to support Risto Ryti who was not among the ones to whom the Soviets objected. Ryti was elected.

The Soviets renewed their demands for the mining concessions in January 1941. The Soviets threatened "to bring order into the situation by the application of certain means" unless the Finns came to a speedy agreement.[35] Rather than intervening directly, the Germans managed to cloud the issues by demanding various guarantees with respect to delivery of ore. While the Soviets broke off negotiations and stopped exports to Finland, they avoided an open breach with Germany. The Soviets agreed to provide Germany with their nickel supplies but Hitler believed that they would only keep their promises so long as it suited them. In a meeting with Mussolini on January 18–20, Hitler stated that he would have gone further to support the Finns and that he could not permit further Soviet encroachment on Finland.[36]

Early Military Interactions

The picture one gets when reading the accounts of Mannerheim, Ryti, and other high Finnish civilian and military officials is that the Finnish government and its military consistently refused to make any promises or enter into agreements with Germany about a war between Germany and the Soviet Union. This is generally true with respect to the visible and formal side of the relationship between Finland and Germany. There is strong evidence, however, that this formal side did not represent the true situation. Not only were there many meetings between the military of the two countries, but some events and movements of military forces into Finland required considerable preparation which translates into early Finnish acquiescence. It is by examining these events that we get a fuller understanding of the special relationship that existed between the two military establishments.

It is impossible to tell when the special relationship between the two military establishments began. To a large extent it may have existed since World War I. This feeling of comradeship was heavily reinforced by the realization of the Finnish military leaders that only Germany could offer them real protection against the Soviet Union. There was also considerable disappointment—even bitterness—towards the Western powers for not coming to their aid during the Winter War. After the presidential election in December 1940, Finnish foreign policy was controlled by what Olli Vehviläinen describes as an "Inner Circle" in which Mannerheim and Ryti were the leading figures.[37]

Whenever the special relationship started, it began to solidify when Veltjens made his visit to Helsinki in August 1940. The transit arrangements that were worked out served both sides. Finland felt more secure from its eastern neighbor since Germany now had a stake in Finland's well-being. Numerous statements by Finnish politicians and public officials demonstrate this newfound feeling of security. For example, at a New Year's reception in Berlin the Finnish ambassador told the German secretary of state that he believed Finland would not stand alone in a future conflict with the Soviet Union. There was also an attempt in February, through the military attaché system, to elicit direct German diplomatic support, since another crisis in Finnish–Soviet negotiations appeared to be in the making.

Germany viewed Finland as a route by which to attack the Soviet Union. An entry to this effect is found in the Halder diary on July 22. This was shortly before Hitler made his decision to attack the Soviet Union. The transit agreements served to tie Finland to Germany and the latter, in the words of the German ambassador, was able to establish a line of supply bases in northern Finland.

Otto Meissner, chief of the German Presidential Chancellery, who was a well-informed individual about what was going on, writes in his memoirs: "Rumania and Finland, in a constant state of tension with the Soviet Union, had agreed ahead of time to participate in a possible war."[38]

This early participation of Finland was asserted at the Nuremberg Trials in the form of a deposition from Colonel Kitschmann. Kitschmann was assigned as the German military attaché to Finland from October 1, 1941 when the regular attaché, Major General Rössing, became ill. Kitschmann was briefed on the secret negotiations that had been carried out between the German and Finnish governments and their respective military leaders. His deposition continues:

In the course of these conversations von Albedill [German major on the attaché staff who briefed Kitschmann] told me that as early as September, 1940, Major General Roessing, acting on an order of Hitler and of the German General Staff, had arranged the visit of Major General Talwel [Paavo Juho Talvela[39]], the Plenipotentiary of Marshal Mannerheim, to the Führer's headquarters in Berlin. During this visit an agreement was reached between the German and Finnish General Staffs for joint preparations for a war of aggression, and its execution, against the Soviet Union. In this connection General Talwel told me, during a conference at his staff headquarters in Aunosa in November, 1941, that he, acting on Marshal Mannerheim's personal orders, had as far back as September, 1940—been one of the first to contact the German High Command with a view to joint preparation for a German and Finnish attack on the Soviet Union.[40]

It was probably not just a coincidence that the National Defense Section of the OKW submitted a plan dealing with operations against the Soviet Union to General Jodl on September 19, 1940. The plan assigned a large role to Finland. It is unlikely that planners would have given Finland such a role unless it had been discussed with Finnish military leaders.

Hitler had a conference with Field Marshal Brauchitsch and General Halder on December 5 to discuss what was essentially the latest draft of Operation *Barbarossa*, the German attack on the Soviet Union. Hitler approved the plan and General Jodl instructed the National Defense Section on December 6 to prepare a directive based on this plan. A meeting between General Nikolaus von Falkenhorst, German Armed Forces commander in Norway, and Halder on December 7 discussed the same plan and here we learn that the Germans planned to use four divisions: two for the Pechenga area and two for the Salla area. The last two would come by rail from central Norway across Sweden.[41]

Major General Talvela again appears on the scene. He made a visit to Berlin in the middle of December 1940. The presence of the Finnish general in Berlin in this period caused Ziemke to suggest the possibility that the Finns may have participated in the development of the *Barbarossa* directive. There is no direct evidence that this was the case although his visit was probably not just a coincidence. The stated reason for Talvela's visit was to maintain the personal contact between Mannerheim and Göring that had been established by Veltjens.

Talvela had talks with both Göring and Halder and the Finn briefed his hosts on the political and military situation in Finland. We have no information about what else may have been discussed except that Talvela tried to get German support for a political union between Sweden and Finland. Such a union had been agreed to by the Swedes provided Finland gave guarantees that it would not engage in a war of revenge against the Soviet Union. Finland accepted this condition. However, a union of Sweden and Finland ran contrary to German interests. They wanted to keep the north divided in order to maximize German influence. A Swedish-Finnish union would also alleviate Finland's isolation and undermine German efforts to secure Finnish participation in the attack on the Soviet Union. It was a serious policy mistake by the Soviet Union to also oppose such a union. The German opposition to a union was conveyed to Talvela by Göring.

This was the second attempt to form a Scandinavian military alliance. It had been proposed earlier in 1940 after the Winter War and

Norway and Sweden were positive to the idea. The Soviet Union also expressed opposition on this occasion although such a defensive alliance was not specifically prohibited by the Peace of Moscow nor was there a requirement for Finland to seek prior approval by the Soviet Union. A Scandinavian military block may have kept all of Scandinavia out of World War II and spared the Soviet Union from having to worry about the north.

Matters of more immediate interest to Germany were also touched on during Talvela's visit. Halder requested information about the time the Finns would need to make an "inconspicuous" mobilization for an attack in the Lake Ladoga area.[42] It is unlikely that Halder would have raised this question if Finnish participation had not already been discussed by representatives of the two countries.

The *Barbarossa* directive (No. 21), signed by Hitler on December 18, 1940, states that Finland would cover the marshalling of German troops transferred to the Rovaniemi area from Norway. In describing the operations in the far north it is again assumed that Finnish contingents would operate with the Germans against the Murmansk Railroad. The described participation of Finland is not hypothetical and since the directive served as the basis for all planning associated with the attack on the Soviet Union we must assume that the Germans had some form of assurance from the Finns and that the question of Finnish participation was a settled issue.[43]

In January 1941, the OKH invited the chief of the Finnish General Staff, Lt. General Erik Heinrichs, to Germany for the stated purpose of lecturing to military audiences on Finnish operations and experiences in the Winter War. General der Infanterie Waldemar Erfurth writes that there was no mention during this visit of German–Finnish military cooperation or the German plans for an attack on the Soviet Union.[44]

It defies logic to believe that there were no discussions—at least hypothetical—of cooperation in case of war in view of what is already discussed in this chapter and subsequent developments. Even Mannerheim's writings, which always deny that Finnish officers made any agreements with the Germans or participated in their planning, wrote this about General Heinrichs' visit to Germany:

> During a formal visit to the Chief of the German General Staff, General Halder, the latter suggested that Finland and Germany

again, as in 1918, might come to the point of fighting together, and that the natural task of the Finnish Army would be to move against Leningrad. The idea was rejected emphatically by Lieutenant General Heinrichs, who said he was convinced that neither the government nor the commander in chief would consent to such an operation—particularly since the Russians had asserted that Finland threatened the security of Leningrad. It deserves to be emphasized that neither the so-called Barbarossa Plan nor any others were shown to Lieutenant General Heinrichs.[45]

The refusal to threaten Leningrad is believable in light of Mannerheim's long-standing view that nothing should be done to validate Soviet concerns and their stated reason for launching the Winter War.[46] However, it is less believable that the Finns showed no interest in military cooperation in view of their strong desire to recover lost territories and to remove the threat from the east.

Helmuth Greiner, who kept the OKW diary, was exceptionally well informed of important conversations and decisions at the highest military levels in Germany. According to him, General Halder told Hitler as early as February 3, 1941, that "The Finns intended to deploy about four army corps in the south, and to assign five divisions from these to the attack on Leningrad, three divisions to Lake Onega, and two divisions against Hanko; however, they needed strong support."[47] This information was obtained by Halder in a "detailed conversation" he had on January 30, 1941 with Lieutenant General Heinrichs in Germany about cooperation between the two countries in case of a war against the Soviet Union.

The First Buschenhagen Visit

Colonel Erich Buschenhagen, chief of staff of Army of Norway, was present in Berlin during General Heinrichs' visit. He was sent to Finland the following month (February). There are divergent statements and claims on what transpired during this visit.

Buschenhagen's description of his mission suggests a coordination visit by the chief of staff of the organization tasked to take part in Operation *Barbarossa* on the northern front. It is very unlikely that the Germans would have sent this officer to Finland for that purpose if the subject of military cooperation had not been discussed in Berlin the previous month.

Buschenhagen's explanation of his visit to Finland is contained in a deposition at the Nuremberg Trials. It was to make a personal contact with the Finnish General Staff to discuss "operations from middle and northern Finland."[48] He held meetings on this subject with Lieutenant General Heinrichs, his deputy, and Colonel Kustaa Tapola, the chief of operations of the Finnish General Staff, and relates that they reached agreement on various issues. He goes on to say that he and Colonel Tapola traveled to central and northern Finland to study "the terrain, the possibilities for deploying and billeting, and for operations in that sector."[49] According to Buschenhagen, these discussions led to the development of a plan by the Army of Norway for operations from Finnish territory. This plan was presented to, and approved by, the OKW.

Mannerheim gives a different version, claiming that the visit dealt primarily with the transit traffic. However, he goes on:

> Besides that, the Colonel wanted to familiarize himself with our operational plans for Lapland and discuss traffic and communications in the north. He also let it be known that Germany would not remain inactive in case of a Soviet attack on Finland. As far as operational plans were concerned, I absolutely refused to disclose them; neither could there be any question of discussing possible German–Finnish operational coordination. On the other hand, there were no objections to discuss the communications system of Lapland within the context of the transit agreement.[50]

The German visitor was interested in Finnish operational plans for the northern part of the country and Mannerheim undoubtedly knew that German interest in this part of the country was due to plans to strike at the Soviet Union from northern Finland with the port of Murmansk and the Murmansk Railroad as the obvious objectives. I believe the Finnish General Staff, possibly with Mannerheim's blessings, did discuss contingency plans. It is otherwise difficult to understand why an army level chief of staff, in the company of the operations officer of the Finnish General Staff, would travel to northern Finland. The transit traffic was operating without problems and had there been any, it would have been more appropriate for lower-level transport personnel from both sides—not two key military planners—to have addressed these problems.

General Hermann Hölter, who was General Erfurth's chief of staff in Finland,[51] writes the following:

> For a group of forces provided for a thrust via Salla in the direction of Kandalaksha, which were not to be transported over the Baltic until shortly before the attack, it was necessary to create supply bases in the harbors of the Gulf of Bothnia and in the Rovaniemi district [for forces planned for the use in the Salla region]. These deployment preparations were served by the negotiations of the Chief of the General Staff of the AOK [Army High Command] Norway, Colonel Buschenhagen, with Finnish command officials in the winter of 1940–41 and his reconnoitering the boundary between northern Finland and Russia.[52]

Later, in discussing operational planning, Hölter quotes Buschenhagen as saying on June 13, 1941, as they traveled together to Finland that "The Finns stood by our side with advice and assistance in planning the operations."[53] A note in the Halder Diary after a conference on Operation *Barbarossa* on March 17, 1941, deals with security in the rear areas and it states "no difficulties in Northern Russia, which will be taken over by Finland." Again, on March 30 Halder notes the following: "No illusion about our allies! Finns will fight bravely, but they are numerically weak and have not yet recovered from their recent defeat. Rumanians are no good at all."[54] General Walter Warlimont, deputy chief of operations at OKW, reported on April 28, 1941 that Finland's part in Operation *Barbarossa* needed to be clarified with "authoritative" Finnish military officials without breaching operational security.[55]

There can be no doubt that much more collaboration was taking place between the Finnish and German military in this period than what is stated by Mannerheim. General Erfurth writes that "Neither negotiations nor discussions concerning a possible future cooperation between the Germans and the Finns took place during this visit of Buschenhagen at Helsinki or anywhere else" and he suggests that Buschenhagen confused the February visit to Finland with a visit he made in June 1941.[56] He admits, however that Buschenhagen had a tour of eastern Lapland. This area had little to do with the transit of personnel but figured prominently in later German operations.

It should be kept in mind that Erfurth only arrived in Finland in June 1941. He spent over three years at the Finnish Headquarters and his friendship with Mannerheim is well known. His statement may therefore have been influenced by the views of the Finns rather than based on any independent knowledge he had about the events leading up to the war. Observations on German Army activities in Finland in the spring of 1941 by Ambassador Blücher, which are quoted earlier, clearly contradict statements by Mannerheim, Erfurth, and Heinrichs.

For security reasons the Germans did not want their relations with Finland to warm too rapidly. Too much activity in this area could alert the Soviet Union that something was afoot. The Finns were eager to acquire a protective umbrella in the form of Germany and Finnish foreign minister Rolf Witting went so far as to suggest to the German ambassador in Helsinki in early April that Finland join the triple alliance. The Germans ignored the suggestion. This worked to the advantage of the Finns since they later found themselves as a cobelligerent with Germany and this was preferable to that of an ally.

General Heinrichs' Visit to Salzburg and Berlin

Karl Schnurre, a special envoy from Hitler to the Finnish president, arrived in Helsinki on May 20.[57] He told Ryti that a tense situation had developed between Germany and the Soviet Union that could lead to war. In view of this hypothetical possibility, he asked that a Finnish military delegation be sent to Germany to be briefed on the situation. According to Mannerheim, President Ryti told the envoy that Finland was resolved not to attack the Soviet Union and he expressed an unwillingness to be drawn into a war between the great powers.[58] Despite this statement, it was decided to send a military delegation to Germany— with the apparent approval of the cabinet and Mannerheim.

The Finnish military delegation, headed by General Heinrichs, left for Salzburg on May 24, 1941. General Heinrichs' instructions, according to Mannerheim, did not authorize him to make any decisions or enter into any sort of agreements.[59] However, the fact that the delegation included the chiefs of operations, mobilization, supply, and the navy's chief of staff give credence to a conclusion that they came not merely to listen to a briefing of the worsening situation in Europe but to actually participate in planning.

It is difficult to determine how much reliance can be placed on the statements of the various parties in such murky circumstances. All present their actions in the very best light but the happenings on the ground—reconnaissance by planners, the establishment of a network of supply installations, strengthening of roads and bridges to support heavy military traffic, and the deployment schedules of units—speak volumes about the veracity of the different actors.

The Germans had made detailed plans for the three-day conference. The primary Finnish account is given by Mannerheim, and is supplemented by German diaries and the information contained in the testimony and documents from the Trials of War Criminals. The Finns were met by Field Marshal Wilhelm Keitel and Major General Alfred Jodl.

Jodl opened the conference and he described the planned attack on the Soviet Union as a preventive action. He portrayed a dangerous build-up of Soviet forces along the border that would allow the Soviet Union to select the time and place for military action. While Germany would try to resolve the issues through diplomacy, Soviet actions had forced the undertaking of certain countermeasures. If diplomatic means were not successful, military measures would become necessary.

The Finns were briefed on the German operational plan that involved the conquest of the Baltic states. Jodl explained that the Soviet defenses were expected to collapse as Army Group North advanced towards Leningrad. The primary task for the Finns would be to tie down Russian forces around Lake Ladoga. The briefing also included plans for the German attack from north Norway across Finnish territory to capture Murmansk and the planned German/Finnish attack across the waist of Finland to capture Salla together with its continuance to Kandalaksha on the White Sea to cut the Murmansk Railroad.

Germany's requests of Finland included:[60]

1. Transport of a German corps headquarters and a reinforced division from harbors in the Gulf of Bothnia by rail to the Rovaniemi area.
2. Small Finnish detachments to assist the attack against Murmansk.

3. Early disguised mobilization of the Finnish Army.
4. Finnish participation in the attack out of central Finland to cut the Murmansk Railroad.
5. Finnish attack on both sides of Lake Ladoga toward the Svir (Syväri) River and the Ladoga Canal.

German friendship and protection, eagerly pursued by the Finns since the Winter War, had blossomed into full-scale participation in plans for a war of aggression at the side of Germany against the Soviet Union. The Finnish leadership must have been fully aware that events would take them in this direction. The talks that had taken place and the composition of the military delegation sent to Germany support this conclusion.

According to Mannerheim, Heinrichs told the Germans that Finland desired to remain neutral but was also determined to resist any Soviet aggression. He allegedly stated that while he was not authorized to make any commitments in operational matters, he believed that in the hypothetical case outlined by Jodl it would be possible for some smaller Finnish units to cooperate with the Germans in the far north.

From Salzburg the delegation traveled to Berlin, where it was received by General Halder, chief of staff of OKH. As chief of staff of the army, he was particularly interested in Finnish participation in the operation against Leningrad and suggested a strong attack on either side of Lake Ladoga. The German Army wanted the Finns to delay their operations for 14 days after the German attack but General Heinrichs opposed such a delay. Again, according to Mannerheim, Heinrichs stated Finland's desire to remain neutral and that Finland would not attack Leningrad under any circumstances, even if attacked by the Soviet Union. Halder asked that the German views be given to the Finnish government and the military high command.[61]

Buschenhagen's Second Visit to Finland

Talks between the German and Finnish military resumed again on June 3, 1941, this time in Helsinki. Colonel Buschenhagen represented the OKW and Colonel Eberhard Kinzel represented the OKH. The German officers discovered that the Finns were willing to accept the proposals made by the Germans at Salzburg and Berlin at the end of May.

Buschenhagen's second visit to Finland is mentioned by Mannerheim in his memoirs, but in a misleading way. He writes:

> From his [Buschenhagen's] remarks to the General Staff it
> appeared that his mission this time was concerned with a dis-
> cussion of practical details in connection with eventual cooper-
> ation in the north if Finland were attacked by the Soviet Union,
> and also with obtaining guarantees for Finland participating in
> the war as Germany's ally. After I had reported to the President
> of the Republic and he had confirmed that he adhered to his
> earlier standpoint, I had Colonel Buschenhagen informed that a
> guarantee for Finnish participation in the war could not be
> given. Finland was determined to remain neutral provided she
> was not exposed to aggression.[62]

It comes as no surprise that there are major differences between the
excerpt of Buschenhagen's testimony below and Mannerheim's statement.

> At these conferences [in Helsinki], which again took place be-
> tween General Heinrichs, General Halder, and Colonel Tapola,
> the details of this collaboration [agreed to the previous week in
> Germany] were worked out, such as the timetable, the schedule,
> measures of secrecy as to the Finnish mobilization. . . . All
> agreements between the OKW and the Finnish General Staff
> had as their sole purpose from the very beginning the participa-
> tion of the Finnish Army and the German troops on Finnish ter-
> ritory in aggressive war against the Soviet Union. . . . There
> was—from the very beginning—no doubt among the Finnish
> General Staff that all these preparations would serve only in the
> attack against the Soviet Union. . . .[63]

A number of Finnish military officers labeled Buschenhagen's deposition false or distorted at the war guilt trials in Helsinki in 1945.[64] Both
Heinrichs and Tapola were among them. The Finnish officers denied
that any agreements had been made with the Germans at any of their
meetings or conferences.[65] In the summary of his testimony Heinrichs
declared:

Neither in conversation with him [Buschenhagen] nor in connection with the visit to Salzburg and Berlin, nor on any other occasion . . . were there made any written or oral commitments or agreements, binding for Finland's government or military leadership.[66]

How much credibility should be given to the testimony of Buschenhagen is a controversial subject. His testimony at the Nuremberg Trials was not given in person but via a deposition taken while he was a Russian prisoner of war. Buschenhagen was released from captivity in 1955 and he did not die until 1994. There was therefore ample time for him to recant the testimony he gave while a Soviet prisoner and thus put the record straight if he had wanted. He never officially changed his testimony.

Greiner's writings support Buschenhagen's testimony. He claims that Finnish refusals to offer formal commitments were essentially meaningless as far as the Germans were concerned:

On this occasion [May 25, 1941], however, no firm agreements were reached, only operative possibilities were discussed in a non-binding manner, but the Finns were officially notified of the German intention, in case of a war against the Soviet Union, of having German troops push forward from northern Norway through the Petsamo region against Murmansk and from central Finland against the Murmansk Railway. . . . At the beginning of June the Chief of Staff of the Armeeoberkommando Norway, Colonel Buschenhagen, was sent to Helsinki to continue discussions with the Finnish General Staff. The Finns now expressed agreement to the transport of the German 169th Infantry Division as early as the first half of June [begun on June 4] from the homeland by sea to Oulu and Kemi and from there move forward by rail into an area of deployment provided east of Rovaniemi.[67]

Colonel Bernhard von Lossberg in the National Defense Section of the OKW expresses views similar to those of Greiner when he writes:

Finland was to cover the deployment of a Northern Group

detached from our Army of Norway . . . and operate in cooperation with it. . . . The final discussion with the Finns took
place at the beginning of 1941 after preliminary discussions in
Salzburg. . . . When the Finns agreed to the question as to
whether they would take part in such a campaign [pre-emptive
German attack on the Soviet Union if that became necessary],
Jodl explained the tasks planned for them within the context of
the overall plan. The Finns basically agreed subject to the con-
currence of their government. . . .[68]

Finally, we should take into consideration a pro memoria which
General Heinrichs gave the German military representatives on June 3,
1941:

The Commander-in-Chief [Mannerheim] wishes to take this
opportunity to say that the interest called forth by these discussions is in no way purely operational or military-technical in
nature.
    The idea [destruction of the Soviet Union] which forms the
basis of the propositions communicated to him by the highest
echelons of the German leadership must arouse joy in the
Finnish soldier's heart and is regarded here as a historic sign of
a great future.[69]

Heinrichs added orally that "for the first and probably the last time
in Finland's thousand-year history the great moment has come in which
the Finnish people can free itself for all time from the pressure of its
hereditary enemy."[70]
    Ziemke's examination of German military records supports
Buschenhagen, Greiner, and Lossberg's accounts and allows us to sum-
marize what was agreed to in Helsinki. The assembly of the main force
of the Finnish Army would—with the Svir River as its objective—be
such that it could attack east or west of Lake Ladoga on five days'
notice. A reinforced battalion would be attached to the German forces
driving towards Murmansk and a corps of two divisions would participate in the attack towards the Murmansk Railroad at Kandalaksha.
The Finns accepted responsibility for occupying the Åland Islands and
pinning down the Soviet forces in Hanko. However, they requested that

a German division be made available to attack and capture Hanko. German documents also affirm that the Finnish government and the Finnish parliament represented by the Foreign Affairs Committee approved the military arrangements between Germany and Finland on June 14.[71]

The Finns appear to have harbored some fears that the Germans might reach an agreement with the Soviets that would avoid war and possibly leave them exposed. In the event of a peaceful settlement between Germany and the Soviet Union they wanted guarantees from Germany of its independence, its borders (preferably the 1939 borders), and economic assistance. Two days before they began general mobilization, the Finns reiterated their demands for guarantees in case war was averted. Field Marshal Keitel authorized the German military attaché in Helsinki to tell the Finns that all conditions they had expressed were accepted and would be fulfilled.[72]

The Finns began a partial mobilization on June 9 and a general mobilization was ordered on June 17. The rapid and efficient mobilization called to duty reservists born between 1897 and 1918 in addition to the 1919 and 1920 year groups. The defense forces involved, including auxiliaries, numbered 630,000.[73] This was a massive undertaking by a nation with a population of less than four million.

General Erfurth and Colonel Buschenhagen arrived in Helsinki on June 13. Erfurth assumed his duty as liaison officer at Mannerheim's headquarters. Buschenhagen traveled to Rovaniemi on June 15 and established the headquarters for the Army of Norway in Finland. The Army of Norway thereafter had two headquarters more than 1,600 kilometers apart, one in Norway and one in Finland. Operational control of the Finnish III Corps, commanded by Major General Hjalmar Fridolf Siilasvuo, also passed to Army of Norway on June 15. In order not to arouse Soviet suspicions about an attack, General Falkenhorst remained in Norway until June 21.

It is impossible to reconcile the increasing interaction between the Finnish and German military from August 1940 onwards with the picture of innocence and reluctance to participate in a war against the Soviet Union painted by Finnish political and military leaders after the war. While the Finnish leaders denied that they participated in war planning with the Germans or had made any commitments to the Germans, the average Finn, watching the hectic German activities in central Finland, must have been fully aware that the country was moving rapidly towards war

While the decision to become a cobelligerent with Germany may have been made by a group of influential political and military leaders, it is safe to conclude that the decisions taken were in tune with the majority of the politicians and the Finnish population.[74] President Ryti undoubtedly expressed the view of many Finns when he told a parliamentary delegation on June 21 that "this war is Finland's only salvation. The Soviet Union will never give up its attempt to conquer Finland."[75]

NOTES

1. C. Leonard Lundin, *Finland in the Second World War* (Bloomington: Indiana University Press, 1957), p.80.
2. Ernst von Born, *Levnadsminnen* (Helsingfors: Söderström, 1954), pp.327–375.
3. Carl Olof Frietsch, *Finlands Ödesår 1939–1943* (Helsingfors, Söderström, 1945), p.244.
4. Earl F. Ziemke, *The German Northern Theater of Operations 1940–1945* (Washington, D.C.: Department of the Army (Pamphlet No. 20-271), 1959), p.115.
5. Wipert von Blücher, *Gesandter zwischen Diktatur und Demokratie* (Wiesbaden: Limes Verlag, 1951), p.194.
6. *Ibid.* pp.194–195, 197.
7. *DGFP*, volume 8, Nos. 310 and 398.
8. Halder's diary for July 22 mentions Finland as one route by which to attack the Soviet Union.
9. Messages from Zotov to Molotov on July 12 and August 1, 1940, as cited in Vehviläinen, *op. cit.,* p.82.
10. Veltjens, a highly decorated pilot, was an old friend of Göring from WWI. He was engaged in what can be called the business of arms dealing.
11. *NSR*, Foreign Office Memorandum w/4646/40g, dated October 8, 1940.
12. Mannerheim, *Memoirs*, pp.399–400.
13. Prime Minister Risto Ryti held two positions at this time. He was Prime Minister but also acting President because President Kyösti Kallio was ill.
14. The delivery of arms to Finland and the presence of German troops on its soil were violations of the spheres of influence established in the secret protocol of the Ribbentrop-Molotov Pact. However, it can be argued that the Soviet Union had already violated the secret protocol when it occupied Lithuania in 1940 since the agreement called for the Soviet sphere of influence to stop at the northern border of that country.
15. Blücher, *op. cit.*, p.198.

16. *Ibid*, p.198.

17. *Ibid*, p.221.

18. Hjalmar J. Procopé, editor, *Fällande dom som friar* (Stockholm: Fahlcrantz & Gumælius, 1946), pp.67–68.

19. Blücher, *op. cit.*, pp.198–199.

20. Mannerheim, *Memoirs*, p.427.

21. Ziemke, *The German Northern Theater of Operations*, p.115.

22. *NSR*, Telegram from Foreign Minister Ribbentrop to Ambassador Schulenburg on September 16, 1940.

23. *Ibid*, Telegram from Foreign Minister Ribbentrop to the German Minister in Finland on September 16, 1940.

24. *Ibid*, Telegram from the German chargé Tippelskirch to Foreign Minister Ribbentrop on September 27, 1940.

25. *Ibid*, Telegram (No 1787) from Foreign Minister Ribbentrop to the German Embassy in Moscow on October 2, 1940.

26. See, for example, Paul Schmidt, *Statist auf diplomatischer Bühne, 1923–45* (Bonn: Athenäum Verlag, 1949); and *NSR*.

27. Paul Schmidt, *Hitler's Interpreter* (New York, Macmillan, 1951), p.212. This is a much-shortened version of the book referenced in note 26, primarily because it leaves out that part dealing with the period before Hitler's rise to power.

28. William L. Shirer, *The Rise and Fall of The Third Reich. A History of Nazi Germany* (New York, Simon and Schuster, 1960), p.805.

29. Winston S. Churchill. *The Second World War. Their Finest Hour* (New York, 1948–1953), p.584.

30. These words are not in the German minutes of the meeting but come from Churchill, *Their Finest Hour*, p.586 based on a later conversation with Stalin.

31. *NSR*, Telegram from Ambassador Schulenburg to Foreign Minister Ribbentrop containing a memorandum (No. 2362, dated November 20) of a meeting with Foreign Minister Molotov. The other conditions included a mutual security pact with Bulgaria, bases in the Black Sea within range of the Straits to include joint military action against Turkey if that country caused troubles, a recognized Soviet sphere of influence in the direction of the Persian Gulf, and a renunciation by Japan of commercial rights (oil and coal) in northern Sakhalin.

32. *NSR*, p.304.

33. The German decision not to participate was actually caused by a misunderstanding since the German Foreign Office did not discover until the end of the month that an option existed and by then it was too late.

34. Blücher, *op. cit.*, pp.211–212.

35. *Ibid*, p.215 and Ziemke, *The German Northern Theater of Operations*, p.118.

36. *Ibid*, p.119.

37. Vehviläinen, *op. cit.*, p.85.

38. Otto Meissner, *Staatssekretär unter Ebert-Hindenburg-Hitler* (Hamburg: Hoffmann und Campe Verlag, 1950), p.572.

39. Major General Talvela was a hero of the Winter War and held important com-

mands in the war that began in June 1941. He commanded the VI Corps from June 1941 to January 1942. He was promoted to lieutenant general in 1942 and assigned as the Finnish representative to OKW and OKH. He served in that position from January 1942 until February 1944 when he took over as the commander of the Maaselkä Front until June 1944. In that month he became commander of the Svir Front for one month (June 16 to July 18). From July to September he was again assigned as the Finnish representative at German military headquarters. General Talvela was a trusted advisor and confidant to Marshal Mannerheim.

40. International Military Tribunal, *Trials of the Major War Criminals* (Nuremberg, 1947), volume VII, pp.327–328.

41. Ziemke, *The German Northern Theater of Operations*, p.122.

42. *Ibid*, p.124.

43. H. R. Trevor-Roper, editor, *Hitler's Wartime Directives 1939–1945* (London: Pan Books Ltd, 1966), pp.93–98.

44. Waldemar Erfurth, *The Last Finnish War* (Written under the auspices of the Foreign Military Studies Branch of the Historical Division, Headquarters, European Command. Washington, D.C.: University Publications of America, Inc., 1979), p.8. Erfurth was Chief, Liaison Staff North, attached to Mannerheim's headquarters as the representative of OKH and OKW from June 1941 to September 1944.

45. Carl Gustaf Mannerheim, *Minnen* (Stockholm: Norstedt, 1952), volume II, p.261.

46. Mannerheim had not always held this view. In 1919, as General Nikolay Nikolayevich Yudenich, Commander of The Northwestern White Army during the Russian Civil War, was approaching Petrograd (later Leningrad), Mannerheim proposed that the Finns attack the city from the north.

47. Helmuth Greiner, *Die Oberste Wehrmachtführung 1939–1943* (Wiesbaden: Limes Verlag, 1951), p.357.

48. International Military Tribunal, *op. cit.*, volume VII, pp.309–311.

49. *Loc. cit.*

50. Mannerheim, *Minnen*, volume II, pp.261–262.

51. General Hölter spent the whole war in Finland. He was chief of staff to General Erfurth from June to September 1941; chief of staff of the XXXVI Mountain Corps from October 1941 to October 1943; chief of staff of the XIX Mountain Corps from November 1943 to February 1944; and the chief of staff of the 20th Mountain Army from March 1944 to the end of the war.

52. As quoted by Lundin, *op. cit.*, p.97 from Hermann Hölter, *Armee in der Arktis. Die Operationen der deutschen Lapland-Armee* (Bad Nauheim, 1953), pp.9f. I did not have access to the 1953 edition but to the somewhat shortened 2nd edition published in 1977: Hermann Hölter, *Armee in der Aktis. Die Operationen der deutschen Lapland-Armee* (München: Schild Verlag, 1977). In this edition a similar statement appears on p.15.

53. Hölter, *op. cit.*, (1977 edition) p.17.

54. International Military Tribunal, *op. cit.*, volume X, pp.947–949.

55. *Ibid*, volume X, p.982.

56. Erfurth, *The Last Finnish War*, p.9.

57. Dr. Karl Schnurre was the chief of the Eastern European and Baltic Section of the Commercial Policy Division of the German Foreign Office with the rank of Ambassador.

58. Mannerheim, *Memoirs*, p.406.

59. *Ibid*, p.408.

60. International Military Tribunal, *op. cit.*, volume X, pp.998–1000.

61. Mannerheim, *Minnen*, volume II, pp.264–267.

62. Mannerheim, *Memoirs*, p.410.

63. International Military Tribunal, *op. cit.*, volume VII, pp.311–313.

64. The War Guilt Trials were not part of the Nuremberg process. Finland was permitted to conduct the trials in Finland under retroactive Finnish laws and with Finnish judges. The law passed by parliament to support the trials limited them to the highest Finnish political wartime leadership, exempting military leaders. It is rumored that the exception of military leaders, including Marshal Mannerheim, was at the direction of Stalin. The trials began on November 15, 1945, and ended in February 1946. The sentences of the eight found guilty ranged from two to ten years. Ryti was sentenced to 10 years' hard labor. Most Finns considered the trials a mockery of justice and all those found guilty were quickly pardoned after the 1947 peace treaty. Ryti was pardoned in May 1949.

65. Procope, *op. cit.*, pp.236–239. Questioned on this subject at his trial, Ryti answered: "To speak plainly, I was a little suspicious, in consequence of some vague rumors that military cooperation might have been prepared for in advance, besides other things, at the Salzburg-Berlin conferences. But I never had sufficient ground to doubt the assurances of the military authorities when I asked many times whether no consent at all had been given to enter into other negotiations or make agreements. . . . I trust the assurances of General Heinrichs that no oral or written declarations of any kind had been made."

66. As quoted in Lundin, *op. cit.*, p.103.

67. Greiner, *op. cit.*, p.357.

68. Bernhard von Lossberg, *Im Wehrmachtführungsstab. Bericht eines Generalstabsoffiziers* (Hamburg: H. H. Nölke, 1949), pp.113–114.

69. As quoted by Ziemke, *The German Northern Theater of War*, p.204, note 33, from official German military documents.

70. *Ibid*, p.204, note 33.

71. *Ibid*, p.134.

72. *Ibid*, p.135.

73. Göran Westerlund, *Finland överlevde. Finlands Krig 1939–1945 i ord och bild* (Helsingfors: Schildts Förlags Ab, 2007), p.65. Finland's army was, since 1918, based on universal military training. The country was divided into nine military regions at the start of the Winter War. Each region was divided into three military districts. A military region was required to form a division when reservists were called up during a mobilization. The division was to consist of three infantry regiments, one from each district. Each region was also required to mobilize one artil-

lery regiment. Other units, such as signal, engineers, support troops, naval, and air units were activated through the efforts of several regions. While the principle of regional mobilization was maintained after the Winter War, the loss of territory required the redrawing of the military regions to support the mobilization of 16 divisions and some independent regiments—see Ari Raunio, *Sotaoimet. Suomen sotien 1939–45 kulku kartoin* (Kustantaja: Ghenimap Oy, 2004), pp.104–107. The number given by Westerlund includes various support and auxiliary organizations including the Lotta Svärd, a voluntary auxiliary paramilitary organization for women. The Lottas worked in hospitals, manned some of the air-raid early warning stations, and carried out other non-combat auxiliary tasks for the armed forces.
74. Westerlund, *op. cit.*, pp.64–65 and M. Jokipii, *Jatkosodan synty. Tutkimuksia Saksari ja Suomen sotilaallisesta yhteistyöstä 1940–41* (Keuruu: Otava, 1987), pp.620–622 and Vehviläinen, *op. cit.*, p.89.
75. As quoted in Vehviläinen, *op. cit.*, p.89.

TWO
PLANS, PREPARATIONS, AND DEPLOYMENTS

War Aims

It is relatively easy to determine Germany's war aims vis-à-vis the Soviet Union. They are spelled out in the *Barbarossa* Directive.

> The mass of the Russian Army stationed in Western Russia is to be destroyed in daring operations, by driving deep armored wedges, and the retreat of units capable of combat into the vastness of Russian territory is to be prevented. In quick pursuit a line is then to be reached from which the Russian Air Force will no longer be able to attack German Reich territory. The ultimate objective of the operation is to establish a defense line against Asiatic Russia from a line running approximately from the Volga River to Archangel. Then, in case of necessity, the last industrial area left to Russia in the Urals can be eliminated by the Luftwaffe.[1]

The German objective was to destroy the military and economic potential of the Soviet Union by conquering and occupying permanently vast regions of that country, including some areas that were to be given to Germany's allies. It was a life and death struggle between two totalitarian systems. It is relatively easy for a dictatorship to set and maintain war aims since public opinion does not factor much into the equation.

It is much more difficult to discern the true Finnish war aims or what the Finns expected from their participation in the war. There are several reasons for this. First, the Finnish civilian and military leaders were careful—as they had been in their dealings with Germany leading up to the war—not to leave a paper trail. Since their statements at the war guilt trials have little credence, we are forced to look at their state-ments and actions before and during the war. Secondly, Finland was a democracy and public opinion played a large role in setting and sus-taining war aims. Like the public in most democracies, the war aims changed with the ebb and flow of the fighting. Success tended to lead to an expansion of war aims while deteriorating military situations often lead to pressure to reduce the scope of those aims and even to terminate the war. This issue is addressed throughout this book. Finally, it is diffi-cult to learn what the motives were since various writers tend to empha-size, de-emphasize, or dismiss some statements and events depending on their political persuasions.

The stated Finnish war aims were limited to the recovery of territo-ries lost during the Winter War; hence they refer to the conflict from 1941 to 1944 as the "Continuation War." However, it is patently obvi-ous from statements and events both before and during the war that they hoped to come out of the war with much more than the territories lost in 1940.

The most ambitious statements of Finnish aspirations appear to be those given by President Ryti to Ambassador Schnurre in October 1941.[2] He let it be known that Finland desired all of the Kola Peninsula and all of Soviet Karelia with a border on the White Sea to the Gulf of Onega (Ääninen). Also included in his wishes were Ladoga Karelia and that the future border should then proceed along the Svir River, the southern shore of Lake Ladoga, and finally along the Neva River to where it entered the Gulf of Finland.[3] Within a couple of weeks of this statement, Ryti told Ambassador Blücher that Finland did not want a common border with the Soviet Union after the war and he requested that Germany annex all territory south of the Archangel region.[4] The views that Ryti expressed in October 1941 may be what prompted Hitler to tell Foreign Minister Witting the following month when he came to Berlin to sign the Anti-Comintern Pact that Germany favored an expansion of Finland to the east, to include the Kola Peninsula as long as Germany shared in the mineral resources. Witting told Blücher after his visit to Berlin that it was necessary for Finland's security to hold on to the captured territories.[5]

This brings up the thorny question of East Karelia (or Far Karelia) and the concept of Greater Finland (Suur-Suomi). The Karelian issue is long-standing and complicated, too much so to allow proper coverage in this book. Suffice it to say that the Karelians were related to the Finns both linguistically and culturally but their area had never been under the control of Finland or Sweden so Finland had no valid historical claims to that part of the Soviet Union.

The fate of Karelia had been a very contentious issue during the War of Independence in 1918. The issue was complicated by a division of opinion among the Karelians themselves. Some wanted to remain under Soviet rule. Others favored outright independence, while still others—mostly conservatives—favored a union with Finland. The issue was further convoluted at the end of the War of Independence—which was in many respects a civil war—by the presence of British and German troops.

General Sir Charles Maynard commanded the Allied Expeditionary Force in Murmansk from March 1918. He did not favor either political independence for the Karelians or the absorption of Karelia by Finland.[6] His views were naturally colored by the presence of German troops in Finland under the command of General Rüdiger von der Goltz. They were there to aid the anti-Bolshevik forces under Mannerheim but remained in the country for some time after hostilities ended.

However, General von der Goltz also opposed the absorption of Karelia by Finland. His goals were to recreate a conservative Russian regime friendly to Germany and to make Finland a dependable German ally. Separating East Karelia from Russia would be as unacceptable to a new conservative Russia as it was to the Soviets. Finland could never achieve a durable independence or security by making claims on territories Russia considered vital to its interests.[7] Despite von der Goltz's views the Finns laid claim in 1918 to the province of Viena and the Murmansk coast. Von der Goltz is alleged to have warned the Finns privately that it was not wise to seek control of Russia's only ice-free port. The German High Command echoed these views by stating that it could not support a boundary dangerous to the vital interests of Russia.[8]

Mannerheim's relationship with General von der Goltz is described as cool and the reason may well have been the German's view on East Karelia. If Mannerheim harbored a burning desire to bring East Karelia into Finland he did not prevail during the War of Independence. His resignation on May 31, 1918, may well be traced back to his differences with the Germans and members of the Finnish government who shared their views. While the Finns did not renounce their claims to East

Karelia they did not pursue that objective and it remained within the Soviet Union.

Mannerheim's memoirs are surprisingly quiet when it comes to Finland's war aims. However, there are several bellicose orders of the day from both the time of the War of Independence and the Continuation War which indicate that he may at least have shared some of the views of those who argued for the conquest of East Karelia. A couple of examples that proved somewhat embarrassing both during and after the war are illustrative. Part of his order of the day on June 28, 1941, reads:

> I call upon you to take part in a holy war against the enemy of our people. Our dead heroes are rising from their fresh, green graves at this moment in order to rejoin us as brothers-in-arms of mighty Germany in a crusade against our enemy to secure the future of Finland. Brothers-in-arms: Follow me for the last time, now that Karelia is rising, and Aurora will light a new day for the Finns.[9]

Finnish radio carried another order of the day on July 7, as the main offensive was about to begin. It proclaimed his intention of conquering the provinces of Viena and Aunus:

> We promise the Karelians that our sword will not rest until Karelia has been liberated. The provinces of Viena and Aunus have waited twenty-three years for the fulfillment of this promise, and since the winter campaign of 1939–40 Karelia has waited for the dawn of the day that is to bring her freedom. Her battalions are now marching in our ranks.
>
> The freedom of Karelia and the Greater Finland is the goal that beckons us in this mighty whirl of historical events. For us this war is a holy war against the enemy of our nation and at the side of mighty Germany we are firmly determined to bring this crusade against our common foe to a victorious end in order that Finland's future may be assured.[10]

What we don't know is whether such statements were only for the purpose of firing up the fighting spirit of the troops or whether they represented the views of a significant segment of the Finnish military and civilian leadership.[11] While only speculation, such expansionist views would explain why certain circles in Finland were so willing to become involved in the military adventure that Hitler was about to launch.

Ambassador Blücher writes that strong differences of opinion existed both in the officer corps and political circles in Finland on the issue of conquering East Karelia and moving as far as the Svir River. Even in September 1941 the Finnish government tried to avoid a discussion of war aims since it would demonstrate publicly the divide that existed between conservatives and liberals. Only great success on the battlefield by Germany and Finland could solve this dilemma.[12]

General Erfurth believed that the majority of Finns at the beginning of the conflict were interested primarily in recovering the territories lost in the Winter War. Those who harbored hopes for a Greater Finland were primarily among the military and younger academics. However, after the great military successes in 1941 and the apparent unstoppable drive of the Germans deep into the Soviet Union, the ranks of the more ambitious increased.[13]

It is rather amazing that the Finns appear not to have realized—by their refusal to participate in operations against the Soviet Union after they had secured the lost territories and East Karelia—that the achievement of their own goals was totally dependent on Germany achieving its goal of destroying the Soviet Union. Germany's failure to do so either because of a military defeat or because of a negotiated settlement would jeopardize Finland's position. If Germany lost the war the very existence of Finland came into question. It therefore made virtually no difference what the Finnish war aims were as they were intrinsically linked to those of Germany.

It is nevertheless extraordinary that the Germans did not press the Finns for more definitive answers regarding their participation in achieving the two main German objectives—operations against Leningrad and the cutting of the Murmansk Railroad. The failure to do so became a major bone of contention, as should have been anticipated. Karl von Clausewitz wrote: "No war is begun, or at least, no war should be begun, if people acted wisely, without first finding an answer to the question: what is to be attained by and in war?"[14]

While the Finns appear to have limited themselves to stating to the Germans that they were only interested in regaining their lost territories, the Germans were probably well aware that a sizable part of military and political circles in Finland had more ambitious ideas. This became obvious when Finland moved into East Karelia. The strong expectation of a short war was probably a major factor in keeping the Germans from insisting on a harmonization of war aims and plans.

It was a grave mistake for the Germans not to insist on a clear understanding about Finnish participation in the achievement of the dual objectives—capture of Leningrad and the cutting of the Murmansk Railroad—before placing some 250,000 troops in a war theater where they would to a large extent be dependent on the actions of their new-found brothers-in-arms. If the Finns had balked at such an understanding, it would have been wise for the Germans not to waste precious resources in this theater of war.

Deficient Command Structure

The OKW was given the responsibility under the *Barbarossa* Directive to make the necessary arrangements to put Romanian and Finnish contingents under German command. There is no evidence that this was seriously tried with respect to Finland. Command and command relationships were discussed during the Finnish delegation's visit to Germany in May 1941. The Germans wanted General Falkenhorst to command the forces in north and central Finland while Mannerheim would command in the south.

German planners had previously assumed that Mannerheim would be given overall command in Finland.[15] This is reflected in the OKW directive on April 7, 1941 (see below). That idea was now dropped, and their chance of bringing Mannerheim, a rather independent individual, under their control was lost as well. In doing so the Germans disregarded another well-known warning of their military philosopher and theorist Clausewitz that the worst situation is where two independent commanders find themselves operating in the same theater of war.

Ziemke and Erfurth speculate that this change came about because of an OKW desire to command in an active theater of operations. There was probably another and more practical reason. Hitler became exceedingly worried about the security of northern Norway and the iron and nickel mines in Sweden and Finland after the British raid on the Lofoten Islands in March 1941 (see below), and began a major force build-up. Mountain Corps Norway was an integral part of the defense of north Norway and Hitler and the OKW may well have been reluctant to place a good part of this area under Finnish command. Falkenhorst was still the German armed forces commander in Norway and it made some sense to also have him as commander in central and northern Finland.

Mannerheim wrote after the war that he received indirect feelers—from General Erfurth to General Heinrichs—about assuming overall command in Finland. There is some confusion in the sources as to when these feelers were made. Mannerheim gives the time of the offer as June 1941 while Erfurth places it in June 1944.[16] Mannerheim writes about the 1941 offer that he was not attracted by the idea and gives as his reason a reluctance to become too dependent on the German High Command. Mannerheim does not mention the 1944 offer in his memoirs but Erfurth writes that Mannerheim replied to it on June 29, 1944, with the statement that he was too old to take over the additional responsibilities that the position of commander in chief of all forces in Finland would entail. The 1944 offer, if made, was probably an attempt to tie Finland firmly to Germany at a time when it was beginning to go its own way.

In addition to failing to settle on an overall commander, operations in Finland came under two separate German headquarters. The German commander in chief in northern and central Finland, whose main focus was on isolating Murmansk, reported to the OKW after Hitler's changes to the command structure following the Lofoten raid in March 1941. OKH—responsible for operations on the Eastern Front—was left to deal with operations in southern Finland. The axiomatic belief in both Germany and Finland that the looming war would be short was probably the greatest contributing factor to this deficient command arrangement. This short-war scenario undoubtedly made many feel that no elaborate command structure or long-range plans were necessary.

There was no joint German–Finnish campaign plan much beyond the initial attacks. The loose and informal nature of the coalition, the lack of long-range planning, and an ineffective command structure posed increasing problems as the war dragged on. These massive violations of long-standing military principles could have been rectified by Hitler and the OKW, but they failed to act.

Directive No. 21—The German Strategic Plan

The planning for an operation against the Soviet Union began as soon as Hitler briefed his military advisors at the end of July 1940. The initial planning effort for the invasion was led by Major General Erich Marcks who was in charge of planning at OKH; he developed the first draft which was presented to OKH on August 5. Major General Friedrich von Paulus replaced Marcks in September when he became assistant chief of staff for operations at OKH. In addition, there was an independent operational study going on at OKW by Lieutenant Colonel Bernhard von Lossberg. While the final OKW position did not differ significantly from the OKH plan presented to Hitler on December 5, the earlier efforts focused on trying to change the overall strategy and therefore the roles assigned to the forces on the northern front.

Finland offered at least two operational possibilities for the German planners.

1. An offensive to isolate Murmansk.
2. An offensive on both sides of Lake Ladoga against the right flank of the Soviet forces in the Leningrad area.

General Marcks undoubtedly recognized the importance of the Murmansk Railroad in providing a link between the Soviet Union and the outside world. Finland, however, did not figure prominently in General Marcks' scheme of things. He envisioned the main assault on the Soviet Union to take place in the south and center. Northern Russia did not figure into the initial assault. He recommended postponing Finnish participation until later since a major German drive through the Baltic States to Leningrad was not part of his overall plan.

A plan that the National Defense Section of OKW submitted to General Jodl on September 19, proposed a significant change to the plan initially worked out by General Marcks. This proposal, probably worked out by Lieutenant Colonel von Lossberg, coincided with General von Paulus taking over General Marcks' job at OKH. The National Defense Section recommended a significant increase in the strength of the German Army's left wing driving northward through the Baltic States towards Leningrad. This strategic change increased the importance of Finnish participation. The altered plan called for almost all German and Finnish forces to concentrate in southeast Finland. These forces would either attack across the Karelian Isthmus in the direction of Leningrad or on the east side of Lake Ladoga in the direction of Tikhvin.

The OKW's proposed revisions to the plan made excellent sense. However, strategic and practical problems led to its abandonment. The Finns would probably resist such a deployment since it would leave central Finland virtually defenseless unless they moved sizable forces to that area. Concentrating the bulk of German forces in southeastern Finland would also cause serious transportation and supply problems. The communications network in southeast Finland would be severely strained to support both the Finnish Army plus a number of German divisions. Finally, it would be nearly impossible to have a large buildup of German forces along with the necessary supplies in this area without alerting the Soviets to a pending attack.

Brauchitsch and Halder presented the army plan for the campaign against the Soviet Union to Hitler on December 5, 1940. Hitler approved the plan and Jodl instructed the National Defense Section on December 6 to prepare a directive based on the approved plan.

From the incomplete records of the conference on December 5 and the more complete record of a meeting between Halder and Falkenhorst on December 7 we get a rather clear idea of what the planners had in mind. The plan for a main German effort in the southeast was dropped, undoubtedly for the reasons mentioned above. The plan that was settled on was one that dissipated the offensive and left the important operations in the southeast totally to the Finns. The German offensive was fragmented. Two mountain divisions would cross the Finnish border in the Pechenga area and conduct operations in the direction of Murmansk. Two additional divisions from central Norway were to cross Sweden by rail. This force would launch operations in the Salla area and advance towards Kandalaksha (Kantalahti) and cut the Murmansk Railroad to isolate Murmansk.

Hitler signed Directive No. 21, the strategic plan for Operation *Barbarossa*, on December 18, 1940. It is a very concise document (nine typed double-spaced pages) when one considers the fact that it was the blueprint for the most gigantic military operation in history. The directive, which the OKW issued as the basis for operational planning by the services, reads as follows regarding operations in Finland:

Finland will cover the advance of the Northern Group of German forces moving from Norway (detachments of Group XXI) and will operate in conjunction with them. Finland will also be responsible for eliminating Hango [Hanko].

It is possible that Swedish railways and roads may be available for the movement of the German Northern Group, by the beginning of the operation at the latest.

. . . *The most important task of Group XXI, even during these eastern operations, remains the protection of Norway* [emphasis in Trevor-Roper's translation]. Any forces available after carrying out this task will be employed in the North (Mountain Corps), at first to protect the Petsamo area and its iron [nickel] ore mines and the Arctic highway [Arctic Ocean Highway], then to advance with Finnish forces against the Murmansk railway and thus prevent the passage of supplies to Murmansk by land.

The question whether an operation of this kind can be carried out with stronger German forces (two or three divisions) from the Rovaniemi area and south of it will depend on the willingness of Sweden to make its railways available for troop transport.

It will be the duty of the main body of the Finnish Army, in conjunction with the advance of the German North flank, to hold down the strongest possible Russian forces by an attack to the West, or on both sides of Lake Ladoga, and to occupy Hango.[17]

The whole German effort in the north was directed at isolating Murmansk—whether in a drive from Pechenga, from Rovaniemi, or from both. The operations in the south and southeast became a Finnish affair.

Paul Carell writes in *Hitler Moves East 1941-1943* that "The very first drafts for 'Operation Barbarossa' list a surprising objective—Murmansk.[18] This little-known place was named alongside the great strategic objectives like Moscow, Leningrad, Kiev, and Rostov."[19] It is true that the Germans contemplated a drive to capture Murmansk but the capture of that city is not listed as an objective in the final version of Directive No. 21. The task of the forces in the north was to cut the Murmansk Railroad and thus isolate Murmansk.

Murmansk became extremely important to the Allied war effort as the major port for bringing supplies and equipment for the Soviet armed forces. But this development was not foreseen by Hitler and the German High Command and was therefore not the reason for according that port on the Arctic Ocean with a population of about 100,000 such importance. The Germans anticipated a quick knockout blow in World War II and the importance of Murmansk as a supply port was considered very minimal in their short-war scenario.

The Russians had begun the construction of an 1,350-kilometer railway line from St Petersburg (Leningrad after the communists seized power) to Murmansk in 1914. This gigantic construction project, completed in 1917, was undertaken by the Russians for the purpose of making use of the only port in that country which had an unrestricted connection to the oceans of the world. Murmansk, located at approximately the same latitude as Point Barrow, Alaska, was ice-free throughout the year with open access to the Atlantic. The other major port on the White Sea, Archangel, was ice-bound for several months each year. The Russians initially used a convict work force but after World War I began, they used some 70,000 captured German and Austrian prisoners. Carell describes the deplorable conditions under which these prisoners worked:

> The hardships of the prisoners-of-war defied description. During the short scorching summer they were mown down by typhoid, and during the eight months of the Arctic winter they were killed by cold and hunger. Within twenty-four months 25,000 men had died. Every mile of the 850-mile long line cost twenty-nine dead."[20]

To Hitler, the danger from the Murmansk Railroad was the ability it gave the Russians to move large military forces from central Russia to their border with Finland along the Arctic Ocean. A major reason for Hitler's invasion of Norway in 1940 was to secure the iron ore from the mining districts in northern Sweden. The nickel mines in Kolosjoki near Pechenga, only 100 kilometers from Murmansk, were also important to the German war industry and a significant reason for Germany's interest in Finland. Of grave concern to Hitler was the possibility that Russia might use the Murmansk Railroad to quickly move significant forces to threaten these valuable sources of iron and nickel. Another worry was that the British would land forces in that area.

Hitler had reason to be concerned. German aerial reconnaissance of the Murmansk area revealed extensive army and air force installations. These, along with massive rail and harbor facilities made Murmansk an ideal Soviet marshalling area for an offensive against northern Finland and Norway. Hitler not only viewed this as a threat against the nickel that the Germans needed in their steel industry but as a strategic threat to the success of *Barbarossa*. Kirkenes in Norway, only 50 kilometers from Pechenga, was an important German base. If the Soviets reached that far, the line of communications to northern Finland would be cut and the whole Finnish front would be outflanked from the north.

Group XXI's Staff Study

The next step in the planning process was the development of a staff study by Group XXI (Army of Norway) for operations in Finland based on Directive 21. The study was expanded by Marshal von Brauchitsch on January 16 to include examining the feasibility of a German–Finnish southeast drive in the area of Lake Ladoga, Lake Onega, and the White Sea. The Army of Norway was asked to make recommendations for supply operations and command relationships. This study, begun in late December, was completed on January 27, 1941, and given the code name *Silberfuchs* (Silver Fox).

The Finnish Army would carry the main burden of the attack. The bulk of their forces would be concentrated in the southeast for an attack east of Lake Ladoga towards the Svir River. The Finnish Army was to defend the frontier north of Lake Ladoga with relatively weak forces, and additionally was responsible for the security of the coast and the Åland Islands. The staff study assumed that the overall command in Finland would be given to the Finns because they were providing the preponderance of forces.

The planning and preparation for *Renntier* was not wasted, but expanded by making it part of the operations assigned to Mountain Corps Norway. The main German attack was a drive from Rovaniemi through Salla to Kandalaksha on the White Sea. This drive would cut the Murmansk Railroad and sever lines of communication between Soviet forces in Murmansk and on the Kola Peninsula from the rest of the Soviet Union.

The forces allocated to the main drive consisted of one German and one Finnish corps. The German corps—XXXVI Corps—consisted of two infantry divisions and SS Kampfgruppe Nord reinforced by a tank battalion, a machinegun battalion, an antitank battalion, an artillery battalion, and engineers. Kampfgruppe Nord would provide security for the assembly of the two infantry divisions. Part of the German forces would turn north when they reached Kandalaksha. In conjunction with one reinforced mountain division advancing from Pechenga towards Murmansk, the forces that turned north would destroy the Soviet forces on the Kola Peninsula and capture Murmansk.

The Finnish corps—III Corps—consisted of two divisions (3rd and 6th) plus border guards. Its main mission was to launch a secondary attack on the German right flank against Ukhta (Uhtua) and then on towards Kem (Kemi) on the White Sea. This drive, if successful, would also cut the Murmansk Railroad. The bulk of the German forces advancing on Kandalaksha would turn south after reaching that town and link up with the Finns in the Kem area for a joint drive southward behind the left wing of the main Finnish Army.

The operations proposed in the *Silberfuchs* staff study assumed that Sweden would allow German troops and supplies to cross its territory from Norway to Finland. It was planned that five divisions (later increased to seven) would be left in Norway for its defense and that the Army of Norway would supply all German units. This would involve large supply, construction, and transportation assets and many of these would have to come from Germany.

The OKH Operation Order

The German Army issued an operation order at the end of January for operations in Finland using the Army of Norway staff study as its basis. Hitler approved the order on February 3, 1941.

The OKH order assigned the defense of Norway as the highest priority of the Army of Norway. Only forces over and above the requirement for the priority mission would be used in Finland where the mission of German forces was limited to the defense of the Pechanga area until Finland entered the war. At that time the order laid out two possible courses of action. The first was that proposed in the Army of Norway staff study, while the second would come into being if Sweden refused transit of troops. If this materialized, the Germans would launch an attack through Pechenga with the mission of capturing Murmansk.

As far as the mission of the Finnish Army, some disagreements had

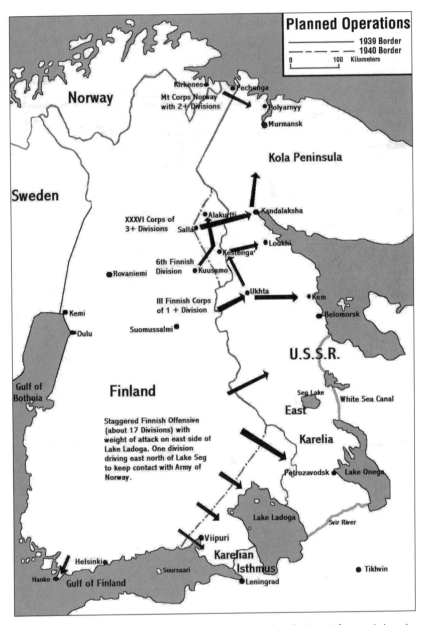

developed and certain things remained unresolved. Finnish participation in the planning had been indirect and remained so because Hitler's order on February 3, 1941 specified that all potential allies should be brought into the planning process only when German intentions could no longer be disguised. The Army order gave the Finnish Army the mission of covering German deployments in central Finland and the capturing of Hanko. The Germans wanted the bulk of the Finnish Army to undertake offensive operations towards the southeast when German Army Group North crossed the Dvina River. The Germans accepted offensives on both sides of Lake Ladoga as long as the main effort was made on the east side of that lake. The Finnish Army was expected to make a sweep around the eastern shore of the lake and isolate Leningrad by affecting a junction with Army Group North in the Tikhvin area.

The Finns, however, preferred to undertake an operation west of Lake Ladoga with the limited goal of recovering the important territory on the Isthmus of Karelia which they had lost in the Winter War. The missions of the Finnish Army were thrashed out in the meeting between General Halder and General Heinrichs on January 30, 1941. The Finns would launch their offensive not later than when Army Group North crossed the Dvina River. The offensive was to take place on both sides of Lake Ladoga with five divisions on the west side and three divisions in the east. The Finns would use two divisions against Hanko. Heinrichs also answered the question that Halder had asked General Talvela in December about Finnish ability to mobilize without drawing attention. Heinrichs stated that to mobilize without causing some attention was not possible.

Resource problems now began to affect the plans in the north. OKH informed the Army of Norway that only a part of the support personnel and transport resources requested in the *Silberfuchs* staff study would be available. In addition, Kampfgruppe Nord was withdrawn from Falkenhorst's order of battle for Finland.[21] The Army of Norway was asked to investigate if it could carry out the OKH order with these limitations. The Army of Norway replied that while the occupation of Pechenga could be carried out, an attack against Murmansk from the Pechenga area alone was not possible because the large force required could not be supported and operational possibilities were also poor. The destruction of Russian forces defending Murmansk was possible providing full use of Swedish territory was granted for both supply and troop movements.

The Army of Norway proposed to execute the plan in the *Silberfuchs* staff study but to delete that part of the plan that called for a southward turn to support the Finnish Army in the Lake Ladoga area because of inadequate logistic and transportation assets. The Army of Norway stated that an operation to the south would be possible only after an adequate supply base had been established in the Kandalaksha area. The OKH accepted the Army of Norway proposal on March 2, 1941.

The Lofoten Raid

On March 4, 1941 the British carried out one of the first commando operations of World War II in the Lofoten Islands in Norway. The operation was code-named *Claymore* and the mission was to destroy a number of fish oil factories that produced glycerin for use in munitions. The factories in the Lofoten Islands accounted for about half of the total production of glycerin in Norway. The naval component of the force consisted of two cruisers and five destroyers. After bombarding the town of Svolvær and sinking several ships in the harbor a force of about 800 was landed. This force consisted of 3rd and 4th Commandos and a force from the Norwegian Army in the UK under the command of Captain Martin Linge.[22] The main factories were destroyed after minor fighting.

The raid had little military significance but it had a considerable psychological effect on Hitler and led him to take action impacting planned operations in Finland. Hitler was extremely proud of having pulled off what he labeled the "sauciest" military operation of the war by his conquest of Norway against virtually all military principles and the views of the German General Staff. He undoubtedly considered Norway a trophy attesting to his military genius and wanted to protect that trophy at nearly any cost. Hitler continued to maintain, "Norway is the zone of destiny in this war" and demanded unconditional obedience to all edicts pertaining to its defense.[23]

Hitler called a conference on March 12 to evaluate the situation in Norway. He expressed the view that the British would start their offensive against the long Norwegian coastline as the German campaign began against the Soviet Union. He expected British action to consist of a number of small raids that would be difficult to counter because of poor internal lines of communication in Norway. These raids could develop into major operations. In view of this danger and the need for the Army of Norway to maintain total security for Norway Hitler made several decisions that impacted on the planned operations in Finland:

1. Strengthen the defenses in Norway with 160 coastal artillery batteries and two garrison divisions.

2. Reduce the number of forces from Norway that had been planned for use in Finland.

3. Re-evaluate the plans for German operations in Finland since Swedish attitude with respect to transit was in doubt.

Hitler's orders led to a revision of the command structure and the OKH order for *Barbarossa*. Falkenhorst had reported to OKW as armed forces commander in Norway and to OKH as commander of the Army of Norway and the planned operations in Finland. Falkenhorst was now placed under OKW in both areas. The additional batteries for coastal defense were to be in place by the middle of May along with increased troop strength in north Norway. The occupation and defense of the Pechenga area was reaffirmed but the planned operation against Murmansk was changed. Murmansk was not to be attacked directly at this stage but only isolated from the rest of the Soviet Union.

The British raid in Lofoten caused the Army of Norway to practically stop its planning for *Barbarossa* while waiting for its missions to be clarified. Some deployments of forces did take place during March. The movement of the 2nd Mountain Division to the vicinity of Kirkenes was begun. The OKH's earlier withdrawal of SS Kampfgruppe Nord from participation in operations in Finland was now rescinded, and the lead elements of this organization were prepared for transport via Sweden to the Kirkenes area. The Swedes were told that the unit was being moved as part of a replacement operation. From Kirkenes Kampfgruppe Nord would proceed south along the Arctic Ocean Highway to its assembly area near Rovaniemi. The reason this unit was again assigned to operations in Finland was that it was the only motorized unit available to the Army of Norway and this facilitated the long trek from Kirkenes to Rovaniemi.

The Army of Norway Operation Order
An OKW directive of April 7, 1941, which implemented the revised OKH order broke the logjam that had existed the previous month and allowed planning and preparations to proceed. The directive provided for the reinforced 2nd Mountain Division to be ready to occupy Pechenga provided its commitment did not reduce the forces available to defend the Narvik-Kirkenes area to below the 18 battalions that had been decided on earlier. It was not certain that enough forces could be gathered for a drive to Polyarnyy to block Kola Bay above Murmansk, but preparations for this possibility were to be made.

The capture of Kandalaksha was still viewed as the first step in isolating Murmansk from the south. Operations after the capture of Kandalaksha would depend on the circumstances at the time. It was assumed that transit through Sweden for the buildup in central Finland would not be possible and other provisions were made. One infantry division was to be sent by sea to Finland and the XXXVI Corps Headquarters and its attachments would come by sea from Norway. An additional division would be sent by rail from southern Norway if Sweden granted transit after the start of the war against the Soviet Union. Again, it was planned to offer the command of all forces in Finland to Marshal Mannerheim.

The Army of Norway submitted its plan of operations to the OKW on April 17 and followed this up a few days later by issuing orders to the Mountain Corps Norway and the XXXVI Corps. The strength of the enemy that these units were expected to encounter was estimated at five infantry divisions and two understrength armored units.

Hitler had a meeting with General der Gebirgstruppe Dietl, the commander of Mountain Corps Norway, in Berlin on April 21. Dietl was an ardent supporter of Hitler, and Hitler was fond of this plain Bavarian who had proved his loyalty by his tenacity at Narvik the previous year. He explained to Dietl the importance of eliminating the threat from Murmansk at the very outset of operations by seizing that city. Dietl explained the difficulties involved in an attack on Murmansk—long and difficult lines of supply, atrocious terrain, severe climate, lack of roads, and the lack of various support troops in his command to overcome these obstacles.

Dietl agreed with Hitler that the Soviets might attack Pechenga since it was much easier for them to do so because they had lateral lines of communication and large supply depots close to their forward positions. He pointed out that it would be much easier for the Germans to cut the Murmansk Railroad further south and that this would place the Soviets at the same disadvantage as the Germans.[24]

Hitler was impressed by Dietl's arguments and asked him to leave his papers so he could think about what Dietl had proposed. While we don't know what caused Hitler not to adopt Dietl's recommendations, the final decision by OKW was, as we shall see, a poor compromise.

Mountain Corps Norway had several missions under the Army of Norway operations order. First and foremost was the defense of Norway north of Narvik. The second mission was to execute Operation

Renntier as discussed earlier. The forces should be ready to carry out this mission on 72 hours' notice. This mission would either be executed separately (in case of a Soviet attack on Finland) or as part of the third mission which was to undertake an offensive along the Arctic coast to Polyarnyy to close Kola Bay north of Murmansk. This operation was code named *Platinfuchs* (Platinum Fox). If conditions allowed, Dietl's forces were to cross Kola Bay and occupy Murmansk.

Dietl had the following forces available for his primary mission, the defense of Norway north of Narvik:

1. The 199th Infantry Division.
2. The 9th SS Regiment.
3. Three machinegun battalions.
4. A police battalion.
5. Some naval units.
6. Coastal artillery.

Dietl had the following forces available for the execution of *Renntier* and *Platinfuchs*:

1. 2nd Mountain Division.
2. 3rd Mountain Division.
3. A reduced-strength antiaircraft battalion.
4. A communications battalion.
5. Two batteries of 105mm guns.
6. A rocket launcher (Nebelwerfer) battery.
7. A construction battalion.
8. An attached Finnish unit of three infantry companies and a battery of artillery. It was referred to as the Petsamo Detachment or the Ivalo Battalion.

The main German attack was to be carried out by the XXXVI Corps against Kandalaksha, code named *Polarfuchs* (Polar Fox). The concept of operations called for the assembly of XXXVI Corps east of Rovaniemi. The corps' main attack would envelop and eliminate the Soviet strongpoints in the Salla area and then drive towards Kandalaksha along the road from Rovaniemi. After taking Kandalaksha and securing its southern flank the corps would push northward along the railroad to take Murmansk in conjunction with Dietl's Mountain Corps.

The following forces were assigned to the XXXVI Corps by the Army of Norway operations order:

1. The 169th Infantry Division.
2. SS Kampfgruppe Nord.
3. 6th Finnish Division, detached from III Finnish Corps.
4. Two tank battalions.
5. Two motorized artillery battalions.
6. A heavy weapons battalion.
7. A communications battalion.
8. Two batteries of antiaircraft artillery.
9. A rocket launcher battery.
10. Two construction battalions.
11. A bridge construction battalion.

All details involving Finnish participation had not been resolved when the Army of Norway issued its order and the part of the order pertaining to Finnish units was therefore tentative.

As described in Chapter 1, on May 25 the OKW began a three-day conference with a Finnish military delegation headed by General Heinrichs. This conference was continued on June 3 in Helsinki. Command relationships in Finland were decided at these meetings. Falkenhorst would command in northern and central Finland (*Silberfuchs*) and Marshal Mannerheim would command in southern Finland. This was a change from earlier German intentions to offer Mannerheim the overall command in Finland.

The Army of Norway issued a supplement to its April order after the problems involving Finnish participation were resolved on June 11. This included an order to the Finnish III Corps,[25] which became attached to the Army of Norway on June 15. The combat elements of III Corps consisted of two infantry divisions and border guards. However, one division—the 6th—was attached to XXXVI Corps. The III Corps (3rd Division plus border guards after the detachment of the 6th Division) was directed to provide security for the right flank of the XXXVI Corps through offensive operations. Its main force was to attack from Suomussalmi towards Kem by way of Ukhta. A secondary attack would be launched against Loukhi (Louhi) via Kestenga (Kistinki). The 6th Finnish Division—attached to XXXVI Corps—

would begin its advance from the Kuusamo area towards Loukhi but instead of going directly to that town, it would swing in a northeast direction east of Salla to Alakurtti on the Tuntsa River. The southern border of the Army of Norway's responsibility was along a line running from Oulu to Belomorsk.

The roles of the German Navy and the Luftwaffe in Operation *Silberfuchs* were limited. Admiral Erich Raeder, the commander in chief of the German Navy, was eager to capture Polyarnyy and Murmansk early. He viewed this as the most effective way to neutralize Soviet naval supremacy and reduce the chances of British naval operations in the north. The navy expected that supply operations along the coast of north Norway might have to be curtailed until Polyarnyy was captured and Kola Bay sealed.

The Luftwaffe participation was very inadequate. The 5th Air Fleet in Norway held back about 200 aircraft for the defense of Norway, its primary mission. A measly 60 aircraft were made available to support *Silberfuchs*. Only 10 of these were fighters. The rest were bombers (40), and reconnaissance aircraft (10). These very small air assets had the nearly impossible missions of providing close air support, destroying the port facilities at Polyarnyy and Murmansk, interdicting the Murmansk Railroad, destroying Soviet airfields, and of operating against the Soviet Navy in the Arctic Ocean.

Marshalling of Forces

The concentration of the Army of Norway forces for *Silberfuchs* was itself a major undertaking. In the far north, only the 2nd Mountain Division was already in the Kirkenes area. Most units that became part of Mountain Corps Norway for defense of north Norway and for *Platinfuchs* had to be transported from southern Norway. Sea transport was the only practical way since Route 50 south of Narvik had to cross several fjords before reaching Bodø and for the 140 kilometers that separated Bodø from Narvik there was no road at all. Route 50 north of Narvik was impossible to keep open in winter with available snow removal equipment. From April to June much of this road became impassable because of the thaw.

The 3rd Mountain Division was already in the Narvik area but had to be brought from there to Kirkenes. The last elements of this division did not reach their assembly area south of Kirkenes until June 17. The

199th Infantry Division, the staff of the 702nd Infantry Division, and various miscellaneous units amounting to several thousand troops had to be transported from southern Norway. The transfer of these units was completed by the end of May. The 8,000-strong motorized SS Kampfgruppe Nord came from southern Norway through Sweden to Narvik and had to be moved from there to Kirkenes. It reached its destination on June 6 and started the long trek via the Arctic Ocean Highway to Rovaniemi on June 7. It reached Rovaniemi on June 10.

The assault elements of Mountain Corps Norway (the 2nd and 3rd Mountain Divisions plus combat support troops) numbered 27,500 men. Mountain Corps Norway was to draw its supplies from a one-year stockpile Hitler had ordered established in Norway in the fall of 1940. These supplies were, for the most part, brought to Kirkenes by ships.

The movement of the main force of XXXVI Corps to Finland was carried out in two sea transport operations: *Blaufuchs* (Blue Fox) *1*, and *Blaufuchs 2. Blaufuchs 1* brought the 169th Infantry Division and assorted support units (20,000 men) from Stettin to Oulu. *Blaufuchs 2* brought the XXXVI Corps Headquarters and corps support troops (10,600 men) by ships from Oslo to Oulu. The first ships sailed on June 5, 1941, and the transfer was completed on June 14.

These large-scale troop movements could not be concealed and their purpose was explained as a relief operation for north Norway. The XXXVI Corps was ordered not to turn eastward from the route Oulu–Rovaniemi until June 18.

The strength of the XXXVI Corps was 40,600 men. This did not include the attached Finnish units. Stockpiles that the corps could draw on had been established with rations for three months, ammunition for more than two months, and petroleum products for two months. The supply operations for both Norway and Finland were managed by *Heimatstab Nord* (Home Staff North). This organization was renamed *Heimatstab Übersee* (Home Staff Overseas) in June 1941.

Negotiations for the transit of one division to Finland across Sweden from southern Norway began in Stockholm on June 23, 1941. The Swedes consented to the transit on June 25 and the 163rd Infantry Division began moving out of Oslo on June 26. The 163rd was replaced in Norway by the 710th Infantry Division from Germany. The intention had been to use the 163rd Division against Hanko but OKW ordered it attached to the Finnish Army in the south where it became Mannerheim's reserve for operations in the Lake Ladoga area.

Seven divisions (about 150,000 troops) were left for the defense of Norway and they were organized and stationed as follows:

1. LXX Corps of three divisions had its headquarters in Oslo.
2. XXXIII Corps of two divisions had its headquarters in Trondheim.
3. Provisional Corps *Nagy* of two divisions with its headquarters in Alta. This organization was originally part of Mountain Corps Norway but was detached on June 28 and thereafter came under the command of the Army of Norway in Oslo. It had 160 batteries of army coastal artillery, 56 batteries of naval coastal artillery, 6 police battalions, an SS-Regiment, and 3 motorized machine gun battalions.

In an elaborate cover operation to shield the upcoming attack on the Soviet Union units in Norway were assigned to an operation called *Harpune Nord* (Harpoon North). Units in Denmark and France were also part of the deception plan (*Harpune Süd*—Harpoon South). The intention was to depict an invasion of England in the making, timed for about August 1, 1941.

Timing of the Attacks

The timing of the attacks out of Finland was left undecided in the operational orders. With respect to the timing of the Finnish attacks in the southeast this was probably due to the fact that the Germans did not want to reveal the starting date of their own operations against the Soviet Union. Another reason was that the Germans wanted to time the Finnish attack for maximum impact in relation to the advance of Army Group North. The Finns requested of the Germans on June 16 that the main Finnish attack be delayed until a few days after *Silberfuchs* started. Erfurth explained that the reason for the Finnish request was that "The Finns wanted to create the impression among their own people and people's representatives of being drawn in by the course of events."[26]

Finland declared neutrality when the Germans attacked the Soviet Union on June 22, 1941. This official position was maintained until the evening of June 25 despite the fact that German aircraft began operations from Finnish airfields on June 23 when the Luftwaffe flew missions against Murmansk and Salla. The Russians retaliated with attacks on Pechenga, Kemijärvi, and Rovaniemi. The Soviets began massive air attacks against cities in southern Finland on June 25 and that night the Finnish government declared that since the country had been attacked, a state of war existed between Finland and the Soviet Union.

Much focus has been directed at the fact that the Soviet Union initiated attacks on Finnish cities before Finnish military operations against the Soviet Union had begun. The Soviets were well aware that strong German military forces were present in Finland and that the Finnish armed forces were mobilized and deploying with the logical intention of joining the Germans in offensive operations. The Finns later admitted that the presence of German forces in the country gave the Soviets compelling reasons for attacking. Tanner recounts a conversation with Mannerheim, Prime Minister Linkomies, the minister of defense, and the chief of staff on August 9, 1943:

> The conclusion of the exchange of opinions can be said to have been that . . . Germany having attacked Russia on June 22, 1941, the Soviet Union had begun bombing places in Finland because there were German troops in the country.[27]

The German Army made its decision as to the location of the Finnish attack on June 24 and this differed somewhat from what had been agreed to earlier. Erfurth was instructed to tell the Finns to prepare for an operation on the east side of Lake Ladoga with at least six divisions, with the weight of the attack on the left. The Finns submitted plans which agreed with the German wishes on June 29. General Halder, based on the fact that Army Group North was approaching the last major obstacle south of Leningrad—the Dvina River—decided on July 4 that the Finns should start offensive operations on July 10.

The Mountain Corps Norway executed Operation *Renntier* on June 22 by crossing the Norwegian–Finnish border with the 2nd and 3rd Mountain Divisions. The Finnish border guards had orders to cooperate and there were no incidents. Mountain Corps Norway stopped short of the Finnish–Soviet border with the 2nd Division on the left and the 3rd Division on the right. Orders were issued to Mountain Corps Norway by the Army of Norway not to cross the Soviet border until June 29. The German move into Pechenga was undoubtedly observed by Soviet forces on the Rybachiy Peninsula at the entrance to Pechenga Bay.

The Army of Norway also issued orders to the Finnish III Corps and the German XXXVI Corps on June 22. The III Corps was ordered to begin cross-border operations at 0200 hours on July 1 and XXXVI Corps was ordered to begin its operations at 1600 hours the same day. The staggered timing in each sector was necessitated by the scarcity of air resources. The air operations in support of Mountain Corps Norway could take place from airfields in Norway—Kirkenes and Banak—but the operations had to switch to Rovaniemi for support of the two corps in the Salla area.

Supply Lines

Some of the serious problems for the Germans with respect to lines of communication were touched on when we discussed the marshalling of their forces. The main supply and support bases for German operations out of Finland were in Norway and the poor lines of communication in the northern part of that country presented the Germans with almost insurmountable problems. There were basically four routes for the Germans to support their forces in Finland:

1. By sea around the northernmost part of Norway to the ports of Kirkenes and Pechenga. This route was exposed to British and Soviet naval attacks and the entrance to Pechenga harbor was within range of Russian shore batteries on the Rybachiy Peninsula.
2. Route 50 from Narvik to Kirkenes. This road did not have an all-weather surface in 1941 and the snow removal equipment proved inadequate to cope with the heavy snowfall.
3. The land route from Norway through Sweden. Reliance on this route was dangerous because its use hinged on Swedish permission. The Swedes became increasingly reluctant to grant permission for its use as the war progressed. Finnish railroads were built to Soviet gauge while Swedish railroads used western gauge. For that reason rail shipments from Sweden had to be trans-loaded at the border.
4. The sea route through the Baltic, either from Norway or Germany. While this route was relatively safe, it was long

and presented problems of its own. The Finnish port capacity in the Gulf of Bothnia was limited and the ports were ice-bound for up to five months each year.

The internal lines of communications in Finland were also inadequate. Almost none of the roads were improved by any stretch of the imagination. Most of the bridges were not built to carry heavy military equipment. The Arctic Ocean Highway was exceedingly important to the Army of Norway as it was the only road link between Rovaniemi and Pechenga and on to Kirkenes. However, it was inadequate for the increased demands and of marginal usefulness since trucks consumed nearly the weight of their cargos in fuel on the 600-mile round trip from Rovaniemi to Pechenga.

Terrain and Weather

Severe climate and extraordinarily difficult terrain characterized the Mountain Corps Norway zone of operations. At Pechenga Bay the influence of the Gulf Stream is still strong enough to permit some summer vegetation near the bay and along the river valley. East of Pechenga the coast is bare. The terrain is a mass of low, rocky hills, and depressions with giant boulders left over from the last ice age. Many valleys have no outlets and the melting ice forms hundreds of lakes. This belt of tundra is rather narrow at Pechenga but as one moves east the effects of the Gulf Stream weaken and the belt increases in width to nearly 100 kilometers or more near Kola Bay and Murmansk. Dietl described the terrain around Murmansk as follows when he talked to Hitler on April 21:

> The landscape up there in the tundra outside Murmansk is just as it was after the Creation. There's not a tree, not a shrub, not a human settlement. No roads and no paths. Nothing but rock and scree. There are countless torrents, lakes and fast-flowing rivers with rapids and waterfalls.[28]

Dietl goes on to describe the tundra belt around Murmansk as one big wilderness and the pathless desert of rocks as impenetrable for military formations.

Inland from the tundra the terrain gradually becomes characterized by coniferous forest. There are mountains with elevations of up to 2,000 feet but the valleys are swampy with numerous streams and lakes. This is the type of terrain found in the Salla area.

The winter lasts from October to May on the Arctic coast. While the temperatures are not as severe as found further south, away from the influences of the Gulf Stream, the winters are characterized by almost continuous storms and blizzards. The temperatures inland frequently reach -45° Fahrenheit in the Rovaniemi-Salla area of southern Lapland and -40° Fahrenheit in Karelia and South Finland.

The summer usually brings a month or more with an average temperature over 50° Fahrenheit. Swarms of mosquitoes thrive in the swampy forests of the interior. Patches of snow and ice survive the summer despite the fact that temperatures may occasionally reach as high as 80° Fahrenheit. The coastal winds bring in banks of fog that persist from a few hours to weeks.

The Plans in Retrospect

A close look at the planning process for German operations out of Finland is quite revealing. Perhaps most important is the fact that the allocation of resources, particularly air assets, reveals that German capabilities were already showing evidence of being overstretched. Germany was not only about to become involved in a life and death struggle with the Soviet Union but had large forces tied down in the Balkans, in North Africa, and in the defense of western Europe. The scarcity of forces may also have contributed to the hesitant planning and frequent changes leading up to and subsequent to the launching of the attack.

Hitler's fixation with the defense of Norway and assigning that the top priority on the northern front severely reduced the forces available for operations in Finland. The ground forces sent to Finland represented only slightly more than half of what was held back for the defense of Norway. The danger he saw to his hold on Norway was in the form of a British attack. It is difficult to square this with Hitler's stated view that Great Britain was defeated and only the hope of Soviet and US help kept its hopes alive. However, there is some validity to Hitler's argument that the garrison troops in Norway were not suited for operations in the Arctic.

The fragmentation of the German effort did not augur well for overall success. While operations began with the main effort correctly identified as the operations of the XXXVI Corps, the allocation of resources failed to underscore this decision. Attacks by the Army of Norway were launched in three sectors with about two divisions in each sector. Generals Hans Feige (commander of XXXVI Corps) and Dietl both argued that the main effort should be made against Kandalaksha and that the forces in this area should be strengthened for that purpose. Dietl even suggested suspending operations in the Mountain Corps Norway sector to achieve a concentration in central Finland. As we shall see, instead of doing so the Army of Norway took action to effectively shift the main effort to the sector of the Mountain Corps. It is curious that the OKW and the Army of Norway continuously violated some of the teachings of Clausewitz, such as concentrating striking power at the decisive point through the reduction of forces elsewhere.

While strategic logic dictated that the main effort should be made in the drive to Kandalaksha, it was important to maintain pressure in other sectors so as to prevent the Russians from shifting forces laterally behind their front from one to the other. They were able to do so because of the Murmansk Railroad. OKH did not become involved in the arguments about a strategy in Finland since the Army of Norway came directly under OKW after the Lofoten raid and because the OKH considered the operations in Finland, except for those of the main Finnish Army, a waste of precious resources.

The Germans allowed themselves to enter into a very imperfect coalition by failing to insist upon the harmonization of objectives and plans. To them the war was total but not to the Finns. These differing aims created difficulty for the cobelligerents from the very start. The greatest potential of the Finnish effort from the standpoint of the Germans was twofold: 1) the quick isolation and capture of Leningrad so that forces tied up in that gigantic operation could be used in other areas and 2) in providing assistance in severing the Soviet Union's overseas supply route. It was up to the political leadership in Germany to achieve a formal agreement from Finland on these points and it was up to the OKW to take steps to establish an effective command structure. Hitler did not intervene and OKW failed to take these rather obvious actions. Without them it was virtually impossible for the Germans to achieve an effective strategic relationship with Finland and its more limited—and politically unstable and shifting—war aims.

NOTES
1. *NSR*, VII, Fuerher Directive 21, dated December 18, 1941.
2. *NSR*, Serial 260, Schnurre, *Aufzeichnung*, October 31, 1941.
3. Ryti is also alleged to have told Schnurre that he favored depopulating the Leningrad area and that Germany should retain it as some kind of "trading post."
4. *NSR*, Telegram from Blücher to the Foreign Office, Serial 260, November 9, 1941.
5. Blücher, *op. cit.*, pp.263–264.
6. Major General Sir Charles Maynard, *The Murmansk Venture* (London: Hodder & Stoughton Ltd., 1928), pp.95–98.
7. Rüdiger Graf von der Goltz, *Als politischer General im Osten* (Leipzig: K. F. Köhler, 1936), p.63.
8. Lundin, *op. cit.*, p.121, quoting several historians.
9. Erfurth, *The Last Finnish War*, p.20. This order of the day is not quoted in Mannerheim's memoirs.
10. Lundin, *op. cit.*, p.127. Also published in the *New York Times*, July 15, 1942 after it had been released by the Germans.
11. At the war-guilt trial in 1945, President Ryti stated that government was not informed of the July 7 order of the day and it did not reflect Finnish policy.
12. Blücher, *op. cit.*, pp.245–246 and pp.249–250.
13. Waldemar Erfurth, *Der finnische Krieg 1941–1944*. (Wiesbaden: Limes Verlag, 1950), p.197.
14. Karl von Clausewitz, *On War* (Translated from the German by O. J. Matthijs Jolles. Washington, D.C.: Combat Forces Press, 1953), p.569.
15. Erfurth, *The Last Finnish War*, p.57 and Ziemke, *The German Northern Theater of Operations*, p.133.
16. Mannerheim, *Memoirs*, p.422; Erfurth, *The Last Finnish War*, pp.187–188; and Waldemar Erfurth, *Problemet Murmanbanan under Finlands senaste Krig*. Translated by Azel Öhman (Helsingfors: Sönderström & Co. Förlagsaktiebolag, 1952), pp.18–19.
17. The source for this translation is Trevor-Roper, *op. cit.*, pp.93–98.
18. Murmansk is a relatively new town, the last founded in the Russian Empire on October 4, 1916. It was first named Romanov-on-the-Murmane, after the Romanov dynasty. It was renamed Murmansk in 1917. Murman is the traditional Pomor name for the Barents Sea. The Pomors were Russian settlers who penetrated the White Sea and Kola regions. The name Murmane derives from the old Russian word for Norwegians. After a considerable increase in population during and after World War II, the population has recently shown a significant decline from 468,039 in 1989 to 336,137 in 2002. It remains the largest city north of the Arctic Circle.
19. Paul Carell, *Hitler Moves East 1941–1943*. Translated from the German by Ewald Osers (New York: Bantam Books, 1966), p.443.
20. Carell, *op. cit.*, p.444.
21. The SS-Kampfgruppe Nord was composed of the 6th and 7th SS Death's Head Regiments. It was a police unit and had just begun military training. It was the only

motorized unit in the Army of Norway.

22. Erling Jensen and Ragnar Ulstein, *Kompani Linge* (Oslo: Gyldendal Norsk Forlag, 1962), p.17.

23. Joseph H. Devins, *The Vaagso Raid* (Philadelphia: Chilton Book Company, 1968), p.202. and Henrik O. Lunde, *Hitler's Pre-emptive War. The Battle for Norway*, 1940 (Drexel Hill: Casemate, 2008), p.550.

24. Carell, *Hitler Moves East*, pp.446–448.

25. Some sources refer to this organization as the Finnish V corps. That was its designation before it was attached to the German command on June 15, 1941 after which its designation became III Corps.

26. A dispatch by General Erfurth quoted by Ziemke, *The German Northern Theater of Operations*, p.136.

27. Tanner, *op. cit.*, p.94.

28. Carell, *Hitler Moves East*, p.447.

THREE
OPERATION *PLATINFUCHS*

The Murmansk Convoys

This is a logical place to digress temporarily before discussion of land operations in order to consider the importance of the Murmansk supply route for the Soviet Union. The actual convoy operations—a magnificent achievement under trying circumstances and atrocious conditions—are outside the scope of this book. These operations are covered in numerous books that are still available.[1]

As the war progressed and it became obvious that the Finns were reluctant to participate in an attack on Leningrad, there were only two possible benefits for the Germans to have Finland at their side:

1. Finnish operations to recapture their lost territories and their operations in East Karelia would draw some Soviet forces away from those facing Army Group North as it approached Leningrad from the south. In addition, Finland's participation in the war assisted in the blockade of the Soviet Baltic Fleet and thus contributed to German control of the Baltic Sea.

2. More importantly, Finnish cooperation to isolate Murmansk was counted on since the Finns had not objected to it during the planning phase and had placed one corps at the disposal of the Germans for that purpose.

The German planners were undoubtedly aware that Murmansk had already gained some importance as a supply route towards the end of World War I. They also knew that the British had a great stake in keeping the Soviet Union in the war and they should have drawn the next

85

logical conclusion: that Great Britain would make every possible effort to that end. German expectation of a short campaign is probably what caused them not to give Murmansk the attention it deserved. They fully expected to knock the Soviet Union out of the war before aid would be of any consequence.

Churchill was no admirer of Communism but in the life-and-death struggle that was now underway he followed the axiom that the enemy of my enemy is my friend. Churchill took to the airwaves on the evening of June 22, the day of the German attack, to pledge the Soviet Union all possible assistance against what was now their common enemy.

Almost a month passed before the Soviet ambassador in London, Ivan Maiski, delivered Stalin's reply on July 18, 1941. The Soviet dictator surfaced a proposal that was to be repeated frequently in the years to come. He wanted Great Britain to open a front against Germany in France or in the Arctic.

In his book *The Second World War*, Churchill expresses considerable irritation at the behavior of the Soviet Union on the subject of aid. From the outset, the Soviet demands were expressed in harsh language and the efforts of the British were constantly belittled. Stalin viewed British efforts in theaters that did not directly benefit the Soviet Union as sideshows. He demanded the lion's share of the Lend-Lease supplies flowing from the United States and although he must have known its virtual impossibility, he clamored for the opening of a second front in the north in 1941.[2] Stalin undoubtedly knew that a landing on the continent in 1941 was out of the question and may have used this harsh approach to obtain the supplies and equipment his armed forces so sorely needed.

Churchill met considerable opposition from the Admiralty when he proposed to send aid to the Soviet Union via the Arctic Ocean. Admiral Sir Dudley Pound, the First Sea Lord, thought the proposed operation flawed and very risky.[3] Churchill viewed keeping the Soviet Union in the war as a paramount objective and insisted that supplying its armed forces to keep them from collapsing was worth the effort and risks. He was haunted by the fear of Stalin making a separate peace with the Germans. His fears were not groundless as demonstrated by the Soviet attempt to offer the Ukraine to Germany.[4]

The worries of the Admiralty were sound. The resources of the Royal Navy and the merchant fleets at the disposal of the British were already strained.[5] In addition to threats from U-boats and occasional sorties by the German fleet, which had most of its surface units in Norway, the convoys would pass perilously close to the Norwegian coast, well within reach of the Luftwaffe. The best time of the year to minimize these dangers was in the summer when the retreating Arctic ice-sheet allows ships to stay further away from the Norwegian coast. However, there is continual daylight at these latitudes in summer and it would be easy for the Germans to locate and track convoys.

In winter there are frequent violent storms and gigantic waves. The seas and mist sweeping over ships froze immediately upon contact with decks and superstructures, forming layer upon layer of solid ice. These were monstrous conditions for the crews and could lead to capsizing when a ship became top-heavy. Navigation was also a serious problem in the darkness superimposed on the fog produced as the cold Arctic air mass joined with the warmer waters of the Gulf Stream.

It was Admiral Sir John Tovey, the commander in chief of the Home Fleet, who was responsible for executing Churchill's order for establishing a convoy system. The port of Archangel would soon be closed by the ice as the inlet to the White Sea froze and that meant all convoys in 1941 and the first months of 1942 would have Murmansk as their destination. While the British were familiar with both places from their efforts there from 1915 to 1919, they had virtually no information about the facilities that had sprung up since then. Admiral Tovey therefore sent Rear Admirals Philip Vian and Geoffrey Miles to discuss matters with Vice Admiral Golovko, the commander of the Soviet Northern Fleet, and to examine the facilities.

Faced with a multitude of problems in the summer of 1941, Churchill saw the need for closer consultations with the United States. President Franklin Roosevelt was also eager to provide aid to the Soviet Union in order to keep it in the war. A conference between Churchill and Roosevelt was arranged to be held off the coast of Newfoundland. Churchill set out for the conference on Britain's newest battleship, *HMS Prince of Wales*.[6]

President Roosevelt, aboard the heavy cruiser *Augusta*, was already in Placentia Bay, Newfoundland, when Churchill arrived on August 9, 1941. The meetings that followed between the two leaders had momentous consequences not only for the conduct of the war but because they laid the basis, through the Atlantic Charter, for the United Nations. For our purposes, the most important result of the meetings was President Roosevelt's commitment of America's industrial might in support of both Great Britain and the Soviet Union.

The first convoy sailed from Iceland on August 21, 1941. It arrived safely in Murmansk. The regular convoys that were to carry the famous PQ or QP designations started a month later, on September 29. Eight convoys of 55 merchant ships reached Murmansk safely by the end of 1941.[7]

The German response to the convoy traffic around north Norway was slow. The reason is likely their belief that the war would be short and that they were therefore of little importance. Lack of adequate air and naval forces in north Norway may also have played a role as did fuel shortages.

The situation had changed by late winter or spring of 1942. It was now obvious to the Germans that the war would not be short and they were becoming seriously concerned about the steady flow of supplies to the Soviets through the Arctic. The volume of this aid was on a far greater scale than had been anticipated.

Hitler issued orders in mid-March to step up operations against the Murmansk convoys. The navy was ordered to increase the numbers of U-boats in north Norway and the Luftwaffe was directed to increase its long-range reconnaissance and bomber forces.

The Royal Navy historian Sir Michael Lewis refers to the Arctic Convoys as a magnificent achievement under almost impossible conditions. This achievement was not without cost. The Allies, mostly the British, lost 18 warships and 1,944 sailors and airmen. Eighty-seven merchant ships and 829 merchant sailors were also lost. Six of the 87 merchant ships lost sailed independently and another five were sunk by German aircraft in Soviet ports. The German Navy lost one battleship, three destroyers, and 32 submarines.[8]

At the end of 1943 the German efforts against the Arctic Convoys essentially came to an end as a result of the sinking of the *Scharnhorst*, the crippling of the *Tirpitz*, and the lack of bombers in Norway after most were moved to other fronts. The U-boats remained a threat but the increased effectiveness of anti-U-boat operations reduced their usefulness. The Germans were waiting for the introduction of a new-type submarine that would overcome this problem.

Magnitude and Importance of Western Aid to the Soviet Union
Hitler placed much emphasis on the early capture of the Soviet industrial area. However, he failed to appreciate the effects of the massive assistance of weapons, ammunition, equipment, and foodstuffs from Britain and the US. This proved instrumental in keeping the Soviet Union in the war.

While the effects of the Lend-Lease program are still hotly debated, it is worthwhile looking at what some writers have to say on this subject. The German historian Paul Carell writes this about the first two years of the aid:

And since Archangel was frozen up from November onward, supplies for the desperately fighting forces outside Moscow and Leningrad had to come via Murmansk. It was an endless stream, a stream which was not to cease again, but grow in volume, a stream which ultimately decided the German-Russian war.

Here are a few figures to prove the point. During the first year of the Soviet aid programme the following supplies were delivered along the northern sea route alone—i.e. through Murmansk and Archangel—in nineteen convoys:

3,052 aircraft: Germany entered the war in the East with 1,830 aircraft.

4,048 tanks: The German forces on 22nd June 1941 had 3,580 armoured vehicles.

520,000 motor vehicles of all types: Germany had entered the war with altogether 600,000 vehicles.

In fact, the American armament supplies during 1942 almost completely made good the material losses of the Soviet Army. The decisive effect of American aid on the destinies of the war could not be revealed more clearly than by this fact.[9]

What arrived in the Soviet Union via Murmansk was only part of the immense flow of aid from the Western democracies. Aid via the Persian Gulf began arriving in 1942 but the flow was small until 1943 when the railway system between Basra and the Caspian Sea area had been expanded sufficiently to accommodate the traffic. The supplies and equipment arriving by this route eventually amounted to about 25 percent of all aid to the Soviet Union.

The largest flow, accounting for about half the aid, came across the Pacific to Soviet eastern ports. The possibility that this route would be disrupted by the Japanese was taken into account and Stalin warned Japan not to interfere.[10] Thus approximately 25 percent of the aid came via Murmansk and Archangel. The total tonnage shipped via the northern route was 3,964,231 out of a total of 16,366.747.[11]

War materials sent via the Murmansk route according to Woodman included:

5,218 tanks (1,388 made in Canada); 7,411 aircraft (3,129 made in America); 4,932 anti-tank guns; 4,000 rifles and machine guns; 4,338 radio sets; 2,000 field telephones; 1,803 radar sets; 473 million projectiles; 9 torpedo craft; 4 submarines; 14 minesweepers; 10 destroyers; and a battleship.[12]

As far as overall aid going by all routes Woodman makes the following listing:

Between March 1941 and December 1945, the United States of America contributed to Russia: 14,795 aircraft; 7,537 tanks; 51,503 jeeps; 35,170 motor bicycles; 8,700 tractors; 375,883 trucks and lorries; 8,218 anti-aircraft guns; 131,633 submachine guns; 345,735 tons of explosives; 1,981 locomotives; 11,155 railway wagons and trucks; 540,000 tons of steel rails; in excess of 1 million miles of telephone cable; food shipments to the value of $1,312 million; 2,670,000 tons of petrol; 842,000 tons of chemicals; 3,786,000 tyres; 49,000 tons of leather; and 15 million pairs of boots. The total value of the above is said to be $11,260,343,603.[13]

The extent to which this aid contributed to the ability of the Soviet Union to halt the German offensive and eventually go on relentless offensives of its own is difficult to quantify and the subject of continued controversy. Soviet writers during the period of the Cold War downplayed the value of Western aid. The aid received was also labeled as consisting of obsolete items of little value. It was claimed by the Soviets in 1948 that the aid amounted to only 4 percent of Soviet production between 1941 and 1943.[14] In the late 1970s Soviet scholars revised the estimate upwards admitting that the number of tanks received amounted to 10 percent of their own production and that the aircraft equaled 12 percent of the production.[15]

However, even after the breakup of the Soviet Union the tendency has been to be less than forthright in admitting the value of Western aid. Many Western historians fell in line with Soviet claims that the aid was of little consequence both because of the amount and the claim that it was of inferior quality.

Most of the tanks provided through 1943 were light tanks and certainly not up to the quality of the home-produced T-34. That some failed to measure up against what the Germans had is understandable but to claim that they were valueless is a total distortion, particularly the large number of Sherman tanks.

Soviet claims that the 14,795 aircraft provided by the United States fell into the useless category is even more questionable. Sixty-seven percent of these were fighters and 26 percent bombers. The Soviet air force lost over 1,800 aircraft in the first day of the German attack and 3,200 aircraft in the first four months. As Chris Bellamy writes, "even obsolescent aircraft were better than none" in a period of heavy losses and with a dramatic cutback in production.[16]

The most valuable aid may have been in the 1941–42 period when the Soviet war industry was moved to the Urals and beyond to keep it from falling into German hands. This was an achievement which contributed immeasurably to the ability of the Soviet Union to stay in the war and begin turning the tables on the Germans. However, production in 1941–42 was at its lowest and insufficient to meet the demands brought about by the enormous losses. Victor Kravchenko, who was involved in the Soviet armaments procurement industry during the war, claims that aid played a prominent role.

It may have been in the areas of logistics, transportation, food, communications, raw materials, and the more sophisticated equipment that the aid had its greatest importance. Bellamy points out that the Soviet armed forces had 665,000 motor vehicles at the end of the war but their own production between 1942 and 1944 was only 128,000. It is therefore obvious that most of them came from American factories and that they provided the Soviets with the capability to motorize their forces.

The 436,087 vehicles, received mainly from the United States, enabled the Soviets to motorize their troops, their logistical support, and their command and control.

The 8,701 tractors, including half-tracks, provided by the US allowed the Soviets to motorize their artillery to keep up with the advancing troops. Without this the Red Army could not have kept its offensives rolling deep into central Europe. The accessories and spare parts provided to keep this vast transportation fleet running, for example, included 3,786,000 tires for the vehicles. In their final drive on Berlin the northern wing of the Soviet forces under Marshal Rokossovskiy crossed the rivers in East Prussia using General Motors Corporation DUKW six-wheel-drive amphibious vehicles.[17]

Nikita Khrushchev wrote in his memoirs:

> Just imagine how we would have advanced from Stalingrad to Berlin without them [US vehicles]! Our losses would have been colossal because we would have no maneuverability. . . . Note by Crankshaw: The Soviet tanks were the finest in the world; but until Stalingrad the Soviet army had virtually no mechanized transport. It was with American and British trucks that it was able to advance swiftly, complete the encirclement of the German forces around Stalingrad, and sweep out rapidly across the steppe to shatter the German armor at Kursk—and on to Berlin and Vienna.[18]

The less sensational items of aid were perhaps the most important. Bellamy reports that only 58 percent of cultivated lands were under Soviet control in 1942, and that, compared to 1940, grain production had fallen by two-thirds; herds of animals had fallen by 33 to 78 percent, depending on type. To compensate for these enormous losses the US provided more than five million tons of food and the British also provided sorely needed foodstuffs although on a much smaller scale. The provision of food and leather as well as 15 million pairs of boots must have been very welcomed assistance that helped feed the Red Army and keep its offensives rolling.[19]

Joan Beaumont believes that perhaps the most important contributions of the Lend-Lease program were in the fields of communications, command and control, and railway equipment. The program provided the Soviets with almost one million miles of telephone cable and about 247,000 field telephones. The US aid included half a million tons of railway tracks that were important in rebuilding the 65,000 kilometers of railway tracks and 2,300 bridges destroyed by the Germans. The aid in this area also included 1,155 railroad cars and 1,981 locomotives.[20]

The Soviets have ridiculed the 2.67 million tons of petroleum received from the US in view of their own output of about 30 million tons per year. What is left out of their commentary is the fact that much of the US-provided petroleum consisted of high-octane aviation fuel, a type that was in short supply in the Soviet Union. The Lend-Lease program also provided much-needed raw materials, including about 75 percent of the aluminum and copper needed by Soviet industry between 1941 and 1944.[21]

On the subjects of food aid and the provision of raw materials, Khrushchev writes:

In addition we received steel and aluminum from which we made guns, airplanes, and so on. Our own industry was shattered and partly abandoned to the enemy. We also received food products in great quantities. . . . There were many jokes going around in the army, some of them off-color, about American Spam; it tasted good nonetheless. Without Spam we couldn't have been able to feed our army. We had lost our most fertile lands—the Ukraine and the northern Caucasus.[22]

Khrushchev makes the following observations on why Soviet historians have failed to give proper credit for the aid received from the West during the war:[23]

Unfortunately, our historical works about World War II have perpetrated an illusion. They have been written out of a false sense of pride and out of a fear to tell the truth about our Allies' contribution—all because Stalin himself held an incorrect, unrealistic position. He knew the truth, but he admitted it only to himself in the toilet. He considered it too shameful and humiliating for our country to admit publicly.

From the very onset of planning for the eastern campaign, the Germans underestimated Soviet strength and resilience. This continued during the war. While they had grown to appreciate the strength and endurance of the Red Army by 1942, their estimates of Soviet productive capability continued to fall far short of what the Soviets achieved. In March 1942 the Germans estimated Soviet steel production at 8 million tons while it turned out to be 13.5 million tons.[24] This faulty estimate of steel production resulted in a much lower estimate of armament production than what was achieved.

The Lend-Lease program from the US and Britain was something the Germans had woefully underestimated. This underestimation badly aggravated German mistakes as far as Soviet production was concerned.

It is in this light that we should view Western aid and the efforts by the Germans to interdict the flow through Murmansk. The compounded German mistakes—underestimation of Soviet production and Lend-Lease aid—may explain why they did not press harder to cut the Murmansk Railroad in 1941. However, in 1942 they were beginning to get a more accurate picture of the vast program of Western aid. Nevertheless, they still continued to rely on inadequate forces for the cutting of the supply route and failed to press the Finns for vigorous efforts in this area.

The Mountain Corps Norway Plan

Operation *Renntier* (occupation of the Pechenga region) was completed without any problems on June 22, 1940. The two divisions of Mountain Corps Norway went into assembly areas just west of the Soviet border and prepared for the start of Operation *Platinfuchs*, the attack towards Murmansk, 90 kilometers to the east of the border. The artillery regiment would support both divisions. The OKW intelligence summary on June 6, 1941 estimated that there was only one Soviet division in the Murmansk area.

The assembly of the two divisions corresponded to their planned employment. The 2nd Mountain Division, commanded by Major General Ernst Schlemmer and consisting of the 136th and 137th Mountain Regiments, assembled east of Pechenga since it would constitute the left wing of General Dietl's drive. The 3rd Mountain Division, commanded by Major General Hans Kreysing and consisting of the 138th and 139th Mountain Regiments, assembled further to the south, in the vicinity of Luostari. It constituted the right wing of the German advance.

The Finnish Petsamo Detachment (also referred to as the Ivalo Battalion) would stage a diversionary attack 90 kilometers to the south, north of the Lutto River. Its mission was to tie down Soviet forces in this area and act as flank security for Mountain Corps Norway. This detachment advanced to within 20 kilometers of Ristikent, southeast of Murmansk. After a number of sharp engagements with Soviet forces, it withdrew back to the Akka River near the Finnish–Soviet border and from then until the end of August it engaged primarily in patrol activities.

The final objective of the 2nd Mountain Division was Polyarnyy on Kola Bay north of Murmansk. The capture of this town would seal Murmansk from the Arctic Ocean. In the first phase of the operation Dietl expected his two divisions to reach a line from Motovka in the south to the Litsa village in the north. The 2nd Mountain Division would use one of its two regiments, after sealing off the neck of the Rybachiy Peninsula with one battalion, to strike southeastward to Titovka and Litsa village. The reinforced second regiment of this division would drive in a southeastern direction to the road between Titovka and Litsa village, interdicting this road east of the Litsa River. The 3rd Mountain Division would attack with one reinforced regiment in a southeast direction from its assembly area past Chapr Lake towards Motovka.

First Attempt to Breach the Litsa River Line
The attack across the border into the Soviet Union began on schedule at 0300 hours on June 29. There was no air support as the area was enveloped in heavy fog. General Erfurth writes that within a short time the Mountain Corps Norway gained 30–40 kilometers.[25] However, the situation was not really that rosy.

The 137th Mountain Regiment had a particularly hard time reducing the pillboxes along the border. Determined Soviet resistance gave the Germans an early taste of what was in store in the days ahead. Thanks to dense fog, the line of pillboxes was finally reduced, with only light casualties. The Soviets, mostly Siberian and Mongolians, fought to the very end.[26] Fewer than one hundred prisoners were taken. There was little Soviet air activity at the beginning of the operation. Despite the fact that the war had begun a week earlier, German bombers caught Soviet biplane fighters unprotected on the airfields near Murmansk, and most were destroyed.[27]

The Germans did not have accurate intelligence of Soviet strength on the Rybachiy Peninsula. The plan had been for one battalion from the 136th Mountain Regiment to peel off and seal the neck of that peninsula to prevent a threat developing against the German left flank. They soon found out that two battalions were required for this task. That left the 136th to make the drive towards Titovka and the Litsa village with only one battalion instead of with the two called for in the plan. However, the 136th captured the bridge over the Titovka River intact and found the airfield and nearby Soviet camp deserted.

Things also began well in the sector of the 3rd Mountain Division. The Titovka River was reached quickly and the Germans were ferrying troops across by 0600 hours. However, the entire situation changed in the next six hours.

Dietl had given Hitler an accurate description of the difficulties facing Mountain Corps Norway when the two met on April 21, 1941. One aspect of his concerns was the total lack of east–west roads. To overcome this obstacle Dietl was assigned Reich Labor Service groups K363 and K376 under the command of Chief Labor Leader Welser.[28]

Dietl received maps of his operational area in May and these showed that things were not as difficult as he had depicted to Hitler. Only a small border strip in the zone of operations showed a complete lack of roads and tracks. A few kilometers inside, the country roads and tracks were marked. The maps showed one road leading from the bridge over the Titovka River to Litsa village. Then there was another road from Lake Chapr to Motovka. Finally, there was a road leading from Motovka north to Litsa village. All these roads connected to the main road leading east to Murmansk. The operational plans of the Mountain Corps were made on the assumption that the roads shown on the maps existed.

It may well be that OKW showed Hitler these maps and this may have caused him to believe that his Bavarian friend had painted an overly pessimistic picture of the transportation problems confronting Mountain Corps Norway. This may have led him to disregard Dietl's recommendation that the main offensive effort take place from Salla towards Kandalaksha and that a defensive posture be adopted on the Arctic front.

By midday on June 29 the Germans discovered that the road shown on the maps from Chapr Lake to Motovka did not exist and aerial

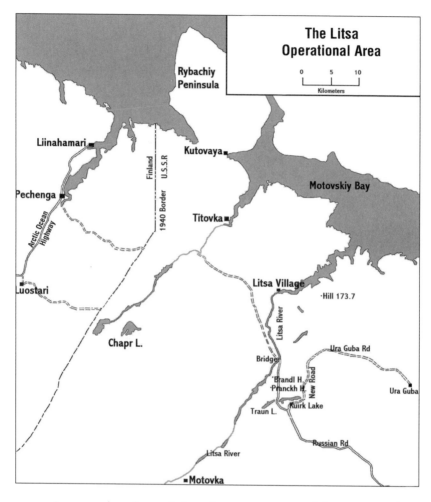

reconnaissance also showed that there was no road from Motovka to the Litsa village. The 2nd Division soon discovered that there was also no road from Titovka to the lower Litsa River. The explanation for this serious miscalculation appears to stem from an analysis of the maps at OKW. The analysts had assumed that the Soviets used the same map symbols as the countries in central Europe. As a result, they had interpreted the dotted double lines on the Soviet maps as depicting roads or tracks. What these maps actually showed were telephone lines and the routes used by the Lapps in their winter migrations.[29]

General Dietl quickly concluded that it would not be possible to supply two divisions moving on parallel routes across the trackless tundra. The advance of the lead elements of the 3rd Mountain Division, which had struggled forward past Chapr Lake, was halted. Major elements of the 3rd Mountain Division were ordered back across the border to take up positions along the Arctic Ocean Highway in the Pechenga area behind the right wing of the 2nd Mountain Division. However, the 3rd Division already had one regiment on the Titovka River. Two battalions from this regiment were ordered to proceed in a northerly direction into the 2nd Division sector while the third battalion was ordered to make a sweep in a northeasterly direction to make contact with the right regiment of the 2nd Division between Titovka and the Litsa River, about five kilometers from the end of the bay. Although this was the main route to Kola Bay, what was expected to be a road was little more than a track.

By the end of the first day of the offensive the Germans were forced to completely revise their operational plan. The right regiment of the 2nd Mountain Division (137th), joined by a battalion from the 3rd Mountain Division, was ordered to push eastward to the bridge across Litsa, southwest of Litsa village. It was hoped that a road from there to Kola Bay would offer some operational possibilities.

One battalion from the 136th Regiment of the 2nd Mountain Division captured Titovka on June 30.[30] The remainder of this regiment was involved in heavy fighting at the neck of the Rybachiy Peninsula. The Soviets had landed reinforcements, supported by warships, on the east shore of Motovskiy Bay at the village of Kutovaya. The 137th Mountain Regiment was able to get one battalion to the right bank of Litsa River on July 1. The fighting near Titovka and in the drive to the Litsa River was heavy. The 95th and 112th Soviet Assault Regiments of the 14th Division suffered heavy losses in the first two days of fighting.

Faulty map reading and a trackless tundra wilderness were not the only problems facing the German mountain troops. German intelligence had, in the first week of June, estimated that there was only one Soviet division of poor quality in the Murmansk area. The Germans now discovered that they were facing two divisions—14th and 52nd Rifle Divisions of the 14th Soviet Army. These were highly motivated and proficient troops amply supported by artillery and air. Two regiments from these divisions were digging in to hold the Litsa River line. Another regiment, supported by a battalion of artillery, was contesting the Germans at the base of the Rybachiy Peninsula. The air resources from the 5th Air Fleet in Norway were inadequate to contest Soviet air superiority since these resources also had to support the XXXVI Corps, 350 kilometers to the south. The exceptionally difficult terrain favored the defenders and made the rate of movement by the German mountain troops very slow, not exceeding one kilometer each hour even when their advance was not contested. It was becoming abundantly clear to everyone, from Dietl to the infantrymen at the front, that the task they were facing was much more difficult than they had anticipated.

The Rybachiy Peninsula was sealed by July 4 but two battalions were required to hold the narrow neck near the village of Kutovaya. The 1st Battalion, 137th Mountain Regiment, secured the Litsa fishing village on July 3. A company from the battalion crossed the Litsa River in rubber rafts just above the estuary.

An attack by both divisions to pierce the Litsa River line was planned for July 6. The 2nd Division would strike from the west bank between the Litsa village and the bridge over the Litsa about 10 kilometers south from that village. The 3rd Division would occupy positions to the south of the bridge. The main effort would be made by both divisions near the bridge—one regiment from each division attacking north and south of the bridge. After securing the river line, both attacks would continue along the Russian Road.

The attack on the Litsa River line was planned for the morning of July 6 but it was delayed until late that day because the 2nd Division assembly area was subjected to heavy Soviet artillery fire and the 3rd Division, because of difficult terrain, had problems getting sufficient forces in place on the west bank of the river. The attacks, when they began, met fierce resistance. By the end of the day the 2nd Division had only one battalion across the river while the 3rd Division had managed to get two battalions into a 1.5 kilometer-wide bridgehead.

The Soviets now launched a serious flank threat to Mountain Corps Norway. Two Soviet transports, escorted by a cruiser and two destroyers, had steamed into Litsa Bay and landed two battalions, one on each side of the bay. The threat from the amphibious landing forced the 2nd Division to send a battalion to screen its left flank.

The Mountain Corps Norway's chief of staff, Lieutenant Colonel von Le Suire, informed Falkenhorst's headquarters that the Soviet amphibious landings threatened the corps flank and operations across the Litsa had to be suspended. The troops on the east bank of the river held their positions on July 7 but after repelling strong Soviet counter-attacks during the night they were ordered to the west bank of the river in the morning of July 8. In a situation report to Falkenhorst, General Dietl demanded increased air support and reinforcements. He asked for at least one additional regiment.

Hitler now intervened indirectly in the operations of Mountain Corps Norway. He was again becoming fixed on the danger of a British landing in north Norway and demanded immediate strengthening of the defenses there as well as around Pechenga. The land forces for Pechenga's defense—one battalion of mountain troops and three artillery batteries—were stripped from Dietl's Mountain Corps.

The offensive strength of Mountain Corps Norway was slowly being frittered away. First, it had to provide two battalions to seal off the Rybachiy Peninsula. Then it had to detach one battalion to screen the left flank of the corps against the threat posed by the Soviet amphibious landing. Finally, a reinforced battalion was sent back to the Pechenga area to act as a defensive force. These detachments represented 30% of Dietl's striking power.

It did not take OKW long to respond to Dietl's urgent request for reinforcements. OKW ordered Falkenhorst on July 7 to transfer troops from the XXXVI Corps—the main effort. Falkenhorst was also asked to contact Mannerheim and request help for Dietl so he could again gather his forces for offensive operations. Falkenhorst provided one motorized machinegun battalion from his own resources and prevailed on Mannerheim to make the 14th Infantry Regiment, minus one battalion, available to Mountain Corps Norway. When it arrived it was used to relieve the German troops sealing the Rybachiy Peninsula.

Dietl had toyed with the idea of resuming the offensive almost immediately after the troops were withdrawn behind the Litsa. This time he intended to use only the 3rd Mountain Division, again in the vicinity of the bridge and along the road. It is not known why he waited until he had withdrawn his troops to the west bank of the river before he decided to resume the offensive. The plan was aborted on July 10 after a dispatch rider carrying the attack orders missed his turnoff to a regimental headquarters near Kutovaya and drove straight into the Soviet lines and was wounded and captured. Because of supply difficulties, it is doubtful if the operation could have succeeded. The divisions were supplied by pack mules but many of them had died from exhaustion. Those left could barely transport rations let alone the large amount of ammunition needed for offensive operations.

Second Attempt to Breach the Litsa Line

On July 12 Dietl shifted the weight of the attack to the left flank of the corps. The 2nd Mountain Division was to attack eastward from its present positions near the Litsa village to the chain of lakes lying in a rough arc about 10 kilometers behind the river. Then it would turn south into the rear of the Soviet forces defending the river's west bank—thereby allowing the 3rd Mountain Division to launch its attack on the river line. With the two divisions advancing along the road the corps hoped to push about 12 kilometers to where the road passes between two lakes—Lake Kuirk and a lake the Germans named Traun.

By the evening of July 13, the first day of the renewed attacks, the 2nd Division had seven battalions on the east bank of the Litsa River and had advanced about three kilometers. Enemy resistance stiffened on July 14 and there were reports of additional amphibious operations not only on the north side of Litsa Bay but at several other points along Motovskiy Bay. Mountain Corps Norway concluded on July 15 that the threats to its left flank would have to be eliminated before the offensive could proceed. The German attacks continued throughout the day of the 15th and one German column succeeded in penetrating the area between Lakes Kuirk and Traun. However, the outlook was not promising. The Soviets launched heavy counterattacks against the German bridgehead from the south and southwest. At the same time, in what appeared to be part of a coordinated effort, the Soviets attacked the German force that held the neck of the Rybachiy Peninsula.

The determined resistance by the Soviet troops on the Litsa line and the amphibious landings on Mountain Corps Norway's undefended left flank presented the Germans with almost insurmountable problems. Instead of having to defend the six-kilometer neck of the Rybachiy Peninsula and a 20-kilometer front on the Litsa River, they now had to worry about a front of almost 70 kilometers from Kutovaya in the north almost to Motovka in the south.

The German logistical situation continued to deteriorate as troops previously used in the supply effort were used in the beachhead to maximize combat power. Dietl informed the Army of Norway on July 17 that he could no longer continue his advance against Murmansk. He intended, instead, to reduce the size of the bridgehead and use the troops thereby freed to mop up Soviet forces that had landed north of Litsa Bay. In summary, Dietl did not believe it would be possible to resume the offensive until he received, as a minimum, one additional division.

On July 18, the 2nd Mountain Division withdrew its troops in the Litsa bridgehead back to a line extending from a point three kilometers south of the Litsa village to a waterfall about six kilometers to the south. The 3rd Mountain Division settled into a line on the west bank of Litsa from the waterfall to a point west of Traun Lake, about five kilometers south of the bridge over the Litsa.

A meeting between General Falkenhorst, his chief of staff Colonel Buschenhagen, Admiral Hermann Boehm (commander of German naval forces in Norway), and General Dietl took place on July 21. They all agreed that with winter approaching, Mountain Corps Norway could not be left where it was. Either it had to be withdrawn to Finland or it had to push through to Murmansk. Falkenhorst favored pushing on to Murmansk and believed that three regiments could be quickly brought to Dietl provided Hitler would allow such a switch. Admiral Boehm, who had already stationed a flotilla of five destroyers at Kirkenes, promised that two submarines would be added to that force. However, he cautioned that there was not much the navy could do to assist Dietl because of Soviet naval superiority east of Varangerfjord (the bay where Kirkenes is located). The danger to the German Navy in the north was also brought home on July 30 when British carrier-based aircraft bombed Kirkenes, Liinahamari, and Pechenga.

Dietl was informed on July 23 that he would receive two battalions from Norway and the Army of Norway ordered him to resume the offensive. Dietl was pessimistic after assessing his situation. He had started the offensive on June 29 with two mountain divisions of two regiments each. The fighting since then had seriously depleted his fighting units to a point where all his regiments were seriously understrength. Three battalions from these regiments were involved in a desperate attempt to cope with the threat to his left flank and one reinforced battalion acted as a mobile reserve for the defense of the Pechenga area. The 3rd Mountain Division was already behind the Litsa River line and the 2nd Mountain Division, fighting off repeated heavy Soviet attacks on its bridgehead, had recommended that it be withdrawn to the west bank of the river. Dietl informed the Army of Norway on July 24 that the only thing he could accomplish after receiving the two-battalion reinforcement was to eliminate the threat to his left flank.

The Army of Norway completed a review—at the request of OKW—of the situation in its three corps in Finland (Mountain Corps Norway, XXXVI Corps, and III Finnish Corps) on the same day as Dietl submitted his pessimistic report of the situation on his front. OKW had intimated that consideration be given to terminating operations in central Finland and moving forces north to reinforce Mountain Corps Norway if the situation in central Finland did not look promising. This would allow Dietl to continue his attack and take Murmansk before the onset of winter. The Army of Norway's comment on the OKW suggestion was that while the situation in the III Corps area did not look good, to adopt a defensive posture in central Finland would allow the enemy to throw his forces against either the remaining forces in central Finland or against Dietl's mountain corps. The Army of Norway still believed that Dietl could take Murmansk if he was assigned another mountain division by the end of August.

Relentless Soviet pressure against the German bridgehead on the Litsa continued at the end of July. Mountain Corps Norway had assembled a force of four battalions for a drive northeastward from the line Titovka–Litsa village to eliminate the flank threat to the corps. This operation, dubbed the *Hofmeister* "unternehmen" (undertaking) after the group commander, was successful. The Soviets had spread their two forward battalions in a thinly manned 15-kilometer line and the German attack, which began on August 2, made rapid progress. One Soviet battalion was destroyed by August 5, and the second battalion was evacuated to the south side of Litsa Bay after sustaining heavy casualties. This success also reduced the pressure on the German bridgehead. It appeared that the Soviets were switching to a defensive posture throughout the Mountain Corps Norway's area of operations.

Hitler ordered the 6th Mountain Division from Greece to the Arctic front on July 30, 1941. It was a long move and the most optimistic scenario had it arriving in the Mountain Corps Norway area during the second half of September. The Army of Norway, worried about early signs of autumn in the Arctic, felt that something had to be done to get the stalled Mountain Corps Norway moving before the arrival of the 6th Mountain Division. Falkenhorst proposed to make two regiments available from the forces in Norway. Hitler denied the request initially, believing that there would still be time to act after the arrival of the 6th Mountain Division. However, after an investigative visit to the Mountain Corps Norway area by Major General Walter Warlimont, chief of the OKW's National Defense Section, Hitler relented. The 388th Infantry Regiment and the 9th SS Infantry Regiment were withdrawn from Norway and attached to Dietl's forces.

Final Attempt to Breach the Litsa River Line

Mountain Corps Norway spent most of August planning for a new drive across the Litsa. It was hoped that a quick penetration of this front would allow for a rapid drive to Murmansk after the arrival of the 6th Mountain Division and before the winter weather made operations impossible. The Germans did not alter their approach but essentially repeated the strategy tried in July. The 3rd Mountain Division with the 388th Infantry Regiment attached would attack frontally across the Litsa River. The 2nd Mountain Division, with the 9th SS Infantry Regiment attached, would push south from the bridgehead behind the forward Soviet positions along the Litsa River. The objective focused on inflicting maximum losses on the defending Soviet forces since this would facilitate the drive towards Murmansk after the 6th Mountain Division arrived.

A debate ensued between Dietl and the Army of Norway about the upcoming attacks. Based on experience in the XXXVI Corps area of central Finland, Falkenhorst wanted Mountain Corps Norway to drive around the Soviet left flank using the 3rd Mountain Division. The experience in central Finland had shown that the Soviets did not yield ground and each position had to be eliminated in costly fighting. Flanking attacks, on the other hand, threw the Soviets into confusion and forced them to retire after their lines of communication were threatened or else face encirclement. This had also been the experience of the Finns in the Winter War. Dietl argued, however, that the tundra terrain in which his troops found themselves did not lend itself to flanking movements that might be appropriate elsewhere. Movement was exceedingly slow in the rugged terrain where there was no concealment or cover and this allowed the enemy ample time to shift forces to meet any envelopment.

The final decision on August 25 was heavily influenced by the views of Major General Hans Kreysing, the commander of the 3rd Mountain Division. Reconnaissance of his front revealed that the Soviets had made significant improvements to their defensive positions. Kreysing viewed the prospects of success in a frontal attack as very poor. He suggested that a better chance of success could result if he moved his forces several kilometers to the south in order to drive around the Soviet left flank.

The plans for the German attack were dependent upon interdicting the existing roads on the east side of the Litsa River. All these roads served as supply routes for the Soviet forces and assisted the movement of their forces behind the front. The most important road was the one the Germans referred to as the "Russian Road," the main route to Kola Bay. This road had been the objective of the earlier operations of the 3rd Mountain Division. The road referred to as the "New Road" branches off from the Russian Road between Lakes Kuirk and Traun, 11 kilometers south of the Litsa Bridge. It runs north for about 16 kilometers to where it intersects with the Ura Guba Road. To call the latter a road is a stretch of the imagination. It was little more than a path in the rocky tundra. The Ura Guba Road continued towards positions occupied by the 2nd Mountain Division after intersecting with the New Road. If the New Road could be reached, it would give the Germans a chance to move behind the Soviet forces on the Litsa front. Dietl planned to begin the attack on September 8.

The 2nd Mountain Division massed two regiments, one mountain regiment and the 9th SS Regiment, on its left flank to attack east for about three kilometers and then swing south behind the chain of lakes to the junction of the two roads—New Road and Ura Guba Road.

The 3rd Mountain Division assembled its two regiments south of its right flank for an attack around the Russian left flank. The drive would take them to the junction of the Russian Road and New Road. From there the two regiments would advance along the New Road to link up with units of the 2nd Mountain Division. It was anticipated that this junction would take place near where the New Road intersected with the Ura Guba Road.

The 388th Infantry Regiment, attached to the 3rd Division, was to launch a frontal attack across the Litsa to capture the two prominent hills about three kilometers from the bridge, which the Germans referred to as Pranckh and Brandl Hills. These hills constituted the anchor positions of the Soviet left flank. After taking these hills, plans called for the regiment to continue eastward and join up with the advance of the two other regiments from the 3rd Mountain Division along the New Road.

The lack of security for the routes of supply and reinforcement was brought home to the Mountain Corps Norway at the end of August. Two German transports carrying replacements for the Mountain Corps were sunk by a Soviet submarine. Much of the 6th Mountain Division was to be brought to north Norway by sea and the likelihood of accomplishing this in face of the naval threat caused the Army of Norway to order Dietl not to wait for the arrival of the entire 6th Mountain Division before he undertook his offensive against Murmansk. The delay of the division was underscored on September 7 when British naval forces attacked a German troop convoy near North Cape. While the transport managed to seek refuge in a fjord, the escorting artillery training ship *Bremse* was sunk.

The outlook for the success of their planned attacks appeared doubtful to the Germans even if major parts of the 6th Mountain Division should arrive. Major General Buschenhagen (promoted from Colonel to Major General on August 1, 1941), the chief of staff of the Army of Norway, told Jodl that he was very pessimistic about the prospects. Whether or not the operation was successful would hinge on the first few days of the offensive. The Army of Norway was already considering the use of the 6th Mountain Division in the drive to Kandalaksha and the only thing that kept them from doing it was Hitler's desire to capture Murmansk at the earliest opportunity.

Dietl informed Jodl on September 5 that even if the attack and advance were successful it would be extremely difficult to reach the west shore of Kola Bay before winter began in early October. Even if his forces, including the 6th Mountain Division, reached Kola Bay he doubted that he had sufficient combat power to cross to the east side of the bay and capture Murmansk. And, should Murmansk be reached and captured, his forces would be cut off from their source of supplies for the remainder of the winter. For Murmansk to be held and his troops to survive the winter would require that Kandalaksha be captured and the Murmansk Railroad north of that town be put into operation for supplies.

There was lack of realism at OKW. Both the Army of Norway and the commander of Mountain Corps Norway had expressed serious doubts about accomplishing the corps' mission at this late date. The best decision would have been to go into winter positions near Pechenga or along the Litsa River. This would have provided ample time for all reinforcements to arrive to take part in renewed operations in the spring.

The attack on September 8 started out with the Germans making good progress. The 2nd Mountain Division, after breaking out of its bridgehead, captured Hill 173.7 and then turned south behind the Soviet units in the forward area. The right flank regiment of the 3rd Mountain Division also made good progress after crossing the Litsa River. By the end of the day it had reached the neck of land between Lakes Traun and Kuirk.

However, the day that started out well did not end well for either of the German divisions. The troubles began with the 388th Infantry Regiment. This unit was to attack across the Litsa River from a position in the left portion of the 3rd Mountain Division's area. Two battalions from this regiment made rapid progress towards the two key terrain features, Pranckh and Brandl Hills. However, the forward Soviet units had not been eliminated by the advancing Germans and they made their reappearance as soon as supporting fire was lifted. This placed them at the rear of the advancing Germans who were taken under heavy fire by the bypassed Soviet units.

Two German companies were heavily mauled by fire from the rear and both flanks. The situation became desperate by mid-afternoon and the commander of the 388th Regiment asked permission to pull his troops back across the Litsa. He informed the 3rd Mountain Division commander that this was the only way to avoid complete destruction of his regiment. One battalion of the regiment had already suffered 60% casualties and was therefore for all practical purposes combat ineffective. The 388th was given permission to withdraw and was back across the river late in the day.

The danger of hasty advances by inexperienced troops was repeated in the sector of the 2nd Mountain Division. Two battalions of the 9th SS Infantry Regiment made quick progress on the left flank of the division, capturing Hill 173.7 and continuing their advance. Again, the Soviets had allowed themselves to be bypassed and opened a devastating fire on the Germans from the rear at the same time as Soviet troops in front of the Germans launched a counterattack supported by artillery.

Panic developed among the SS troops and they broke and ran. Control was restored only after the 2nd Division committed mountain troops to recapture the lost ground.

The 2nd Mountain Division managed to push about five kilometers to the south on September 9, but then its advance was halted by heavy Soviet counterattacks. The 3rd Division advanced with one regiment forward and reached to within a few hundred yards of the junction of the New Road and the Russian Road. Here they encountered a Soviet regiment in prepared positions. The advance came to a halt while artillery and supplies were brought forward. Bringing supplies forward was a laborious task and the 3rd Division estimated that it would not be ready before September 11. Both mountain divisions were tied down in repelling heavy Soviet counterattacks on September 10.

The 3rd Mountain Division was not ready to resume its attack on September 11. The commander set September 13 as a resumption date but he had to delay the attack for another day because the Soviets hit the division with a strong counterattack as it was getting ready. The 2nd Mountain Division did resume its attack on September 12 but advanced only a little over one kilometer against determined resistance. Most of the ground gained during the day was lost to Soviet counterattacks during the night.

Bringing supplies forward continued to be a serious problem. Pack mules were used but their numbers had again dwindled from exhaustion and exposure. There were only enough mules available to keep the two divisions supplied for defensive operations.

The 3rd Mountain Division resumed its offensive on September 14 with both regiments. While they were able to secure the area around the lakes, the exhausted condition of the troops and the inclement weather (cold, rain, and sleet) took its toll. Both divisions were so worn down that their activities on September 15 and 16 were limited to patrols and minor offensive operations to frustrate Soviet counterattacks.

While the main reasons for stopping offensive operations had to do with determined Soviet resistance, the lateness of the season, and supply difficulties, other problems also had a great impact for the Army of Norway and OKW. Mention has already been made of the loss of two German transports on September 12 and 13. The German Navy then halted all shipping to ports east of North Cape. This coincided with an inventory of supplies on hand in the Mountain Corps Norway. While there were sufficient rations and fuel on hand to last until the end of September, ammunition was critically short.

The realization began to set in at the Army of Norway that the supply difficulties in the Mountain Corps Norway sector would only increase with the arrival of the 6th Mountain Division. The prospects of capturing Murmansk under these circumstances were very dim. While the Army of Norway proposed to move the 6th Mountain Division to central Finland to take part in the attack on Kandalaksha, Hitler did not agree.

In a conference with General Falkenhorst in Berlin on September 15 Hitler agreed that the effort to reach Murmansk in 1941 should be abandoned. However, in a poor compromise, he insisted that the attacks in progress should be allowed to run their course and that the 6th Mountain Division should be moved up to relieve the 2nd and 3rd Mountain Divisions. The 6th Mountain Division was expected to hold the line during the winter and prepare to resume the attack against Murmansk in the spring.

After Falkenhorst left Berlin, Hitler decided—with Jodl's support—to use battleships to clear the sea–lanes in the far north. This view was probably supported by General Falkenhorst, who considered that the threat from the British Navy posed the greatest danger to the shipping route. Actually, the presence of eleven Soviet submarines stationed off the Norwegian coast was a more immediate danger. Falkenhorst may not have known about the deployment of that many submarines in the area around the North Cape or he may have felt that they could be countered by an increase in the number of lighter German naval units.

Admiral Raeder refused to use his battleships in a defensive role as escorts for convoys. He pointed out that the enemy could quickly muster superior forces and that the clearing of the sea–lanes would only be a temporary measure as the naval threat would quickly reappear.

British naval operations in the far north had a primarily political objective: the demonstration of support for the Soviet Union. Sea operations in the far north to support land operations were basically viewed by the British as a waste of precious resources that promised little payoff. This was their experience in late July when, in response to a Soviet request, the British had sent two aircraft carriers, two cruisers, and six destroyers into the area. Aircraft from the two carriers bombed Pechenga, Liinahamair, and Kirkenes. The damage inflicted was relatively minor and the losses in aircraft high.

A smaller British naval force—two cruisers and two destroyers—was sent into the area on August 19 but its primary mission was to evacuate the residents of Svalbard and destroy the coal mines located there. A third incursion into the Arctic Ocean took place at the end of August. This force consisted of two cruisers, an aircraft carrier, and a freighter loaded with fighter aircraft bound for Archangel. While these British operations were not intended to interdict German sea routes, one German freighter was sunk on the task force's return voyage.

Generals Dietl and Buschenhagen decided to halt the Mountain Corps Norway offensive on September 18. The conditions already described led to this decision, chief among them the critical supply situation. In addition, the Soviets had not only replaced their losses but intelligence reported they had brought forward a unit designated as the Polyarnyy Division. This unit was understrength and composed mostly of prisoners, labor-camp workers, and sailors. Buschenhagen again put forward his earlier idea of transferring the 6th Mountain Division to central Finland but Dietl stated that this unit was needed in the north since his two mountain divisions were worn down and needed to be relieved.

The German attack had meanwhile entered its final phase. The 3rd Mountain Division captured Pranckh and Brandl Hills on September 17. This achievement was short-lived. A fresh Soviet regiment approached the division's southern flank and the following day, September 18, was spent in repelling repeated Soviet attacks. The situation for General Kreysing's troops was reaching a crisis stage as the Soviets brought up two regiments from the Polyarnyy Division. The 3rd Division was soon under heavy attack from two directions. It occupied a long triangle-shaped front from the Litsa River to the lake region and Pranckh and Brandl Hills with the northern part of the salient running back to the Litsa River south of the bridge. Because the front was long, the defensive positions thinly occupied, and casualties continuing to mount, General Kreysing did not believe his division could hold its position. He requested permission to withdraw to the west bank of the Litsa in order to avoid its complete destruction. Dietl approved the request and by September 26, the whole division was again back behind the Litsa.

The Army of Norway cancelled offensive operations in the Mountain Corps Norway sector on September 21 and a directive by Hitler approved the Army of Norway order on September 23. The 2nd Division was allowed to continue operations in order to acquire good defensive positions for the winter.

In his directive canceling the offensive operations of the Mountain Corps Norway Hitler raised the possibility of operations to secure the Rybachiy Peninsula before winter. The Army of Norway and Mountain Corps Norway opposed such an operation as it would lengthen the defensive lines considerably.

Mountain Corps Norway became busy constructing winter positions. The 6th Mountain Division moved into the area in the middle of October. The 2nd Mountain Division was moved back to the area around Pechenga. The 3rd Mountain Division, which had been in the Arctic since it landed at Narvik on April 9, 1940, was moved to southern Finland and from there to Germany.

The transfer of the 3rd Mountain Division was apparently a political decision. The morale in this unit had suffered considerably due to the heavy fighting and setbacks during the summer. Ziemke writes the following about this transfer:

> One of the current rumors had it that the 3rd Mountain Division was being kept in the Arctic as part of a plot to exterminate the Austrians. (Most of the division personnel were Austrian.) Finally, one of the soldiers who was a Nazi Party member complained to the party authorities; and, since there were at the same time signs of unrest in the Austrian provinces, the matter was taken through party channels to Hitler, who ordered the division transferred.[31]

End of Operation Platinfuchs

The Germans did not have much to show for their strenuous efforts on the Arctic front. They began their operations with their objective— Murmansk—at a distance of 90 kilometers. After two-and-a-half months of attacks by some of the most elite troops in the German Army, they were still 66 kilometers from their objective. The corps had suffered 10,290 casualties, a high price for little gain.

In retrospect, it is relatively easy to see where mistakes were made.

However, some of the problems should have been foreseen.

Hitler's fixation with the defense of Norway, where no real threat existed, did much to doom *Platinfuchs* to failure. The force made available for the operation was dictated, not by what was required for its success but by what could be spared from Norway. Faulty planning and preparations led to logistics levels that were barely able to support Dietl's two divisions. A quick logistics fix to support a larger force level from the Kirkenes/Pechenga base area was not possible because the means of transportation over poor and insecure routes were lacking.

The shortage of forces led the Germans, according to Ziemke, to modify their goals for the operation. However, this observation in itself is erroneous since whether Polyarnyy or Murmansk was the goal made little difference. The force required for a drive to Polyarnyy would be essentially the same as that required for a drive to Murmansk. The planners must have realized that the Soviets fully understood that the capture of Polyarnyy would eliminate Murmansk as a gateway to the world, and that they would therefore resist its capture as strenuously as they would a direct attack on Murmansk.

Hitler's preoccupation with the defense of Pechenga also played a role in the failure of Operation *Platinfuchs*. Again, the problem can be traced back to the faulty planning that failed to factor in security forces for Pechenga at an early date. Stripping forces for that purpose from the attacking divisions was a poor solution.

The Germans underestimated the difficulties posed by the terrain despite having been informed by experts. Dietl had sought out the opinions of knowledgeable Scandinavians, and all had expressed the view that the terrain between Pechenga and Polyarnyy was totally unsuitable for offensive military operations, even in summer. This was reported by Dietl to OKW as early as May 15, 1941. Jodl brushed this aside by stating that the difficulties were well known to OKW and that the accomplishment of anything above the defense of Pechenga should be considered a gift. Such statements reveal doubts about prospects for success from the commander on the ground to the highest level in the German command structure and should have been sufficient to question the wisdom of wasting two of Germany's finest divisions in an operation pre-ordained to fail.

The fact that the Soviets employed much larger forces, including armor, in this area in late 1944 does not change this conclusion. They had a reasonably good road leading up to the Litsa River and they had upgraded that road along with others in the area between 1941 and 1944.

The Germans underestimated the skill and tenacity of the Soviet soldiers in defensive operations. This was undoubtedly influenced by the poor showing of the Soviet Army during the Winter War. They failed to give proper weight to the fact that the Soviets confronted an enemy in the Finns who were ideally suited to fight in the kind of terrain found in their homeland. They undoubtedly also underestimated the interim improvements that had been made in the Soviet military.

German intelligence estimates were faulty. They expected to be confronted by one division of the 14th Soviet Army but they faced two divisions, which had increased to three by the time they made their last effort to pierce the Litsa River line. There was a strong feeling within Mountain Corps Norway that this came about because of the staggered starting time for operations out of Finland. Major General M. Kräutler refers to the week from June 22 to June 29 as the neglected or lost seven days (*Die versäumten sieben Tage*).[32]

The Soviets were fully aware of the significant buildup of forces in north Norway during the spring and summer of 1941 and that sizeable portions of this force moved into the Pechenga area on June 22. The movement into the Pechenga area signaled the Soviets that they should expect an offensive and gave them a week to increase their force level between Pechenga and Murmansk to thwart the operation.

The faulty interpretation of Soviet map symbols between the Finnish border and the Litsa River at OKW was a grievous error. However, it is unlikely that a correct interpretation would have changed anyone's mind about the operation. It was not surprising that the Soviets decided to make their stand along the Litsa River. They had a relatively good road (Russian Road) leading into that area from Murmansk while a more forward deployment would have presented them with supply problems similar to those of the Germans.

In addition, the Soviets made full use of their naval dominance and amphibious capabilities in Motovskiy Bay to launch threats against the German flanks. This was apparently not anticipated by the German planners and the woefully inadequate Luftwaffe resources made available for operations in Finland could not counter this threat.

It can be argued persuasively that the operations of Mountain Corps

Norway should have been terminated with the first failure to crack the Litsa River line on July 17. It appears that this was what General Dietl had in mind. Instead of doing so Hitler and the OKW made the capture of Murmansk a stated objective of the continued offensive.

Ziemke concludes that the interdiction of the sea routes around North Cape led to the failure of Operation *Platinfuchs*.[33] While this caused a delay in the arrival of the 6th Mountain Division and decreased the flow of supplies by sea, the addition of another division that needed to be supplied in the roadless tundra may only have exacerbated those difficulties. Dietl had concluded that he would not have been able to break through to Murmansk even with the 6th Mountain Division because the Soviets could mount a defense in depth and keep supplied via the relatively good road from Murmansk and by sea.[34]

NOTES

1. I recommend, for example, the excellent work by Richard Woodman, *Arctic Convoys 1941–1945* (London: John Murray Ltd, 1994).
2. Churchill, *The Second World War*, volume III, pp.378–380. Stalin wanted a landing in the north and, "if the British were afraid he would be willing to send round three or four Russian army corps to do the job."
3. Woodman, *op.cit.*, p.9.
4. *Loc. cit.*
5. An amazing achievement of the war was the mass construction of Liberty Ships in the United States based on a British concept. 2,751 of these ships were built between 1941 and 1945. The construction of each ship was incredibly fast. The average time from the laying of a keel until the ship was launched was 42 days. The fastest recorded was that of the *Robert G. Perry*, launched in Richmond, California on November 12, 1942, 4 days and 15½ hours after the keel was laid. (Woodman, *op. cit.*, p.20). The Allied effort was also greatly assisted by the availability of the Norwegian merchant fleet—some 223 modern tankers and over 600 cargo vessels. Churchill wrote that they were "worth a million soldiers." (Woodman, *op. cit.*, p.22).
6. *Prince of Wales* was not to survive long. She was sent to the Far East in October 1941 and sunk by Japanese bombers operating from Saigon along with the battlecruiser *Repulse* on December 10, 1941.
7. Stephen Wentworth Roskill, *The War at Sea 1939–1945* (London: HMSO, 1954), volume II, p.143.
8. Woodman, *op. cit.*, p.447.
9. Carell, *Hitler Moves East*, pp.456, 465–466.
10. Woodman, *op. cit.*, p.14.

11. *Ibid*, p.444.
12. *Ibid*, p.443.
13. *Ibid*, p.444.
14. Chris Bellamy, *Absolute War. Soviet Russia in the Second World War* (New York: Alfred A. Knopf, 2007), p.440.
15. *Loc. cit.*
16. *Ibid*, pp.440–441.
17. *Ibid*, pp.441–442.
18. Nikita S. Krushchev, *Khrushchev Remembers*. With an introduction, commentary and notes by Edward Crankshaw. Translated and edited by Strobe Talbott (New York: Bantam Books, Inc., 1971), p.239 and note 43.
19. Bellamy, *op. cit.*, p.443 and Woodman, *op. cit*, p.444.
20. Joan Beaumont, *Comrades in Arms: British Aid to Russia 1941–45* (London: Davis Poynter, 1980), pp.212–213.
21. *Ibid, op. cit.*, pp.213–214.
22. Krushchev, *op. cit.*, p.239.
23. *Ibid*, p.237.
24. Bellamy, *op. cit.*, p.444.
25. Erfurth, *The Last Finnish War*, p.25.
26. M. Kräutler and K. Springenschmidt. *Es war ein Edelweiss. Schicksal und Weg der zweiten Gebirgsdivision* (Graz: Leopold Stocker Verlag, 1962), p.165.
27. Carell, *Hitler Moves East*, p.451.
28. *Ibid*, p.449.
29. *Ibid*, p.452.
30. Kräutler and Springenschmidt, *op. cit.*, p.169.
31. Ziemke, *The German Northern Theater of Operations*, p.154. This was based on a 1957 review of the draft of Ziemke's work by General Erich Buschenhagen.
32. Kräutler and Springenschmidt, *op. cit.*, pp.152–153.
33. Ziemke, *The German Northern Theater of Operations*, p.155.
34. Gerda-Luise Dietl and Kurt Hermann, *General Dietl*, München: Münchner Buchverlag, 1951, pp.231–233.

FOUR

OPERATIONS IN CENTRAL FINLAND

The Central Finland Operational Area

While about 350 kilometers south of the Mountain Corps Norway area of operations, Salla is still 50 kilometers above the Arctic Circle. The terrain in this area, while there were patches of tundra, was characterized by vast virgin coniferous forests and rocky hills with elevations up to and over 2,000 feet. The valleys were swampy with numerous rivers, streams, and lakes. Ziemke observes that it was particularly hot in July 1941 with the temperature rising to above 85° Fahrenheit on 12 days, twice reaching 97°.[1] Swarms of mosquitoes flourished in the hot swampy forests and made it virtually impossible to work except during the cool nights.

A large triangular area running east from Salla was ceded to the Soviet Union after the Winter War. The town of Salla was included in a corner of this triangle. The Kuola River is on its north and flows into the Salla River to the west of that town. To the south of Salla is a range of hills with their highest peak at 2,156 feet. The mountain slopes were bare.

The Soviets had completed a railroad from Kandalaksha to the new Finnish border. By the terms of the treaty in March 1940 the Finns were obligated to construct a connecting line from Kemijärvi. The Finns were in no hurry to complete this line since they viewed it as a threat by which the Soviets could cut across central Finland to the Swedish border. However, as it became clear that it now could be used by German and Finnish forces to regain the lost territory, the Finns became energized and rapidly pushed the project towards completion.

In the period since March 1940 the Soviets had fortified the Salla area and the town had become a defensive strongpoint. The Germans

and Finns did not have accurate information on enemy forces. They estimated enemy strength opposite north and central Finland at five infantry divisions and two weak armored units. They had identified one division, the 122nd Rifle Division, in Salla with about 50 tanks and believed
there was another division, possibly two, at Kandalaksha.

The Soviet forces in the north operated under the 14th Army,
commanded by Lieutenant General Valerian Alexandrovich Frolov. Its
major combat formations, in addition to artillery and other units, consisted of the 104th and 122nd Rifle Divisions and the 1st Tank Division
which came under the XLII Corps as the operation progressed. In addition there were the 14th and 52nd Rifle Divisions in the Murmansk
region. The 23rd Murmansk Fortified Region, an artillery regiment, several border guard detachments, and the 1st Mixed Air Division also
came under his command.

The 6th Finnish Division, attached to the XXXVI German Corps,
was located north of Kuusamo and therefore did not have to make a
lengthy move in preparation for the offensive. The two German divisions of XXXVI Corps, the 169th Infantry Division and the SS Division
Nord, moved up close to the border opposite Salla at the end of June.

The III Finnish Corps constituted the right wing of the Army of
Norway front and occupied a 100-kilometer stretch of the Finnish–
Soviet border between Kuusamo and Suomussalmi. With the 6th Finnish Division attached to the XXXVI German Corps, it had only one
division—the 3rd—plus some miscellaneous units. This corps was commanded by Major General Hjalmar Fridolf Siilasvuo. He was one of the
heroes of the Winter War when, as a colonel commanding the forces at
Suomussalmi, he conducted one of the most classic shallow encirclement operations in military history, leading to the virtual annihilation of
two Soviet divisions.[2]

General Siilasvuo had reorganized the 3rd Division in anticipation
of the upcoming operation. The division was divided into two groups—
labeled F and J. Each group consisted of one regiment and assorted
attachments, including border guards. One regiment was kept back as a
corps reserve. The corps had attached one battalion from the 6th
Finnish Division as well as a German tank company.

The command setup in central Finland plagued operations almost
from the very beginning. General Falkenhorst[3] came under the direct
control of OKW. German operations in Finland were begun with inad-

equate forces and reinforcements had to come from the OKH and OKL (Oberkommando der Luftwaffe—Air Force High Command) not the OKW. OKH and OKL were reluctant to provide substantial reinforcements that would detract from the main effort against the Soviet Union, particularly after it became obvious that the Finns would not assist the Germans against Leningrad.

Another problem already mentioned in Chapter 2 was the failure to achieve unity of command within the theater. While the Finnish III Corps was under the operational control of Falkenhorst, it had also a direct line to Marshal Mannerheim and this soon caused problems. When you add to this the German failure to firmly designate a main effort within their theater, you had a recipe for failure.

Plans

The XXXVI Corps planned to capture Salla by a double envelopment as the first step in a quick drive to Kandalaksha to cut the Murmansk Railroad. The main attack would be carried out by the 169th Infantry Division making up the northern envelopment. The 169th Division, commanded by Lieutenant General Kurt Dittmar, was organized into three task forces, each approximately one regiment in strength, as follows:

1. The northern or left task force would advance eastward 13 kilometers to the north of Salla. Its primary mission was to screen the corps' northern flank. At the appropriate time it would become the northern pincer in another envelopment the Germans planned in the Kayrala area.
2. The center task force was also to advance eastward to the north of Salla, but only eight kilometers to the north. It would drive in a southeastern direction to the road between Salla and Kayrala. When reaching that road it would turn southward and become the northern pincer in the Salla envelopment.
3. The southern or right task force of the 169th Division would jump off from a location just north of the road leading from Salla to Savukoski. It would assault the border fortifications frontally.

Two regiments from SS Division Nord would start out from positions to the south of the road from Rovaniemi to Salla. They would bypass Salla on the south and then swing in behind that town and become the southern pincer of the Salla envelopment.

The German XXXVI Corps had grave doubts about SS Division Nord. The unit was officially formed on February 24, 1941 as SS Kampfgruppe Nord and commanded by SS Brigadeführer Richard Hermann. Both its regiments—6th and 7th SS Infantry Regiments—had been in Norway since April 1940. They were equipped with Czech arms. SS Kampfgruppe Nord was officially renamed SS Division Nord (motorized) on June 17, 1941. At the same time the command was transferred to Major General of the Waffen SS Karl-Maria Demelhuber. The unit strength was 8,150 when it arrived in Finland. Artillery and antiaircraft components from Germany joined the division in Finland. The units of the division had not worked together and were poorly trained. Erfurth writes that the division "consisted of elderly men without combat experience and was an improvised unit over which hovered an unlucky star. During transport 105 casualties had occurred as a result of a fire on board ship."[4] Ziemke makes the following observation:

The march from northern Norway had been so poorly executed and revealed such a profound ignorance of military procedures that it resulted in the relief of the commanding general and his operations officer. The new commanding general, after looking over his troops, reported on 23 June that he could not assume responsibility for committing them in battle.[5]

General der Kavallerie Hans Feige, commander of XXXVI Corps, was reluctant to use the SS Division against Salla, particularly after the report by its commander on June 23. Falkenhorst appears to have overruled Feige on this issue. It may be that Falkenhorst and the Army of Norway underestimated the quality of their opponents.

The 6th Finnish Division, attached to XXXVI Corps, would cross the Finnish–Soviet border about 70 kilometers south of Salla. The division would advance in a northeast direction, making a deep penetration towards the town of Alakurtti while sending part of its force to attack Kayrala from the south. The 6th Finnish Division would thus become the southern pincer in the second planned envelopment.

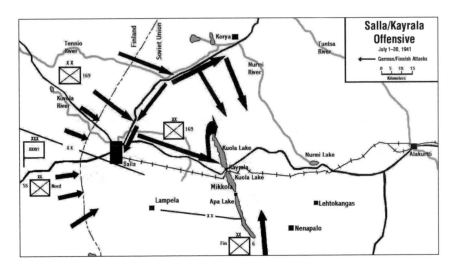

Group J of III Finnish Corps, commanded by Lieutenant Colonel Johannes Turtola, assembled south of Kuusamo in preparation for the attack. Its immediate objective was Kestenga. Group F, commanded by Lieutenant Colonel Arne Somersalo, assembled further to the south, just east of Suomussalmi. The final objectives of the groups were Loukhi (Group J) and Kem (Group F), both on the Murmansk Railroad.

Attack on Salla

The 6th Finnish Division was the first unit to cross the border at 0200 hours on July 1. The 169th Infantry Division and the SS Division did not cross the border until 1600 hours on July 1. It is unclear why the attacks were staggered but it may have had something to do with the scarcity of air support.

The timing of the attacks by the main elements of the XXXVI Corps also took into consideration the fact that there were 24 hours of daylight and that in the afternoon the sun was in the face of the defending Soviet troops. July 1 was a hot day with temperatures in the high 80s (Fahrenheit). The air and artillery bombardment started forest fires and the smoke reduced visibility to near zero in some places.

Any doubts that the Germans may have had about the quality of the Soviet troops were soon dispelled. The right flank task force of the 169th Infantry Division, advancing on the fortifications in front of Salla with two battalions, was stopped dead in its tracks 500 meters east of the border. A sharp Soviet counterattack threw the lead German battalions back to the border, briefly creating panic in the rear echelons of the task force.

The other two task forces in the 169th Division, however, made good progress. By the end of the day the northernmost task force had gained over three kilometers. The center task force was even more successful and by the end of July 1 it was closing in on the road between Salla and Kayrala.

The questions about the combat effectiveness of SS Division Nord were answered on the first day of battle. Against determined Soviet defenders the division broke and ran. Panicky SS troops streamed past the Corps headquarters on the road between Rovaniemi and Salla. There was total confusion at the front. The division operations officer could only account for two of the six battalions. Major General Demelhuber declared that his division was not fit for combat operations in the morning of July 2. Losses in the SS Division on July 1 included one regimental commander, one battalion commander, and 600 men.

The enveloping units had made good progress initially but that came to an end on July 2. The Soviets realized that encirclements were in process and threw everything they had at the center task force— whose mission was the northern pincer in the planned encirclement of Salla. The Soviet attack was assisted by armor and air support. The task force, which had reached the Salla–Korya (Korja) road, was forced to fall back. The 169th Division reinforced the center task force with two infantry battalions and a tank company on July 3 but also changed earlier plans. The mission of the left task force under the original plan was to screen the division's north flank and thereafter advance on Kayrala. The Kayrala advance was now cancelled and the left task force was ordered to turn south behind Salla along the Salla–Korya road.

The left task force moved south on July 3 and the center task force also regained the Salla–Korya road and pushed down along the Tennio River. The Soviets hit the German front with no fewer than seven counterattacks. Their main effort was in the area north of Salla. The Germans were able to repel the attacks, but the heavy fighting was beginning to take its toll on the German infantry.

On the following day, while the left task force moved south, the center task force regained the road and pushed down to the Kuola River. The division also committed the third regiment in the river crossing and assault on Salla. The crossing of the river was set for July 6.

The SS Division was moved into defensive positions behind the Finnish border after its panic on July 1. Now, while the 169th Infantry Division was assembling its forces for a crossing of the Kuola River and the assault on Salla, there was another panic in the SS Division. This particular incident, which happened in the morning of July 4, is described by Ziemke but not mentioned by Erfurth. The episode evidently started when General Demelhuber, believing that his division was under an armored attack and having no confidence in his troops, ordered a withdrawal that turned into the panic described by Ziemke:

> Early on the morning of the 4th the XXXVI Corps headquarters staff witnessed an astonishing scene as the motorized SS-Division came streaming down the road toward Rovaniemi swearing Russian tanks were at its heels. For several hours the corps staff, including the chief of staff and Feige himself, was out on the road getting the SS-men headed back toward the front. Some of the vehicles were stopped and turned back at the Army of Norway advanced headquarters halfway down the road toward Kemiyärvi, and a few went the full 50 miles to Kemiyärvi where an SS-man urged the local commandant to blow the bridge across the Kemi River to hold up the Russian tanks which he claimed were in hot pursuit.[6]

Feige decided to remove the SS Division from the frontline on July 6. He had to abandon this plan when Hitler, very annoyed at the behavior of the SS troops, ordered the division to remain at the front. After the virtual disintegration of the SS Division, the XXXVI Corps decided that it no longer had the strength to complete the encirclement of Salla since it also had to hold the front west of Salla. The Army of Norway offered up its reserves—a Finnish battalion, a motorized machinegun battalion, and a battalion of the SS.

The 163rd German Infantry Division was on its way to Finland from Norway, by way of Sweden. It was planned to attach this division to Mannerheim's army as his strategic reserve. General Feige, the XXXVI Corps commander, now asked Falkenhorst to request that a regiment from this division be attached to his corps. The last regiment of this division was still at Torino on the Swedish–Finnish border. Hitler approved Falkenhorst's request on July 5.

General Erfurth is rather critical of Falkenhorst's request and OKW's acceptance of that request. He notes that the additional regiment was not required since Salla was captured on July 7, before the requested regiment was in place on the Salla front. He goes on to say that the 163rd Division was "torn into two parts" by the decision.[7]

The virtual disintegration of the SS Division caused plans to be changed that had far-reaching consequences for the Salla offensive. General Feige became concerned about the 6th Finnish Division attached to his corps. That division began its advance from a position about 70 kilometers south of Salla. General Feige's concern was that the 6th Division, moving cross-country, would be exposed to Soviet attacks against its northern flank now that the German drive through Salla was stalled. Feige ordered the 6th Division to abandon its deep penetration to Alakurtti and turn its whole force north towards Kayrala.

The safety of the 6th Division was not Feige's only concern. The 169th Infantry Division was worn down after having fought for Salla almost single-handedly after the collapse of the SS Division. It would need considerable help if it were to carry out the second envelopment.

The 169th Division was meantime ready to cross the Kuola River and assault Salla from the east. It hoped to trap the Soviet forces in Salla by crossing the terrain behind the town to the hills in the southeast. With dive-bomber and artillery support, the attack made progress against stubborn resistance and at noon the right-flank regiment was within a half-mile of Salla. The northern wing of the attack reached the fork in the road east of Salla where one road leads to Kayrala and the other to Korya.

The Soviets launched fierce counterattacks that were repelled. The Kuola River was crossed in the evening of July 6. The intensity of the fighting is attested to by the fact that 50 destroyed Soviet tanks littered the battlefield by the end of the day. The division's right flank task force entered Salla in the evening but was thrown back in a strong counterattack. The withdrawal threatened to become another panic until the commanding general and two of his regimental commanders personally intervened.

Salla was captured in the evening of July 7. The bulk of the 122nd Rifle Division disengaged on the morning of July 8 and withdrew through the southern part of the planned encirclement. The area through which the Soviets withdrew was supposed to have been closed by the SS Division but it was still not closed.

German-Finnish Drive Stopped at Kayrala

The pursuit of the Soviets withdrawing from Salla was left to the SS Division, not a particularly good choice in view of its earlier performance. However, the Germans did not have much choice since they were afraid that the Soviets would make a stand in the narrows of the chain of lakes in the Kayrala area; they needed their best unit, the 169th Infantry Division, to try to prevent the Soviets from establishing themselves in these narrows.

The Finnish 6th Division had already reached Apa Lake and was pressing northward along its eastern shore. This division was lacking some of its punch as it had to leave all its artillery behind on its long diagonal trek across the wilderness from the border. The Finns encountered prepared Soviet positions south of Mikkola. General Dietl's need for reinforcements in his attempt to penetrate the Litsa River line now took its toll on the XXXVI Corps as it was ordered to detach its motorized machinegun battalion and send it north to be attached to Mountain Corps Norway.

The line of advance of the XXXVI Corps was through the lake narrows west of Kayrala, an area that the Soviets had fortified as a fallback position since their takeover of the region in 1940. In the more northern part of this front—around the Maaseljaen Hills—defensive positions were blasted from the rocky hillsides.

The Germans soon learned that a frontal attack would not succeed. The Soviets had brought up a new division that held the Kayrala narrows—the 104th Rifle Division—while the 122nd Rifle Division had withdrawn behind the chain of lakes to regroup. The 1st Soviet Tank Division, which had forward elements in Salla, was in positions between Kayrala and Alakurtti. This division consisted of two tank regiments, a motorized infantry regiment, and artillery. The units holding the Kayrala positions and deployed between Kayrala and Alakurtti were grouped under the command of the XVII Soviet Corps. The drives of the Germans and Finns were stopped. The 6th Finnish Division managed to cut the road and railroad leading east from Kayrala on July 9, but vigorous Soviet counterattacks from the north and east drove it back.

Over the next five or six days the Soviets kept pouring in reinforcements via Kandalaksha that brought the 122nd Division back to full strength. These came primarily by sea from Archangel. The Luftwaffe failed to hinder the sea transport but carried out attacks as Soviet troops moved from Kandalaksha to the front.

After their initial repulses on July 9 and 10, the Germans concluded that they needed to resort to envelopments to have any chance of success. Since the XXXVI Corps had only two effective divisions (169th and 6th Finnish) the envelopment had to be limited in both size and scope. To avoid the risk of defeat in detail it was limited to trapping the Soviet forces holding the lake narrows.

The main effort was assigned to the 169th Division. The plan called for sending one regiment north along the Salla–Korya road and then for it to turn south and strike the Soviet right flank at a point about 13 kilometers north of Kuola Lake. This operation took some time since the regiment had to traverse the heavily wooded and hilly country between the Salla–Korya road and the Soviet positions east of the Kuola Lake. After having eliminated these positions, the regiment was to complete the northern prong of the encirclement. Two battalions from another regiment of the 169th Division were to work north along the western shore of Kuola Lake, around the northern tip of that lake, and strike the Soviet right flank. The Finnish 6th Division constituted the southern prong of the encirclement.

The northern prong of the German encirclement met stiff resistance as soon as it turned southeast from the Salla–Korya road. XXXVI Corps added another regiment and two battalions from its reserve—the 324th Infantry Regiment from the 163rd Infantry Division—to the northern encirclement force.

The Army of Norway had wanted a much wider envelopment—extending as far as to the Nurmi River—to ensure that the Soviet divisions in the lake region were trapped and destroyed. The XXXVI Corps maintained that such a deep encirclement was beyond its capability. This hotly disputed difference of opinion between the two headquarters led to a compromise involving the strengthening of the northern encircling force.

The troops of the northern prong of the encirclement struggled mightily in the difficult terrain and against repeated Soviet counterattacks. The two regiments were advancing abreast and they had to cut roads through the wilderness as they moved forward.

The Soviet reinforcements were beginning to make themselves felt by launching continuous counterattacks against the northern pincer movement and against the Finns east of Apa Lake. Falkenhorst viewed an immediate attack as the only solution to the XXXVI Corps problem. However, General Feige and the commander of the 169th Division were pessimistic since the 169th lacked the strength to cut the Kayrala–Alakurtti road.

Falkenhorst, running out of patience, visited the left flank of the 169th Division in person on July 23. In a one-sided conversation he had with General Dittmar, the commander of the 169th Division, he angrily castigated the division commander for having allowed two or three Soviet regiments, badly mauled at Salla, time to recover. As far as poor roads were concerned, he observed that they were boulevards compared to those in the Mountain Corps Norway area.[8]

Back at his headquarters, Falkenhorst composed a pointed message to General Feige describing the negative impressions he gained from his visit to the 169th Division. He stated that the time for debate and assessments were over and concluded with two directives and a warning: 1) An immediate end to any talk about stationary warfare or he would ask OKW for a more aggressive corps commander and 2) The establishment of a firm date for the resumption of the attack. Feige got the message and set the date and time of the attack for July 26 at 2300 hours.

The XXXVI Corps attack began on schedule but bogged down quickly against stubborn Soviet defenses. The 169th Division launched its attack with two regiments forward. The Soviets launched a counterattack against the left flank regiment before it got out of its attack positions. The other regiment gained less than two kilometers before it was also stopped and pinned down. The 6th Finnish Division was given the mission of tying down Soviet forces in the south until the 169th Division had broken through the northern defenses. Initially, the 6th Division made good progress but was then thrown back by a Soviet counterattack.

Feige informed Falkenhorst on July 27 that his attacks could not achieve any decisive results. Colonel Buschenhagen, the Army of Norway chief of staff, told Feige that the attacks had to continue because Hitler wanted to cut the Murmansk Railroad in at least one place. Feige thereupon committed his two reserve battalions to the attack on the northern flank but it failed.

The attacks by the XXXVI Corps had come to a complete standstill by July 28. The Army of Norway ordered the corps to conduct only limited offensive actions to keep Soviet forces tied down so that they could not be switched against the III Finnish Corps or against Mountain Corps Norway. The Army of Norway reported to OKW that the offensive could not be resumed unless it was assigned an additional division. Hitler validated the Army of Norway action on July 30 and ordered the termination of the XXXVI Corps offensive, an offensive that had started a month earlier with high hopes of success. The results of the hard-fought actions of the XXXVI Corps were meager and high in costs. The corps had advanced across the border to a distance of 20 kilometers and had suffered 5,500 casualties, 3,296 of them in the 169th Division.

III Finnish Corps Captures Kestenga

Führer Directive Number 34 on July 30 ordered that the attack in the direction of Kandalaksha be halted and the switching of the main effort by the Army of Norway to the Finnish III Corps' drive to Loukhi. Only enough forces would be left with XXXVI Corps for defense of the terrain it had captured and as deception of future offensive operations. If operations against Loukhi also failed, the German forces with III Finnish Corps were to be withdrawn and transferred to the Karelian front.[9] Falkenhorst had been a proponent of the idea that the Murmansk Railroad could be reached and cut most quickly at Loukhi.

Major General Siilasvuo had divided 3rd Division into two groups—F and J. The SS units had not yet been attached to III Corps. Siilasvuo sent Group J, consisting of one reinforced regiment, across the border in the direction of the town of Kestenga. Group F, consisting of two regiments, crossed the border east of Suomussalmi and advanced in the direction of Ukhta. The corps, in accordance with the Army of Norway plan, placed its main effort with Group F. The two regiments crossed the border at different points, about 60 kilometers apart, for a converging attack on the village of Voynitsa. The Soviet forces opposing III Corps, consisting of the 54th Rifle Division, split to meet the drives of both Finnish groups.

Numerically, the attackers and defenders were about equal but the advantage was with the attacker who presented multiple threats over a relatively wide area. The III Corps offensive therefore made good progress against weak and disorganized resistance. Group J reached

Makarely, about 27 kilometers from the border, on July 5, and the southern prong of the concentric advance of Group F had reached Ponga Guba, 45 kilometers east of the border. The two regiments of Group F reached Voynitsa on July 10, one from the west and one from the south. Here they encountered a tough center of resistance, which they encircled and destroyed by July 19.

On that day, elements of Group J reached the 13-kilometer long Sofyanga River connecting Pya Lake and Top Lake. The river was a major obstacle and defended in strength by the Soviets. Lieutenant Colonel Turtola was confident that if he could seize the narrows between the two lakes he could then advance on Kestenga without worrying about flank threats. A good road covered the 67 kilometers between Kestenga and Loukhi. It appears that the actual commander of Group J was Major General Väinö Henrik Palojärvi after major elements of SS Division Nord were attached.

Colonel Buschenhagen, the Army of Norway's chief of staff, visited Group J on July 18. He was surprised by the relative rapidity of the Finnish advance. They had covered over 65 kilometers and built a road as they advanced. Finnish expertise in forest warfare had been obvious.[10]

Colonel Buschenhagen discussed his observations with General Falkenhorst when he returned to headquarters. This discussion led to a decision to reinforce success by sending an infantry regiment and an artillery battalion from SS Division Nord to reinforce Group J. General Siilasvuo also contributed to strengthening Group J by moving two infantry battalions from Group F and attaching them to Group J. This group now had the strength of about three infantry regiments. Further SS reinforcements were provided at the end of July when the Army of Norway became concerned about partisan activities and the exposed northern flank of Group J.

Group F was also making good progress in its advance to Ukhta. After having eliminated the encircled Soviet forces in the Voynitsa area the group continued along the road to Ukhta via Korpijärvi, which was reached on July 23.

The group again split into two major columns. One approached Ukhta on both sides of the Korpijärvi–Ukhta road while the second column advanced southeast and then east along the north shore of Verkhneye Kuyto Lake. This column reached Enonsuu across Stredneye Kuyto Lake from Ukhta on August 2. The northern columns reached

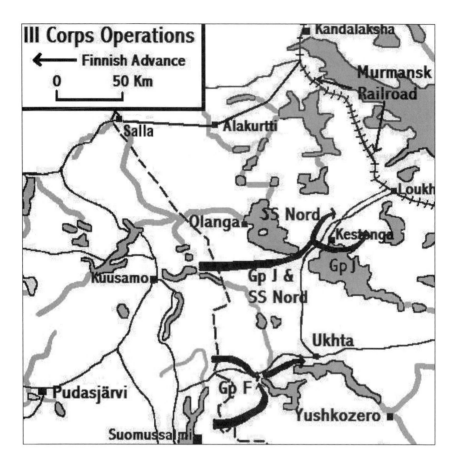

the Yeldanka Lake area on July 28. This put them about 19 kilometers northwest of Ukhta. By August 2, at the same time as the southern group reached Enonsuu, the northern group drew up to the Kis-Kis River line, about 10 kilometers from Ukhta.

Group J began its assault on the Sofyanga River line on July 30. While the main force attacked the river line near the village of Sof-Porog, one battalion crossed the western tip of Top Lake by boat to attack the Soviets in the rear. Group J penetrated the Sofyanga River line after three days of hard fighting. The town of Kestenga fell on August 7. The Finns and Germans believed that the Soviets had thrown their last reserves into the defense of Kestenga.[11]

On August 11, a Finnish regiment of Group J reached a point about

32 kilometers southwest of Loukhi, in the narrows between Lakes Yelovoye and Lebedevo. The Soviets had rushed the 88th Rifle Division to the Loukhi front from Archangel in order to keep the Murmansk Railroad from being cut. The Finns met heavy resistance in the lake narrows and the resistance became even more determined in the next few days as the 88th Division reached the front.

Group F had become stalled on the Kis-Kis River line. Attempts at envelopments from the north failed against heavy resistance. The front stagnated and the actions boiled down to patrolling and probing attacks. The Army of Norway cancelled the offensive operations of Group F on August 19. An infantry battalion from Group F was ordered to join Group J in order to increase the weight of the attack against Loukhi.

One reason for further increasing the strength of Group J was that there were indications that enemy resistance in that area was weakening. However, the Finnish and German troops were also exhausted after nearly two months of offensive operations. Their losses were also significant. Group J managed to encircle and trap a Soviet regiment south of the Kestenga-Loukhi road but because of exhaustion and lack of strength they were unable to eliminate the trapped troops. General Siilasvuo informed General Falkenhorst on August 25, 1941 that he did not believe it possible for his troops to complete their drive to Loukhi without significant reinforcements. He asked to be assigned another Finnish division used to forest fighting.

General Siilasvuo's assessment of the situation led to a hurried meeting between Generals Falkenhorst, Buschenhagen, and Siilasvuo at Kuusamo on August 29. Siilasvuo told his guests that both Group F and J were stalled. The six Finnish and three SS battalions in Group J faced 13 Soviet battalions in prepared defensive positions. Two of his SS battalions together had an effective strength of only 280 men. It now appeared possible that the Soviets would be able to strike southward from the Loukhi area to Kestenga. If successful, this could bring about the collapse of Group J. General Siilasvuo stated that it was an error to have stopped Group F before it reached Ukhta since it now found itself in poor defensive positions.[12]

General Siilasvuo's pessimistic assessment of the situation in the III Corps area led Falkenhorst to make yet another change in the operational plans. His decision was basically to start up again the attack on

Ukhta while Group J held its positions. To bolster the strength of Group J, the last two infantry battalions of the SS were assigned to that group. A motorized machinegun battalion was added in the mix. A regiment from the 6th Finnish Division would be released to increase the striking power in the attack on Ukhta. The exact date for the transfer of this infantry regiment was left undecided. It would be done as soon as conditions in the XXXVI sector permitted its detachment. Until that time, Group F was expected to remain on the defensive.

The Kayrala Encirclement
The attack on the Kayrala–Mikkola line by the XXXVI Corps had met initial failure by July 28 and the Germans limited themselves to minor offensive actions to keep the Soviets from switching their forces against III Finnish Corps.

The sharp differences between Generals Falkenhorst and Feige noted earlier continued. At times they became acrimonious. Feige, in accordance with earlier instructions from the Army of Norway (and also in accordance with Hitler's directive of July 30), ordered his two divisions on August 3 to tie down the opposing enemy forces and await a favorable opportunity for resuming the offensive after reinforcements had arrived.

The Army of Norway immediately countermanded Feige's order. It directed XXXVI Corps to prepare to resume its offensive with the weight of the attack in the sector of the Finnish 6th Division in the south—without waiting for reinforcements that could not be counted on for some time.

There is no doubt that Falkenhorst ignored the July 30 directive as far as the XXXVI Corps is concerned. In his defense it must be pointed out that OKW did not issue an implementing order for that directive and until they did Falkenhorst may have felt free to set XXXVI Corps in motion.

The Soviets withdrew the 1st Tank Division (minus one regiment) from the Salla front on August 1 and transferred it to the Leningrad front. This led the Army of Norway to order the XXXVI Corps to execute a deep envelopment to the road-railroad line just west of the town of Alakurtti. The XXXVI Corps viewed this as impossible because of lack of sufficient forces in terrain that did not lend itself to wide and deep envelopments. It insisted that the envelopment should not aim at a point further to the east than Nurmi Lake, halfway to Alakurtti.

The XXXVI Corps intended to send the 6th Finnish Division on a thrust to Nurmi Mountains as the southern prong of the envelopment. The Finns—the main effort—would advance with one regiment forward and two in reserve against the Nurmi Mountains and take up blocking positions. One regiment of the division would advance eastward along the Alakurtti road at Vuoriyarvi (Vuorijärvi). A German task force of two infantry battalions and six companies of mixed SS and engineer troops would cross the Nurmi River behind the left wing of the 169th Division and drive towards Nurmi Lake as the northern arm of the envelopment. Other units from the 169th Division would take over the 6th Division's defensive positions to make the Finnish drive possible. Two regiments (one German and one Finnish) constituted the corps reserve.

The regrouping of forces for the offensive was a major task. It required the construction of a road from Lampela to the southern point of Apa Lake in order to bring artillery into the Finnish sector. This road was completed on August 14. Units of the 169th Division, which were to take over the Finnish defensive positions, were pulled back through Salla and sent south to where the Finnish 6th Division had crossed the border. From here they moved northeast along the route the Finns had followed in early July. While this maneuver may have confused the Soviets, it was a trying experience for the troops in the 169th Division. The straight-line distance from their start point to their new area of operations was only 28 kilometers. Now—because of the lack of lateral roads near the front—they had to make a strenuous move of 175 kilometers to arrive at the same destination.

The Finnish 6th Division began its northward attack in heavy rain and fog on the morning of August 19. The main attack made good progress and reached Lehtokangas, about halfway to Nurmi Lake, the same afternoon. A Russian pocket of resistance northeast of Lehtokangas was destroyed. The right flank regiment, however, met determined resistance and its progress was slow. The German regiment on the left barely managed to get out of its starting positions. The main Finnish force reached the railroad south of Nurmi Lake on August 20. The Finns had five battalions in defensive positions south of Nurmi Lake and across the road and railroad leading east from Kayrala, the route that the trapped forward Soviet forces would have to take in a retreat.

The infantry battalions from the 169th Division which were to drive south along the east shore of the Nurmi River to Nurmi Lake were making slow progress and this left the Soviets an escape route. It was imperative to close the pincer as rapidly as possible and troops in the forward German positions west of Kayrala were reduced to the minimum in order to increase the striking power of the northern pincer. Poor weather conditions kept the Luftwaffe grounded until August 25.

The Finnish 6th Division tried to move forces northward in order to link up with the Germans moving south but in the meantime the Soviets had begun to make their escape via an unknown east–west road north of Lake Nurmi. The advancing Finns did not reach and cut this road until August 25. The right flank Finnish regiment had captured the village of Vuoriyarvi, about 20 kilometers southwest of Alakurtti on the previous day.

The Soviet defenses north and south of Lakes Kuola and Apa were collapsing and Soviet soldiers from the forward areas were in headlong retreat to the east in order to avoid the trap that was about to close on them in the Lake Nurmi area. While a clear-cut victory was achieved, the failure of the German drive from the north to close the encirclement allowed the bulk of the trapped Soviet soldiers to escape although most of their vehicles and equipment were abandoned in the process.

Even as late as the morning of August 27 the Soviets managed to keep the encirclement from closing in desperate and bloody defensive fighting northeast of Nurmi Lake. The XXXVI Corps ordered a relentless pursuit of the beaten enemy in the direction of Alakurtti. A major reorganization for the pursuit was undertaken. The units that had earlier been detached from the 169th Division were now reattached. In addition, three SS battalions were attached to the Finnish 6th Division to make sure that unit had sufficient weight to overcome anticipated desperate Soviet rearguard actions. The pursuit made good initial progress and reached a point about seven kilometers from Alakurtti by the end of August 27.

The Soviet defenders held a narrow bridgehead on the western banks of the Tuntsa River and this bridgehead, with prepared positions, held the Germans and Finns at bay for several days despite vigorous frontal and flanking attacks. The bridgehead was finally eliminated on August 30 and the Soviets destroyed the road and railroad bridges over this formidable obstacle as they withdrew to the eastern bank of the river.

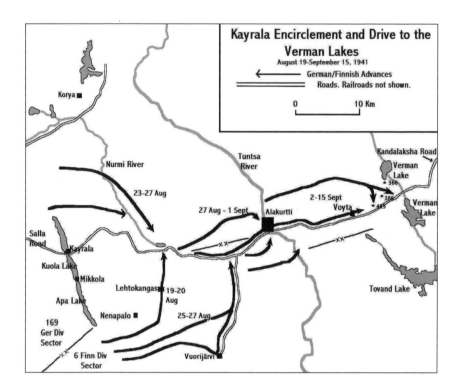

In their withdrawal to the east bank the Soviets neglected to destroy a footbridge north of the main east–west road, which a regiment of the 169th Division used to cross the river. There followed a day of hard fighting in town before the Soviets suddenly withdrew in the evening of September 1, 1941. They withdrew to the river running through the village of Voyta 10 kilometers to the east of Alakurtti.

As the Germans and Finns were pressing on east of Alakurtti, the Army of Norway redeployed some units that reduced the strength of the XXXVI Corps. Two SS battalions from the 7th SS Infantry Regiment were transferred to the Finnish III Corps while one battalion from the 9th SS Infantry Regiment, which had earlier been transferred to the XXXVI Corps from Mountain Corps Norway, was now sent back north to General Dietl.

It was thus a reduced-strength corps that closed on the Voyta River line on September 2. This had been the border between the Soviet Union and Finland prior to March 1940 and the old Finnish border fortifications were now manned by five Soviet regiments. Some of these regiments—from the 104th and 122nd Rifle Divisions—were at a severely reduced strength from the previous two months of fighting. One motorized regiment from the 1st Tank Division had been attached to the 104th Rifle Division. It held the center of the Soviet defensive line. The Soviets were also bringing forward a steady flow of replacements from Kandalaksha.

The XXXVI Corps halted along the west bank of the Voyta River for four days with the 169th Division on the left and the 6th Finnish Division on the right. The Germans and Finns began their assault across the river on September 6. Four regiments made the frontal assault while one regiment enveloped the enemy's north flank and headed for Hill 366 just southwest of the northernmost of the two Verman lakes. While the frontal attack by the four regiments was repelled, the enveloping regiment made rapid progress towards Hill 366 (elevation in meters). This was one of several places where high ground dominated the road and railroad to Kandalaksha. Faulty intelligence from a reconnaissance two days earlier had made the Germans believe that Hill 366 was unoccupied. They now discovered that it was occupied and strongly fortified. The German regiment found itself in a dangerous position, over eight kilometers behind the Soviet line along the Voyta River. This situation led to heated exchanges between the regiment and corps and illustrated the raw nerves symptomatic of exhausted units.[13] Much of the recrimination dealt with the lack of artillery and air support, priority for which was still with Mountain Corps Norway.

The attack by the XXXVI Corps on September 7 made no progress due to heavy rainstorms. Intercepted Soviet radio traffic indicated that the Soviet troops had orders to hold their positions at all cost, even at the risk of encirclement. The corps decided to abandon the frontal attacks and concentrate on what had started out as a promising northern envelopment. However, as we have seen, the regiment in the north was in trouble. It had managed to take Hill 366 on September 7 and also reported securing Hill 386 to its south. It was learned the following morning that Hill 386 had in fact not been secured. The corps ordered an additional regiment forward on the north flank and sent a Finnish regiment to take up a position northeast of Hill 366 to cover the corps' left flank. Another Finnish regiment was at the northern tip of Tolvand Lake to cover the southern flank.

The German attack bogged down in front of the high ground east of Voyta for two days until Hill 386 was captured on September 10. The corps ordered the new regiment it had sent forward to push east along the road to Verman River. The regiment, which had been in this area since the beginning of the attack, was ordered to move west and attack the Soviet defenses in the Voyta area from behind. The regiment hesitated for almost a day and moved out only after General Feige intervened personally. The 169th Division managed to push a battalion across the Voyta River on September 11 and contact with the regiment approaching from the east was established on September 12. While the road to the east was now open, the Soviet forces to the south of that road clung to their positions and it took the Finnish 6th Division one week of heavy fighting to reduce those positions.[14]

As the XXXVI Corps drew up to the line of the Verman Lakes, they again found themselves facing the same foes as they had since operations began—the 122nd and 104th Soviet Rifle Divisions. Over 8,000 replacements had joined these two units by September 15, bringing them up to 80% of full strength.

These two divisions occupied prepared positions along the Verman River that flows between the two lakes by that name. The Soviet positions were anchored in the north on the North Verman Lake and in the south on Tolvand Lake. The Soviets, who had a much better appreciation of the importance of Murmansk to their war effort—were obviously committed, at all costs, to preventing the Germans and Finns from reaching the Murmansk Railroad. Forced labor had been working for months on three additional fortified defensive lines between the two lakes and Kandalaksha.

As the XXXVI Corps drew up to the Verman Lake line the Army of Norway made another change in its strategy that brought relations between Generals Feige and Falkenhorst to breaking point. With the failure of the last attack across the Litsa River in the Mountain Corps Norway's area of operations, the Army of Norway switched the effective main effort in Finland back to the XXXVI Corps—just a few days after two battalions of the 7th SS Infantry Regiment were transferred to the Finnish III Corps, and one battalion from the 9th SS Infantry Regiment was sent north to Mountain Corps Norway.

The XXXVI Corps had suffered 9,463 German casualties since the campaign was initiated and was hardly in a position to become the main effort. The 169th Division was so worn out and depleted that it was hardly capable of performing defensive missions, much less offensive operations. The Army of Norway proposal elicited some very unusual harsh comments from General Feige. The XXXVI Corps characterized the proposal as "grotesque" and "hardly calculated to arouse confidence in the higher leadership."[15]

General Feige did not limit himself to pointing out the futility of switching the main effort to the XXXVI Corps. He leveled—in an appreciation of the situation on September 16—some harsh criticism against the Army of Norway for having missed excellent opportunities in the past. He pointed out that, by the earlier emphasis on the operations of Mountain Corps Norway to the detriment of reinforcing the XXXVI Corps, two good opportunities had been missed within a month—one after the Kayrala encirclement and another as the corps drew up to the Verman line. He concluded his assessment with the statement that the corps could advance no further with the forces it had assigned. While there was still a possibility of reaching Kandalaksha before winter, Feige stated that to do so he needed another Finnish division and a German mountain division. However, time was of the essence since the Soviets were improving their defenses with each passing day.

General Feige must surely have been aware of the efforts made by the Army of Norway to obtain additional forces, although those efforts were late. Falkenhorst had requested the two remaining regiments of the 163rd Division on August 25, 1941 and on September 4 General Buschenhagen had requested the use of the 6th Mountain Division. On September 14 Falkenhorst had again requested the remainder of the 163rd Division and the 6th Mountain Division. There was no reply to the August 25 request for the 163rd Division and, as we saw earlier, both Hitler and Dietl were determined to use the 6th Mountain Division in the far north. With respect to the second request for the 163rd Division on September 14, OKW promised a reply as soon as the operations around Leningrad were sorted out.

The request for the 163rd Division on August 25, even if OKW had acted on it, came too late to add much punch to the pursuit after the Kayrala encirclement. It would take some time to withdraw the 163rd Division from East Karelia and move it and its support base several hundred miles. The request for the 6th Mountain Division on September 4 was likewise too late. The division was still on its way from Greece by

way of Norway and was not expected to reach the Mountain Corps
Norway's area of operations until sometime in October.

The Army of Norway instructed XXXVI Corps on September 17 to
rest its troops for the time being on the Verman River line. Feige was
promised two battalions from an organization referred to as Schützenverband Oslo. This was a regimental-size unit of two battalions organized in Norway. The unit was not yet available; it was on the way to
Finland from Norway and the quality of this makeshift organization
was open to question. General Feige predicted that the operations of his
corps had come to an end since winter was fast approaching.

Hitler's War Operational Directive Number 36, issued on September 22, still called for the XXXVI to continue its offensive against
Kandalaksha in October.[16] The Army of Norway was told that
Mannerheim would be asked to release the 163rd Division in time to
take part in the offensive. The directive also called for the release of all
German troops from the Finnish III Corps and for them to be reattached to XXXVI Corps. Finnish III Corps was to halt all its offensive
operations. This was yet another change to German strategy in Finland
and the promised additional forces were too little and too late. It was
soon learned, for example, that the 163rd Division was not expected to
join the XXXVI Corps for four to five weeks, after the full fury of winter had set in on the central front in Finland.

This realization led to yet another shift in strategy by the Army of
Norway. Falkenhorst disregarded Directive 36 since the premise on
which it was based—the timely arrival of the 163rd Division—was no
longer realizable. Instead of terminating operations by III Finnish
Corps, Falkenhorst began withdrawing troops from the XXXVI Corps
for use in the Finnish III Corps area. Offensive operations in the XXXVI
area were delayed until winter.

This was not the end of the back-and-forth about strategy in
Finland between the Army of Norway and the OKW. On October 8 the
OKW ordered a stop to all operations in the Army of Norway sector.
This resulted in a call from the Army of Norway to OKW for an expla-
nation. This was at a time when the great encirclement battles by Army
Group Center at Bryansk and Vyazma had been concluded with Soviet
losses estimated at 300,000 killed and 700,000 captured.[17] With Army
Group Center beginning its final drive against Moscow a sense of un-
warranted optimism prevailed in Berlin. OKW believed that the military

collapse of the Soviet Union was imminent. In view of this, it was felt that it was not necessary to push things in central Finland. This is essentially the explanation given to General Buschenhagen by General Jodl. It was confirmed by Führer Directive Number 37 on October 10, 1941.[18]

Offensive operations by the Army of Norway were to cease and its mission reverted to protecting the nickel mines and making preparations for seizing the Rybachiy Peninsula and Murmansk. It was planned to give Mannerheim control of the Finnish III Corps as part of his planned reorganization of the Finnish Army and the XXXVI Corps was instructed to detach its Finnish units and have them revert to III Corps control and at the same time transfer the SS Division Nord to the control of the XXXVI Corps.

Finnish III Corps Operations

The operations in the Finnish III Corps area had also turned decisively against the Army of Norway. The Soviets had increased their forces confronting both Groups J and F. The 88th Soviet Rifle Division was moved into the Group J area along with an ad hoc unit referred to as Independent Brigade *Grivnin*. This unit was made up of one regiment from the 54th Rifle Division and a unit referred to as Special Regiment Murmansk. Group F, west of Ukhta, confronted the 54th Rifle Division (short one regiment). Under constant pressure, Group J had to abandon its forward positions and fall back. It ended up in new defensive positions about 13 kilometers east of Kestenga. Group F attempted to resume its offensive but was stopped dead in its tracks by the 54th Rifle Division.

As the situation in the Group J area looked very threatening, possibly necessitating a further withdrawal, the Army of Norway asked for an additional Finnish regiment for this sector on September 9. Ziemke writes that General Erfurth, the chief German liaison officer at Mannerheim's headquarters, refused to relay the request to the Marshal.[19] Erfurth does not mention this in his book. He only observes that the difficulties in the Army of Norway area caused Falkenhorst to ask the Finns for help. He also observes that the frequent changes in German plans decreased Finnish willingness to heed the German requests.[20]

On September 12 the Army of Norway pulled the SS Reconnaissance Battalion out of the XXXVI Corps sector in order to provide the

Finnish III Corps with a reserve. The transfer of the regimental head-quarters and one battalion of the 14th Finnish Regiment from Pechenga to the III Corps area were also ordered. This reshuffling of forces to the III Corps area took place while the main effort was still assigned to the XXXVI Corps and while that commander was virtually begging for reinforcements. It underscores the lack of an overall strategy and may well have contributed to a Finnish refusal of a second request from Falkenhorst for a fresh regiment. Mannerheim did promise to provide 2,800 troops as replacements for losses in III Corps.

Relations had soured between Falkenhorst and subordinate Finnish commanders. The transfer of the SS Reconnaissance Battalion to the Finnish III Corps brought virtually all SS Division Nord units into that corps. General Siilasvuo, the III Corps commander, had split the SS Division and assigned its units to his two groups—primarily Group J. This left General Demelhuber, the commander of SS Division Nord, and his staff as mere onlookers. The SS Division had improved since its debacle at Salla but the Finns still considered it an unreliable unit if left on its own. Demelhuber had obviously complained about this state of affairs to Falkenhorst who now insisted to General Siilasvuo that all SS units be placed under the command of General Demelhuber with their own sector of operations. While General Siilasvuo resisted, Falkenhorst was not about to have a German division commanded by a Finnish colonel. Siilasvuo appealed the decision later in the month but Falken-horst refused to reconsider.

A trip by Falkenhorst to Hitler's headquarters on September 14 resulted in yet another change of plans for the Army of Norway. Falken-horst was ordered to stop the attack by Group F against Ukhta and have Group J and SS Division Nord take up defensive positions. These orders were later confirmed in Führer Directive 36.

Intelligence from prisoner interrogations convinced III Corps at the end of September that Soviet morale was poor among the forces in the area between Kestenga and Loukhi. III Corps planned to resume its advance against Loukhi and asked the Army of Norway for reinforce-ments. Falkenhorst agreed with the request despite Hitler's orders on September 14 to halt all offensive operations in the III Corps sector and he offered Siilasvuo the following units:

1. One regiment from the 6th Finnish Division.

2. The two infantry battalions that constituted Schützenverband Oslo.
3. The 9th SS Infantry Regiment from Mountain Corps Norway.
4. One regiment of artillery.
5. The last battalion of the 14th Finnish Infantry Regiment, also from the Mountain Corps Norway sector.

The Army of Norway issued orders for the III Corps attack on October 6 but had to cancel the order on October 8 since OKW, in accordance with Hitler's earlier instructions, ordered that all offensive operations cease. The cancellation order came as the troop deployments were underway. The 9th SS Infantry Regiment and the lone battalion from the 14th Finnish Infantry Regiment were allowed to move into the III Corps sector but remained under Army of Norway control.

Generals Falkenhorst and Siilasvuo had a meeting on October 11, 1941. The purpose of the meeting was to discuss developments in the left sector of III Corps. It had been learned that one of the major units facing Group J and SS Division Nord—Independent Brigade *Grivnin*—had been dissolved. One of its regiments was moved south to join the 54th Rifle Division while another regiment had been identified in the XXXVI Corps sector. Both generals agreed that the prospects for an attack were good but, in view of Hitler's orders, it was decided to characterize their planned attack as an attempt to improve the defensive positions of Group J and SS Division Nord.

Major General Siilasvuo reported to Falkenhorst on October 23 that he believed the attack discussed on October 11 would prove to be a complete success. Falkenhorst asked if Siilasvuo believed that a drive directly to Loukhi was possible. The Finn gave an affirmative answer. Falkenhorst's question to Siilasvuo is a clear revelation of his intention. He saw a chance to accomplish the Army of Norway's mission of cutting the Murmansk Railroad and grabbed it despite Hitler's instructions on September 14 and the OKW order on October 8. The redeployment of forces that the Army of Norway had ordered on October 6 gave Siilasvuo and Falkenhorst the extra forces they believed necessary for the new offensive.

Major General Siilasvuo set the objectives for the attack. It involved a close encirclement of the Soviet forces along the front and then a quick drive to Loukhi. The SS Division Nord was given the mission of tying down the Soviet forces on their front while three Finnish regiments and the 9th SS Infantry Regiment broke through the Soviet positions along the railroad. The breakthrough forces would then turn north and encircle the Soviet troops tied down by the SS Division Nord. A task force of two Finnish battalions would bypass the southern Soviet flank and advance to Verkhneye Lake south of Lebedevo Lake.

The attack began on October 30 and by November 1, III Corps had encircled the Soviet regiment holding the front in the SS Division Nord sector. It had been General Siilasvuo's intention to destroy the encirclement as quickly as possible while the bulk of his forces pushed on to seize the narrows between Lakes Lebedevo and Yelovoye on their way to Loukhi. However, there was a sharp change in his intention soon after the encirclement was completed. He insisted to the Army of Norway that he needed time to eliminate the Soviet pocket before he could resume his advance.

A message from OKW on October 9 requested information about Falkenhorst's intentions and reminded him pointedly about Führer Directive Number 37, which had prohibited offensive operations in the III Corps area. In its reply, the Army of Norway pointed to the successes already achieved: the destruction of two regiments of the 88th Soviet Rifle Division and the seizure of the narrows between Yelovoye Lake and Lebedevo Lake. This area provided an excellent starting point for operations against Loukhi.

The Army of Norway also received a message from General Erfurth. The message requested that III Corps cease offensive operations as soon as possible because Mannerheim wanted to proceed with the reorganization of the Finnish Army (to be discussed in Chapter 6). This message elicited the logical question from the Army of Norway—what was meant by as soon as possible? Erfurth replied that the timing was left up to the Army of Norway but Mannerheim wanted to proceed with his reorganization plans quickly.

The cleaning out of pockets of Soviet soldiers was completed by November 13. Over 3,000 dead were reported as well as 2,600 prisoners. While the Soviets had moved reinforcements into the area in form of the 186th Rifle Division, it was not viewed as a serious obstacle since it was less than 3,000 men strong. It was in fact the Polyarnyy Division, which had made an appearance in the Mountain Corps Norway sector in September. It had been renamed and moved south when operations on the Litsa front came to an end.

Despite the successes achieved, General Siilasvuo made no move to exploit them. In fact, he grew downright gloomy in his assessment. On November 16 he reported that his troops were facing 17 enemy battalions and his conclusion was that further attacks by his corps would produce no results. This was followed by a report on November 18 that his corps was not capable of continuing the operation and that he would instead adopt a defensive posture. His immediate subordinates, the commanders of Group J and SS Division Nord, disagreed openly with Siilasvuo's assessment and felt that the prospects for a continued offensive were good. The German liaison officer at III Corps reported that the commander of Group J, as late as November 18, considered his unit fully capable of continuing the offensive and his regimental commanders concurred. The drawbacks of coalition warfare were beginning to haunt Falkenhorst's efforts.

Major General Buschenhagen, Falkenhorst's chief of staff, traveled to Helsinki on October 15 to try to sort out various aspects relating to the Army of Norway and to visit Major General Warlimont from OKW. It probably came as no surprise to Buschenhagen that OKW was upset with the activities by the Army of Norway in view of earlier directives not to engage in offensive operations. Warlimont repeated General Erfurth's earlier arguments that Mannerheim wanted control of his troops in order to carry out his reorganization plans. Warlimont told Buschenhagen that the Germans had to start removing their troops from III Corps no later than December 1, 1941. He also told Buschenhagen that Heinrich Himmler wanted the SS Division Nord sent back to Germany with a rather vague promise that he would provide replacement units.

Although the Finns maintained that the reason for halting offensive operations was to facilitate Mannerheim's plans for reorganizing the Finnish Army, it is more likely that the primary reason was political. Diplomatic relations between Great Britain and Finland were broken on July 31, 1941. A note from the British government to the Finnish government sent via the Norwegian Embassy in Helsinki on September 22 demanded that Finland end hostilities and pull its troops back to the 1939 borders. If the Finns continued their advance into Soviet territory the British would treat Finland as a hostile nation. After lengthy discussions within the Finnish government, in which Mannerheim participated, the Finns politely rejected the British note.[21]

What may have had a more decisive impact on Finnish behavior as far as III Corps operations were concerned was an intervention by the US (although not a belligerent at this time). The US ambassador to Finland presented a memorandum from the US government to President Ryti on October 27, 1941. The note included the following demands:

> Insofar as the Finnish government is anxious to preserve the friendship of the United States now and in the future, the United States government must be given satisfactory assurances that the intention of the Finnish government is immediately to cease operations against Russian territory, and that Finnish forces will immediately be withdrawn (in principle) from Russian territory to a line corresponding to the 1939 boundary between Finland and the Soviet Union.
>
> In the event that attacks are made against shipments of military supplies from the United States en route to Russia via the Arctic Ocean, and such attack is presumably made or may be claimed to be made from Finnish-controlled territory, it must be assumed that in view of the public opinion now prevailing in the United States such an incident must be assumed to lead to an immediate crisis in Finnish–American relations.[22]

The US warning was elaborated on in another memorandum on October 30 and at a press conference by Secretary of State Cordell Hull on November 3, 1941. The October 30 memorandum stated that Finnish military operations (presumably against the Murmansk Railroad) "constituted a definite threat to the security of the United States."[23]

While the Finnish government rejected the US demands, we may assume that Finland did not want a Finnish unit (III Corps) under German command posing the only serious danger to the route by which American military equipment and supplies were delivered to the Soviet Union. It was therefore important to stop the offensive operations of III Corps, return the German units under its control to the Army of Norway, and bring III Corps back under Finnish control. This is also what Falkenhorst suspected as the reason for the unusual attitude of Major General Siilasvuo who was probably briefed by Mannerheim.[24] Mannerheim, in his memoirs, is silent on this subject.

German Command and Organizational Changes

Mannerheim was not the only one contemplating organizational changes. Führer Directive Number 37, issued on October 10, ordered the Army of Norway to go over to defensive operations. It is not surprising that Falkenhorst fell by the wayside in the wake of this directive. It was the inevitable price for the failure of the Army of Norway to achieve its main objectives—the capture of Murmansk or its isolation. Falkenhorst was also a demanding officer with rough edges who frequently ruffled feathers of fellow Germans as well as his Finnish "brothers-in-arms."

Falkenhorst did not leave in disgrace—he remained as commander in chief in Norway until December 18, 1944—and he may have been pleased by the change. Up to now he had been saddled with enormous responsibilities, and had to operate two army headquarters more than 1,600 kilometers apart. In Norway he commanded a single army with a very specific defensive mission.

The selection of General der Gebirgstruppe General Eduard Dietl as a replacement for Falkenhorst was also almost pre-ordained. He was an early supporter of Hitler. He and his company stood ready to support Hitler and his followers during the Beer Hall Putsch on November 9, 1923. His stubborn defense of Narvik for two months in 1940 when many, including Hitler, were ready to give up the game gave him an almost legendary status. Dietl was one of the few generals that Hitler had grown to like and trust over the years. He was loved by his troops and had a personality and charm well suited for dealing with the Finns who also admired him.

The instructions issued on November 7, 1941, by the OKW directed an early transfer of command. Falkenhorst and the Headquarters, Army of Norway, would return to Norway. Dietl would assume command of all German forces in Finland and northern Norway and establish a new headquarters, designated the Army of Lapland.

Everyone appears to have been pleased by the new command arrangement—except Dietl. He was basically a troop commander, not a manager, and was happiest when he was at the front with his troops. A briefing at the Army of Norway headquarters brought home to him the enormity of the job he was about to assume and he may well have sincerely doubted his own abilities to deal with this managerial task. Dietl wrote a letter to General Jodl on November 24 asking that his assignment as commander, Army of Lapland be withdrawn. This unusual action by an officer who was being promoted resulted in an order for him to report to Hitler's headquarters. In the end, Hitler and Jodl prevailed on him not to give up the command to which he had been appointed.

Analysis of Operations in Central Finland

The OKW and the Army of Norway made a number of serious strategic and tactical mistakes in 1941 that are complex in nature and difficult to understand. Most have their inception in the planning and preparations for operations out of Finland. Ziemke attempts to explain the problems in a different way. He writes:

> In the first place, the objective of the Army of Norway [with respect to Murmansk and the Murmansk Railroad] was political and psychological rather than strategic. . . . There is some reason for believing that the operation was directed more against Great Britain, to demonstrate its isolation and helplessness, then against the Soviet Union. Under those circumstances it became worthwhile to disregard sound tactics and attempt to stage a quick march along the arctic coast to Murmansk.[25]

Hitler's obsession with the defense of Norway—where no real threat existed in 1941—played a large part in his decisions regarding Finland. Hitler's views regarding Murmansk were heavily influenced by his concerns for the security of the nickel mines near Pechenga—and the iron mines in north Sweden—shown by the arguments he used in his meeting with Dietl in April 1941. He viewed Russian troops in Murmansk as a threat to those mines and to northern Norway. Therefore, it is unlikely that a demonstration of Great Britain's helplessness was foremost in Hitler's mind when it came to Murmansk.

Ziemke is definitely right in his observation that the operations in Finland were begun with inadequate forces and that OKH was correct in not providing substantial reinforcements that would detract from the main effort in Russia. Substantial forces could, however, have been provided from those seven divisions that sat idle in Norway but here again we are confronted with Hitler's obsession with the defense of Norway.

When it comes to German operations in Finland in 1941 we are again faced with a complex and confusing picture. One is forced to conclude that there was a great amount of uncertainty in the Army of Norway and at the highest level in Germany, caused by a lack of a coherent strategy. This resulted in constant changes. Some of these changes originated with the Army of Norway but others were caused by OKW meddling in the operations of that army.

Seven divisions (five German and two Finnish) were employed at four different points and the effective main effort kept shifting throughout 1941. Two German divisions and one Finnish regiment were used in the far north. Two German divisions and one Finnish division were used initially on the Salla front. SS Division Nord was subsequently fragmented and eventually sent to the III Corps area. The III Finnish Corps, with one division initially, was employed 140 kilometers to the south of Salla. It was subsequently reinforced in driblets by units from the SS Division Nord. Finally, the badly split 163rd German Infantry Division was used in the far south, in Mannerheim's main offensive.

Although a main effort was designated initially, the force levels in each of the three areas reveal that no main effort existed. In failing to come up with a strategy supported organizationally within the German armed forces, the Germans let a golden opportunity for decisive results slip away in 1941. The Finns, seeing shifting plans and the lack of progress, became increasingly difficult to deal with, a situation aggravated by outside influences on the Finnish government.

The blame for the lack of a coherent strategy cannot be laid at the feet of Falkenhorst alone as Erfurth and Feige appear to do. Much of the fault can be traced back to inadequate planning and preparation and OKW meddling. The shifting of forces from one area to another to exploit opportunities rather than to create opportunities was not wise in view of the enormous transportation and supply difficulties in northern and central Finland.

Falkenhorst had a thankless job. He did not have the complete control of operations that you would expect of an army commander. He did not control air operations in his area of responsibility—the 5th Air Fleet in Norway answered to Göring and if he did not want to cooperate he had the ear of Hitler. Similarly, the SS Division he had assigned had a direct channel to Himmler. The commander of the Finnish III Corps had a direct line to Mannerheim who kept a close eye on the happenings in the Army of Norway area since Finnish troops were heavily involved.

Falkenhorst's force requests were submitted to OKH. That headquarters, completely absorbed with operations in the Soviet Union proper and North Africa, increasingly viewed the operations by the Army of Norway as a drain of valuable resources that were sorely needed elsewhere.

Finally, there was a surprising disregard for the chain of command within the army. Dietl was subordinate to Falkenhorst but in Chapter 3 we saw that he frequently dealt directly with OKW on operational matters. He even took positions opposing those held by the Army of Norway (for example, the use of the 6th Mountain Division).

It has already been noted that Generals Feige and Dietl felt that the real main effort should be in the Kandalaksha sector. Dietl had felt this way since April 1941 and never changed his views. Falkenhorst, on the other hand, was a proponent for cutting the Murmansk Railroad further south at Loukhi, from the III Corps sector. Feige and Dietl were correct from a tactical standpoint and also on strategic grounds. The place to cut the Murmansk Railroad for the most decisive results was at Kandalaksha. Cutting it further south—between Kandalaksha and Belomorsk—would not be as effective since the Soviets could bring supplies and equipment by rail to Kandalaksha and from there across the White Sea to Archangel or Onega by ship. Cutting the line south of Belomorsk would serve no purpose because a recently completed rail line from Belomorsk connected with the line from Archangel, thus avoiding the use of the southern part of the Murmansk Railroad from Belomorsk to Volkhov.[26] The Kandalaksha sector was also the only one of the three that had a relative good road and rail network that could logistically support the large forces required to interdict the Murmansk Railroad.

General Erfurth was a strong proponent of achieving relative superiority. In his book, *Die Überraschung im Krieg*, published in 1938 he writes "To achieve relative superiority somewhere is the main objective of almost all military movements and the essential purpose of generalship."[27] It is therefore surprising that he supported the movement of the 163rd Infantry Division to Karelia—where it accomplished virtually nothing—and was very critical of the decision to give one of its regiments to Falkenhorst. Giving the whole division to Falkenhorst might have given him the necessary forces to carry out his mission.

Erfurth argued later that General Siilasvuo would probably have reached Loukhi if he had been given an additional division in a timely manner and that Marshal Mannerheim had expressed the same opinion on several occasions.[28] By an additional division they are undoubtedly referring to the 6th Finnish Division attached to XXXVI Corps, and they are probably right. However, Falkenhorst had already given Siilasvuo SS Division Nord and, in view of the condition of the 169th Division, he had no further forces to spare based on security require- ments in XXXVI Corps' sector. The presence of the whole 163rd Division would have allowed him to release the 6th Finnish Division.

In an article published in *Wehrwissenschaftliche Rundschau* in 1952 and cited by Ziemke, General Erfurth suggested that the Army of Norway failed to follow OKW orders on several occasions. Falkenhorst did deviate from plans and orders several times to seize opportunities. The prerogative and expectation that a commander would do so had been part of German military doctrine since the late 1600s. The concept was referred to as *Selbständigkeit der Unterführer* (Independence of Subordinates).

Erfurth also claims in the same article that the orders violated were intended to create a main effort. The orders to which he must be refer- ring are the ones issued on July 7 and 30. It is somewhat misleading to characterize those as establishing a main effort. If anything, they were disruptive.

The July 7 OKW order dealt with the transfer of forces to Mountain Corps Norway after the capture of Salla. Dietl needed reinforcements— he had asked for one regiment. There is no indication that this repre- sented a change in the main effort. The other order to which Erfurth is referring must be the Führer Directive of July 30. It stopped the XXXVI Corps offensive and directed increased efforts in the Mountain Corps Norway and III Corps sectors. By this time Falkenhorst had unfortu- nately already switched his efforts to the Mountain Corps Norway and Finnish III Corps sectors. If the July 30 directive did anything, it appears to have blessed actions already taken by Falkenhorst. The effort in the far north was stopped by atrocious terrain and lack of lines of com- munication. The effort in the III Corps sector also had poor lines of communication but here the effort collapsed through Finnish refusal— probably on political grounds—to carry it out.

The frequent movement of regiments and battalions from one sector to another during the summer and fall point to uncertainty in German headquarters caused by a lack of cohesive strategy. However, Ziemke's explanation for the shifting of forces should be kept in mind as it was obviously a contributing factor:

> Falkenhorst maintained consistently and correctly that to relax the pressure at any one point meant giving the Russians an opportunity to exploit the superior maneuverability which the Murmansk Railroad afforded them to pull out troops and shift them to one of the other sectors. With the troops at its disposal the Army of Norway could not create a true main effort any- where without defeating its own ends in the process and could not shut down any single sector without creating a potential threat elsewhere.[29]

This observation in turn reveals the fact that the Germans were overcommitted. When overcommitted, the judicious use of available forces is more important than ever. The correct place for judicious offensive action was opposite Kandalaksha. General Erfurth agrees despite his above support for an increase of forces in the III Corps sec- tor.[30]

The Germans underestimated both the difficulties that the terrain posed for an attacker, and the capabilities and determination of their foe. These were surprises for the Germans and had a devastating effect on some of the poorly trained units that were sent to Finland.

Finally, when it comes to air operations—a factor that cannot be overemphasized in the spectacular string of German victories up to this point—the resources were not up to the demands placed on them. This again supports the observation of overcommitment. They had to sup- port operations of three corps separated by great distances. If the Murmansk Railroad could not be seized, adequate air assets should have been provided so as to render the railroad and trans-shipment facilities useless for considerable periods of time.

When Dietl assumed command of the Army of Lapland, his com- mand had been forced into a defensive posture in all sectors and the out- look for the future was bleak. After about 100 days of fighting the Germans had suffered nearly 22,000 casualties and the Finnish forces in the German areas had close to 7,000 casualties. Those who had watched the performance of the German Army in Finland with a sense of disillusionment were hoping that the Hero of Narvik could turn the situation around.

NOTES
1. Ziemke, *The German Northern Theater of War*, p.166, note 12.
2. Condon, *op. cit*, pp.80–103.
3. General Falkenhorst was not a stranger to Finland. In 1918, at the end of WWI, he had served as operations officer of General Rüdiger von der Goltz' forces in Finland. In this capacity he had undoubtedly encountered Marshal Mannerheim and some of the other key military leaders.
4. Erfurth, *The Last Finnish War*, p.26.
5. Ziemke, *The German Northern Theater of Operations*, p.158. If Ziemke is right, the transfer of command on June 17 must have been a relief of command.
6. *Ibid*, p.160.
7. Erfurth, *The Last Finnish War*, p.27.
8. Ziemke, *The German Northern Theater of Operations*, pp.165–166.
9. Trevor-Roper, *op. cit.*, p.147.
10. One additional advantage of Finnish experience, which became obvious as the war progressed, dealt with encirclements. The Germans favored wide encirclements but in an area of dense forests such encirclements were time-consuming and difficult to seal. The Finns, on the other hand, favored smaller and tighter encirclements that were easier to accomplish and seal in difficult terrain. These types of encirclements were made famous in the Winter War and gave rise to a new military term—*motti*.
11. Ziemke, *The German Northern Theater of Operations*, p.169.
12. This after-the-fact assessment may be right but it should be remembered that it was weakening Soviet resistance in Group J's sector that led to its reinforcement with one regiment and an artillery battalion from SS Division Nord and General Siilasvuo himself contributed to the strengthening of this group by taking two battalions away from Group F. Both groups were fought to a standstill by the Soviets. The Army of Norway order stopping Group F's offensive came after that unit's offensive had bogged down. There may have been a difference between the Finns and the Germans as to which group should constitute the main effort but at least as late as the end of July there seems to have been a consensus that it should be with Group J.
13. Ziemke, *The German Northern Theater of Operations*, p.174.
14. The Soviets threatened the whole XXXVI Corps on September 15 when they briefly recaptured Hill 366.
15. Ziemke, *The German Northern Theater of Operations*, p.176.
16. Trevor-Roper, *op. cit.*, pp.155–159.
17. Bellamy, *op. cit.*, p.277.

18. Trevor-Roper, *op. cit.*, pp.159–163.

19. Ziemke, *The German Northern Theater of Operations*, p.179.

20. Erfurth, *The Last Finnish War*, pp.44, 47.

21. Mannerheim, *Memoirs*, pp.432–433.

22. Wuorinen, *op. cit.*, pp.136–137.

23. Ibid, p.137.

24. Bellamy, *op. cit.*, p.269.

25. Ziemke, *The German Northern Theater of Operations*, p.185.

26. Jukka Juutinen provided the following translation of a passage from Juri Kilin and Ari Raunio's article *Sodan taisteluja 2: Jatkosota*, pp.12–13: "On February 5, 1940, the central committee of the Soviet Communist Party and the Soviet government approved the decision to lay an additional railway to the Kirov [Murmansk] railway. . . . The Belomorsk–Obozersk railway that was to be of decisive importance to the end result of the Great Patriotic War was being constructed with the forces of the NKVD Gulag of Belomorsk. In July 1940 about 60,000 prisoners worked on the site. According to the report the railway was temporarily opened on December 28, 1940, that is 2 days before the completion deadline. After reporting having finished the work NKVD opened a railway that was basically unfit for traffic, a railroad which wasn't fully operational until over a half year later in the summer of 1941."

27. Waldemar Erfurth, *Surprise*. Translated by Dr. Stefan T. Possony and Daniel Vilfroy (Harrisburg, Pennsylvania: Military Service Publishing Company, 1943), p.5.

28. Erfurth, *Problemet Murmanbanan*, p.14.

29. Ziemke, *The German Northern Theater of Operations*, p.187.

30. Erfurth, *Problemet Murmanbanan*, pp.5–6.

FIVE
THE FINNISH OFFENSIVES

Military Situation and Operational Concept

The Finns were much better prepared for war in 1941 than in 1939. They had an officer and noncommissioned officer corps of proven leaders with solid experience from the Winter War. These men, who had proven themselves in the past, faced the prospect of another encounter with their traditional foe with confidence. Furthermore, they were not alone as they had been in 1939. They were now entering the fight at the side of Germany, the world's leading military power.

The Finnish leaders, realizing that the imposed peace of 1940 was not the end of their troubles with the Soviet Union, had done all that could be done to prepare themselves for a new conflict. The stocks of supplies and equipment, exhausted in March 1940, had been replenished with German assistance. The increase in automatic weapons for the infantry had significantly improved their firepower. Heavy field artillery batteries, lacking in the Winter War, were now available. Air defenses had been improved and strengthened, however, although the Finnish Air Force was in better shape than during the Winter War, it was still inadequate in size for the tasks that lay ahead.

One of the most important improvements dealt with mobilization. New procedures instituted in the short period since the end of the Winter War resulted in the ability to field almost twice as many operational units. By the time the ground war began Finland had about 500,000 men under arms, an amazing feat for a country with a population of four million. When military construction and men and women auxiliaries are included, the number of individuals involved in the military or military-related activities amounted to 630,000 or over 15% of the population.[1] Even with such a massive mobilization it is highly questionable whether the Finns could have conducted their offensives in the south had it not been for the fact that the Germans had relieved them of the responsibility for defending a 500+ kilometer stretch of frontier in Lapland. In addition, the northward advance of German Army Group North served as a magnet that drew Soviet forces away from the Finnish front.

Such a large military was unsustainable in a prolonged war and it strongly suggests that Mannerheim and other Finnish leaders expected the war to be short. They, like so many others, were highly impressed by the string of spectacular German victories in Scandinavia, western Europe, and the Balkans and probably expected the Soviet armed forces to quickly crumble. When this did not materialize in the first six months of the war the large Finnish military establishment became a serious economic liability that had to be rectified.

The Finns had asked for a few days' delay in the attack by their main army until operations in the far north and around Salla had begun. As related in Chapter 2, Erfurth explains that the Finns wanted to create the impression among the people and members of parliament that Finland was being drawn into the war by events outside its control. This accorded well with the wishes of OKH. That headquarters wanted the Finns to strike from the north at the most effective time, as Army Group North approached the last natural obstacle south of Leningrad—the Dvina River, which was reached on a wide front on July 1, 1941. By July 4 the OKH had sufficient confidence in the continued progress of Army Group North to ask the Finns to launch their attacks on July 10.

The general concept of operations by the main Finnish army had been thrashed out on January 30, and again in the period June 24–28. The Finns, despite Mannerheim's disclaimer below, appear to have initially wanted to undertake operations west of Lake Ladoga with the goal of recovering the important territory on the Karelian Isthmus, which they had lost in the Winter War. The Germans, on the other hand, wanted the Finns to attack on both sides of Lake Ladoga, with the main effort in the east. This wish was again expressed by OKH on June 24 and reflected in the Finnish plans submitted on June 28, 1941.

Mannerheim writes that, despite the wishes in some Finnish circles for the immediate reconquest of the Karelian Isthmus, he opposed this idea from the beginning. He explains that by initiating operations on the

Karelian Isthmus the Soviets would believe that he was aiming at Leningrad and would marshal strong forces in opposition at a time when Army Group North was still far to the south. Mannerheim writes "It was my firm opinion that such an undertaking was against the interest of the country, and from the beginning I had informed the President of the Republic and the government that under no circumstances would I lead an offensive against the great city on the Neva."[2]

Mannerheim describes the development of the concept of operations by the Finnish Army as follows:

> Instead of attacking on the Karelian Isthmus, I decided to commence an offensive north of Ladoga on either side of Lake Jänisjärvi, with the beach of the Ladoga west and east of the town of Sortavala as its first objective, and the next one the frontier. A thrust north of Lake Jänisjärvi towards the Suojärvi area formed part of the main operation. The aim was to sever the way of retreat for the Russian forces concentrated west of Sortavala, and to roll up the enemy's position north of Vuoksi, thereby creating a favourable initial situation for a later offensive against Viipuri and the Isthmus.[3]

While—as Lundin points out—the sources are murky, imprecise, and contradictory, there is no doubt that Mannerheim's memoirs imply that the concept of operations was his, not that of the OKH.[4] German sources claim that the initial wish of the Finns was for an offensive on the Karelian Isthmus and that this issue was thrashed out in the meetings between General Heinrichs, the chief of the Finnish General Staff, and General Halder, the chief of staff of OKH, on January 30 and the results were as expressed by the OKH on June 24.

General Waldemar Erfurth, the chief of the German liaison staff at Mannerheim's headquarters, relates a completely different story from that told by Mannerheim:

> As the Finns saw it, based on the experience of all former wars against Russia, the main theater of war had to be the Karelian Isthmus. . . . It was, therefore, quite natural that the thoughts of the Finnish Commander-in-Chief were occupied chiefly with the Karelian Isthmus as the main theater of war of the planned

Finnish offensive. The deployment of Finnish forces was carried out mainly in accordance with this idea.[5]

Erfurth continues:

The German brothers-in-arms had other plans, however. The greater the success of the German offensive in western Russia, the more pressing became the demands of the German High Command that Marshal Mannerheim should not direct the main thrust of his army by way of the Karelian Isthmus toward Leningrad, but east of Lake Ladoga toward Lodeynoye Pole on the Svir. The German Army High Command desired that the strongest possible Finnish forces advance to the Svir and there unite for a decisive operation with Army Group North, which was proceeding across the Volkhov River.[6]

General Hermann Hölter, who was present in Finland at the time, supports Erfurth's story. He writes:

During the first consideration of operations by the Finns, the Karelian Isthmus was instinctively in the foreground of strategic wishes. The wish of the German High Command, however, that the Finns should make their principal thrust east of Lake Ladoga, in order to "join hands" with the German Army Group on the Svir, led to the operations of the "Finnish Karelian Army" under General Heinrichs through Ladogan Karelia to the Svir.[7]

It is not clear why Mannerheim elected not to conduct simultaneous offensives on both sides of Lake Ladoga and across the Karelian Isthmus, or what the German views were on this issue. Mannerheim may have hoped that the German Army Group North's continued drive towards Leningrad would cause the Soviets, in an effort to halt the German advance, to substantially reduce their forces on the isthmus. A delayed Finnish advance in this area would encounter less opposition. This appears to be what eventually happened. There may also have been logistical reasons for staggering the offensives.

It was important for the Finns to quickly occupy both Ladogan Karelia and the Karelian Isthmus. Soviet air attacks against Finnish towns presented a serious problem. Enemy bombers usually approached Finland across the Gulf of Finland from their airfields in Estonia. There was not much the Finns could do about this threat since their air force was too weak to prevent the raids. The Finns hoped that the advance of Army Group North would soon eliminate this threat.

The Soviets had expanded old airfields and built new ones in the territory they had conquered in the Winter War on the Karelian Isthmus and in the area east of Lake Ladoga. Soviet aircraft using these fields presented a difficult problem for the Finnish early warning network and their air defense forces. Since the removal of this threat could be accomplished only with Finnish ground offensives, their elimination played a prominent part in Finnish planning.

Order of Battle

The Finnish forces were deployed generally along a line from Hanko on the Gulf of Finland to an area around Lieksa, southwest of Belomorsk (Sorokka). Along this line the Finns had deployed five army corps as follows:

1. IV Corps, commanded by Major General Karl Lennart Oesch, had its right wing on the Gulf of Finland west of Viipuri and its left wing on the Vuoksi River. It consisted initially of three divisions—8th, 12th and 4th—and the 2nd Coastal Brigade. The 10th Division was apparently in a reserve status to the rear of the boundary between IV Corps and II Corps.[8]

2. The II Corps, commanded by Major General Taavetti Laatikainen, occupied a front north of the Karelian Isthmus and Lake Ladoga stretching from the left flank of IV Corps to the right flank of VII Corps. It consisted initially of three divisions—the 2nd, 18th, and 15th.

3. The Army of Karelia occupied the front from the left flank of II Corps opposite the narrows between Lakes Pyha and Ladoga in the south to just north of Ilomantsi in the north. Under normal circumstances Finnish corps were directed by the Finnish High Command without the interposition of an army headquarters. An exception was made in this case as it appeared doubtful that a multi-corps advance into Karelia

could be effectively directed from Mannerheim's headquarters. The decision was made to create an army—the Army of Karelia—under the command of Lieutenant General Heinrichs, Mannerheim's chief of staff. He retained his job as chief of staff but the duties were actually performed by deputies, first by Major General Viljo Einar Tuompo, chief of the command section and later by Major General Edvard Fritjof Hanell, chief of fortifications. The major units of the Army of Karelia were two corps, one light corps-size group, and an army reserve.

   a. VII Corps, commanded by Major General Johan Woldemar Hägglund, occupied the right wing of the Army of Karelia, from Lake Pyha to the outskirts of Vyartsilya (Värtsilä). It consisted initially of two divisions—the 19th and 7th.

   b. VI Corps held the center of the Army of Karelia from Vyartsilya to Korpiselkya (Korpiselkä). It was commanded by Major General Paavo Juho Talvela and consisted initially of the 11th and 5th Divisions.

   c. Task Force Oinonen occupied the left wing of the Army of Karelia, positioned north of the Ilomantsi area. It consisted of the cavalry brigade and the 1st and 2nd Jäger Brigades.[9] The task force was commanded by Major General Woldemar Oinonen.

   d. The 1st Division was in reserve behind the Army of Karelia.

4. The 14th Division covered the left flank of the Finnish Army and filled the gap between that army and the Army of Norway. It was commanded by Colonel Erkki Johannes Raappana and stationed in the Lieksa area. This division was directly subordinated to Marshal Mannerheim.

5. The 17th Division had the mission of sealing off Hanko.

6. The 163rd German Infantry Division (minus one regiment) arrived in early July and Mannerheim stationed it initially at Joensuu behind the Army of Karelia as his reserve.[10]

The composition of the corps changed frequently during the war as corps headquarters were moved around and divisions and brigades were detached from one corps and attached to another.

The Soviet forces facing the Finnish Army were part of Marshal Klimenti Voroshilov's Northwest Front. The 32nd Soviet Army[11] was responsible for the area north of Lake Onega. It consisted of five divisions. In the Army of Karelia sector north and east of Lake Ladoga the Soviet 7th Army had three divisions forward and one in reserve. The Soviet 23rd Army on the Karelian Isthmus had four divisions of stationary troops manning the border fortifications and three divisions in reserve. The Soviet troops at Hanko consisted of two infantry brigades plus a number of specialized units. At the outset of the war the Soviets had the equivalent of 18 divisions at the fronts in Finland and they faced 15 Finnish and four German divisions.[12]

German pressure from the south forced the Soviets to weaken their forces along the Finnish border in order to make units available to contest the advance of Army Group North. By the time the Finns began their operations, the Soviets had redeployed nearly all their reserve formations. The Finns were thus confronted by only seven divisions plus the two brigades at Hanko, giving them a 4:1 superiority in infantry and a 9:1 superiority in artillery.[13] They could also remain relatively assured that the forces opposing them would not increase markedly in the near future as the Soviets were throwing all they had at the approaching Germans.

Ladoga Karelia Offensive

The Finns planned to attack on both sides of Yanis Lake (Jänisjärvi). They hoped this would split the Soviet defensive line, allowing the Finns to advance along the east shore of Lake Ladoga through Olonets (Aunus) to Lodeynoye Pole (Lotinapelto) on the Svir River. Both IV and II Corps would hold on the border initially but II Corps was to be ready to advance on orders towards the northwest shore of Lake Ladoga.

The Finns commenced offensive operations from the area between Lake Pyha in the southwest and Ilomantsi in the northeast on July 10. The offensive had the conquest of Ladoga Karelia as its objective.[14] Small units had operated behind enemy lines before that date. The main Finnish effort was in the VI Corps sector between Vyartsilya and Korpiselkya (Korpiselkä), northeast of Yanis Lake. General Talvela organized two battle groups to cover his flanks. Battle Group South attacked from the area between Lakes Pyha and Yanis with the mission of penetrating the isthmus between Lakes Yanis and Ladoga. Battle Group North was to attack from the area between Korpiselkya and Ilomantsi in the direction of Tolvayarvi (Tolvajärvi) and Muanto.

Despite stubborn local resistance, Soviet defenses quickly collapsed under the weight of the Finnish attack in the Vyartsilya–Korpiselkya sector; and it became apparent that the main Finnish thrust had hit a weak sector in the Russian front. Colonel Ruben Lagus' 1st Light Infantry Brigade from Group Oinonen was brought in and it managed to break through the Soviet defenses rather quickly.[15] Through the gap thus created, the light Finnish infantry, some equipped with bicycles, penetrated deep into enemy territory in the direction of the village of Tolvayarvi. After hard fighting, the town of Kokkari was stormed on July 12 and the village of Tolvayarvi further to the southeast was occupied on the same day. Continuing its exploitation, the light infantry brigade moved on the town of Muanto, which it captured on July 14.

The advance of the right-flank units of VI Corps driving south through Vyartsilya met stiff opposition in the hilly landscape east of Yanis Lake. The VII Corps, expected to advance southward on the west side of Yanis Lake, met heavy opposition and made little progress. Soviet resistance along the east shore of Yanis Lake was eliminated on July 16 and VI Corps swept around the southern end of the lake and set up positions facing west along Yanis River.

Mannerheim ordered several units redeployed on July 16. The 1st Division, which had been his reserve, was ordered forward to protect VI Corps' eastern flank near Loymola (Loimola). It was commanded by Colonel Paavo Paalu. The 17th Division, which had sealed off Hanko, was moved to the Vyartsilya area. It was commanded by Colonel Otto Snellman. The mission of sealing off the Soviet forces in Hanko was left to coastal defense units and a battalion of Swedish volunteers. Finally Mannerheim committed the German 163rd Infantry Division, commanded by Lieutenant General Erwin Engelbrecht, to the east with the mission of capturing the town of Suvilakhti. This town, located at the southern end of Suo Lake, was a road and railroad junction. By these redeployments Mannerheim effectively increased the forces available to the Army of Karelia by three infantry divisions. The stage was set for a rapid advance towards the Svir River.

While units of the VI Corps secured their positions at Tolvayarvi against possible Soviet attacks from the east, the main body continued southward. General Talvela saw an opportunity and immediately committed all his mobile forces to capture Loymola. This would allow the Finns to interdict the railroad from Petrozavodsk (Petroskoi). A Finnish armored infantry battalion captured Loymola on July 15.

An even more promising opportunity presented itself to General Talvela. This involved a quick thrust to the shores of Lake Ladoga near the town of Koirinoja. A successful drive to the shore of Lake Ladoga would isolate the forces holding Sortavala and contesting the Finnish advance on both sides of Lake Yanis. While flank security forces were sent to the east the bulk of the troops were committed in the direction of Koirinoja on the northeast shore of Lake Ladoga. That town fell to Finnish forces on July 16. Colonel Lagus' 1st Light Infantry Brigade completed its 110-kilometer contested drive with the capture of Koirinoja.

General Talvela sent two strong columns on a drive towards the east and south. One column was sent eastward to the Tulm Lake area while the main force advanced south along the east shore of Lake Ladoga. The Soviets had reorganized some of its forces and brought in reinforcements from the Karelian Isthmus. Units from the 452nd Motorized Infantry Regiment had reached the front and set up defensive positions around the town of Salmi, where the Tulm River empties into Lake Ladoga. Colonel Lagus' troops crossed the Tulm River five kilometers north of Salmi, isolating the Soviet defenders. Salmi was captured on July 21 after some heavy fighting and only a small number of the defenders managed to escape the encirclement. The corps crossed the 1939 border on July 23 and on July 24 Mannerheim ordered it to halt along the Tuloksa (Tuulos) River and take up defensive positions.

The Soviet forces facing the Finns on the Ladogan front had reorganized on July 21. The 7th Army had been organized into two groups. One, called the Petrozavodsk Group, was commanded by Lieutenant General M. Antonjuk. Its main combat units consisted of an infantry regiment, two motorized regiments, and an armored regiment. The other group was referred to as Group South under Lieutenant General V. Tsvetajev. It consisted of a marine brigade, two motorized regiments, and some smaller units.

The old border marker erected by King Gustav II Adolphus at Aajakontu was reached by troops of the VI Corps on July 22. General Talvela's message to Mannerheim reads in part: "After the capture of

Manssila today at 1130 hours, the Russians have been chased out of Finland in the operational area of the VI Corps. The area, whose rear boundary is formed by a line Korpiselkä–Jänis River, has been freed from our hereditary foe."[16]

The Finnish columns advancing inland from Lake Ladoga were also making good progress. One column crossed the historic boundary on its way to Lake Tulm. The northern settlement on this lake was captured on July 18 and the rest of the settlements along the lake during the following two days. The Soviets put up strong resistance in the Rajakonru area and it was not overcome until July 23 when a Finnish column advancing from the southern part of Lake Tulm towards Vidlitsa (Vitele) threatened the Soviet line of retreat along the shore of the lake. This threat caused the Soviets to withdraw and both Vidlitsa and Rajakonru were taken after light fighting on July 24. The Finnish forces, in accordance with orders from Mannerheim, took up defensive positions.

While the reasons for Mannerheim's decision to cease offensive operations in Karelia may have been complex, he had ample operational reasons to worry about this front. The rapid advance of the 5th Division along the eastern shore of Lake Ladoga had exposed a 100-kilometer stretch of shoreline in his rear that could be interdicted by the Soviets from the sea. Furthermore, strong Soviet forces were still present in the area north and northeast of Lake Ladoga and in the important Lake Suo area.

Mannerheim's concerns were soon validated by Soviet actions. Heavy counterattacks by an armored regiment and parts of four infantry regiments in the Vidlitsa area resulted in ten days of heavy fighting before the Finnish front was stabilized about 10 kilometers east of Lake Vidlitsa. Meanwhile, Major General Pavlov, the Soviet commander of the coastal defense forces on Lake Ladoga launched a night amphibious assault in the rear of the Finnish 5th Division at the same time as a strong attack was launched against the Finnish line at Tuloksa. The landing took place on the two small islands of Lukulansaari and Mantsi, just offshore from the town of Salmi. General Talvela had to scrape together whatever forces were at hand, including support troops, in order to keep the Soviets from establishing themselves on the two islands. The Finns were able to destroy four of the 15 ships used in the landing and managed to split the Soviet marines into three encircled pockets, which were eliminated by the evening of July 26. The Soviets made another landing on Mantsi on July 27 and almost succeeded in capturing the islands before enough Finnish forces could be brought in to reinforce the defenders. The fighting was heavy before the Soviet landing force was eliminated on July 28.

The 163rd German Infantry Division, on the Army of Karelia's left flank, ran into difficulties north of the rail line between Loymola and Suvilakhti. This area is interspersed with numerous lakes that channel any advances and therefore favored the Soviet defenders. The German soldiers, not used to fighting in a forest wilderness, had difficulties from the start. An attempt on July 16 to capture Suvilakhti by forces advancing from Loymola failed.

The VI Corps sent a force from the Tulm Lake area to help the Germans. This force cut the railroad between Suvilakhti and Petrozavodsk east of Suvilakhti on July 26. However, the German division was still unable to resume its advance at the end of July and Mannerheim sent Group Oinonen with its two brigades to its assistance—the cavalry brigade and the 2nd Light Infantry Brigade under Colonel V. Sundman. These forces had assembled in the Ilomantsi area in preparation for their missions in the Ladoga Karelia offensive. During the first part of that offensive the cavalry brigade and light infantry brigade slowly made its way in the direction of the upper Aitto River east of Suo Lake against stiff Soviet resistance.

The attack in the Lake Suo area by German and Finnish forces from two directions (south and west) needed systematic preparation and several weeks passed before it was executed. The Finnish forces from Group Oinonen were merged with the 163rd Division and named Battle Group Engelbrechtunder, under the command of Lieutenant General Engelbrecht. Even this combined force found the going difficult. It was not until August 4 that the 2nd Light Infantry Brigade and the German 307th Infantry Regiment began their attack on the village of Aglajarvi east of Tolvayarvi, which was captured the following day. The Finnish Cavalry Brigade cut the road between Alajarvi and Tolvayarvi and made contact with the 2nd Light Infantry Brigade on August 6. The Soviets retired behind the Aitto River to avoid encirclement.

The 11th Finnish Division was located to the south of Battle Group Engelbrecht and it moved northward and reached the Petrozavodsk railroad on August 19. This unit continued northward and captured

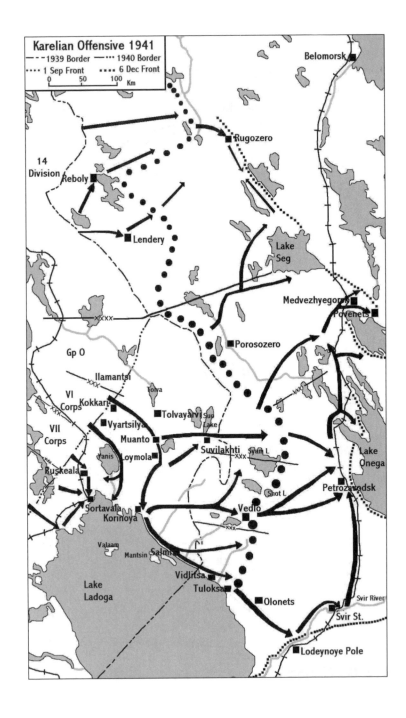

Karelian Offensive 1941
- - - 1939 Border · · · 1940 Border
· · · · 1 Sep Front · · · · 6 Dec Front

0   50   100
              Km

Suvilakhti on August 21. The 2nd Light Infantry Brigade, the Cavalry Brigade, and the German 307th Infantry Regiment crossed the Aitto River on 19 August. The Cavalry Brigade tried to encircle the enemy forces east of the river but the Soviets recognized the danger and withdrew before the 11th Division cut their last escape route at Tsalkki on August 23. While VII Corps established a front in the narrows between Lakes Syam and Shot, the 163rd Division was withdrawn from the front and stationed at the rear of the Army of Karelia as Mannerheim's strategic reserve.

On the right wing of the Army of Karelia, the VII Corps also began its offensive on July 10, but its advance was not as spectacular as that of VI Corps. Its offensive was launched from the area between Lakes Pyha and Yanis. VII Corps pressed the stubborn enemy slowly southward and by the end of the month had reached the town of Ruskeala. A division detached from VI Corps occupied defensive positions along the Yanis River between the lake by that name and Lake Ladoga. The Soviets were facing and fighting in two directions—against the forces at Ruskeala in the north and the division along the Yanis River in the east. Under constant pressure and in order to avoid encirclement, the Soviets withdrew slowly in the direction of Sortavala.

The Army of Karelia had gone into defensive positions on orders from Mannerheim on July 19 and after minor local advances ended up along a line with Group Oinonen in the north, VII Corps in the center, and VI Corps in the south. General Talvela, commander of VI Corps, was not happy with the halt as indicated by a conversation he had with General Engelbrecht, commander of the 163rd German Division, on September 2. Ziemke quotes the operational log of the 163rd Division pertaining to this conversation:

> Talvela said he regretted that his sector had been left completely inactive for the past several weeks even though he had repeatedly tried to get permission to resume the attack. He regretted the inactivity the more since the impact of his first advance had thrown the Russians into a panic which in his opinion would have made it "positively easy" at that time to push to the Svir and, possibly, create a bridgehead across it. The entire advance to the Tuloksa River line, he said had cost the VI Corps 3,500 casualties; the period of inaction since had cost as many.[17]

On the Army of Karelia's right flank, II Corps occupied the border between Vuoksi River and Pyha Lake. It did not begin its offensive until July 31. The corps' immediate objective was the railroad junction at the town of Khitola. Its capture would completely isolate the Soviet forces in the Sortavala area. The offensive made excellent progress and Mannerheim, who had earlier detached the 10th Division from the IV Corps as his reserve, committed that division on August 6 to exploit the success. In a rapid advance the 10th Division reached the shore of Lake Ladoga at the town of Lakhdenpokhya (Lahdenpohja). The main force of II Corps captured Khitola on August 11, the same day that a more southern column from the corps reached the shore of Lake Ladoga between Kegsgolm (Käkisalmi) and Khitola.

The Soviet forces, caught in a pocket between the forces of VII Corps in the east and north and those of II Corps in the west and north, were split into two groups by the advancing Finns. A group of about two divisions found itself isolated by II Corps forces in the vicinity of the town of Kyrikiyoki. The Soviets put up a fierce resistance despite their desperate situation. Many managed to withdraw to Kilpola (Kilpolansaari), a large island connected to the mainland by a causeway. The Soviets were evacuated by sea in mid-August but suffered heavy losses in men and ships. The fighting at Kilpola was concluded on August 24. The area of the Karelian Isthmus between Lake Ladoga and Vuoksi River was now in Finnish hands.

The Russian division fighting in the area west of Sortavala was pressed against the shore of Lake Ladoga between Lakhdenpokhya and Sortavala. After fierce resistance it was surrounded at Rautalahti. Resistance ceased on August 20. Some of the Soviet troops managed to escape by ship to Valaam Island.

Mannerheim made some further organizational changes before moving against Sortavala. He moved the VII Corps Headquarters to the area between the VI Corps and the 163rd German Infantry Division. The units that had been under VII Corps control—7th and 19th Divisions—were placed under the control of the newly created I Corps, as was the 2nd Division from II Corps. It was I Corps that took over the attack on Sortavala. The Soviet forces defending the city could not hold out against simultaneous Finnish attacks from three directions and Sortavala was captured on August 16. Most of the Soviet troops escaped by sea to Valaam Island and from there they were transported to the Leningrad area. Finnish and German aircraft could not prevent the Soviet evacuation.

The Karelian Isthmus Offensive

The front between the Gulf of Finland and Lake Pyha was relatively quiet during the month of July. The discussions at Finnish Headquarters about action on the Karelian Isthmus assumed increasing importance towards the end of the month. General Erfurth notes that Mannerheim was not prone to make hasty decisions and observes that the inactivity of the Finns west of Lake Pyha allowed the Soviets to shift forces not only against the approaching German Army Group North but also to move forces to the area east of Lake Ladoga to contest the advance of the Army of Karelia.[18]

Mannerheim ordered General Laatikainen's II Corps to begin its attack on July 31. The initial phases of this attack were related under the Army of Karelia offensive since its mission to clear the northwest shore of Lake Ladoga was more in support of the operations of that army than a separate offensive on the Karelian Isthmus. Nevertheless, by capturing Khitola and reaching the shore of Lake Ladoga between Kegsgolm and Khitola on August 11, the forces were in an ideal position to continue their advance southward on the Karelian Isthmus.

Ziemke writes that "the Finnish plan of operation underwent a fundamental change" during the first half of August.[19] He notes that General Erfurth, the German liaison officer at Mannerheim's headquarters, had reported as early as July 14 that he had detected opposition on the part of Mannerheim to operations east of Lake Ladoga but that this warning had been dismissed by OKH. That headquarters changed its mind in early August. On August 2, OKH requested that the Finns resume their offensive towards Lodeynoye Pole to coincide with the final push towards Leningrad by Army Group North. Mannerheim refused and in his reasoning shifted the blame back to the Germans by stating that the Army of Karelia could not resume its advance as long as the 163rd German Division had failed to take Suvilakhti. The OKH thereupon proposed on August 10 that the Finns conduct an offensive towards Leningrad on the Karelian Isthmus. Mannerheim accepted this proposal.

There is little reason to believe that the Soviet forces in the Lake Suo area were capable of preventing a resumption of the offensive east of Lake Ladoga. It may be that Mannerheim, as noted by the Germans, was a pessimist and that unexpected developments, such as the inability of the 163rd German Division to eliminate Soviet resistance in its area of operations, could have influenced him more than it should.

However, two other possibilities are more likely to have affected his plans. One was his wish—and that of the government and the vast majority of the Finnish people—to recover lost territories and to incorporate areas in East Karelia. The second reason is that the performance of German units in Finland had disappointed Mannerheim and may have colored his views of the progress of Field Marshal Wilhelm Ritter von Leeb's Army Group North. This Army Group had made rapid progress through the Baltic States mainly because Marshal Voroshilov did not intend to make a stand in those areas and had successfully withdrawn his forces virtually intact. There were no great encirclement battles as in other areas on the Soviet front. Voroshilov began to offer stiffer resistance when the Germans reached Russian territory. The countryside was unfavorable for the use of armor between Lakes Ilmen and Peipus and the advance of Army Group North slowed to a crawl. Leeb planned to begin his final push from the area west of Lake Ilmen and Hitler reinforced him with an armored corps from Army Group Center. It was this drive that the Germans wanted the Finns to support, first by an attack east of Lake Ladoga and finally by an attack towards Leningrad over the Karelian Isthmus.

After clearing out the northwest shore of Lake Ladoga, Mannerheim ordered II Corps to turn south against Pakkola, at the narrowest part of the Vuoksi River. That river was crossed north of Pakkola on August 18, and before long the Finns had a sizable bridgehead that favored both a continued advance southward and a move to the northwest to threaten Soviet forces facing IV Corps. At the same time another column on the left flank of II Corps drove southward from Kegsgolm, clearing the east shore of Lake Ladoga as they advanced.

The IV Corps began its offensive on August 22. The nine-day delay between the time II Corps was turned south and east and the launching of the attack by IV Corps made excellent military sense. Those nine days allowed II Corps to get on the flank and rear of the Soviet forces facing IV Corps. In fact, the Soviets became so unnerved by developments that they began destroying their own border fortifications on August 21. There was little resistance at the outset of the attack and the Finns reached Kilpenjoki on August 23. A northwest drive by II Corps from its bridgehead north of Pakkola got to within 12 kilometers of Viipuri.

The Soviets had three divisions in the Viipuri area. Their plans were to hold the city with one division while the other two launched a drive

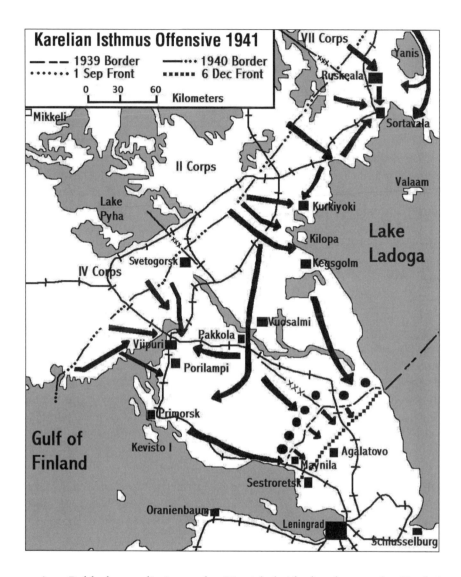

Karelian Isthmus Offensive 1941
— — — 1939 Border ——···· 1940 Border
········ 1 Sep Front ▪▪▪▪▪▪ 6 Dec Front

0   30   60
⊢——⊣——⊣ Kilometers

VII Corps
Yanis
Ruskeala
Sortavala
Mikkeli
II Corps
Valaam
Lake Pyha
Kurkiyoki
Kilopa
Svetogorsk
Kegsgolm
IV Corps
Lake Ladoga
Vuosalmi
Pakkola
Viipuri
Porilampi
Primorsk
Gulf of Finland
Kevisto
Agalatovo
Maynila
Sestroretsk
Oranienbaum
Leningrad
Schlusselburg

against Pakkola to eliminate the Finnish bridgehead over the Vuoksi River. It was planned that a division coming from Kilpola Island to the northeast would join them in the Pakkola attack.

The Finns acted so rapidly that the Soviets were unable to put their plan into operation. The city of Viipuri was quickly encircled. The 12th Finnish Division under Colonel Einar Vihma advanced southwards along the right bank of the Vuoksi River and made contact on August 22 with the 18th Division from II Corps, coming from the southeast from the bridgehead north of Pakkola. This put the whole right bank of the Vuoksi River in Finnish hands.

The Soviets launched a counterattack with two divisions—123rd and 115th—against the Finnish forces east of Viipuri on August 24. They managed to push the Finns back about five kilometers without breaching the front. The Soviet forces were pushed back to their starting positions the following day when the Finnish 26th Infantry Regiment from the 12th Division was committed. On the same day that division succeeded in cutting the railroad between Viipuri and Leningrad.

The 8th Finnish Division, commanded by Colonel Winell, had been engaged in clearing operations along the western shore of the Bay of Viipuri in preparation for crossing that bay. The crossing of the bay to Lihaniemi Peninsula began on August 24 with the 3rd Battalion of the 45th Infantry Regiment leading the way. The peninsula was secured by the end of the day. Forces from the 8th Division expanded their beachhead the following day and cut the railroad from Viipuri to Primorsk running along the shore of the Gulf of Finland. The 12th Finnish Division had also continued its advance. On August 27 it cut the main road from Viipuri to Leningrad, effectively sealing off Viipuri from the outside world.

The Supreme High Command of the Soviet Armed Forces (STAVKA) recognized the hopeless situation in the northwest corner of the Karelian Isthmus and permitted the 23rd Army to withdraw from Viipuri to a new defensive line near where the Mannerheim Line had been located in the Winter War. They gave up trying to defend Viipuri, which was occupied by Finnish forces on August 29. However, the withdrawing Soviet forces soon found their route of retreat to the south blocked by the 8th Finnish Division. They managed to force several convoys of trucks through before the Finns permanently closed that escape route. The retreating Soviet troops were encircled about 10 kilometers south of Sveklovichnoye (Porlampi). They defended themselves desperately and a sizable part of the force—about 12,000 men—managed to break through the western encirclement force and escape to Koivisto Island after abandoning most of their vehicles and equipment. They remained on that island until they were evacuated in November. The remaining Soviet forces in the encirclement were cleared out by the Finns on September 1. At least 9,000 surrendered to the Finns and over 7,000 were killed in the fighting. A large amount of equipment was captured, including 306 artillery pieces, 55 tanks, 673 trucks, and approximately 4,500 horses.

The rapidity of the Finnish advance—particularly that of the 12th Division—kept the 23rd Soviet Army from carrying out its plan to make a stand in the vicinity of the old Mannerheim Line. They continued their fighting withdrawal towards the lower part of the Karelian Isthmus. Finnish forces continued their advance across the Karelian Isthmus in the direction of the town of Koivisto (Primorsk) without encountering serious opposition. Units of IV Corps reached the old border on August 31 and Koivisto on September 2.

The Finnish advance along the western shore of Lake Ladoga towards the old border had also continued. Mannerheim shifted I Corps headquarters, under Major General Einar Mäkinen, from Sortavala to the eastern part of the Karelian Isthmus on August 24. It was assigned two divisions from II Corps—the 10th and 15th—and given the mission of clearing the Ladoga side of the isthmus south of the Vuoksi River. It reached the border on August 31, as did the 2nd Finnish Division. The whole stretch of the old border was secured by September 2.

In a one-month offensive the Finns had driven the 23rd Soviet Army out of Finland and recaptured their lost territory on the Isthmus of Karelia. Only a few islands off Koivisto and in Lake Ladoga were still in Soviet hands. The islands of Valaam and Konevitsa on Lake Ladoga were captured at the end of September 1941.

Mannerheim and the Finnish government now had to consider whether their offensive should stop at the border or, as the Germans pressed for, continue southward. This question had both political and military ramifications. There was opposition within the Finnish government, particularly from the Social Democrats, to continuing the offensive past the border on the Karelian Isthmus. These opponents also wanted to rein in Mannerheim's offensive plans for East Karelia. This split was reflected in the cabinet. Blücher, the German ambassador to Finland, claims that this opposition was just a passing thing and that the Finnish cabinet almost immediately returned to favoring an aggressive pursuit of the war.[20]

Mannerheim had already decided, on September 1, that the offensive should continue across the frontier far enough that his troops would be able to occupy favorable defensive positions. The new, more defensible line ran from the mouth of Sestra (Rajajoki) River northeast to Lake Ladoga—basically a diagonal line a short distance north of the towns of Sestroretsk and Agalatovo. There was little fighting involved in moving to the new positions except a sharp engagement in the sector of I Corps where the 10th Division managed to encircle and destroy the 941st Soviet Infantry Regiment. The whole length of the new defensive line had been reached by September 9.

East Karelian Offensive

Up to this point, the Finns had basically recaptured territories taken from them during the Winter War. While their forces had crossed the pre-1940 borders in some places, particularly in Ladoga Karelia and the area to the west of Seg Lake (Seesjärvi), those incursions into pre-1940 Soviet territories could be justified on military grounds as providing flank protection or as an attempt to obtain positions better suited for defense. This all changed with the commencement of what is commonly referred to as the East Karelian offensive, in September 1941.

Offensive operations into East Karelia had actually begun before the Ladoga Karelia offensive. The unit undertaking this operation was the 14th Finnish Division, under the command of Colonel Erkki Raappana. It began its operations from the Lieksa area, approximately 200 kilometers north of the northernmost point of Lake Ladoga. The 14th was not part of the Army of Karelia, but a separate division answering directly to Mannerheim.

The 14th Division formed a link between the Army of Karelia operating against the Svir River and the III Finnish Corps, which was part of the Army of Norway. The border between the Finnish and German sectors ran southwest from Lake Oulujärvi in Oulu Province to the border. This link was rather tenuous since large tracts of virgin, roadless forests separated it from both the Army of Karelia and the right flank of the Army of Norway. While a north–south railroad running from Oulu on the Gulf of Bothnia to Sortavala and on to Helsinki came within 20 kilometers of the border in the 14th Division's area, there was no east–west railroad and the east–west roads in the area were few and can hardly be described as roads. The 14th Division was therefore in a difficult logistic position and had to rely on its own resources. Mannerheim directed Colonel Raappana to advance eastward to the town of Rugozero (Rukajärvi) on the road to Kotshkoma on the Murmansk Railroad. Colonel Raappana initiated operations several days before the Army of Karelia in the south opened its offensive against Ladoga Karelia. Patrols crossed the border on July 1 and the main advance began two days later. The Soviet forces that initially opposed the advance of the 14th Division consisted of the 337th Infantry Regiment of the 54th Soviet Infantry Division and the 73rd Border Guard Detachment.

The 14th Division captured Reboly (Repola) on July 6 and the advance continued. The Finns crossed Lake Leksozero (Lieksajärvi) northeast of Reboly on July 11. The village of Lendery was captured by another column. The advance in the wilderness was slow because the 14th Division lacked light infantry. Nevertheless, it managed to score a brilliant tactical victory by encircling major Soviet forces in the isthmus areas of this lake country. The encirclement at Omelia was completed on July 23 and Soviet attempts to break out of the pocket were only partially successful. Over 100 drowned in an attempt to cross one of the lakes and 300 were captured. The troops in the encirclement surrendered on July 24.

The 14th Division encountered stiff resistance at the Ontrosenvaara Hills west and south of Rugozero. The fighting for these hills took place between July 30 and August 12. The Soviets had brought in reinforcements in the form of the 137th Regiment from the 54th Division and the 71st Border Guard Detachment. These forces were unable to halt the Finnish advance and a new Soviet division—the 27th—was formed. The Soviets had well-prepared positions at the Rukavaara Hill and were able to halt the Finnish advance for three weeks.

The Finns initiated an encirclement of the Rukavaara Hill, forcing the Soviets to abandon their positions on September 8. Rugozero was captured on September 11. The 14th Division had accomplished the mission assigned it by Mannerheim with comparatively small losses. The division crossed the Onkajoki River just east of Rugozero and took up defensive positions.

At the beginning of September 1941 the Army of Karelia was deployed with Group Oinonen on the left from the 1939 border to Syam (Syamozero) Lake. The Group consisted of one cavalry brigade and the

2nd Light Infantry Brigade. The VII Corps was located just east of Lakes Syam and Vedlo. It consisted of two divisions—the 1st and 4th. The VI Corps, consisting of three divisions (5th, 17th, and 7th) and the 1st Light Infantry Brigade, was located on the right between Vedlo Lake and the point where the Tuloksa River empties into Lake Ladoga. The 163rd Division was located behind the VI Corps as Mannerheim's reserve.

The offensive began on the night of September 3–4, with the heaviest artillery preparation of the war. This allowed the 5th Division of VI Corps to cross the Tuloksa River seven kilometers from the coast. Finnish units managed to cut the coastal road by noon on September 4 but were hit by a Soviet counterattack, which created a dangerous situation until the corps reserve was committed. After blunting the Soviet counterattack the Finns drove to the shore of Lake Ladoga behind the Soviet defenders along the south bank of Tuloksa River. The trapped Soviet forces—3rd Marine Brigade and two infantry regiments—were practically destroyed.

The successful attack by the 5th Division opened the road to Olonets for Colonel Lagus' Task Force—1st Light Infantry Brigade and one infantry regiment. The task force passed through the 5th Division and captured Olonets after a brief fight on September 7. A Finnish detachment from Task Force Lagus continued the eastward advance and captured the northern end of the railroad bridge at Svir Station on September 8. This severed the rail connection between Murmansk and Volkhov and took place on the same day as Army Group North captured Schlusselburg in the southwest corner of Lake Ladoga.

The 17th Finnish Division in the corps center was less successful in its attack. The 3rd Soviet Division was able to stop the Finnish attack. The 7th Finnish Division, on the left flank of the VI Corps, had more success. The 13th Infantry Regiment reached and cut the road from Olonets to Petrozavodsk. The 34th Infantry Regiment moved south along this road at the same time as the 44th Infantry Regiment, which had been attached to Task Force Lagus, moved north. Both advances were aimed at the town of Nurmoyla, which was captured on September 7.

The capture of Nurmoyla meant that all road connections to the 3rd Soviet Division were severed. The Soviet division tried to recapture Nurmoyla but failed. It was trapped but most of the personnel managed to slip out of the pocket by abandoning their vehicles and equipment. After reaching the Svir River, the 7th Finnish Division began clearing both banks. The Soviets had reinforced the area with the 314th Division and the clearing operation was slow. The Finns succeeded in establishing a bridgehead on the southern banks of the Svir by September 22. The bridgehead was approximately 40 kilometers wide and 5–10 kilometers deep.

The Finns were organizing a multidirectional attack against Petrozavodsk, the capital of Soviet Karelia. The 1st Light Infantry Brigade was approaching the city from the south along the railroad. The VII Corps on the left wing of the Army of Karelia, reinforced by the 4th Division from the Karelian Isthmus, was moving against Petrozavodsk from the west. The corps captured the important road junction at Krasnaya Pryazka, 40 kilometers west of Petrozavodsk on September 8. Major General Hägglund sent the 1st Division on a very strenuous march eastwards against Petrozavodsk through the great trackless forest south of the road, a task that it completed with considerable speed. Group Oinonen and II Corps, under Major General Laatikainen, which had been transferred to East Karelia from the Karelian Isthmus, approached Petrozavodsk from the northwest.

The concentric Finnish attack on Petrozavodsk began on September 18. The Soviets soon recognized the gravity of the situation and began to evacuate forces from the city. By the time the 11th Finnish Division cut the main road and railroad leading north from the city on September 30, most of the Soviet troops had been evacuated by sea across Lake Onega. The city fell to Finnish troops on October 1, 1941.

The 3rd Soviet Division, which had offered stubborn resistance to the northward drive along the road and railroad, now found itself completely isolated. Equipment and vehicles had been abandoned and the remaining troops began a southward trek through the forest with the Finnish 30th Infantry Regiment in pursuit. Only a few hundred men from the division managed to escape two weeks later across the Svir River.

The VI Corps had meanwhile crossed Svir River at its Lake Onega end. The Finnish bridgehead across the Svir was expanded to 100 kilometers in width and 20 kilometers in depth. This expansion was necessitated by the need for better defensive positions before the onset of winter.

Capture of Medvezhyegorsk

Mannerheim decided the Army of Karelia should continue the north-ward offensive towards the town of Medvezhyegorsk (Karhumäki) despite signs of an early and hard winter. The first objectives were the string of lake isthmuses along the Suna River. The Finnish divisions advancing from Petrozavodsk and Porosozero (Porajärvi) were able to maneuver the Soviets into the rough lake and river country between Medvezhyegorsk and Lake Seg. II Finnish Corps reached and cleared the Suna River line on October 19, and units from this corps also reached the area west of Lake Seg. Finnish forces from the south captured Kondopoga (Kontupohja) on November 3 and met the forces from the north at Lizhma Lake on November 5. Soviet forces tried desperately to prevent this juncture. When they failed to stem the multipronged Finnish advance, they withdrew to Medvezhyegorsk.

Finnish troops were beginning to show the strain of months of continuous operations. The early onset of winter did not help. It appeared that their offensive strength had reached its limit. The planned transfer of one division and several heavy artillery batteries to East Karelia from the Karelian Isthmus for the attack against Medvezhyegorsk could not be carried out because of rail transportation problems.[21] The terrain around Medvezhyegorsk had become almost impassable due to deep snow. An attack by the 4th Division from the north was stopped only four kilometers from the town center. The attack by the 1st Division was also stopped. It appeared that the Finnish offensive had come to an end in front of Medvezhyegorsk.

At the urgings of their corps commander, General Laatikainen, the Finns began another supreme effort on November 29, successfully breaching the outer Soviet defenses on December 2. The Finns launched their final attack on the morning of December 5 with the 4th Division from the north and the 1st Light Infantry Brigade, followed by the 2nd Light Infantry Brigade, from the west. Advancing in bitter cold, and with snow up to their knees, the Finns breached the final defensive line and entered Medvezhyegorsk. The town of Povents (Poventsa) on the Stalin Canal was captured by Colonel Lagus' 1st Light Infantry Brigade on December 6, 1941. A large Soviet force was surrounded south of Medvezhyegorsk and destroyed on December 8.

The Finns established a defensive line on the Maaselkä, the watershed between the Gulf of Finland and the White Sea. This watershed ran across the isthmus between Lake Seg and the northern point of Lake Onega. The Finnish defensive positions overlooked this isthmus. With the capture of Medvezhyegorsk, active operations ended on the Finnish front.

The Finnish victories in the south were impressive. But the cost in lives was high. Total Finnish casualties by the end of the year had reached 75,000, including 25,500 who had paid the ultimate price. Vehviläinen points out that the number who fell was almost equivalent to a whole year group of conscripts.[22]

Operations in the Gulf of Finland

There are some aspects of the war in southern Finland that cannot be covered in the same detail as the land operations because of space considerations. They were nevertheless important and deserve to be mentioned. Both naval operations in the Gulf of Finland and air operations fall into this category.

The small Finnish Navy was divided into two branches, coastal artillery, and naval ships. The latter were few in number—two coastal defense ships, five submarines, and a number of smaller ships. German naval units in the Baltic had the primary mission of protecting the sea route for the iron ore that came from Sweden. Support of operations in Finland was accorded a lower priority.

Recognizing their own inferiority to the superior Soviet Navy, the Finns and Germans had agreed before the war to rely primarily on mine warfare to neutralize the enemy surface fleet. This fleet was substantial—2 battleships, 2 light cruisers, 19 destroyers, and 68 submarines. In addition there were over 700 naval aircraft. Furthermore, the Soviet naval base at Hanko was to be besieged from both land and sea. Belts of mines were laid in the Baltic and Gulf of Finland beginning shortly before the commencement of hostilities. The German/Finnish tactics proved very successful and the Soviets were unable to make use of their naval superiority. The fleet remained bottled up in the Bay of Kronstadt. The Finnish Navy thereby accomplished its primary mission of neutralizing the much superior Soviet fleet.

As Army Group North advanced through the Baltic states, the Soviets were forced to make a number of sea evacuations along the coast. The German and Finnish navies tried to interfere with these evacuations by laying mines in the approaches to and from the seaports. A total of 3,000 mines were laid outside Tallinn to interfere with the large-scale evacuation from that city. A fleet of 160 ships evacuated 28,000 personnel and 66,000 tons of matériel. This evacuation began on August 27, 1941, despite heavy and almost constant attacks by German aircraft and artillery. The Soviet ships ran into the heavily mined area near Cape Jumida on August 28 while under attack by Finnish and German torpedo boats. Sixty-five of the 160 ships were lost and a large number damaged. Personnel losses were heavy with 16,000 perishing.

Both the German and Finnish navies suffered serious losses on September 14. Three German minesweepers exploded in Helsinki harbor due to unknown causes. On the same day, the Finnish coastal defense ship *Ilmarinen* struck a mine and sank southwest of Hanko with the loss of 271 sailors.

The Soviets evacuated the islands off Koivisto before the Gulf of Finland froze. These islands would have been very difficult to defend after the ice became thick enough to support troops. The Finns occupied the islands in early November.

Things remained relatively quiet at the leased Soviet naval base at Hanko, which had begun to lose its importance for the Soviets in view of the northward progress of Army Group North. The Soviets did not have the strength to undertake any offensive operations and the Finns confined themselves to keeping the place blockaded from both land and sea. The Soviets decided to evacuate Hanko when the Gulf of Finland began to freeze. They may have assumed that the Finns had delayed any offensive operations against Hanko pending the freeze, which would prevent Soviets from sending reinforcements.

A strong Soviet naval force from Kronstadt Bay set out for Hanko on November 3, 1941. They managed to avoid the minefields and brought off the garrison without interference from the Finns who were taken by surprise. Several Soviet ships heading back to Kronstadt Bay struck mines and sank with heavy losses. The Finns occupied Hanko on December 4.

German naval assault units attacked and occupied the Osmussar Islands off the Estonian coast. They also planned to occupy Suursaari Island (Gogland), important for controlling shipping traffic because of its location more or less in the center of the Gulf of Finland east of Helsinki. The operation was postponed because the necessary forces for a continued occupation were lacking.

The plan to occupy the islands in the Gulf of Finland was revived in early March 1942, this time at the urging of Army Group North. The Finns were also eager to occupy Suursaari Island before the ice disappeared from the Gulf. Suursaari was important for the air defense of Finland and in blockading Leningrad. The participation of German troops in the operation became doubtful by the middle of March since the situation in Army Group North's area did not permit a withdrawal of forces.

Marshal Mannerheim decided on March 17, 1942 to act alone against Suursaari. Forces from the 18th Finnish Division, commanded by Major General Aaro Olavi Pajari, were assembled near Kotka. German participation was limited to air support.

The Finnish attack on Suursaari began at night on March 26 and the island was secured on March 27. Tytaersaari (Bolshoi Tyuters), a smaller island about 20 kilometers south of Suursaari, was also captured on April 1. A German garrison relieved the Finns on Tytaersaari on April 4 and the Soviets chose that time to launch an attack on the island, which was repulsed. This island remained occupied by the Germans, while Suursaari was occupied by the Finns. These difficult operations were carried out quickly and with relatively light losses. Any delay would have made the operations impossible since the ice in the Gulf of Finland lost adequate carrying capacity within a few days.

Air Operations

The Finnish Air Force was seriously outnumbered by the Soviets but was nevertheless very successful in its operations. Finnish fighter planes contested Soviet air superiority and their pilots showed great ability and courage in numerous air fights. Finnish aircraft gave excellent support to ground operations.

The Finnish anitaircraft artillery forces were stronger and better equipped than they had been in the Winter War. However, their limited size and the vastness of the territory to be defended prevented them from giving adequate protection to some of the cities. For example, an air attack on Helsinki on November 3, 1941, caused severe damage.

The Finnish Air Force had great success over the Gulf of Finland in early 1942. Bitter air battles were fought after the Finnish attacks on Suursaari and Tytaersaari Islands. Finnish fighter planes downed twenty-seven Soviet planes on March 28, 1942. During the entire war,

Finnish aircraft and pilots proved themselves superior to their Soviet opponents.

The German Luftwaffe had the dual missions of supporting the fight for Leningrad, and at the same time, conducting air warfare in the arctic. German bombers from the 5th Air Fleet made numerous attacks on Soviet installations along the Murmansk Railroad, trains, the port of Murmansk, and Soviet installations and bases on the Rybachiy Peninsula. The 1st Air Fleet, supporting Army Group North, also flew numerous missions in support of Finnish operations in the Lake Ladoga area and to interdict the Soviet supply route after Lake Ladoga froze in December. It was bombed regularly by German planes.

The Germans, because of their own stretched resources, made frequent requests for Finnish Air Force support in the spring of 1942. The 1st Air Fleet requested Finnish assistance in providing air cover over the Gulf of Finland on April 5. On the same day the 5th Air Fleet (in Norway, and responsible for supporting operations of German forces in Finland) requested that the Finnish Air Force support Army of Lapland operations. The Finns were not able to meet these requests but it revealed to them the fact that the Luftwaffe was overextended as a result of the Soviet winter offensive.

The Finns turned down a request by the Germans to station two bomber groups at the Malmi Airport near Helsinki. The reason for the German request was that stationing the aircraft there would allow them to approach Leningrad from the north. Mannerheim turned down this request for political reasons and to avoid exposing the Finnish capital to Soviet air attacks. The Finns offered the Germans the use of Utti Airport, just east of the town of Kuovola and around 80 kilometers northeast of Helsinki. The 1st Air Fleet used Utti until the end of October 1942.

The 5th Air Fleet had begun an extensive program to enlarge and strengthen its ground support elements in Finland. This program put a strain on the Finnish economy because of the large requests for building material. The Finns were engaged in large programs to fortify the areas they had captured and the German requests competed with these projects.

Lieutenant General Jarl Fritjof Lundquist, the commander in chief of the Finnish Air Force, a very outspoken individual with a growing skepticism about the outcome of the war, gave the German liaison officer at his headquarters an earful about the constant German changes in plans and their extravagant demands on the Finnish economy:

> The Finns are beginning to be fed up with being led by the nose by the Germans. Considering the large ground organization needed by the Luftwaffe, we Finns cannot adapt ourselves every four weeks to another plan. . . . For the time being we shall do nothing but wait and see how the situation develops.[23]

Lundquist let it be known that the Finns were becoming leery about German ability to encircle Leningrad and thus provide the Finns some security.

General Hans-Jürgen Stumpff, commander of the 5th Air Fleet in Norway, came to the Finnish headquarters in Mikkeli on January 17, 1942, primarily to discuss operations against Belomorsk with the Finnish General Staff and General Lundquist. Both General Stumpff and General Erfurth, who also attended the meetings, came away with the distinct and uneasy impression that the Finnish officers were unusually reserved and noncommittal on all issues.[24]

NOTES

1. This would be the equivalent of the United States today mobilizing 45,000,000 individuals for its armed forces.
2. Mannerheim, *Memoirs*, p.416.
3. Mannerheim, *Memoirs*, p.417.
4. This is also the impression given by Vehviläinen, *op. cit.*, p.93, in 2002. He does not mention that German sources tell a different story.
5. Erfurth, *The Last Finnish War*, p.20.
6. *Ibid*, pp.20–21.
7. Hölter, *op. cit.*, p.16.
8. Westerlund, *op. cit.*, pp.72–73. There is disagreement in the sources as to the location of the 10th Finnish Division. Westerlund has it located as a reserve behind corps IV and II. Colonel K. J. Mikola, *Finland's Wars During World War II (1939–1945)*, p.XXIII, locates it behind II Corps. Ziemke, *The German Northern Theater of Operations*, p.189, and Erfurth, *The Last Finnish War*, p.23, has it as part of IV Corps. Ari Raunio, *op. cit.*, p.117, appears to give the 10th Division a separate sector between IV Corps and II Corps, under V Corps. The explanation may be that these sources depict the location of the division at different times leading up to the offensives.

9. The Jäger brigades were highly mobile light infantry units ideally suited for the heavily forested areas in Finland. Their functions were those that are normally performed by armored cavalry regiments in more open country. The Germans were very impressed by these units and General Falkenhorst repeatedly tried to have one of the brigades assigned to the Army of Norway.

10. Original plans had called for the 163rd Infantry Division to be used in the attack against the leased Russian naval base at Hanko. This would have allowed the 17th Finnish Division, which had sealed off Hanko, to be used by Mannerheim for other purposes.

11. The size of a Soviet Army can be more accurately compared to a corps in the German Army.

12. *Jatkosodan historia* (Porvoo: WSOY, 1988–1994), volume I, p.193.

13. Vehviläinen, *op. cit.*, p.93.

14. The area is variously referred to as Far Karelia, Aunus (Olonets) Karelia, or Ladoga Karelia. Aunus is the main town in the southern part of the isthmus between Lake Ladoga and Lake Onega.

15. It appears that General Talvela was not satisfied with the aggressiveness of Colonel Eino Koskimies' 5th Division at Korpiselkya and relieved him of his command.

16. Erfurth, *The Last Finnish War*, p.33.

17. Ziemke, *The German Northern Theater of Operations*, p.193, note 9.

18. Erfurth, The *Last Finnish War*, p.36.

19. Ziemke, *The German Northern Theater of Operations*, p.192.

20. Blücher, *op. cit.*, pp.246–248.

21. Erfurth, *The Last Finnish War*, p.43.

22. Vehviläinen, *op. cit.*, p.96.

23. Erfurth, *The Last Finnish War*, pp.47–48.

24. *Ibid*, p.68.

SIX

COALITION PROBLEMS AND SOVIET COUNTEROFFENSIVES

The First Six Months of War

Despite impressive Finnish military successes that achieved all their stated war aims, neither the Finns nor the Germans were satisfied with the events of 1941, and the Finns faced 1942 with considerable doubts and apprehensions. The Germans in Finland had accomplished none of their objectives. They had failed to interdict the Murmansk Railroad or capture Murmansk. They had failed to take Leningrad and the planned linkup with German forces on the Svir had not materialized. The Germans had not succeeded in convincing their cobelligerent to participate in the attack on Leningrad or even to take aggressive action to tie down Soviet forces north of Tikhvin and Leningrad. Finally, Finnish participation in operations to cut the Murmansk Railroad was coming into question.

While the Finns were awed and impressed by the crushing German victories in the first months of the war they must have been equally impressed by continued stiff Soviet resistance. Between July and November, the German armies in the east conducted one of the greatest sustained offensives in military history. The Soviets suffered some three million casualties, half of these being prisoners. But the German losses had also been heavy—about 800,000 men. Despite the enormous Soviet losses, their armies had not been destroyed and they successfully traded space for time and awaited the approaching winter, which proved to be especially severe.

The misfortunes of the German armies on the eastern front in December 1941 could not be shielded from the Finns and they began to fear that they could be on the losing side in this brutal war. They had assumed that the war would be short and that the Soviet Union would collapse under the German onslaught. It was the short-war illusion that had caused the Finns to mobilize the maximum force for its prosecution, a decision that was now haunting the Finnish economy. The accord and smooth relations that had existed between Finns and Germans at the outset of the war were also beginning to fade. Finally, the relations with the Western democracies worsened.

This worsening of relations began with a German demand in July 1941 that Finland break diplomatic relations with Great Britain. The Germans based their demand on the claim that the large British contingent at their embassy in Helsinki served as an intelligence-gathering apparatus for the Soviets. The British made no move to close its embassy and the repeated German urgings finally led Finland to announce on July 28 that it intended to close its embassy in London. The matter was decided on July 31 when British aircraft bombed Pechenga. Both countries broke diplomatic relations.

The United States had taken a wait-and-see attitude, watching whether Finland, despite its official statements, would carry the war beyond its 1939 borders. In mid-August the Soviet Union authorized the US to inform Finland of its willingness to make peace with territorial concessions. This offer was communicated by Under Secretary of State Sumner Wells to the Finnish ambassador in Washington on August 18, but no reply was received from Finland.[1]

The rebuff infuriated Stalin and he demanded that Great Britain use its influence with Finland to have the operations stopped or, failing that, to declare war on Finland. The British warned Finland through Mr. Michelet, the Norwegian Ambassador to Finland, against invading Soviet territory. US Secretary of State Cordell Hull gave a similar warning to the Finnish ambassador to Washington, Hjalmar J. Procopé, on October 3.

As mentioned in Chapter 4, the US presented a note to Finland on October 25, 1941, when it became worried about the Murmansk supply route for Lend-Lease supplies. Finland delayed its answer until November 11 and in the meantime the US made public both the Soviet offer from August and its own note to Finland. The Finnish answer on November 11 rejected the US note, stating that they were waging their own separate war, and refused to suspend what they called fully justified military operations.

The US publication of the Soviet offer of peace caused some friction in German–Finnish relations. The Finns had never given their "brothers-in-arms" a complete version of the offer. The Anti-Comintern Pact was due to be renewed at the end of November 1941 and Germany now pressured Finland to become a signatory. Germany's action was probably aimed at complicating Finnish relations with the Western democracies.

The Finns were in no position to refuse the German demand. They had recently asked Germany for help with their railroad transportation problems and had also found it necessary to request 175,000 tons of grain to help them through the winter.

Unable to avoid signing the Anti-Comintern Pact, Finland wanted to do so with as little fanfare as possible. However, this was not in Germany's interest. The Germans insisted that Foreign Minister Witting participate in the well-publicized ceremony in Berlin on November 25, 1941 when Germany, Japan, and Italy also signed the pact. In a long post-signing audience with Hitler the Finns were promised their territorial aspirations, the Kola Peninsula, and more grain (260,000 tons) than they had actually requested.[2]

Foreign Minister Witting found a British ultimatum waiting for him when he returned to Helsinki on November 28. The note demanded that Finland cease active operations by December 5 and withdraw from hostilities. There was no demand for the withdrawal of troops and a private letter from Winston Churchill to Mannerheim had the added suggestion that "Surely your troops have advanced far enough for security during the war and could now halt and give leave. It is not necessary to make any public declaration, but simply leave off fighting and cease military operations, for which the severe winter affords every reason, and make a de facto exit from the war."[3]

The British, having received no reply from Finland, declared war on Finland on December 6, which happened to be Finland's Independence Day. It was also the day after Finnish forces captured Medvezhyegorsk and the same day that the Finnish parliament formally annexed the recaptured territories.

The many reports flowing into Mannerheim's headquarters in December 1941 made it obvious that a crisis situation had developed for the Germans in the east. The German Army communiqué on December 17 allowed the Finns to infer that the Germans were retreating involuntarily. One passage read "Improvements and shortening of various sectors of the eastern front have at present become necessary owing to the transition from offensive operations to winter trench warfare." Hitler's order of the day on December 31, 1941 was unusually frank in stating: "The year 1941 now lies behind us. It was a year of most difficult decisions and extremely bloody fighting."[4]

Hitler undertook a house cleaning as a result of the setbacks in the late fall of 1941. Field Marshal Gerd von Rundstedt, commander of Army Group South, was relieved on December 1 for withdrawing his forces against Hitler's orders. Army Group Center's senior officers were hit hard for their failure to capture Moscow. The Army Group commander, Field Marshal Fedor von Bock, was relieved on December 18. Over the next three weeks, about 40 high-ranking officers from Army Group Center were relieved including three of the six army commanders and four of the 22 corps commanders. Field Marshal von Brauchitsch, commander in chief of the German Army, bit the dust on December 19. His job was taken over by Hitler himself. Field Marshal Leeb asked to be relieved in January 1942.

This wholesale relief of some of the best officers in the German Army underscored for the Finns the magnitude of the German failure on the eastern front. Hitler's decision to assume personal command of the German Army was anything but reassuring for the Finnish military leaders who had known many of those who were sacked.

Finnish–German Friction

Friction between Finns and Germans had begun in 1941 with General Siilasvuo, commander of III Finnish Corps attached to the Army of Norway, declining to continue offensive operations in his sector. Further friction that year developed between Mannerheim and Falkenhorst—see Chapter 7. The triple errors by the Germans before the war—failure to harmonize war aims with the Finns, failure to insist on a joint campaign plan, and failure to set up an effective command structure—were clearly demonstrated in 1942. Even General Erfurth wrote in 1952 that the failure to solve these issues before the onset of hostilities was "incomprehensible."[5]

Army Group North's drive towards Leningrad resumed on August 10, 1941, after a short pause, and it was rapidly approaching Leningrad. The question about what to do with Leningrad was now raised in OKW and this impacted on what they wanted the Finns to do. It had

Adolf Hitler and Field Marshal Mannerheim when Hitler visited Finland on June 4, 1942 to honor Mannerheim on his 75th birthday. *Source: Wikimedia*

Finnish troops crossing the pre-1940 border into Soviet territory during Operation *Barbarossa* in 1941. *Source: Wikimedia, Sa-kuva*

Finnish soldiers marching towards the border near Raate in Suomussalmi, July 1941. *Source: The Finnish Defence Forces*

German tanks on their way to the frontline, Vasonvaara, July 1, 1941. *Source: The Finnish Defence Forces*

Finnish soldiers crossing the river in the area of Pajarinjärvi,
August 8, 1941. *Source: The Finnish Defence Forces*

A Soviet soldier surrenders as Finnish soldiers capture a Soviet pillbox,
Termola, September 10, 1941. *Source: The Finnish Defence Forces*

Marshal Mannerheim visiting the city of Aunus, September 10, 1941.
Behind him are Lieutenant General Erik Heinrichs, commander of
the Army of Karelia, and on the right, Major General Paavo Talvela,
commander of the Finnish VI Corps in Karelia.
Source: The Finnish Defence Forces

Heavy artillery on a narrow and slippery road, Juustjärvi,
October 21, 1941. *Source: The Finnish Defence Forces*

Finnish troops crossing the Murmansk railway, as part of battles in the Käppäselkä area, October 27, 1941. *Source: The Finnish Defence Forces*

General der Gebirgstruppe Eduard Dietl, commander of the Army of Lapland, congratulating Major General Hjalmar Siilasvuo (commander of the Finnish III Corps) on Siilasvuo's 50th birthday on March 18, 1942. *Source: The Finnish Defence Forces*

General Erik Heinrichs, chief of the Finnish General Staff, and Heinrich Himmler in Mikkeli, July 1942. *Source: The Finnish Defence Forces*

Finnish soldiers in their machine gun pillbox, in snowbound Sunku, March 28, 1942. *Source: The Finnish Defence Forces*

Snow tunnel on Route 50 in north Norway. Snow tunnels are used for movement in areas where snow is likely to form deep drifts, or where there is a danger of snow avalanches. The climate in this theater was often as dangerous as the enemy. *Source: M. Kräutler, Es war ein Edelweiss. Schicksal und Weg der zweiten Gebirgsdivision*

German *gebirgsjäger* in the sap, taking cover from Russian fire in the area of Loukhi, May 15, 1942. *Source: The Finnish Defence Forces*

This German staff car is mired in the deep mud of a road near Kiestinki, northern Finland, in April 1942. The spring thaw restricted effective movement of troops on or off road. *Source: The Finnish Defence Forces*

German *gebirgsjäger* advancing in the forest towards Loukhi,
May 15, 1942. *Source: The Finnish Defence Forces*

Generaloberst Eduard Dietl and Colonel Oiva Willamo, head of the
Finnish liaison staff at the 20th Mountain Army Headquarters.
Source: Wikimedia, Mikko Uola/SA-kuva

The trench leading to a famous battlefield Sormenkärki, Ollila. May 1944. *Source: The Finnish Defence Forces*

Soldier moving carefully in a trench. The sign says: "Beware of the sharpshooters," Rajajoki. April 18, 1943. *Source: The Finnish Defence Forces*

Finnish heavy mortar on the east side of Ihantala, July 7, 1944. *Source: The Finnish Defence Forces*

Finnish troops disembarking at Tornio in October 1944.
Source: Wikimedia, Kallioniemi, Lapin sota 1944–1945

Finnish soldiers from Infantry Regiment 12 passing a destroyed Soviet T-34 tank on the Imatra road in Tali-Ihantala. The two soldiers carry Panzerfausts on their shoulders and the one to the right carries a Finnish-made Suomi M31 machine gun as a personal weapon. *Source: Wikimedia*

Heavy mortar firing on German positions near the Tornio–Kemi road. October 3, 1944. *Source: The Finnish Defence Forces*

Finnish troops on a badly damaged bridge over the river Raumo during
the German/Finnish fighting near Tornio in October 1944.
Source: The Finnish Defence Forces

The Germans had almost completely destroyed Rovaniemi,
October 19, 1944. *Source: The Finnish Defence Forces*

German message in burned Muonio, photographed October 31, 1944.
The sign says: "Als dank für nicht bewiesene Waffenbrüderschaft"
(Thank you for not being real brothers in arms).
Source: The Finnish Defence Forces

Finnish soldiers planting their flag on the border stone between Finland, Sweden and Norway on April 27, 1945. By then the Germans had left Lapland. *Source: The Finnish Defence Forces*

Finnish political leaders tried at the War Guilt Trials in 1945. Left to right: Henrik Ramsay, Tyko Reinnika, Antti Kukkonen, Edwin Linkomies, J. W. Rangell, Risto Ryti, Väinö Tanner, and T. M. Kivimäki. *Source: Wikimedia, Osvald Hedenström*

been decided that the population in the north of the Soviet Union—including Leningrad with several million inhabitants—were consumers of raw materials and food products that were needed by the Germans and the "productive" people in the industrial and agricultural part of the Soviet Union.

In line with his warped ideology Hitler decided that Leningrad should not be occupied. Its population would be reduced through a process of starvation and bombardment. In the end, it was expected that the city would be leveled to the ground. The Finns had allegedly expressed a desire to have the Neva River as their southern border and Hitler agreed that the territory north of the river should be given to them.[6]

The OKH took an unfavorable view of the OKW decisions on Leningrad but its own recommendations were certainly not based on any high moral principles. The main worry at OKH had to do with the adverse morale effects that a wholesale slaughter of civilians would have on German troops. Their "solution" to the dilemma was to let starvation and shelling do the work and then let the survivors evacuate through German lines.

Pending a final decision of the issue, Army Group North was ordered to encircle Leningrad but not to enter the city or accept surrender. To carry out its order to isolate Leningrad, Army Group North planned to cross the Neva River near Schlusselburg. It would then establish contact with the Finns on the Karelian Isthmus. It also intended to drive north to Volkhov and Tikhvin and link up with the Army of Karelia near the Svir River.

To assist in the accomplishment of its mission, Army Group North wanted the Finns to advance south on both the Karelian Isthmus and from the Svir River to meet the Germans moving north. These proposals were contained in a letter from Field Marshal Keitel to Mannerheim on August 22, 1941.

It seems doubtful that Mannerheim or other Finnish leaders had any knowledge of the ongoing conversations at OKW and OKH about the fate of Leningrad and its population. Mannerheim denies any knowledge in his memoirs.[7] Ryti, as related earlier, did advocate that the Leningrad area be depopulated and turned into a German "trading post." In any case, Keitel's proposals resulted in a refusal by Mannerheim based on some gloomy observations:

1. The Finns had 16% of its population in the military and this was beginning to have serious repercussions on the country's economy.
2. The Finnish casualty rate had been considerably higher in this war than during the Winter War.
3. Mannerheim had been forced to reduce the number of platoons in each company from four to three in August, and he intended to disband one division in September, in order to provide replacements.
4. The Soviet defensive positions along the 1939 border on the Karelian Isthmus were very strong, and Mannerheim suggested they should be taken from behind by German forces.
5. Strong resistance was expected when the offensives in Ladoga Karelia resumed, and Mannerheim doubted that the Finns could cross the Svir.

Mannerheim writes that he showed Keitel's letter to President Ryti. He told Ryti that he did not believe it was in Finland's interests to cross the Svir River or launch an offensive against Leningrad. Mannerheim claims that Ryti agreed.[8]

Major General Hanell, Mannerheim's acting chief of staff, elaborated on Mannerheim's reply to Field Marshal Keitel in a conversation with General Erfurth. He told Erfurth that the Finnish constitution required a political decision by the government if Finnish forces were to advance beyond the country's borders. Permission had been granted for the area east of Lake Ladoga and Hanell stated that he was confident that a similar permission would be granted, if requested by Mannerheim, for the Karelian Isthmus. He suggested that such permission would be requested when "the German Army rapped loudly and clearly on the door of Leningrad."[9]

With respect to the crossing of the Svir River, the ball was also thrown back to the Germans by Hanell stating that Mannerheim's outlook would become more positive after the Germans demonstrated that they did not intend to stop along the Volkhov River. Erfurth concluded that pessimism had taken control of Mannerheim's views and he recommended that an award of a German decoration would help restore his morale.[10]

The letter from Mannerheim to Keitel and Erfurth's gloomy report about Mannerheim's wavering confidence in Germany caused mild consternation at OKW and OKH. It resulted in an immediate message to Army Group North from OKH ordering it to link up with the Finns as quickly as possible, even at the cost of delaying the encirclement of Leningrad.

Mannerheim informed Erfurth on September 1, 1941, that he had secured permission from President Ryti to cross the Karelian Isthmus border as far as a line between Sestroretsk and Agalatovo. When Erfurth writes that Mannerheim's decision to move his defensive line into Soviet territory "went along with the German point of view" he is being less than candid.[11] The move was very short, and the Germans did not want the Finns to revert to a defense and had so indicated on numerous occasions.

The Soviets quickly realized that the Finnish offensive on the Karelian Isthmus had ended. They had remnants of six divisions and several separate battalions and regiments defending Leningrad from the north. They quickly withdrew two of these divisions on September 5 and committed them against the Germans.

When Keitel informed Field Marshal Leeb about the Finns moving their front south on the Karelian Isthmus on September 3, 1941, it elicited a rather cool response. Leeb observed that a mile or two of territory was of no importance and what was essential was to have the Finns undertake operations to tie down the maximum number of Soviet troops on their fronts. If they did not do that the Soviets could create serious problems for the Germans by withdrawing substantial forces from the Finnish front for use against his Army Group.[12]

OKW decided to send a senior German officer to Helsinki to have a discussion with Mannerheim. The choice fell on General Jodl, the Chief of Operations at OKW. He arrived in Mikkeli on September 4, and, in accordance with the earlier suggestion by Erfurth, carried all three classes of the Iron Cross for Mannerheim. While Erfurth describes the long meeting between Jodl and Mannerheim as very cordial and productive, it is difficult to see what was productive about it.[13]

The most important announcement that came out of the meeting was that the Finns would resume their offensive towards the Svir River that very day. Erfurth must have known that this was not a move by the Finns to accommodate the Germans. The operations in Karelia had been previously planned and the fact that its start date coincided with Jodl's visit was simply a coincidence. For the Finns, the most important result was a promise by Germany to fulfill an emergency request for grain.

Marshal Mannerheim's account of the meeting is considerably cooler than that of Erfurth. He states that his previous attitude on future Finnish operations did not change as a result of the meeting—leading Jodl to exclaim "Can't you then do anything to show yourself co-operative."[14] He goes on to explain that in order not to put undue strain on the relations with the Germans or jeopardize the negotiations for grain he "unwillingly" agreed to a limited advance (to the Mustapuro River) on the right flank of the Karelian Isthmus. This advance was never carried out. According to Ziemke, Mannerheim had agreed to more by promising to cross the whole length of the border up to the permanent Soviet fortifications and that when he informed Keitel three weeks later that the Finnish forces had crossed the border to the depth promised, he was only temporizing by avoiding the real issue.[15] The limited advance fell far short of Field Marshal Leeb's wishes.

Army Group North Runs Out of Steam

Army Group North arrived in the Leningrad area in September 1941 at the same time as the Finns reached the Svir River and began their drive into East Karelia. This first week in September was a momentous one for the Germans and the course of the war. Despite signs of an early winter and the exhausted state of his troops, Hitler decided on September 6 that the time was right to resume the German offensive against Moscow. This decision involved removing the 4th Panzer Group from Army Group North and transferring it to Army Group Center.[16] This left only one mechanized formation in Army Group North, the XXXIV Corps.

Schlusselburg fell to the Germans on September 8, 1941, and they now had a foothold on Lake Ladoga and the city of Leningrad was encircled.[17] This was the moment when OKW had planned that Field Marshal Leeb should send the XXXIV Corps on an eastward drive to Volkhov and Tikhvin. Leeb protested that the operation would dissipate his strength at a time when he needed to make the ring around Leningrad secure. He prevailed for the time being. OKH ordered him to cross the Neva River and link up with the Finns on the Karelian Isthmus. The army group's operation against Volkhov and Tikhvin was put off pending the arrival of reinforcements.

The Soviets upset the German plans by launching heavy counterattacks against Schlusselburg. Field Marshal Leeb pointed out to OKH on September 15, 1941, that the Soviets were withdrawing forces from the Finnish front and using them against the Germans. He urged that the Finns resume their offensive on the Karelian Isthmus and predicted that if they did this the battle for Leningrad could be decided within a few days. If they did not, he could not predict when he would be able to cross the Neva River in view of the exhausted and weakened condition of his army group.

There can be little doubt that Leeb was correct. The handful of mauled Soviet divisions north of Leningrad could have been brushed aside easily by the Finns, particularly if they had not transferred forces to East Karelia or if those transfers had been delayed until after the requested German operations on the Karelian Isthmus. Such operations would also have closed the one opening in the German encirclement— across the southern part of Lake Ladoga.

The OKH answered Leeb on September 18, 1941. General Halder assured him that the Finns intended to resume their attacks both on the Karelian Isthmus and south of the Svir River. However, the Finns were hedging their bets by some well-concealed conditions, indicating that they were well informed of what was going on at OKH. The offensive on the Karelian Isthmus would be undertaken as soon as the Germans had crossed the Neva River. The drive out of the Svir beachhead would be undertaken as soon as the effects of a German drive to the east became observable. These conditions doomed the hoped-for cooperation from the Finns since the drive to the east had been cancelled temporarily and Leeb had just stated that he did not have the strength to cross the Neva River in force.

The personal correspondence between Field Marshal Keitel and Field Marshal Mannerheim resumed in the second half of September. Keitel requested that Mannerheim move the 163rd German Infantry Division to the mouth of the Svir River and allow it to cross the river to link up with Army Group North at the appropriate time. This idea appears to have originated with General Erfurth who considered that the use of the 163rd Division in this manner would strengthen the resolve of the Finns and that their forces would join in the venture.[18]

It is difficult to see how two understrength infantry regiments could have made much difference in the situation south of the Svir River.

Mannerheim, a very perceptive individual, must have realized the difficult situation in which the Germans found themselves. He agreed to the request but stipulated that the timing of the move should be left to him.[19]

The issue about what the Finns planned to do was not resolved. While Keitel did not mention it in his letter, Mannerheim's long reply on September 25, 1941, did. Mannerheim informed Keitel that he intended to take Petrozavodsk and thereafter advance to Medvezhyegorsk. He also told the Germans about his plans to reorganize the Finnish Army after the capture of Medvezyegorsk. He intended to change the divisions into brigades and the surplus troops would be released from service to alleviate the acute labor shortage in the civilian economy, now dangerously close to collapse. This explanation was probably made to discourage any further requests from the Germans to reconsider his refusal to participate in their operations south of the Svir or on the Karelian Isthmus.

The German front south and east of Leningrad was stabilized by the beginning of October despite continued heavy Soviet counterattacks. Field Marshal Leeb decided that the time was right for the long-contemplated offensive against Volkhov and Tikhvin. He pulled the XXXIX Corps, commanded by General Hans-Jürgen von Arnim and consisting of two armored and two motorized infantry divisions, out of the front east of Leningrad.

OKW ordered Leeb to attack eastward on October 14, although there was no evidence that the Soviets had reduced their force levels in the Leningrad area to counter the offensive against Moscow. The plan was to drive eastward and envelop the Soviet forces south of Lake Ladoga. It was expected that the XXXIX Corps would link up with the Finns in the area between Tikhvin and Lodeynoye Pole. It appears from this that the Germans still harbored hopes that the Finns would undertake operations south of the Svir River despite Mannerheim's flat refusal to do so in his September 25 letter.

The XXXIX Corps began its advance on October 16, 1941. The advance was slow due to strong Soviet resistance and the onset of rain that turned the roads and earth into mud. The mud and soft ground was so bad that the armored divisions were forced to leave their tanks behind after a few days. The situation appeared so bleak that Hitler wanted to cancel the operation but OKH persuaded him to continue.

Field Marshal Leeb also favored continuing the operation when he visited Hitler but cautioned that his troops would probably only be able to advance as far as Tikhvin.

By the first week in November the Germans were still 10 kilometers from Tikhvin. They planned one final push on November 6. The attack succeeded and Tikhvin was captured on November 9, 1941. Thereupon, one division was turned north along the railroad towards Volkhov.

However, the situation in the Tikhvin salient turned downright dangerous for the Germans by the end of November. The Russians were not giving up the fight for the town and began a counteroffensive against Army Group North with new forces. Some of these forces, according to Erfurth, had been withdrawn from the Army of Karelia front.[20]

The Soviet forces soon succeeded in virtually encircling the Germans and Field Marshal Leeb found it necessary to commit two additional divisions to the operation to hold the flanks of the Tikhvin salient. Any plans of linking up with the Finns in the Lodeynoye Pole area or for a continued advance to Volkhov were out of the question.

On December 3, 1941 General von Arnim reported that he would not be able to hold Tikhvin. Field Marshal Leeb gave him a "be prepared" order to withdraw on December 7 but not to execute it until Hitler had given his permission. Both OKW and OKH warned against a withdrawal and Keitel even claimed that the Finns were going to establish contact from the north.[21] This must have been wishful thinking unless he had received erroneous information from General Erfurth or the Finnish liaison officer at his own headquarters.

Hitler issued an order on December 8, 1941 to stop all offensive operations on the eastern front. The same order directed Army Group North to hold Tikhvin. With respect to Army Group North, Directive 39 reads:

Army Group North will shorten its eastern and southeastern front north of Lake Ilmen, while still denying the road and railway from Tikhvin to Volkovstroi and Kolehanavo. This will make it possible, after the arrival of reinforcements, to clean up the area south of Lake Ladoga. Only thus can Leningrad be finally enclosed and a link with the Finnish Karelian Army established.[22]

The order was amended, as far as Army Group North was concerned, on December 11. All offensive operations by the group were to be delayed until 1942.

Events on the ground made Hitler's orders obsolete in the Leningrad sector. The XXXIX was fighting desperately to hold on to Tikhvin in the middle of a blizzard with temperatures below zero. Field Marshal Leeb notified OKW that he intended to withdraw the XXXIX Corps and Hitler grudgingly agreed, provided the railroad between Volkhov and Leningrad was held.

Tikhvin was evacuated on December 9 and Leeb decided to withdraw behind the Volkhov River, despite Hitler's insistence that he should establish his new front closer to the town of Volkhov. Hitler relented on December 15 after Leeb told him that a failure to withdraw behind the Volkhov River would lead to the destruction of XXXIX Corps. The XXXIX Corps was behind the river on Christmas Eve. They had sustained heavy losses in the fighting for Tikhvin and in the withdrawal.

The Military Situation in Finland in early 1942

The situation in the Army of Lapland area was precarious in early 1942. Mannerheim had refused, in December 1941, to assume responsibility for the sector of the III Finnish Corps (see Chapter 7). He also demanded that those Finnish units attached to the Army of Norway in 1941 be returned to Finnish control. To replace these forces the Germans had decided to bring in two mountain divisions—the 5th and 7th. However, transportation problems slowed their arrival to a trickle. While the 7th Mountain Division began arriving at Hanko on January 14, 1942, only the lead elements had arrived by January 27 when ice closed all Finnish ports. The rest of this division and the 5th Mountain Division could therefore not be transported until spring.

Not only did the ice situation in the Baltic interrupt the flow of reinforcements but it seriously interfered with the flow of supplies to the German troops in Finland, brought the armament shipments for the Finnish armed forces to a standstill, and stopped the grain shipments for the Finnish civilian population.

The deployment plans for the two mountain divisions changed numerous times. Initially, they were to replace the Finnish forces and SS Division Nord that were to be withdrawn from the Lapland Army. After

Mannerheim proposed an operation against Belomorsk in mid-December 1941, the OKW quickly decided to move the 7th Mountain Division to East Karelia upon its arrival in Finland to support the proposed Finnish attack toward Belomorsk. This was soon changed to employing it on the Karelian Isthmus to relieve Finnish units that could then be sent to East Karelia. The change in thinking allegedly had to do with bringing supplies to the German division, a task that would be much simplified if it were located near the coast instead of the interior.

There were probably other unstated reasons. The German troops had not proven themselves well qualified to operate in the terrain they would face in East Karelia. Probably more important was the fact the Mannerheim did not want German participation—despite his earlier polite acceptance of the German offer—since it would give them more control of events than he wished if the operation were to be actually launched.

Mountain Corps Norway had a change of command when General Dietl was moved up to take over the Army of Lapland (formerly Army of Norway) on January 14, 1942. The commander of the 6th Mountain Division, Lieutenant General Ferdinand Schörner, assumed command of Mountain Corps Norway. His previous position as 6th Mountain Division commander was filled by Lieutenant General Philipp Christian.

General Schörner is described as a "hard core" officer, particularly in adverse situations. Probably because of this quality, he rose rapidly in rank and was promoted to Field Marshal in April 1945, in command of one of the army groups defending Berlin and the rest of Germany against the advancing Soviet armies. Ziemke writes that "His [Schörner's] ruthless generalship, especially in the later stages of the war, earned him the enmity of his own troops, and he became the most unpopular general in the German Army."[23]

In the southern sector of the Army of Lapland area there had also been a reorganization of forces. The XXXVI Corps was renamed the XXXVI Mountain Corps. Its commander, General Feige, was replaced in November 1941 by General der Infanterie Karl F. Weisenberger.

The OKW sent a directive to the Army of Lapland on January 8 directing it to release the 6th Finnish Division to the Army of Karelia. The OKW directive made it clear that Mannerheim wanted the forces released to his command as quickly as possible. A quick execution was made difficult by the situation at the Kestenga front. The Soviets had brought up reinforcements and although the Finnish 6th Division—minus one regiment—began leaving the Army of Lapland area on February 15, 1942, the move of the last units was considerably delayed.

The Finnish III Corps Headquarters was still present in the Army of Lapland sector. With the departure of the 6th Finnish Division it was left only with the 3rd Finnish division and Finnish Division J. This former Group J had been reinforced to divisional status by the addition of two regiments—the 14th Finnish Infantry Regiment and the one regiment left behind by the 6th Division. Division J and SS Division Nord held the Kestenga area. SS Division Nord, which had only three infantry battalions in the Kestenga area, was reinforced with two motorized machinegun battalions. The 9th SS Infantry Regiment had been sent back to Germany. The Finnish 3rd Division held the Ukhta sector.

When it became apparent that the Belomorsk operation was delayed indefinitely (see Chapter 7), the reason for moving the 7th Mountain Division to the Karelian Isthmus no longer existed. It was now decided to have this division and the 5th Mountain Division, which followed it, gradually take over the sector of the Finnish III Corps. The Army of Lapland developed a plan to be implemented when the Baltic was reopened for navigation, and this plan was approved by Mannerheim on June 9, 1942. Planning for the use of the two mountain divisions had now come full circle. The XVIII Corps Headquarters was brought from Germany to replace the Finnish III Corps Headquarters.

The reorganization of the Finnish Army did not proceed as planned and produced few of the military benefits that Mannerheim had hoped.[24] The Army of Karelia Headquarters was disbanded in January 1942. General Heinrichs returned to his former job as Army chief of staff. The Army was divided into three fronts and the redesignations and regrouping of forces became effective on March 4, 1942:

1. The Karelian Isthmus front under Major General Oesch. Before the change was instituted Oesch was given the Svir front and Major General Harald Öhquist took over on the Karelian Isthmus.
2. The Svir front with Major General Öhquist the designated commander. The commander was later changed to Major General Osech. Öhquist had been the Finnish liaison officer

at OKW and he was replaced by General Talvela.
3. The Maaselkä front with Major General Laatikainen as its commander.

The lull in the fighting after the middle of January 1942 was used by the Finns to begin their planned reorganization of divisions into brigades. The reorganization resulted in a reduction in the strength of the Finnish forces. Older men were released. Some were sent home but others were organized into new units behind the fronts and given a not too glorious name in the popular vernacular of the day—the "senile battalions." The number of troops dismissed came to 111,500 according to Erfurth but Mannerheim places the number at 180,000.[25]

The planned conversion of divisions into brigades proceeded very slowly, and other than the release of older age groups, did not produce the hoped-for advantages. The plan was finally abandoned by Mannerheim on May 16, 1942, after two divisions had been converted.[26] These units retained their brigade status even after Mannerheim's decision to discontinue the reorganization.

Over the late fall of 1941 and winter of 1942, the Soviets had slowly increased their forces opposite the Germans and Finns in northern and central Finland as well as opposite the Finns in East Karelia. The Soviets had created the Karelian Front just before the onset of winter. This new army group was responsible for the area from Murmansk to Lake Onega and directed the operations against the Germans in Lapland and against the Finns in the Maaselkä and Rukajärvi sectors. The 14th Soviet Army was given responsibility for a shortened part of the new army group front from Murmansk to Kandalaksha, while the 26th Soviet Army was given responsibility in April for the old southern part of the 14th Army sector opposite the Finnish III Corps.

The magnitude of the Soviet winter buildup is demonstrated by the fact that, by the middle of April 1942, they had the following forces arrayed against the Germans and Finns in the Murmansk and Lapland sectors:

1. Against the Mountain Corps Norway they had two divisions, two infantry brigades, two brigades of ski troops, three border regiments, and two machinegun battalions.
2. Against the XXXVI Mountain Corps and Finnish III Corps

they had six divisions, two infantry brigades, two border regiments, and five brigades of ski troops.

The Soviets were able to do this despite the loss of about three million men on the eastern front in 1941, and the enormous resources of men and matériel they were pouring into their operations in central and southern parts of the Soviet Union. This realization must have had a sobering effect on both Finns and Germans.

The Germans recognized that their lateral transportation problems in Lapland could only be rectified by building railroads or roads linking the east and west within the various sectors, as well as by building a railroad between Rovaniemi and Pechenga. The Finns agreed to an OKW proposal in September 1941 for the building of the north–south railroad provided the Germans supplied the materials and labor. The project met with so many difficulties that it was finally abandoned. As an alternative, the Germans undertook to improve the road between Rovaniemi and Pechenga. This project became an important factor in late 1944 as the Germans began a fighting withdrawal from Finland.

Soviet Offensives against the Finns

The Finnish front was mostly quiet during the winter except in the Maaselkä area where the Soviets made several limited attacks in January. The Finns had three divisions (1st, 4th, and 8th) and one brigade (the 3rd) in this sector. The 3rd Brigade constituted the reorganized 12th Division and had been stationed on the Karelian Isthmus. It was moved into the Maaselkä area after the Finns detected a Soviet buildup in progress.

The Soviet offensive began in the Maaselkä area between Povents and Lake Seg on New Year's Day. Bitter fighting took place until January 11, 1942. The Soviet attacks took place mainly across the frozen lakes and rivers and the fighting was particularly heavy on the peninsula near Povents. Although the Soviet attacks were repulsed, they succeeded in pushing back the Finnish front in the area closest to the Murmansk Railroad. Their advance formed a salient, which the Finns attacked—resulting in the restoration of their original front as well as the destruction of a Soviet division.

In the third week of January a very strong ski combat patrol from the 14th Finnish Division, led by Colonel Joose Olavi Hannula, penetrated Soviet territory. Reaching the Murmansk Railroad south of Kochkoma, the Finns disrupted rail traffic for some time. The Russian supply base at Segesha was destroyed, but because they had insufficient forces to hold their position, the Finns withdrew to their own lines.

With the approach of spring and the melting of the snow and ice, the Soviets launched an offensive against the Finnish front on the Svir River. The main thrust was in the area between Lake Onega and Lodeynoye Pole. The Finnish defenders were able to repel the attacks while inflicting heavy losses on the attackers. The Soviets managed to make a 10-kilometer penetration in a heavily forested area where the Finnish line was thinly held. The Finns counterattacked and in ten days of heavy fighting succeeded in virtually annihilating the Soviet troops in that salient. The Svir front was again stabilized by April 21 as the rains ushered in the spring thaw.

Soviet Offensives against the Germans

Army of Lapland plans to undertake offensive operations in late winter were nullified by three events:

1. The unexpected Soviet spring offensive.
2. The failure to reach an agreement with the Finns for joint operations (see below).
3. The failure of promised reinforcements to arrive as scheduled—the 7th and 5th Mountain Divisions.

One regiment of the 7th Mountain Division was diverted "temporarily" to Army Group North on March 2, 1942, before it sailed from Germany. The same happened to a regiment from the 5th Mountain Division a week later. The German lack of reserves for the eastern front was impacting operations in Finland.

The Army of Lapland was slow in noticing Soviet preparations for a spring offensive. Part of this failure is attributable to the preconceived notion that the Soviets would not undertake offensive operations in the period of the spring thaw, when the rains and the melting snow made roads that were not hard-surfaced impassable and the ground too soft for vehicles of any kind. Aerial reconnaissance discovered that there were 700–800 railcars in the Loukhi rail yards on 13 April and this caused III Corps to cancel its own plans for offensive operations.

However, nothing happened over the next ten days and this brought a false sense of security.

Contrary to German expectations, the Soviets timed their attacks to take advantage of the looming thaw. By attacking as late as possible before the onset of the spring thaw they hoped to achieve their initial objectives before its effects reached a point where offensive operations were no longer possible. Having seized their initial objectives they hoped that the thaw, then underway, would prevent or seriously complicate German and Finnish counterattacks for several weeks. The Soviets calculated that the thaw would make the long Finnish and German supply lines impassable while they themselves would have the luxury of a rail line directly to the front.

Hitler's continual concern for the northern areas of Norway and Finland complicated things for the Army of Lapland. Dietl was informed by OKW at the end of February that the main mission of the Army of Lapland was the defense of the Pechenga area against both amphibious and overland attacks. The OKW was also concerned about the threat posed by the Soviet troops on the Rybachiy Peninsula and Dietl was ordered to prepare plans to seize the peninsula. However, no time frame for this operation was established. Still preoccupied with the amphibious threat in the north, Hitler ordered the Army of Lapland in the middle of March 1942 to transfer three battalions to Mountain Corps Norway as a mobile defense force along the arctic coast in Finland, a further reduction of forces in the area of the main effort.

Kestenga Front

The Soviets launched their offensive on the Kestenga front on April 24, 1942. They began with an attack by the 23rd Guards Division and the 8th Ski Brigade against a thinly defended part of the line on the left flank of the Finnish III Corps east of Kestenga. As the attack got underway during the day, the Soviets also attacked in the center. The corps' left flank began to give way on April 26 and it became obvious from intelligence that the Soviets intended to overwhelm the corps or drive it back to the area west of Kestenga.

The Army of Lapland did not have adequate reserves, but General Dietl committed all he had to stem the Soviet offensive. This included one tank battalion with obsolete Panzer I tanks, a company from the Brandenburg Regiment, and a battalion of the 139th Mountain Regiment from the XXXVI Mountain Corps. Finnish III Corps also brought in one battalion from the Ukhta sector. The 5th Air Fleet had been ordered to concentrate its efforts on the Murmansk convoys and the Murmansk Railroad. Since this was a crisis situation, the 5th Air Fleet fighters and bombers were switched from their bases at Banak and Kirkenes to Kemi behind the III Corps front.

When the Soviet offensive reached a point north of Kestenga, Dietl asked Mannerheim on May 1, 1942 for the 12th Finnish Brigade as reinforcement for III Corps. This brigade was the nearest major Finnish unit to the III Corps sector. Mannerheim refused to provide Finnish troops to the German operation (it was actually Finnish III Corps that needed help) but instead made a counteroffer. He offered to replace the 163rd German Infantry Division, committed on the Svir front, with Finnish forces withdrawn from the Maaselkä sector. The 163rd Division would then be brought forward to the Army of Lapland area provided the Germans returned the 14th Infantry Regiment from the Kestenga sector. This regiment had operated under German command since July 8, 1941 and Mannerheim was anxious to get it back under his own control. Exchanging these units would also further his goal of removing Finnish forces from German command as well as German forces from his own command. Mannerheim also offered to take responsibility for the Ukhta sector along with the forces currently located there, something he had refused in December 1941.

Mannerheim's proposal was not to Dietl's liking since the promised help would be too late to affect the situation he was confronting. Nevertheless, he accepted since it would provide him with an extra division for the long haul and would also relieve him of the responsibility for the Ukhta sector.

In early May, the Soviets brought in reinforcements in the form of the 186th Rifle Division and the 80th Rifle Brigade. These units were added to the forces opposite the left flank of III Corps to add weight to the Soviet envelopment. The Germans scrambled to find forces to meet the increased threat. The two remaining battalions of the 139th Mountain Regiment were brought in from the XXXVI Mountain Corps and another battalion was brought in from the Ukhta front. Two battalions from the right flank of III Corps were also committed against the Soviet advance that now consisted of two infantry divisions and two brigades with nine battalions.

The situation reached a crisis stage on May 3, when the Russians attempted a wide envelopment from the north using a brigade from the 186th Rifle Division and the 8th Ski Brigade. The goal of this envelopment through dense virgin forests was to come down from the north behind the German positions and cut the road west of Kestenga. The commander of III Corps, General Siilasvuo, proposed abandoning Kestenga and establishing a new defensive line further west between Lakes Paya and Top. Dietl rejected the proposal because he felt that losses in such an operation would be heavy. He ordered III Corps to hold its position even if its line of retreat to the west was severed.

The two Soviet enveloping units almost succeeded in isolating III Corps. Advance units were only three kilometers from the road leading west from Kestenga on May 5. Here, however, the Soviet offensive ran out of steam in the swampy forests northwest of Kestenga. The initiative switched to the Germans and Finns, and by May 7 German and Finnish units were able to encircle the two Soviet brigades. The two Soviet units took severe losses in the very intense fighting. The 8th Ski Brigade, for example, was virtually destroyed and down to a strength of 367 men. The 186th Rifle Division saw a 40 percent reduction in strength. The situation was not much better for the two divisions that had not participated in the envelopment—the 23rd Guards Division and the 80th Rifle Division.

The German–Finnish defensive operations were partly successful because the Soviets, with decisive superiority in numbers, attacked piecemeal and failed to orchestrate and coordinate their attacks. Dietl concluded that the danger had passed and decided to counterattack.

The counterattack was not launched until May 15, 1942, because of the spring thaw. The Soviets had used the interim period to construct formidable fortifications. The Germans were forced to launch frontal attacks against the Soviet lines after three battalions of Finns making a flanking attack became bogged down in impassable terrain. The frontal attacks breached the Soviet lines on May 21 and Soviet resistance began to collapse. III Corps had almost regained its former front line when General Siilasvuo halted the advance on May 23, before the troops had reached the most advantageous defensive positions. In doing so, Siilasvuo acted against General Dietl's orders.

Dietl decided not to challenge General Siilasvuo's almost incomprehensible decision. He did so primarily because he was afraid that the

Finns would pull their forces out of the front and leave the Germans in the lurch. He limited himself to issuing an order restricting Siilasvuo's authority to withdraw troops from the front line. This action did not prevent the feared action by the Finns. General Siilasvuo disregarded Dietl's order and on May 24 he ordered all Finnish forces withdrawn from the German sector. This was accompanied by a Finnish demand that the Germans return all Finnish horses and wagons within three days. If fulfilled, this demand would deprive the Germans of the assets they needed to keep their troops supplied. Dietl appealed to Siilasvuo not to leave his German comrades in a hopeless position on the battlefield. The "brotherhood-in-arms" concept was beginning to show serious cracks.

Dietl saw the handwriting on the wall and he took immediate action to make German units independent of Finnish support as quickly as possible. He also asked the OKW to speed up the arrival of the 7th Mountain Division. In this last effort he was disappointed because Hitler had just decided that the units from the 7th Mountain Division sent to Army Group North earlier would remain with that organization for the time being.

Lead elements of the XVIII Mountain Corps headquarters began arriving in Finland on June 3, 1942. Dietl planned to have this corps headquarters take over the Kestenga front in the middle of June but General Siilasvuo refused to relinquish his command until the majority of the Finnish troops were out of the area.

It is unlikely that General Siilasvuo would have stopped the counterattack, demanded the return of transportation resources, and refused to relinquish command until most of the Finnish troops were out of the area unless he was ordered to do so or had the acquiescence of Mannerheim—despite denials by the Finnish liaison officer at the Army of Lapland that any pressure had been exerted on General Siilasvuo by his Finnish superiors. The Army of Lapland in its assessment on May 23, 1942, noted that "In the course of the last three weeks the army has received the growing impression that the Commanding General, III Corps, either on his own initiative or on instructions from higher Finnish authorities, is avoiding all decisions which could involve Finnish troops in serious fighting."[27]

On June 18, 1942, Mannerheim agreed to an exchange of command by the end of June as long as the 14th Finnish Regiment and elements of the 3rd Finnish Division were returned to his control. This agreement allowed XVIII Mountain Corps under General Franz Böhme to take command of the Kestenga front on July 3. One Finnish regiment remained in its sector pending the arrival of the last elements of the 7th Mountain Division. This did not happen until the middle of September 1942.

Although the Soviets reportedly had 20,000 replacements at Loukhi, they did not resume their attacks and the front remained relatively quiet. The Germans and Finns had achieved a clear defensive victory although it had been a close call. The Soviets had paid a heavy price in casualties in their attacks in the Kestenga area and this may have led them to break off the offensive. III Finnish Corps claimed to have counted 15,000 dead enemy soldiers in its area. To this can be added substantial losses in the Soviet rear area from artillery and air strikes. The 85th Soviet Brigade, for example, was decimated by German air strikes before it reached the front. The German and Finnish casualties were relatively light—2,500.

The only event that broke the relative quietness that followed in central Finland was an attack by the XVIII Mountain Corps in July to seize a key piece of terrain that had not been secured when General Siilasvuo stopped the advance of III Corps.

The transfer of the 163rd German Infantry Division to the XXXVI Mountain Corps was completed in June and SS Division Nord was renamed SS Mountain Division Nord. Another in the series of unit redesignations without any apparent purpose took place at the end of June when the Army of Lapland was renamed the 20th Mountain Army. It may have been a way to honor Dietl who Hitler promoted to full general (generaloberst) when he visited Finland on June 4, 1942.

A new boundary between the Finnish Army and the 20th Mountain Army came into being as a result of the Finns taking over the Ukhta sector. The 20th Mountain Army still retained responsibility for the rest of the front in central Finland and it was organized into two sectors:

1. Loukhi sector was the responsibility of the XVIII Mountain Corps with two divisions assigned—7th Mountain Division and SS Mountain Division Nord. The preponderance of the XVIII Corps was located between Lakes Top and Kovd.
2. Kandalaksha sector was the responsibility of the XXXVI

Corps. It had two infantry divisions assigned—the 163rd and 169th.

Murmansk Front

The Soviet offensive in the Mountain Corps Norway sector began three days after the Soviet offensive in the Kestenga area. The situation in this area also became very serious for the Germans but did not reach a crisis point as it had in central Finland.

The Soviets launched two divisions and several brigades against the 6th Mountain Division bridgehead on the Litsa on April 27, 1942. The 10th Guards Division—along with the 8th and 6th Ski Brigades—attacked the German right flank while the Soviet 14th Rifle Division attacked the left flank. The Soviets also carried out an amphibious operation with the 12th Naval Brigade on the west shore of Litsa Bay. This unit moved against the German open left flank. The amphibious operation caught the Germans by surprise and it may have succeeded in rolling up the German line if the Soviets had committed more troops.

The fighting in the vicinity of the Arctic Ocean took place under very severe weather conditions. The worst snowstorm of the year hit the area at the end of April and raged with incredible force, stalling operations by both the Germans and the Soviets for several days. The troops on both sides suffered tremendous hardships. Both attacks and counterattacks required superhuman efforts.

The initial Soviet attacks made penetrations in the German lines and the Germans were required to counterattack to restore the cohesiveness of the front. Generals Dietl and Schörner decided on 9 May to gamble on a quick decision by moving the entire 2nd Mountain Division to the front and stripping all available forces in the region from their defensive missions and adding them to the counterattack force. Parts of the 2nd Mountain Division had already moved to the front before the decision. Both generals knew they were taking personal risks by reducing the defensive forces between Tanafjord in Norway and Pechenga Bay to only four battalions since it was an area of great concern to Hitler.

The Luftwaffe also committed all its available forces in the arctic and achieved considerable success. The Soviets contested the German air assault but came out on the short end despite their superiority in numbers in the hotly contested air battles that took place. In one action on May 11 German fighters downed 27 Soviet planes, losing only one of their own. German bombers were also active against Murmansk, the Murmansk Railroad, and against Soviet shipping, particularly in Motovskiy Bay.

The German air offensive convinced the Soviets that the situation for the 12th Naval Brigade, which had landed in Litsa Bay and posed a threat to the German left flank, was untenable. Its sea supply lines had for all practical purposes been severed by the German air offensive and the Soviets ordered its withdrawal.

While the Soviets had reinforced the arctic front with a fresh division—the 152nd "Ural" Division—they halted their attacks after they decided to withdraw the 12th Naval Brigade. The condition of the 152nd Division after it finally reached the front may have played a role in the decision to end the offensive. The division had not received its winter equipment in time and entire companies froze to death on the tundra on their way to the front. Of the 6,000 troops of this division only about 500 reached the front.[28]

The German counterattack was meanwhile underway but it also ground to a halt as the troops were totally exhausted. The vicious fighting ended on May 15, 1942, with the Germans having restored the original front all along the line. The fighting in the north was a clear German defensive victory. Mountain Corps Norway claimed that 8,000 Soviet troops had been killed in the fighting, not counting Soviet rear area casualties or the losses in the 152nd division underway to the front. The price was also heavy for the Germans since they listed their losses on the Litsa front as 3,200.

The Army of Lapland had informed OKW before the start of the Soviet spring offensive that it considered offensive operations during the summer unfeasible since the promised reinforcements would not arrive in time. The OKW accepted Dietl's assessment and gave the Army of Lapland two tasks to be completed during the summer. One involved operations in the Kestenga area to restore the old front. After that was accomplished, all units that could be spared were to be moved to the Mountain Corps Norway area where the army would make its main effort. The Mountain Corps Norway was assigned two missions:

1. Defend against any British and US invasion attempts. This was to be the primary mission.
2. Prepare to seize the Rybachiy Peninsula that the OKW con-

sidered key to operations in the far north. The date for that operation—code-named *Wiesengrund* (Meadowland)—was left open and to be determined by the availability of forces and the supply situation.

Hitler visited Finland in June 4, 1942 to pay honor to Mannerheim (who was promoted to Marshal of Finland) on his 75th birthday. Hitler also met with General Dietl (promoted to full general) who told him that his army did not have the troop strength to seize the Rybachiy Peninsula, or to hold it since it would lengthen his front. Hitler, still preoccupied with the perceived British/US threat, was reluctant to abandon the Rybachiy operation and ordered Dietl to proceed with his plans and preparations.

As summer began, it looked as though the troop strength situation was solved. The Finns were taking over the Ukhta sector and this would free the 5th Mountain Division for a move to the Mountain Corps Norway sector. That promising situation did not last long. In early July OKW informed the Army of Lapland (now the 20th Mountain Army) that the 5th Mountain Division would not be moved to the Pechenga area because it could not be supported logistically—sufficient stores for another full-strength division could not be brought forward from either Norway or central Finland. Instead, the OKW intended to send sufficient static troops—without transport—to relieve the 6th Division on the Litsa line. This would make both the 2nd and 6th Mountain Divisions available to undertake *Wiesengrund*. The OKW was obviously out of touch with the conditions on the arctic front. Dietl quickly intervened; pointing out that the Litsa front was no place for poorly trained and equipped third-rate troops. The OKW backed off and *Wiesengrund* was postponed.

The strengthening of other defensive forces in north Norway and north Finland also continued. The 20th Mountain Army moved five fortress battalions to the coastal areas for which it was responsible. The work on emplacing 21 coastal artillery batteries between Tanafjord in Norway and Pechenga Bay in Finland was completed in August and the headquarters of the 210th Infantry Division was brought in to command the coastal defense forces.

Another British commando raid on the Norwegian coast at Vågsø in December 1941 had, like the Lofoten raid in March 1941, refueled

Hitler's concern for Norway. This time the raid was better organized and included elements of all three services. Concern about Norway was the reason for ordering the battleships *Scharnhorst*, *Gneisenau*, and the heavy cruiser *Prinz Eugen* to make the famous Channel dash in February 1942 and for subsequently stationing most of the German fleet in Norway.[29] Hitler even wanted to move all submarines to Norway and relented only when it was pointed out to him that the ones operating in the western Atlantic were achieving excellent results along the eastern US seaboard.

While Hitler's worry about a British landing in north Norway in March 1941 had been completely unreasonable considering the state of the British armed forces, the situation had changed by the winter and spring of 1942 as a result of the US entry into the war. Both the OKW and General Falkenhorst in Norway now shared Hitler's worries about Norway. They considered it very likely that Norway would become the scene of major and decisive operations after winter had passed.[30] The repercussions of a successful Allied landing in north Norway or along the narrow coast south of Narvik could be devastating. The supply route for the German forces in north Norway and north Finland would be severed and the units isolated. Finland might re-evaluate its participation in the war and Sweden would come under Allied influence and could be induced to become a participant on their side. Every convoy destined for Soviet ports had to be viewed as a possible amphibious invasion force.

Churchill, whose interest in Norway almost rivaled that of Hitler, had in fact proposed a plan—Operation *Jupiter*—that called for landing troops at Pechenga and Banak to operate in cooperation with the Soviets. The overriding objective was probably to eliminate the German air bases that threatened the Murmansk convoys. The intention was to land a division at Pechenga and to use one additional brigade against the airfield at Banak.

Again, as in the case of Norway in 1940, Churchill underestimated the difficulties of such an operation. The Germans had moved most of their navy to Norway by the summer of 1942 and had significantly increased their air forces, not only to support ground operations in Finland, but to interdict the convoys sailing through the Arctic Ocean. The Allies would have encountered strong defenses along the coast at Pechenga, and would have confronted a division-size force in the Banak area. Churchill's plan withered because it did not have the support of his own military advisers or of the US.

Summer also brought organizational and deployment changes in the Murmansk sector. Some have been mentioned already.

Mountain Corps Norway (renamed XIX Mountain Corps in November 1942) had two mountain divisions assigned—the 2nd and 6th. The major corps troops consisted of a signal battalion, an engineer battalion, and two construction battalions. In addition, the following units assigned to 20th Mountain Army were located in, or earmarked for, the far north:

1. 388th Infantry Regiment.
2. 93rd Infantry Regiment.
3. 4th Machinegun Battalion.
4. 13th Machinegun Battalion.
5. 67th Bicycle Battalion.
6. 12 Army coastal batteries and some naval units.
7. Five Finnish frontier guard (light infantry) battalions.

Additional forces were added in the far north between the fall of 1942 and the spring of 1943. These included:

1. 210th Infantry Division with five fortress infantry battalions.
2. Division Group Petsamo under the 503rd Luftwaffe Field Regiment staff.
3. 139th Mountain Infantry Regiment.
4. Naval Command Kirkenes with eight coastal batteries.

The two mountain divisions were stationed along the Litsa line with the 2nd Mountain Division in the south and the 6th Mountain Division in the north. The other two divisions were stationed along the coast with Division Group Petsamo in the east and the 210th Division on the left where it tied into the 230th Division from Army Group Norway.

The mission of Mountain Corps Norway remained the protection of the nickel mines at Kolosjoki (including hydroelectric plants and transmission lines), security of the Arctic Ocean Highway, and protection of the arctic coast. For supplies the corps relied entirely on the stocks that had been built up in north Norway.

The 20th Mountain Army was responsible for an enormous front. It extended from just north of Loukhi to Pechenga, a distance of over 650 kilometers. Then it ran along the coast from Pechenga to Gamvik in Norway, another 600 kilometers. This very long front could not be occupied in strength. Between XXXVI Corps in central Finland and Mountain Corps Norway there was a 300-kilometer gap in the front. Even on the Litsa front there were gaps as the Germans organized a chain of strong points with considerable distances between positions. Stores for extensive combat were located in these strongpoints with all-around defenses. South of the Litsa the gaps in what was referred to as the security line were much greater. For example, the Finnish Petsamo Battalion was responsible for the southernmost part of the security line and they held a front of about 110 kilometers. To supply the southern portion of the security line—in a virgin forest wilderness—the Finns built a 120-kilometer road running east from the town of Ivalo.

The coastal front ran from Titovka Bay on the Motovskiy Bay side of the Rybachiy Peninsula to Gamvik in Norway. This front was responsible for protecting German shipping from Kirkenes to Liinahamari, the air bases used to attack the arctic convoys, and the Litsa front against amphibious assaults.

The Germans had gone to great length to insure adequate supply of the Murmansk front. Depots to support 100,000 troops for 12 months had been ordered by Hitler. Giant depots and cold-storage plants were established in the area and cold-storage ships were located in Kirkenes.

The Luftwaffe had four operational fields in the Mountain Corps Norway sector. They were located at Kirkenes in Norway, and at Luostari, Salmijärvi, and Nautsi in Finland. A forward headquarters for the 5th Air Fleet was established at Kemi.

NOTES
1. William L. Langer and S. Everett Gleason, *The Undeclared War, 1940–1941* (New York: Harper, 1953), p.551.
2. Blücher, *op. cit.*, pp.260–262.
3. Mannerheim, *Memoirs*, p.435.
4. Erfurth, *The Last Finnish War*, p.61.
5. Erfurth, *Problemet Murmanbanan*, p.15.
6. Ziemke, *The German Northern Theater of Operations*, pp.195–196. For more

on this issue see also Lossberg, *op. cit.*, pp.131–134; Adolf Hitler, *Hitler's Secret Conversations 1941–1944*. Translated by Norman Cameron and R. H. Stevens (New York: Farrar, Straus and Young, 1953), pp.325, 505; and Lundin, *op. cit.*, p.151.

7. Mannerheim, *Memoirs*, pp.429–430.
8. *Ibid*, p.427.
9. Ziemke, *The German Northern Theater of Operations*, p.198.
10. Message from Erfurth to OKW on August 26, 1941 as quoted by Ziemke, *The German Northern Theater of Operations*, p.198 and note 16. Erfurth does not mention this request or the basis for it in his book. Likewise, he omits the conversation he had with General Hanell.
11. Erfurth, *The Last Finnish War*, p.40.
12. An entry in the War Journal (Kriegstagebuch) of Army Group North as quoted by Ziemke, *The German Northern Theater of Operations*, p.198 and note 20.
13. Erfurth, *The Last Finnish War*, p.41.
14. Mannerheim, *Memoirs*, p.427.
15. Ziemke, *The German Northern Theater of Operations*, p.199.
16. Mannerheim, *Memoirs*, p.430 claims that the Finns were kept in the dark about the transfer. It would be odd for the Finnish liaison staff at OKH not to inform Mannerheim since such an important decision could not be kept from them.
17. The encirclement was not total. There was a 25–40 kilometer area between the Neva River and the Finnish front on the Karelian Isthmus that allowed for communications across Lake Ladoga to areas under Soviet control outside the German encirclement. This route across the lake became known as the "Ice Road" in winter and in summer it was used by numerous boats. Operation *Klabautermann*, discussed in Chapter 7, was an attempt to interdict this summer traffic.
18. Based on a message from the operations section of the German Liaison Group at Mannerheim's Headquarters to OKW on September 15, 1941 cited by Ziemke, *The German Northern Theater of Operations*, p.201 note 25.
19. Ziemke, *The German Northern Theater of Operations*, p.201.
20. Erfurth, *The Last Finnish War*, p.52.
21. Ziemke, *The German Northern Theater of Operations*, p.202.
22. Trevor-Roper, *op. cit.*, p.167.
23. Ziemke, *The German Northern Theater of Operations*, p.221.
24. To say that it is highly unusual for an army to undertake a major reorganization in the middle of a campaign is an understatement. The only positive result of the reorganization effort was to return a considerable number of troops to the civilian economy. It would appear that this could have been achieved through a process of attrition by dismissing elderly year groups as new inductees became available. It would have avoided the disruption caused by the reorganization. From a Finnish standpoint, the reorganization produced other positive results. It was a convenient reason to end the intermingling of units and brush aside German requests for more active prosecution of the war.
25. Erfurth, *The Last Finnish War*, p.71 and Mannerheim, *op. cit.*, p.441.

26. Erfurth, *The Last Finnish War*, p.76.
27. Army of Lapland War Diary entry for 25 May 1942, as cited by Ziemke, *The German Northern Theater of Operations*, p.227.
28. Carell, *Hitler Moves East*, p.469.
29. Devins, *op. cit*, p.202.
30. Ziemke, *The German Northern Theater of Operations*, p.215.

SEVEN

ABORTED PLANS AND DASHED HOPES, 1941–42

The Belomorsk Issue

There is considerable disagreement in the sources when it comes to Finnish views on interdicting the Murmansk Railroad. On some issues they are absolutely contradictory. General Erfurth, for example, writes that the issue between the German and Finnish high commands was not over the question of whether to attack the Murmansk Railroad but over how best to do it. This may have been true in the beginning but it changed drastically during the course of the war. In his memoirs Marshal Mannerheim wrote: "I had never intended to continue the advance from the Maaselkä Isthmus towards the Murmansk railway."[1] It is hard to square this statement with what follows below.

Operations against the Murmansk Railroad were agreed to during the planning leading up to war and were one of the issues discussed by Mannerheim and General Jodl when the latter visited Finland on September 4, 1941. Mannerheim opined that the simplest solution would be to reinforce General Siilasvuo's III Corps and send it against Loukhi. After capturing that town General Siilasvuo should advance north to Kandalaksha and roll up its defenses from the south since General Dietl's Mountain Corps Norway needed that railroad north of Kandalaksha for supplies after it reached Murmansk.[2]

On September 23, 1941, Field Marshal Keitel wrote a letter to Mannerheim where he stated, "The Führer is adamant about the goal of such operations being the Murmansk Railroad. The enemy along the route must be annihilated and the Murmansk area captured."[3] Keitel goes on to explain that Hitler feared that a British or Canadian force could establish itself in the Murmansk area and bring in large quantities of war matériel.[4]

213

In a very detailed answer on September 25, Mannerheim explained his intentions for the winter. For Finland, the most important goal in the near future was to capture and secure Petrozavodsk. Furthermore the northern flank had to be secured and this could be accomplished best at Medvezhyegorsk. He did not see possibilities for any far-ranging operations before winter but indicated that he should be able to concentrate eight or nine brigades for other operations after the fall of Leningrad. Mannerheim suggested that the attack by these brigades should have as their first objective Belomorsk (obviously from the Maaselkä area) and Kem thereby cutting the railroad between Murmansk and Archangel, completely isolating enemy forces to the north. He goes on to suggest that irrespective of whether the Murmansk Railroad was first reached via Kandalaksha or Loukhi, the troops should facilitate the advances in neighboring sectors by advancing along the railroad.[5]

This proposal certainly belies Mannerheim's later claim, above, that he never intended to advance against the Murmansk Railroad from Maaselkä. Mannerheim's proposal that the operational objective of the Finns should be Belomorsk became the dominating element in future German–Finnish discussions involving the interdiction of the Murmansk Railroad.

Marshal Mannerheim's proposal of September 25, 1941, for a winter offensive against Belomorsk on the Murmansk Railroad may have been intended to soften the blow of his refusal to continue the offensives over the Svir River and across the border on the Karelian Isthmus. He also proposed that the Finnish and German troops in III Finnish Corps be exchanged and that the advance towards Loukhi and Kandalaksha be continued. The whole proposal was neatly tied to German success at Leningrad by stating that the brigades would be available *after* that city had been captured.[6]

Erfurth, who devotes considerable space to Mannerheim's proposal, writes:

It is greatly to be deplored that the OKW did not adopt the proposal of the Finnish Commander-in-Chief. Now would have been the moment for Mannerheim, at the request of the Germans, to take supreme command within the whole area of Finland's war operations and thereupon carry his plan to completion. It can be asserted with great probability that the

German goal of controlling the whole Murmansk Railway would thus have been achieved and the war in the North would have taken a different course.[7]

The OKW, as indicated below, showed great interest in Mannerheim's proposal. However, Erfurth fails to note that its preconditions were that the Germans first capture Leningrad and link up with the Finns along the Svir River. So, what is the meaning of Erfurth "deploring" that OKW did not adopt Mannerheim's proposal? He was probably referring to the command relationships in Finland. To understand this we have to move forward six weeks to a meeting between Generals Warlimont, Buschenhagen, and Erfurth in Helsinki on November 15 and 16, 1941.[8] The idea of offering Mannerheim the overall command in Finland was discussed. This is probably what led Erfurth to bring up the subject in a meeting with Mannerheim on November 20, 1941.

Erfurth writes that Mannerheim maintained at this meeting that the whole front from the Svir River to the arctic should be considered a single front and be under a single commander. Taking advantage of this opening, Erfurth proposed that the logical solution was to place the German Lapland Army (newly renamed from the Army of Norway) under Marshal Mannerheim. According to Erfurth, Mannerheim agreed enthusiastically and underscored that he did not do so from personal ambition but on practical grounds.[9]

It strikes me as odd that Mannerheim would now "enthusiastically" support a proposal that he had rejected five months earlier on the grounds that he would come too much under the control of the Germans. That situation had not changed. It is particularly surprising that he would do so after Finland had received warnings three weeks earlier from the US—amounting to a virtual ultimatum—to refrain from attacking shipments to the Soviet Union from "territory under Finnish control." I believe that his decisions to take III Corps from German control, and for removing German units from Finnish commands, were largely influenced by the US note. If he ended up commanding all forces in Finland, including those trying to capture or isolate Murmansk, he could not escape the charge that the attacks were made from Finnish-controlled territory. On the other hand, a German attack on the Murmansk Railroad by forces not under his command would give him a thin fig leaf of protection.

The proposal in Mannerheim's letter of September 25, 1941 did cause great interest in the OKW since it offered the prospect of restarting offensives against the Murmansk Railroad that had stalled in the Army of Norway sector. The German agreement is reflected in Führer Directive 37 on October 10.[10] While the directive ended the Army of Norway summer offensive, it directed General Falkenhorst to prepare a winter offensive against Kandalaksha in conjunction with a Finnish offensive against Belomorsk and possibly Loukhi.

As opposed to the OKW, the Army of Norway was very cool to the idea of a winter offensive. It pointed out that conducting a winter offensive with the regular infantry divisions at its disposal would not be possible. Falkenhorst insisted that he needed at least two German mountain divisions and one or two Finnish brigades. OKW tried to accommodate Falkenhorst by offering him the 5th and 7th Mountain Divisions. One of these divisions was in Crete and the other was still being organized in Germany. OKW requested two brigades from Mannerheim. Finally, Falkenhorst was directed to begin training his existing units in winter warfare.

The perennial transportation problems that plagued the war in Finland soon made themselves felt and it became impossible to carry out the plan. The problems with the Finnish railroads ruled out bringing in more than one of the two mountain divisions and it would not be in place before the end of March 1942. Since March 1 was considered the latest starting date for the offensive in order to avoid the spring thaw, Falkenhorst concluded that the operation could not be carried out.

Since the Army of Norway was about to have a change in commanders and since Dietl was considered more expert in winter warfare than Falkenhorst, Dietl was ordered to make a personal reconnaissance and report his conclusions. He agreed with Falkenhorst that transportation and supply problems ruled out the offensive and he also doubted the effectiveness of retraining the infantry divisions for winter warfare.[11]

In the conversation Mannerheim had with Erfurth on November 20, 1941 they also discussed the future conduct of the war in Finland. Erfurth, speaking of Mannerheim's opinions, writes:

> According to his view, Murmansk, Kandalaksha, and Soroka [Belomorsk] must be taken during the present winter—the

sooner, the better. He advocated the beginning of January as the best time to launch a winter offensive to the eastward—simultaneously, be it noted well, against all three of the aforementioned objectives on the railway.[12]

Erfurth also reports that Mannerheim was eager to have the Germans capture the important rail junction at Vologda, north of Moscow, the junction through which the line from Archangel passed. "It is the decisive point for military operations on the whole Russian front. If we have Vologda, Soroka, Kandalaksha, and Murmansk in our hands, the Anglo-Americans can no longer get at us."[13]

In a letter to Keitel on December 4, 1941, Mannerheim described the cutting of the Murmansk Railroad as a matter of the highest importance. If Vologda had not fallen to the Germans before then, the railroad north of it should be heavily attacked from the air to hamper the movement of Soviet reinforcements. His letter, which is not part of the memoirs, reads in part:

> The importance of the Murmansk Railway for the Soviet Union's ability to wage war is undoubtedly great, not only with respect to the importation of war materials and food from America and England, but also by the morale role it plays as the main communication route between Russia and its allies. A prompt severing of this connection is of paramount importance.[14]

Then he went on to throw the ball back into the German court by stating that his proposal on September 25, 1941 was conditioned on the fall of Leningrad and the Germans establishing contact with Finnish forces along the Svir River. Those preconditions had not been met and the conditions of the Finnish troops and the economy had in the meantime deteriorated. Mannerheim believed that the German attack on Kandalaksha should begin before March 1, 1942, so that it would be completed before the spring thaw. If the situation permitted, Finnish troops would then begin their advance on Belomorsk with two brigades. His letter makes the Finnish advance on Belomorsk not only dependent on the success by Army Group North, but also on that of the Army of Norway.

General Erfurth believed that the Finns were anxious to get control of the Murmansk Railroad because it might then cease to be a problem in their relations with Great Britain and the US. This seems a peculiar view since the result of interdicting the Murmansk Railroad is likely to have had the opposite effect.

It appears that both Mannerheim and Erfurth believed that simultaneous attacks should be made against Murmansk, Kandalaksha, and Belomorsk in order to keep the Soviets from exploiting the lateral movement capability that the Murmansk Railroad provided them.[15] This is not what Mannerheim stated in a meeting with Falkenhorst less than two weeks later.

Mannerheim and Falkenhorst, with key staff officers, met at the Army of Norway Headquarters in Rovaniemi on December 14, 1941. The meeting dealt primarily with the separation of forces in the Army of Norway sector. Falkenhorst was in a dilemma. He had been directed to cooperate with Mannerheim in the exchange of forces so that the Finns could proceed with their reorganization and also undertake a winter offensive against Kandalaksha. Finally, he had been directed to prepare SS Division Nord for movement to Germany. While replacements were promised, they were not in place. Falkenhorst told Mannerheim that he was therefore in no position to release the Finnish units. Mannerheim, on his side, told Falkenhorst that he would take over the Ukhta sector only if it contained the same number and strength of units as it had earlier. In other words, he would not take over the sector until the requested separation of Finnish and German forces had been carried out. The end result was that Mannerheim refused to take responsibility for the Ukhta sector.

Mannerheim also took a dim view of undertaking operations against Kandalaksha before the beginning of March 1942. He stated that the Murmansk Railroad had increased in significance since the British declaration of war on Finland on December 6, 1941, and the state of war between Germany and the US. He concluded that the railroad had to be cut and suggested that the best way to cut it was by a converging attack on Belomorsk from the south and west by German and Finnish forces. Cutting the railroad at Belomorsk would also cut the branch line south of the White Sea to the interior of the Soviet Union via the Archangel–Vologda route. Successfully cutting the railroad hub at Belomorsk would completely isolate Murmansk.[16]

The OKW accepted Mannerheim's suggestion immediately and offered him the 7th Mountain Division for the operation. This was not the end of the problems associated with cutting the Murmansk Railroad at Belomorsk.

Erfurth reports that Mannerheim was "deeply distressed" by the outcome of his meeting with Falkenhorst. While he made Erfurth understand that he was willing to move against Belomorsk with Finnish troops alone if he had to, the precondition was as before—that the situation south of the Svir River be cleared up by the Germans since the forces he needed for the operation and protection for the Finnish right flank had to come from the fronts in the south.[17] He knew that the situation was critical for the Germans east of Leningrad and he learned, upon return to his headquarters, that the Germans had been driven out of Tikhvin and that the situation east of Leningrad had worsened. On December 26, 1941, the Germans requested that the Finns mount a diversionary operation on the Karelian Isthmus.

It is difficult to determine from the contradictory sources what motivated Mannerheim to make his proposal for a converging attack on Belomorsk or the reasons for his later vacillation. The first indication that the Finns had second thoughts about the proposed operation came in a conversation Ambassador Blücher had with President Ryti on January 1, 1942.[18] Ryti indicated that the operation against Belomorsk posed difficulties for the Finns when it came to availability of forces and supplies. He indicated that the operation would require thorough preparations and he did not see how it could take place before March of that year. Blücher assumed that Ryti's views were based upon those of Mannerheim.

We should keep in mind that the overall military situation on the eastern front had undergone a dramatic change in the month preceding this report. The German reverses in front of Moscow and in other parts of the front had had a sobering effect on the Finns and their outlook on the war. Mannerheim appears to have been so alarmed by these developments that he sent his chief of staff, General Heinrichs, to Germany on January 6, 1942. His mission was two-fold. First, he was to get a clearer overall picture of the situation on the eastern front. With respect to the military situation, Mannerheim wanted answers to two questions. Would the German retreat in Russia be brought to a halt and would the Germans resume and conclude their operation against Leningrad?

Mannerheim may have been concerned that when the Germans eventually stopped the Soviet offensive they would direct their main efforts in the south at the expense of Leningrad. Heinrichs received reassuring promises from Keitel and Jodl at OKW, and from Halder at OKH.

The second part of Heinrichs' mission was to get assurances from OKW that the Finnish III Corps would be replaced by German forces in order to deploy it to the Medvezhyegorsk area. This amounted to an end-run around the German command in Finland—which operated directly under OKW—after the conference between Mannerheim and Falkenhorst had reached an impasse on December 14. This may in fact have been the main purpose of Heinrichs' visit. The OKW, without giving adequate consideration to the situation on the ground, agreed to the Finnish position on the exchange of forces. The Germans apparently received nothing in return as it pertained to the Belomorsk operation.

The dose of cold water that Ryti threw on the prospects for the operation was soon followed by confirmatory reports from General Erfurth. On January 20, 1942 he reported that the Belomorsk operation was completely up in the air. Erfurth noted that Mannerheim would not make a decision unless the situation on the German front in the Leningrad area improved and he recommended that everything necessary be undertaken by the Germans to persuade the recalcitrant Finns to act. He noted that other Finnish officers were less pessimistic than the marshal but that they had little or no influence.

Based on this alarming assessment, Field Marshal Keitel wrote a letter to Mannerheim on January 28, 1942, where he again raised the question of the joint Finnish–German operation against Belomorsk that Mannerheim had proposed on September 25, 1941, and again on December 14, 1941. He tried to minimize what was happening on the eastern front by writing that the Soviets were wearing themselves out in their attacks and would likely exhaust their reserves before spring.

The new commander of German forces in Finland, General Dietl, paid a courtesy visit to Marshal Mannerheim at Mikkeli on February 2, 1942. The Belomorsk operation was the main topic discussed. The politically astute Finn avoided refusing to undertake the operation but repeatedly made it clear that such an operation would be difficult, if not impossible, until the Germans had taken Leningrad. He also stated that any winter offensive under the existing circumstances was out of the question.

Dietl pointed out to Mannerheim that the delay in the arrival of the 7th Mountain Division and the uncertain arrival schedule of the 5th Mountain Division made it impossible for him to relieve the Finnish III Corps in the Kestenga sector since he lacked forces to do so. The lack of forces would also prevent the Germans from supporting the Belomorsk operation by attacking in their own sectors. Dietl told Mannerheim candidly that he did not believe that sufficient forces would be available to him until late spring or early summer.[19]

Mannerheim's description of the meeting is short. He writes that Dietl was "full of enthusiasm for bringing about a united operation in which the Finnish Army was to capture the town of Sorokka [Belomorsk] on the White Sea—hopes which I had to dash."[20]

Erfurth, who participated in the meeting between the two commanders, reported his impressions to the OKW. He concluded that Mannerheim was influenced by internal politics in Finland as well as by his own negative assessment of the military situation. Mannerheim and the government had repeatedly assured the Finns that the end of the war was in sight. An operation against Belomorsk would throw doubts on this optimism. Should the Soviet winter offensive in Russia continue, even a temporary setback could prove fatal to the required Finnish popular support. Further complications, which should have been foreseen, arose. The Baltic froze at the end of January and brought the flow of reinforcements for the Germans and supplies and arms for both the Germans and Finns to an end.

These were the conditions when Mannerheim finally answered Keitel's letter on February 3, 1942. The letter, couched in very polite terms and not ruling out anything, sounded very pessimistic to the Germans. Mannerheim stressed that unless there was a favorable turn in the general situation, he doubted that he would have sufficient forces for a winter offensive, but would not rule it out.

Erfurth interpreted Mannerheim's reference to "favorable turn" as the German capture of Leningrad. Until Leningrad was captured he would not move sufficient forces from the Karelian Isthmus and from the Svir front to undertake offensive operations against Belomorsk. Erfurth believed that Mannerheim, by not ruling out an operation against Belomorsk, was resorting to a diplomatic gesture designed to appear polite and cooperative.

OKW agreed that Mannerheim had ruled out an operation against

Belomorsk—although not specifically stated in his letter—since the situation on the front around Leningrad had not changed. The operations against the Murmansk Railroad were therefore postponed indefinitely.

This would have been the appropriate time for the German High Command to be brutally frank with their recalcitrant coalition partner. They should have pointed out to the Finns that the quickest way to clear up the situation around Leningrad and thereby make forces available for use against the Murmansk Railroad would be for the Finns to close the ring around that city from the north. The Germans could also have pointed out to the Finns that German operations from central Finland were a waste of precious resources if the Finns refused to cooperate in operations against the Murmansk Railroad. In such a situation the Germans would be compelled to reevaluate the commitment of forces in central Finland. The Finns were well aware that they would be hard-pressed to hold on to their conquests in the south if they also had to hold central Finland. Such an approach at this time might have galvanized them into action.

Mannerheim writes in his memoirs that he turned down the German proposal "based on military as well as political considerations."[21] While he considered the operation feasible, he feared that the Soviet reaction would be so strong that it was doubtful that the railroad could be held. He also viewed the political repercussions as detrimental to Finnish interests because "the enterprise would have been likely to draw us into world politics, providing difficult problems for our government." He goes on: "My attitude to the German suggestion of participation in operations against the Murmansk railway therefore continued negative, as I repeated to President Ryti on a visit to Helsinki." Mannerheim was willing to make a limited change to the front in the northeast but rejected a proposal from his own staff to move north to Paradova, about 50 kilometers from Belomorsk since such an advance would give the Soviets the impression that the Finns were moving against the railway. Mannerheim also writes that he informed President Ryti about his decision.

Mannerheim had originally proposed the Belomorsk operation to Field Marshal Keitel on September 25, 1941, and to General Falkenhorst on December 14, 1941. But in his memoirs he makes it sound as if it were a German initiative that he had never favored. As far as becoming embroiled in world politics, that became a fact when Finland entered the war. His account also does not square with a letter that President Ryti wrote him on March 24, 1942, and Ryti's testimony at the War Guilt Trials where the letter was introduced as evidence. It reads, in part:

> On March 24, 1942, the Commander-in-Chief visited me in Helsinki and produced a plan for an operation which, however, was in the beginning only to be directed towards Paradova. He further mentioned that the greater part of the troops were already in readiness.[22]

The Finnish publication about the trial contains, according to Lundin, the following extract from Ryti's diary on March 24, 1942:

> Marshal at Helsinki with Lieutenant Colonel Viljanen presenting a plan for an attack in the direction of Sorokka, towards which he must in the immediate future start the troops which are already for the most part in a state of readiness for it. He requested my view of the matter. I promised to think about the matter overnight and write my opinion the next day and send it by courier to Headquarters. My answer negative.[23]

In his memoirs, Mannerheim writes that he was astonished to receive a letter from President Ryti in which the President claims his views as his own. Mannerheim explains the incident "as due either to misunderstanding or lapse of memory."[24]

Ambassador Schnurre came to Finland in February 1942 to extend the Finnish–German commercial treaty. He visited Mannerheim at Mikkeli on February 15. They discussed the Belomorsk operation and he reported that Mannerheim had stated flatly: "I shall not attack any more." Schnurre was not sure whether Mannerheim was only referring to the present situation or whether his statement should be given a broader interpretation.[25] In any case, the OKW was alarmed by the news.

Mannerheim paid a visit to Dietl in Rovaniemi on April 2, 1942 and again reiterated that he would not undertake the operation against Belomorsk until Leningrad had fallen to the Germans. To soften his rejection he observed that he did not consider the operation against

Belomorsk feasible, because of the terrain, until winter.

Erfurth observes that in early March 1942, the US began to exert diplomatic pressure on the Finns to have them reach an agreement with the Soviets or at least refrain from attacking the Murmansk Railroad. Erfurth is right but the pressure from the US had begun much earlier, in late October and early November 1941, when they passed on a peace feeler from the Soviet Union accompanied by a warning of the dire consequences for US–Finnish relations if the Murmansk Railroad was attacked from territories under Finnish control. That happened at least six weeks before Mannerheim met with Falkenhorst at Rovaniemi.

The US pressure on Finland in March 1942 came at a time when the Finns and Germans were deeply involved in discussions about the offensive against the Soviets in Kandalaksha and Belomorsk and undoubtedly influenced the outcome of these negotiations. Erfurth believes that the timing was not accidental and that a leak of the discussions may have been picked up by the Swedes who in turn informed the US.[26]

Erfurth wrote about Mannerheim's vacillations in the 1950 German version of his book. This part is missing from the English version, published in 1979 under the auspices of the US armed forces:

> It is extraordinary that the plan for an offensive against Soroka [Sorokka/Belomorsk], to which Mannerheim had grown skeptical as early as the beginning of the year because of the deteriorating situation on the German eastern front, was no longer considered viable beginning in March for reasons of foreign policy. In discussions with the OKW at the time, Mannerheim very skillfully placed priority on military considerations, by not rejecting continual German demands to attack the Murmansk Railway, by making them conditioned on the prior capture of Leningrad by the Germans.[27]

The Army of Lapland made another proposal for a German–Finnish operation against the Murmansk Railroad on April 8, 1942. Dietl requested the participation of III Finnish Corps as well as the 14th Finnish Division. The Finns turned down the proposal based on political considerations. This was undoubtedly a reference to Finland's relations with the US.

The proposed operation against Belomorsk was discussed during

Hitler's visit to Finland on June 4, 1942. Keitel related later that the Finns had stated that Belomorsk was of special importance to them not only militarily, but because of the establishment of postwar frontiers. They expressed their regrets at not having been able to undertake it during the past winter but did not think it feasible during the summer. They were considering it for the winter of 1942–43.[28]

Operation Lachsfang

The discussions over an operation against Belomorsk were not totally dead but they became hopelessly entangled in two other operations— Operation *Lachsfang* (Salmon Catch) and Operation *Nordlicht* (Northern Light).

Dietl, having finally received reinforcements and eager to carry out offensive operations, began to argue again for a double drive against the Murmansk Railroad. One part of the drive would be undertaken by the XXXVI Mountain Corps against Kandalaksha, and the other by the Finns against Belomorsk.

A conference between Generals Dietl and Erfurth took place in Rovaniemi on July 9, 1942. The conference was designed to discuss the situation in 20th Mountain Army but developed into an impulse for new operational planning based upon General Dietl's concept. It appeared very illogical to the two generals that the German and Finnish forces between Leningrad and the Arctic Ocean—amounting to about 600,000 men—remained inactive while the German forces on the eastern front were engaged in a life and death struggle to bring about a final decision in the campaign.[29] The German summer offensive of 1942 had begun in the last days of June with the main effort in southern Russia. No mission of any consequence had been assigned to the Finnish-German forces by the OKW.

General Jodl visited General Dietl's headquarters on July 13, 1942 and he was brought in on the discussions. Jodl expressed agreement and carried Dietl's proposal back to Hitler who gave his approval on July 21, 1942 in Führer Directive No. 44. The directive reads in part:

> We must now cut the northern supply route which links Soviet Russia with the Anglo-Saxon powers. This is principally the Murmansk railway, along which by far the largest proportion of supplies from America and England were delivered during the

winter months. The importance of this supply route will increase further when the season and weather conditions prevent successful operations against the northern convoys.

20th Mountain Army therefore proposes, in cooperation with the 5th Air Fleet, to prepare an offensive this autumn to seize the Murmansk railway near Kandalaksha.[30]

The directive also states that it was desirable that the attack by the 20th Mountain Army should be coordinated with a Finnish advance on Belomorsk. It goes on to list the two assumptions, which were that Leningrad would be captured in September 1942 at the latest, thereby releasing Finnish forces and that the 5th Mountain Division would arrive in Finland by the end of September.

Directive 44 puts brakes on Dietl's planned operation by stressing that the "most important task" of the 20th Mountain Army remained the protection of the Finnish nickel mines. On this issue, it reads:

It must once again be stressed, with the greatest emphasis, that without deliveries of Finnish nickel Germany could probably no longer manufacture the high-grade steel necessary above all for aircraft and submarine engines. This could have decisive effects upon the outcome of the war.[31]

The 20th Mountain Army was directed to be ready at all times to send reinforcements to Mountain Corps Norway to fulfill the task of protecting the mine production. The 5th Air Fleet was likewise ordered to be prepared to subordinate all other missions to the protection of the mines if they were attacked.

The directive also postponed the operation against the Rybachiy Peninsula (*Wiesengrund*) by stating that the operation would not take place in 1942, but that Mountain Corps Norway would continue to be reinforced so that it could be launched on an eight-week notice in the spring of 1943. Hitler directed that particular attention should be given to the development and strengthening of air and supply bases, essential not only for the successful execution of *Wiesengrund* but also for meeting an enemy offensive in the north.

There was no unanimity of opinion on whether the prospects for an operation against the Murmansk Railroad offered better prospects in the Kandalaksha sector or in the Kestenga sector. OKW opinion was divided on this issue as were the opinions of senior officers in the 20th Mountain Army. Dietl favored the Kandalaksha sector as did the commander of the XXXVI Corps but Dietl's chief of staff favored the Kestenga sector.[32] An attack from the Kandalaksha sector was chosen.

The XXXVI Mountain Corps started planning for *Lachsfang* on July 22, 1942. The planners realized that success depended on a quick breakthrough of the Verman river/lake line followed by a rapid thrust to Kandalaksha before the Soviets could mount another defense. The XXXVI Corps planned to use both infantry divisions in the breakthrough, one along the road and one along the railroad. The plan also called for a sweep by a mountain division (the yet-to-arrive 5th) around the Soviet right flank to prevent them from establishing and occupying a second defensive line. The plan involved about 80,000 troops, double the number of troops involved in the 1941 summer offensive. The 5th Air Fleet agreed to provide 60 dive–bombers, 9 fighters, and 9 bombers for the operation. This was more air support than had been available in the summer of 1941.[33]

Timing was all-important because of the weather and terrain. The XXXVI Mountain Corps believed it would require four weeks from start to finish. To avoid a winter campaign or a campaign during the spring thaw, it was decided to launch *Lachsfang* so that military operations would essentially be completed by November 15, 1942.

Both Dietl and OKW considered a Finnish attack against Belomorsk an essential prerequisite for the success of *Lachsfang*. General Erfurth was ordered to get the Finnish reaction to Führer Directive 44. He first approached General Heinrichs, the chief of the Finnish General Staff. As expected by the Germans, Heinrichs delivered a "yes, but" answer—the "but" being that Leningrad had to be captured before the operation could be undertaken. However, the Finns brought up a new prerequisite that surprised the Germans. Heinrichs stated that it was necessary also for Army Group North to advance east to the middle Svir River south of Lake Onega.

Erfurth writes:

From whatever side one looked at the problem, one was caught in the vicious circle of a situation in which a free hand in the east could only be obtained after first getting a free hand in the south. Leningrad remained the key to all planning at the Finnish-German front.[34]

General Heinrichs also told Erfurth it would be preferable to have German troops be the first to cut the Murmansk Railroad in order for Finland to avoid difficulties with the US that would probably lead to a declaration of war.[35]

Erfurth writes that the Germans hoped that the news from the fronts in Russia would convince the Finns that things were improving. In fact, the Finns were seeing the German summer offensive in the southern part of the Soviet Union rolling from one success to another. The lower part of the Don River had been crossed on a 250-kilometer front by German troops and their allies and the spearheads of the German drive were 180 kilometers south of the Don. On August 9, 1942, German troops reached the northern slopes of the Caucasus on a 400-kilometer wide front and on August 12 the Germans announced that General Paulus' forces had encircled and destroyed a Soviet army in the great Don bend. The operations in North Africa also looked very promising. German and Italian forces had taken Tobruk on June 21, 1942, and Field Marshal Erwin Rommel's forces were pursuing the defeated British towards the Libyan–Egyptian frontier and had captured Mersa Matruh on June 30. News also arrived in Finland that Erich von Manstein's 11th Army was on the way to the Leningrad area with its impressive siege artillery—280 batteries of 817 guns ranging in caliber from 75mm to 800mm—from the successful siege of Sevastopol. It was hoped that these events would influence the Finnish decision.

Mannerheim's written answer to General Erfurth was delivered on August 2, 1942. In typical fashion, Mannerheim expressed agreement "in principle" with the German proposal for an attack towards Kandalaksha along with a Finnish drive on Belomorsk. In other words, he was willing to cooperate but set a very high threshold. The letter left no doubt that Finnish participation depended on Leningrad being captured first. He also repeated General Heinrichs' prerequisite of an eastward offensive by Army Group North towards the Svir River. Added to the prerequisites was that the Belomorsk operation be supported by the Luftwaffe and that a very large amount of fuel be made available to the Finns.[36]

Under these stipulated conditions the Finnish commander in chief agreed to make the following forces available for an operation against Belomorsk:

1. Two divisions from the Karelian Isthmus and the 3rd and 12th Brigades in the Medvezhyegorsk area.
2. The armored division currently being formed west of Lake Seg.
3. Two more divisions from the Karelian Isthmus and the 14th Division in the Rukajärvi area.
4. The two divisions presently at the Maaselkä front (1st and 4th Divisions) were to follow as a second wave.

In other words, Mannerheim promised to make available the equivalent of 10 divisions for the operation and to do that he would have to strip away the units on the Karelian Isthmus north of Leningrad. The redeployment of the four divisions on the Karelian Isthmus could not take place until Leningrad was in German hands and the redeployment itself would take four weeks because of poor roads. Implicit in his promise to make these forces available was that this rather immense force was needed for the operation to be successful. It was undoubtedly assumed that the Germans would not be so bold as to challenge this implicit assumption.

General Talvela, the Finnish liaison officer to OKW and OKH, delivered the German answer on August 15, 1942:

1. The occupation of Leningrad would be carried out as requested by Marshal Mannerheim.
2. The OKW granted the Finnish request for Luftwaffe support in the attack on Belomorsk.
3. The very large fuel requests were also granted.
4. However, if Mannerheim insisted on an advance by Army Group North to an area south of Lake Onega prior to the offensive, the entire Operation *Lachsfang* would be cancelled. The 5th Mountain Division, slated for movement to the 20th Mountain Army would under these circumstances be assigned to Army Group North.

Erfurth writes that Mannerheim, "like a skilled fencer . . . obliged to make a clear decision by paragraph four of the German reply, evaded a precise written answer and ordered his Chief of Staff to discuss [in Germany] the matter verbally."[37] General Heinrichs arrived in Germany on August 24, 1942 and he and General Talvela gave their explanations to the OKW. The Germans appear to have accepted them—there was not much else they could do unless they were willing to threaten to withdraw the 20th Mountain Army from central Finland. Though it is not certain whether the Finns dropped their demand for an eastward advance by Army Group North, they most probably did since Operation *Lachsfang* was not cancelled.

Marshal Mannerheim devotes only a few lines to these important and complicated negotiations about a Belomorsk operation in his memoirs and has nothing at all to say about his acceptance as long as specific conditions were met. He is also less than candid in describing the requested Finnish participation as limited to tying down Soviet forces in support of a German attack on Kandalaksha. He writes in his memoirs:

> At the end of July, the Germans again raised the question of a Finnish attack on the Murmansk railway, which this time was to commence from the direction of Rukajärvi and the object of which would be to hold down the adversary while they themselves were to attack in the direction of Kandalaks [sic]. I informed President Ryti of the proposal, and it was declined for the same reasons as before.[38]

President Ryti's statement on this issue does not deviate much from what Mannerheim wrote:

> In July–August 1942 an offensive in the direction of the White Sea became a matter of present concern again, since the Germans planned the capture of Leningrad and the improvement of their positions in the direction of Kandalaksha. We succeeded this time, too, after long and involved discussions, in extricating ourselves from participation in these war operations.[39]

The statement makes no mention that the German operation in the direction of Kandalaksha was intended to cut the Murmansk Railroad and that a large part of that plan was an operation by very strong

Finnish forces against Belomorsk. Erfurth writes that the Finnish president was fully informed by Mannerheim's headquarters on several occasions in August and September 1942 about the offensive plans against the Murmansk Railroad and Leningrad.[40] The above statement does show that the Finns were insincere in their dealings with their "brothers-in-arms." Their preconditions were obviously intended to avoid having to participate in the German effort to interdict the Murmansk Railroad.

As in the case of the planning and actions that led up to the war, when it comes to the negotiations for the operations against Belomorsk and Leningrad, there are irreconcilable differences between the Germans and the Finns based on German records, writings of German participants, and statements made by Finns after the war. This applies as well to the differences between what Erfurth (who had considerable sympathy for Finnish views) writes and what Mannerheim writes.

Lundin makes some rather pointed observations about the differences in the accounts by Mannerheim and Erfurth:

> One of the men is a liar, or has too poor a memory to write reminiscences. The question is important for more than the matter of personal veracity: it deals with a central problem of the war. Throughout his book Mannerheim presents himself as the man who reluctantly assumed the burden of fighting a defensive war, nursed no national imperialist ambitions, and avoided rash military ventures which might create irremediable difficulties with Russia by threatening its vital interests. In the episode we have been considering, Erfurth presents the Marshal as a general who was quite willing to fight more than a defensive and limited war for Finland, who would have been glad to take such a decisive step as cutting the chief supply artery of the Soviet Union, but who was deterred by practical considerations of the strength of his armies and the crumbling position of the Waffenbruder [brother-in-arms].[41]

The Finnish attitude on getting involved in costly military operations must also be viewed against the number of casualties they had already suffered—in what some were beginning to believe was a futile cause. The Finnish losses as of September 30, 1942 had risen to about

118,000 of which over 32,000 had been killed. This was almost double the casualties suffered in the Winter War—about 67,000.

Operation Nordlicht

Operation *Lachsfang* was totally dependent on German forces first capturing Leningrad. This was a stipulation made by the Finns for their participation and they consistently maintained that it was militarily necessary in order for them to have the requisite forces available. The German plan to capture Leningrad—Operation *Nordlicht* (Northern Lights)—was rather simple. After a preliminary softening of the enemy by the Luftwaffe and massive artillery, the Germans planned to advance across the Neva River above Leningrad, link up with the Finns if possible, and then capture the city.

The southern fronts in the Soviet Union had been accorded the highest priority in the summer offensive and Army Group North had its forces spread over an extensive area in a defensive posture. Army Group North was now promised an additional five divisions and the heavy siege artillery of Manstein's 11th Army.

The 18th Army, in the Leningrad sector, estimated the Soviet forces confronting it at 13 divisions and three armored brigades. This was in addition to the forces confronting the Finns on the Karelian Isthmus and along the Svir River. The 18th Army had five divisions and it would have five more with the arrival of the 11th Army. It was still eight divisions short of what it believed was necessary for Operation *Nordlicht*.

Field Marshal Georg von Küchler, the new commander of Army Group North, briefed Hitler on Operation *Nordlicht* on August 8, 1942. He pointed out that the Germans were outnumbered two to one in the Leningrad area and requested additional divisions. Hitler answered that Küchler would have to do with what he had since he could not give him divisions that he did not have. Küchler indicated that he would be ready to launch *Nordlicht* at the end of October. Jodl objected and pointed out that it would have to be launched earlier because it was not an end in itself but a preparatory operation for *Lachsfang*. Hitler set September 10, 1942, as the date of the offensive.

No one was happy with either the outcome of the conference on August 8, or Jodl's later recommendation that the mission of taking Leningrad be given to Manstein's 11th Army. Hitler did not take action on this recommendation until two weeks later when he approved Jodl's suggestion. Küchler protested that a switch in the command of Operation *Nordlicht* at this stage would only create confusion in view of all the plans and preparations made by the 18th Army. This did not change Hitler's mind.

However, Manstein, who also had grave misgivings, stated in his first meeting with Küchler on August 28, 1942 that he did not believe artillery bombardment would break Soviet resistance. He concluded that *Nordlicht* would be difficult and that the main attack should be made from the Karelian Isthmus or from both directions.[42]

The lack of forces continued to plague the operation. The 5th Mountain Division, now part of Army Group North, was scheduled to take part in Operation *Lachsfang*. That division would have to be released before August 15 if it were to reach its new staging area in time. Küchler declared this impossible because he had no forces to replace it with and could not risk weakening any part of his front to make reserves available. The problem was kicked up to Hitler and he took a week to make the decision to leave the 5th Mountain Division with Army Group North and instead move the 3rd Mountain Division from Norway to take part in *Lachsfang*.

Despite these difficulties, preparations for *Nordlicht* proceeded well and it held out great promise if successful. However, fate decided otherwise. The Soviets launched an offensive from the east along the south shore of Lake Ladoga against what was referred to as the "bottleneck" on August 27, 1942. The bottleneck was that part of the Army Group North front which projected like a wedge from Schlusselburg in a southwest direction. This wedge was vulnerable to attack from both the west and east and had grown very narrow, only a few miles across in certain locations. The objective of the offensive was to lift the siege of Leningrad by opening a land route through the wedge. The Soviets quickly achieved local breakthroughs and the OKW had to watch helplessly as their own offensive plans evaporated.

As usual, there was a scramble to find forces to restore the situation. The 3rd Mountain Division, already at sea from Norway to Finland, was diverted to the Army Group North front on August 31, 1942. Four divisions planned for use in *Nordlicht* should have assembled southwest of Leningrad but had to be moved to the bottleneck area.

The 18th Army reported that it would have its hands full with containing the Russian offensive for weeks and that Operation *Nordlicht* could not be undertaken as planned. The OKW and OKH agreed and cancelled *Lachsfang* for 1942 and made the execution of *Nordlicht* dependent on the situation east of Leningrad and the availability of forces.

The OKW informed Mannerheim about these decisions and requested immediate Finnish participation in *Nordlicht*. Even Erfurth was surprised at this request based on Mannerheim's attitude during the past year about participating in an attack against Leningrad. A change in Mannerheim's attitude could only be expected through a spectacular German success, not as a result of problems and dire straits.

As usual, Mannerheim did not flatly decline Finnish participation in Operation *Nordlicht* in his answer of September 4, 1942, but he might as well have. The answer was couched in the usual polite terms. Mannerheim agreed to participate "in principle" but pointed out that the capacity of the Finnish Army was limited. Finnish forces would not become available to meet German requests until Operation *Nordlicht* had been successfully carried out. Greiner writes that Finnish participation was limited to moving "artillery into position as a demonstration."[43] Erfurth writes that the capture of Leningrad by German forces "remained the Alpha and Omega of all Finnish planning."[44]

In his memoirs Mannerheim makes no mention of the German request for assistance or the Finnish answer. In fact, he makes no direct reference to Operation *Nordlicht*. He does mention a note received from the US minister in Helsinki, Mr. Schoenfeld, on September 25, 1942. The notes expressed fears that the Finns would give way to German pressure and allow themselves to become involved in offensive operations. Mannerheim writes that the note was probably in reference to Leningrad and that the US wanted to make sure that there would be no Finnish participation in an attack on that city by requesting a statement to the effect that Finland had no intention of advancing beyond its present front. He writes that while Finland could not bind itself to remaining inactive, the answer was written in a friendly tone.[45]

The prospects for *Nordlicht* did not appear promising. The Germans were able to restore the old front in a counteroffensive between September 29 and October 15, 1942. After their experience the past winter the Germans, including Hitler, were wary about any offensive extending into the winter season. The great assembly of artillery was to be used to support incremental advances in the front around

Leningrad as long as that could be done without a great commitment of troops.

General Erfurth contacted Field Marshal von Manstein to get a clearer picture of the state of affairs in the area around Leningrad. He received a discouraging answer on October 12, 1942 that the attack on Leningrad would be postponed indefinitely. Manstein was considering tightening the encirclement of the city and stated that limited Finnish participation was desirable. Erfurth approached General Heinrichs informally on this issue. Erfurth writes this about Heinrichs' reaction:

> He [Heinrichs] drew attention to the "solemn promise" which the Finnish government at the hour of birth of the Finnish state had given the capitals of Europe and the United States, to the effect that no inconvenience should ever be caused the Russian capital by the proximity of the frontier of the newly created Finnish state. Participation of the Finnish Army in Operation *Nordlicht*, even in the modest form proposed by Manstein, could not be expected.[46]

At the end of October the 11th Army was placed under the direct control of OKH and given its own sector between Army Group North and Army Group Center. *Nordlicht* was postponed indefinitely and it was never again seriously revived.

The information that Operation *Nordlicht* was postponed indefinitely was only part of the alarming news that flowed into Finland in late 1942. This news had profound negative impact and further eroded Finnish belief in an eventual German victory.

The spectacular success of the German Army in the southern part of the Soviet Union during the summer had expanded the territory conquered by German arms to the greatest extent of the war. However, the Germans had not achieved their primary aim, the destruction of the Red Army. The Soviets had learned to avoid encirclements.

The military situation that had looked so good and hopeful for the Germans during the summer had turned downright deplorable by the end of the year. In the last week of October the British began their counteroffensive in North Africa which eventually led, after heavy fighting, to a lengthy German/Italian westward withdrawal at the same time as US troops landed on the North African coast in November

1942 and started a drive to the east.

By the middle of November, the situation at the front in southern Russia became critical for the Germans and their allies. A large-scale Russian offensive began northwest and south of Stalingrad on November 19, 1942, by vastly superior Soviet forces. The Romanian 3rd Army was routed and overrun. Disasters quickly followed on the neighboring fronts on the Don and Volga and the Soviet avalanche brought Italian, Hungarian, and also German divisions into the whirlpool of defeat. Battles of tremendous size developed in the last third of November between the Volga and Don.

The situation on the German central front in Russia became grave when on November 25, 1942 the Soviets began their expected offensive on a wide front south of Kalinin. The fact that the Red Army retained the capability to launch so many large-scale offensives after suffering repeated defeats and enormous losses during the summer was dismaying to the Germans and Finns and a surprise to the world.

The German eastern front slowly became more and more disrupted. German islands of resistance, bypassed by the waves of the enemy offensives, were surrounded by the Red Army and had to be supplied by the Luftwaffe.

Operation Klabautermann

At the end of May 1942 the Germans concluded, based on Finnish reports, that the Russians had begun evacuating the population of Leningrad by boats across the southern end of Lake Ladoga. During the winter there was a steady traffic in both directions. Large columns of trucks crossed the ice on several routes on Lake Ladoga, bringing critically needed supplies to Soviet soldiers and civilians in Leningrad. Nonessential civilians were brought out on the return trips across the lake.

The Germans and Finns were both interested in stopping this traffic. The large amounts of military supplies and foodstuffs that were brought in and civilians brought out would lead to a prolongation of the siege. Hitler was concerned about the flow out of the city since, if most of the population could be evacuated in this manner, Leningrad would lose its importance to Stalin and he would switch the forces in and around the city to other fronts. Hitler ordered the evacuation stopped by all available means.

The idea of using small naval craft to interdict the traffic—suggested in late 1941—was revived in 1942. A Luftwaffe officer, Lieutenant Colonel Fritz Siebel, had invented a flat-bottomed doubled-hulled aluminum landing craft. The Luftwaffe planned to bring a number of these to Lake Ladoga after a conference in Finland in June 1942. The German navy was also involved, promising a number of German E-boats and Italian Mas-boats. The operation was code-named *Klabautermann* (Goblin).

The Finns gave the Germans a free hand to conduct the operation and had no role except to provide bases along the shore of Lake Ladoga and some limited air cover. The German Navy had their boats in place and was ready to begin operations on July 1. The Luftwaffe brought in their Siebelcraft in August.

The Germans had still not learned the lessons of joint operations and both the Luftwaffe and the German Navy claimed overall command. There was no German headquarters in this part of Finland to command or coordinate the operations so the elements from the two services operated with sturdy independence and reported to their respective service headquarters in Germany. The two groups could not even agree on how to best accomplish their missions of stopping the traffic across the lake.

Klabautermann had limited success not only because of the lack of a uniform command structure, but because the lake was in many places too shallow even for the Siebelcraft, and because of inadequate air cover. The German crews began to advocate a withdrawal from Lake Ladoga as early as August. Mannerheim felt it absurd to withdraw the boats at the very time that the two planned operations that would benefit from their activities, *Nordlicht* and *Lachsfang*, were under consideration. The interruption of Soviet supply lines would be especially important in a decisive battle for Leningrad.[47]

Mannerheim's opposition postponed the withdrawal but plans to return the boats to Germany surfaced again at the end of September, this time at the urging of Göring, the commander in chief of the Luftwaffe. Since the prospects of *Nordlicht* looked rather dim at this time, Mannerheim did not object to withdrawing the boats. A Finnish proposal to buy some of the boats for their own use resulted in negotiations that delayed the withdrawal until November 6, 1942.

In sharp contrast to the uninterrupted heavy fighting on the eastern

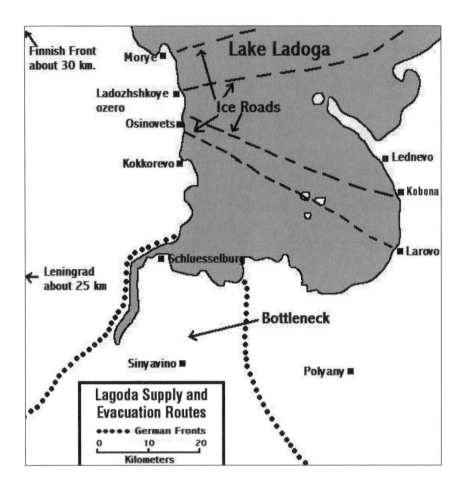

front there was virtually no fighting on the German-Finnish front between the Gulf of Finland and the Arctic Ocean during the summer and fall of 1942. Fighting in Finland was limited to isolated places and had little importance. Days passed without a shot being fired in some sectors.

In an order from OKW on October 7, 1942, the 20th Mountain Army was directed to limit itself to defensive operations. Plans for the capture of the Rybachiy Peninsula were also cancelled for the year. OKW told General Dietl that he should expect an additional division in spring 1943 that might be used to execute *Lachsfang* during the summer of 1943. The main effort of the 20th Mountain Army remained with Mountain Corps Norway but there were no significant changes in its mission. The strength of the 20th Mountain Army at the end of 1942 stood at 172,200 men. By Hitler's orders this was to be increased by one Luftwaffe field regiment and a police regiment.[48]

As winter began, little was left of the hopeful plans that had been discussed between the Germans and Finns since July 1942. Few in Finland, Germans as well as Finns, viewed the coming year with any sense of optimism.

NOTES

1. Mannerheim, *Memoirs*, p.435.
2. Erfurth, *Problemet Murmanbanen*, pp.27–28.
3. *Ibid*, p.30.
4. *Ibid*, pp.30–31.
5. *Ibid*, pp.32–34.
6. Message from the Operations Section of the Finnish Liaison Staff at Mannerheim's Headquarters to OKW on September 25, 1941 as quoted by Ziemke, *The German Northern Theater of War*, p.208 and note 54.
7. Erfurth, Problemet Murmanbanen, p.34.
8. Erfurth, *The Last Finnish War*, p.57.
9. Erfurth, *Problemet Murmanbanan*, pp.39–40.
10. Trevor-Roper, *op. cit.*, pp.159–163.
11. The Army of Norway implementing decision for Directive 37, message from the Army of Norway to OKW on November 21, and a telegram from Dietl to Jodl on November 24, referenced by Ziemke, *The German Northern Theater of Operations*, p.209 notes 57–59.
12. Erfurth, *Problemet Murmanbanan*, p.38–40.
13. *Ibid*, p.40.
14. Lundin, *op. cit.*, p.152; Hölter, *op. cit.*, p.64; and Erfurth, *Problemet Murmanbanan*, pp.5–6.
15. Message from Erfurth to OKH on December 5, 1941 as cited by Ziemke, *The German Northern Theater of Operations*, p. 210 and note 62.
16. Erfurth, *The Last Finnish War*, p.60. This would be true only if Kandalaksha were to be captured as well.
17. Erfurth, *Problemet Murmanbanan*, p.46.
18. Blucher, *op. cit.*, pp.271–272.
19. Erfurth, *The Last Finnish War*, p.70.
20. Mannerheim, *Memoirs*, p.443.
21. *Ibid*, pp.443–444.
22. *Ibid*, p.444.
23. Lundin, *op. cit.*, p.154, note 16.

24. Mannerheim, *Memoirs*, p.444.
25. Erfurth, *The Last Finnish War*, p.71.
26. *Ibid*, p.156.
27. Waldemar Erfurth's *Der Finnische Krieg*, pp.201–202.
28. Ziemke, *The German Northern Theater of Operations*, p.230 and note 42.
29. Erfurth, *Problemet Murmanbanan*, p.50.
30. Trevor-Roper, *op. cit.*, pp.191–193.
31. *Ibid*.
32. Erfurth, *The Last Finnish War*, p.84.
33. Ziemke, *The German Northern Theater of Operations*, p.232.
34. Erfurth, *The Last Finnish War*, p.84.
35. Erfurth, *Problemet Murmanbanan*, p.52.
36. *Ibid*, p.53.
37. Erfurth, *The Last Finnish War*, p.86.
38. Mannerheim, *Memoirs*, p.456.
39. Lundin, *op. cit.*, p.160.
40. Erfurth, *The Last Finnish War*, p.91.
41. Lundin, *op. cit.*, p.162.
42. Army Group North War Diary entries from August 8, 21, and 28 as cited in Ziemke, *The German Northern Theater of Operations*, p.234.
43. Greiner, *op. cit.*, pp.405–406.
44. Erfurth, *The Last Finnish War*, p.87.
45. Mannerheim, *Memoirs*, pp.457–458.
46. Erfurth, *The Last Finnish War*, p.89.
47. A southward advance by the Finns on the Karelian Isthmus would have closed this all-important route of supply for the Soviets in Leningrad.
48. Ziemke, *The German Northern Theater of Operations*, p.235.

EIGHT
FRONT WITHOUT COMBAT ACTIVITY— JANUARY 1943–JUNE 1944

The period from early 1943 to June 1944 was a time of total stagnation in Finland and a period of increased friction between the coalition partners extending from disagreement on military and operational matters to political and economic issues. The topics ranged from direct and indirect Finnish negotiations with the Soviets (without informing Germany)—to such seemingly mundane but highly important issues as the activities of the Finnish free press, the increasingly active peace movement, Finnish support for the Estonians, the disbanding of the Finnish SS Battalion, the Jewish issue, and German demands on the Finnish economy. Most of these issues are beyond the scope of this book while others are woven into the text at appropriate points. Many had their origins in waning German fortunes on other war fronts.

It is not unusual in a democracy for the public to be highly supportive of a military venture at the outset when effectively explained by the government as being absolutely necessary for a nation's security or its vital interests. Public support invariably declines as a conflict becomes protracted, as reverses are encountered, as losses mount, and when the original reasons for the conflict become questionable. In Finland's case the situation was infinitely worse since it was in coalition with and dependent for its very survival on a dictatorial government in Germany, where there was little or no understanding at the highest levels for the role public support played in Finland. German expectations that the Finns would deal decisively with public dissidence ran into well-ingrained democratic values in Finland.

Leningrad and Other Fronts in 1943
Things looked bleak for the Germans on the eastern front at the start of

241

1943. The fate of the German 6th Army was being sealed in the momentous and decisive battle of Stalingrad. According to General Erfurth, Marshal Mannerheim had by now lost faith in German fortunes and began preparing himself and the nation for an unsuccessful end to the war.[1]

The Finns had a special interest in what was happening in their immediate neighborhood—the Leningrad front. They were therefore alarmed when General Jodl issued the OKW estimate of the situation on January 2, 1943 that brought the unwelcome news that a German attack on Leningrad was not possible at this time. Instead, the German High Command expected a major Soviet offensive on the Leningrad front in the near future.

The Soviet offensive to open a land-bridge to Leningrad began on January 16. While they broke through the "bottleneck" and managed to open a corridor to Leningrad on January 19, the ferocious fighting lasted until the end of March and cost the Soviets 270,000 casualties. The Germans managed to restrict the Soviet corridor to a width of six miles, which could be brought under artillery fire thus reducing its usefulness.

Vague communiqués from the OKW were slow to arrive in Finland and they were viewed with increasing skepticism as the Finns compared them with what was reported by radio from Stockholm and Moscow. Anglo-American and Russian communiqués published in the free Finnish press spurred the desire for a separate peace. The news about breaking the Leningrad siege was followed by news of the destruction of the German 6th Army at Stalingrad, the retreat of German armies and those of their allies from the Volga and Don to the Dnieper, and the precarious German-Italian situation in North Africa.

All this news had damaging psychological effects in Finland. Senior Finnish officers viewed the struggle in the east and the unfavorable course of events in Africa with increasing alarm. They saw the industrial power of the Western Allies joined with the vast manpower of the Soviet Union as an unbeatable combination for Germany and its allies.

The day after Stalingrad fell, there was a high-level policy meeting at Finnish military headquarters which included Mannerheim, Ryti, and several influential members of the cabinet. Those assembled concluded that there had been a decisive turning point in the war and that Finland should conclude peace at the earliest opportunity. Parliament was briefed in a secret session on February 9, 1943, to the effect that Germany could no longer win the war. Mannerheim explains that the briefing "had the effect of a cold shower" on the members of parliament.[2]

The Germans were fully aware of the importance of Leningrad for the Finns. On March 13, 1943, Hitler therefore ordered Army Group North to prepare an offensive in late summer to capture Leningrad. This was wishful thinking. Army Group North, fighting a defensive battle, was primarily worried about what the Soviets would do. It was especially fearful that the Soviets would strike at the boundary between Army Group Center and Army Group North south of Lake Ilmen. This could split the German front and pin Army Group North against the Baltic coast.

Nevertheless, Army Group North proceeded to plan for the capture of Leningrad—code-named Operation *Parkplatz*. Much of the siege artillery brought north by the 11th Army was still in place but Army Group North needed eight or nine divisions in order to launch the offensive. These were promised only after Army Group South had completed its operation to pinch off the large Russian salient at Orel west of Kursk—Operation *Zittadelle*.

Operation *Zittadelle* was launched on July 5, 1943 but after initial successes, fortune quickly turned against the Germans as the Soviets launched a strong counteroffensive and the conflict developed into the largest tank battle in history. The Germans were forced to retreat and the much hoped-for success turned into a serious German defeat.[3] As the fighting spread the Soviets broke through the German front on the Donets River by the end of July. In August and September the German armies were driven back from the Donets River to the Dnieper River. By the end of September the Soviets had captured Kharkov and Günther von Kluge's Army Group Center had been forced back to the edge of the Pripet Marshes.

Disastrous news for the Germans was piling up during the summer and fall of 1943. Sicily was invaded on July 9 and by August 17 the island was in Allied hands. Hitler's ally Benito Mussolini was overthrown on July 24, 1943 and an armistice was signed with Italy.

With their offensives making rapid progress in the south at enormous losses, the Soviets turned their attention to Army Group North. A full-scale offensive to lift the siege of Leningrad was launched on July

22, 1943. Repeated Soviet attacks south of Lake Ladoga were repulsed by Army Group North in July and August. However, the Germans knew that this offered only a temporary respite; OKH ordered Army Group North to prepare a new defensive line along the Narva River and Lake Peipus, 200 kilometers southwest of Leningrad. These positions eventually became the Panther Line. This spelled the end of Operation *Parkplatz.*

OKW asked the 20th Mountain Army for its opinion about a possible withdrawal to the Panther Line. The answer stated that a withdrawal should not take place. The 20th Mountain Army argued that the Finns already felt let down by the failure of the Germans to capture Leningrad despite repeated assurances to the contrary. Dietl pointed out that after such a withdrawal the Finnish fronts on the Svir River and at Maaselkä would become indefensible and the Finns would be forced to withdraw.

Dietl went on to caution that a likely result of a withdrawal to the Panther Line would be a Finnish approach to the Soviet Union for peace. If an acceptable peace was offered, the 20th Mountain Army would be cut off and a retreat over bad roads in wintertime to Norway would be extremely hazardous. Dietl's warning was followed by a Finnish notice through Blücher, the German ambassador to Finland, that a withdrawal would have serious consequences for Finland.[4] This could only be interpreted by the Germans as a warning that Finland would be forced to leave the war if the Germans withdrew to the Panther Line.

Mannerheim also expressed concerns to General Erfurth about reports of a pending German withdrawal. OKW sent an explanatory message on October 3, 1943, where it stated that there were no intentions to withdraw but that rear positions were being constructed in case of an emergency. It was anticipated that the Finns would accept this since they had themselves been busy for weeks building secondary defensive lines.

Partisan Activities

Partisan or guerrilla warfare made its appearance in Finland, but not to the same extent as in other war theaters. The possibility of conducting effective warfare behind enemy lines became possible with the appearance of new technologies, particularly aircraft and radio communications. This new phenomenon of partisan warfare in World War II necessitated making rear-area security part of all operations and it often required substantial forces.

The problems in rear-area security during the first year of the war in Finland were limited to periodic engagements with dispersed elements of Soviet units hiding out in the forested areas as the Finnish Army advanced, particularly in Karelia. These emaciated individuals were forced by hunger and cold to make their appearance and were quickly captured and disarmed by the Finns.

The rather dormant situation changed in the summer of 1942 with partisan warfare most profound in the rear areas of the 20th Mountain Army, especially in the Salla area. Organized guerrilla units were sent through German lines by the Soviets. Long stretches of the 20th Mountain Army front were guarded only by patrols or outposts. The German units in the Kandalaksha sector, for example, had no contact with adjacent units and it was therefore relatively easy for Soviet guerrilla bands to bypass the German corps on their flanks in that area and on the Litsa River. These guerrilla bands made surprise attacks on German and Finnish outposts. Traffic behind the front soon became insecure.

The Germans instituted security measures. Special companies and battalions were sent into the border wilderness off the flanks of the corps. These mobile units carried out antiguerrilla warfare, trying to sever the return routes of the guerrilla bands. This was a difficult task in the trackless wilderness during the summer but it became much easier in the fall after the first snow had fallen.

The Finnish border police and raider battalions were particularly well suited for antiguerrilla warfare since they were recruited from the border population. These men were predominantly settlers, lumberjacks, trappers, and reindeer breeders living along the border. They were far superior to the German soldiers in this kind of warfare.

These Finnish irregular battalions were particularly appreciated by General Dietl, himself an experienced mountaineer and hunter. Four of these battalions (plus the Ivalo Battalion on the Murmansk front) were left under the control of the 20th Mountain Army after the relief of the III Finnish Corps. The Germans considered these battalions indispensable assets and they strenuously resisted efforts by Marshal Mannerheim to bring them back under Finnish control.

Partisan activities increased significantly in the rear area of the 20th

Mountain Army after the thaw set in during the spring of 1943. Traffic on the Arctic Ocean Highway was no longer safe and the lives of Finns and Germans even deep in the rear areas were in jeopardy. It made little difference whether a person was military or civilian.

Both the 20th Mountain Army and the Finnish High Command wrestled with this problem. In trying to come up with effective counter-measures the continuous discussions between the two headquarters resulted in friction. General Dietl suggested that the Finns chose between two alternatives. The first was to reinforce the frontier guards. The second was to evacuate the civilian population from the border region east of the road leading from Kuusamo through Salla to Ivalo.[5]

Mannerheim turned down both German proposals. He maintained that the increase in the strength of the border guards could only be accomplished by a reduction in the army and the evacuation of the border area would encounter much opposition from the populace and disrupt the economy. The Finns decided to activate a motorized unit for the protection of traffic along the Arctic Ocean Highway. This unit was placed under the command of Colonel Villamo, the Finnish liaison officer at Dietl's headquarters. As a long-standing member of the border guards he was well suited for the job. The Finns also issued weapons to the civilian population in the border regions.

On January 11, 1943 Mannerheim requested that General Dietl return four of the five irregular battalions attached to the 20th Mountain Army. Mannerheim's request resulted in weeks of discussions.

Dietl considered the issue very important since the units in question were not only needed for rear-area security but for out-posting and patrolling the gap between the northern and southern parts of his sector. No progress was made in the negotiations between Mannerheim and Dietl and the OKW became involved. Not wanting to ruffle the feathers of the Finnish marshal at this critical juncture in the war, OKW directed General Erfurth to work out a compromise.

Mannerheim upped his demand on February 7, 1943 to include the fifth battalion—the Ivalo Battalion. After lengthy negotiations Mannerheim dropped the demand for the Ivalo Battalion but only after the 20th Mountain Army agreed to return the other four to Finnish control. Dietl, while having to accept the results, felt that he had made a bad bargain. OKW may not have fully appreciated the importance of these battalions to the 20th Mountain Army and decided not to get involved in an argument with the Finns over a few battalions at a time when their support was beginning to waver.

OKW Planning Conferences

At an OKW planning conference on January 14, 1943, it was decided not to give the 20th Mountain Army any offensive missions in 1943. The planned operation against the Rybachiy Peninsula—Operation *Wiesengrund*—could not be executed because XIX Mountain Corps lacked the necessary strength. Operation *Lachsfang* against Kandalaksha required an offensive by the Finns against Belomorsk at the same time, which the Germans had finally come to view as something that could not be expected. Furthermore, such an operation required an additional division plus two regiments which could not be spared in the dire circumstances in which German Army found itself.

The OKW planning conference also made a complete revision of its view of Finland as a cobelligerent. It amounted to writing Finland off as an ally that could be counted on to carry its own weight. This estimate must have been heavily influenced by the refusal of the Finns to take part in any offensive operations over the past year since nothing else of consequence had transpired on the ground to warrant the negativism contained in the estimate. The Finnish operations in 1941 and 1942 had been very successful and achieved virtually all goals. The revised estimate concluded that the Finns would not be able to prevent setbacks in case of a major Soviet attack because their defenses were poorly constructed, they had few reserves, and the Finnish units were "not imbued with the spirit of holding to the last man."[6]

A planning conference for the whole Scandinavian region took place at OKW in mid-March 1943. It included representatives from the OKW operations staff, the chief of staff of the 20th Mountain Army, and the operations officer of the Army of Norway. The conferees agreed that a British-American landing in north Norway was possible but they also agreed that such a landing would only imperil the German position in Scandinavia if it were accompanied by a Soviet offensive. It was concluded that this was not likely on the rather shaky ground of mistrust between the Soviets and the Western Allies. A more logical reason for the unlikelihood of a Soviet offensive was provided by the 20th Mountain Army. It reported that the Soviets had withdrawn three divisions and two brigades from the northern front. This was a strong indication that the Soviets did not plan an attack or anticipate one by the Germans. The conference recognized that the fall of Stalingrad had caused a decisive shift in Finnish opinion and that the Finnish government and the Finnish military leaders no longer believed in a German victory. The conferees agreed that a major reason for the defeatist attitude of the Finnish military leadership could be found in the pessimistic reports provided by the Finnish liaison officer at OKH, General Talvela. The chief of staff of the 20th Mountain Army opined that the Finns were preparing to exit the war and could only be prevented from doing so by a convincing German military victory in the summer of 1943 or by their inability to obtain acceptable peace terms from the Soviets. General Jodl was more optimistic. He believed that the Finns would keep faith with Germany.

Stagnation

In striking contrast to what was happening in other theaters of the war, the fronts in Finland remained very quiet after the Soviet spring offensives in 1942. This situation is exemplified by a silly and aimless argument between the 20th Mountain Army and the OKW about how best to designate the front. OKW favored labeling it "the front without combat activity" (*Front ohne Kampfhandlungen*) while the 20th Mountain Army favored, because of continued minor casualty figures, "the front without significant combat activity" (*Front ohne ghrössere Kampfhandlungen*).[7]

Whatever action took place was limited to very light trench warfare. Neither side made any effort to increase combat activity. The troops spent their time improving positions, living quarters, and their supply routes. The front lines remained essentially as they had been at the end of the summer of 1941.

The OKW believed that a major Soviet offensive could be launched against the 20th Mountain Army at the end of the winter 1943, probably in the Murmansk sector. Dietl expected a Soviet offensive as early as the beginning of February 1943. Jodl's letter conveying the OKW estimate promised reinforcements, including a division from Norway if the situation so dictated.

While the Finns were beginning to search for a way out of the war, they had to prepare for the eventuality that the price could be unacceptable. Therefore, they continued to call additional year groups to the colors. The second half of year group 1924 was inducted on March 8, 1943, and the first half of year group 1925 was inducted four days later. The second half of the 1925 year group was called to the colors on October 12, 1943. Individuals from older age groups were called up two weeks later. On October 28, 1943, the Finnish military headquarters announced the activation of three new mixed brigades. They also requested enough artillery from Germany to activate eight more artillery battalions. Most of the requests were granted by OKW but not delivered in time for the activation of the brigades at the end of the year. These brigades initially had to do without artillery.

The Finns suggested a modification to the boundary between Finnish and German forces in central Finland. They proposed that the boundary be shifted northward and the 20th Mountain Army agreed. The new boundary ran through the southern part of the German area in the Kestenga sector and necessitated a shift in forces by the XVIII Mountain Corps. The left flank of the Finnish forces became anchored on the Poposero River.

It is ironic that the ratio of forces on the Finnish fronts was decisively in favor of the Germans and Finns precisely at the time when decisions on offensive operations had become gridlocked.

The Soviets began their withdrawal in the spring of 1943 and an estimate of the situation by the Finnish High Command on September 15, 1943 reported that 400,000 Finnish troops were confronted by 160,000–180,000 Soviet troops. The 20th Mountain Army with its 200,000 men faced about 90,000 Soviet troops. In the whole theater the Finns and Germans numbered over 600,000 while the Soviets had only about 270,000 troops. The ratio was at least 2:1 and a more favorable condition for successful offensive operations never existed during the entire war. When the quality of the troops on both sides is factored in the Germans and Finns held a decisive advantage.

A joint Finnish-German offensive would have had a great chance of success in late 1943. The Finnish refusal to exploit this advantage has been harshly criticized both during and after the war by German and Finnish officers.

An offensive by the Finns and the 20th Mountain Army in the fall of 1943 would not have seriously influenced the deteriorating German position. They could undoubtedly have broken through the Soviet defenses and relieved Army Group North by driving south from both Ladogan Karelia and the Karelian Isthmus. This would have afforded Army Group North a badly needed but only temporary relief. The Germans and Finns could, without doubt, have cut the Murmansk Railroad in late 1943 but that link to the outside world was no longer vital for the Soviet Union. Its potential loss was more than compensated for by a great increase in Soviet production, by supplies flowing into ports in the Far East, and the opening of a new supply route through the Persian Gulf.

It is not an exaggeration to state that the German and Finnish forces in Finland were practically on a peacetime status from the summer of 1942 to the summer of 1944. The quietness of the fronts in Finland must have struck the soldiers as ominous since it could be interpreted as a Soviet decision to let them wilt while their fate was decided elsewhere.

Führer Directive No. 50

War is an extension of politics and must remain subordinate. This is invariably a problem, particularly in coalition warfare. Finnish leaders were fully aware that an offensive beyond the current positions would result in an immediate declaration of war by the US, their only friend of any consequence in the Allied camp. The US was viewed as Finland's best hope in securing an acceptable settlement with the Soviet Union. Taken together with the view that Germany could no longer prevail in the war, this conclusion dictated a policy designed to keep the US from declaring war. Finnish insistence that their current war was a purely Finnish–Soviet affair—continuation of the Winter War—was unrealistic but colored their outlook on events. Finnish military leaders exercised great care not to put themselves in a position where they could be blamed by the government and parliament for a US declaration of war.

We can safely assume that Germany, the Soviet Union, and the United States were fully aware of the Finnish dilemma. Germany's knowledge of the state of affairs is undoubtedly the reason they did not press the Finns to undertake offensive operations in 1943. The Soviet Union's knowledge allowed them to take the risk of removing great numbers of troops from the German-Finnish fronts in 1943. The US was the trump card and Ziemke is probably right when he writes that an offensive by the Finns in late 1943 "would in the long run have been suicidal for the Finnish nation."[8]

The OKW operations staff informed Hitler on September 25, 1943 that there were increasing signs that Finland desired to leave the war and it was expected that they would take action in this direction if Army Group North was forced to withdraw. This warning resulted in the OKW issuing Führer Directive No. 50 three days later (September 28). It dealt with a possible Finnish collapse and the preparations required by the 20th Mountain Army for a withdrawal to north Finland and north Norway. Parts of the directive read:

> It is our duty to bear in mind the possibility that Finland may drop out of the war or collapse.
>
> In that case it will be the immediate task of 20th Mountain Army to continue to hold the Northern area, which is vital to our war industry, by moving back the front to a line running through Karesuando, Ivalo, and the sector at present held by the 19th Mountain Corps. 230th and 270th Infantry Divisions will come under its command in due course.[9]

The anticipated operation involved withdrawing the two corps in central Finland (XXXVI Mountain Corps and XVIII Mountain Corps) northward and simultaneously swinging their eastward orientation to one more southerly. The two corps would tie into the XIX Mountain Corps along the new line and the army's mission would become one of defending the nickel mines. The directive ordered that preparations for carrying out the operation begin immediately and authorized direct coordination between the 20th Mountain Army and the Army of Norway. The implementing plans and preparations by the 20th Mountain Army are covered in Chapter 11.

Finnish recognition of the dangerously deteriorating military situation on the Russian front found its expression in a request on October 6, 1943 to General Erfurth for permission to reconnoiter defensive positions in the rear of the 20th Mountain Army. The Finns intended to construct fortifications in the rear of the German front. The request was based on the possibility of a German withdrawal from Lapland. General Erfurth quickly reported the Finnish request to OKW on October 7 and recommended that a top-level representative be sent to brief Marshal Mannerheim.

General Jodl's Visit to Finland
This was the background for General Jodl's visit to Finland on October
14 and 15, 1943. He had orders from Hitler to give Mannerheim a complete orientation on the overall military situation and to discuss questions of mutual interest. He also carried a personal letter from Hitler to
President Ryti, which was delivered by Ambassador Blücher. Hitler
scolded Ryti for the anti-German attitude of the Finnish press and the
lack of supportive internal policies in Finland. Ryti replied to Hitler at
the end of the month in a positive tone but without making any specific commitments.[10]

Jodl was well received and had a lengthy meeting with Mannerheim
on October 14, 1943. It was a far-ranging discussion in which the
German tried to calm some of the Finnish fears. Jodl explained that the
defection of Italy had little military significance since that country had
never been a strong partner in the alliance. The Germans expected an
invasion in France but they were confident that it would result in a disastrous defeat for the British and Americans. In fact, the Germans were
eager to deal with that threat since it would put an end to the fear of a
second front and allow Germany to move troops that were now tied
down in France to the eastern front. Jodl acknowledged that the situation in the sector of Army Group North was dangerous and there had
been discussions of pulling back its northern flank. Such suggestions
had been rejected out of consideration for the Finns. For his part,
Mannerheim continued his insistence on reconnoitering the area behind
the 20th Mountain Army with the intention of building fortifications.
The OKW agreed to this request on October 26, 1943.

Jodl pointed out to the Finns that Germany knew about Finnish
efforts to get out of the war. Commenting on this Jodl stated: "No
nation has a higher duty than that which is dictated by concern for the
existence of the Homeland. All other considerations must take second
place before this concern, and no one has the right to demand that a
nation shall go to its death for another."[11] Jodl went on to lay out
Finnish possibilities as he saw them. One was to continue the war at the
side of Germany which he viewed as the least risky. The other possibilities were to conclude a separate peace with the Soviet Union, conclude
an armistice with the assistance of the Western Allies, or to join the
Russians in the final battle against Germany. With respect to a separate
peace or armistice, he did not expect that Finland would be shown

much mercy at the clutches of Stalin. As to the last possibility, Jodl found it incompatible with the Nordic conception of loyalty and honor. Mannerheim writes that he was favorably impressed by the frankness of General Jodl and the regard he had for Finnish difficulties. Nevertheless, Mannerheim notes that the strategic perspective which Jodl laid out failed to influence his own view of the situation.[12]

Both the Finns and Germans made short speeches at the dinner that followed the meeting between Jodl and Mannerheim. Jodl closed his with these remarks: "We shall never surrender. We will never betray our allies. We will fight to the final victory." According to Blücher, these remarks were welcomed by those present by great applause.[13] Mannerheim was apparently so satisfied by Jodl's explanations that he asked him to delay his return to Germany so that he could brief General Walden, the minister of defense.

A few days after Jodl's visit, General Dietl visited Helsinki and Minister of Defense Walden asked to see him. In a lengthy meeting General Walden told Dietl that he disapproved of the groundless writings in the Finnish press about a separate peace and he assured his visitor that Finland would remain faithful to its brotherhood in arms with Germany.[14]

The 20th Mountain Army availed itself of Jodl's visit to argue strenuously against Führer Directive 50. The objections by the 20th Mountain Army dealt primarily with the supply situation. While it recognized that it was the best-supplied German army and had eight or nine months of supplies stockpiled in Finland and Norway, it viewed its ability to hold out in northern Finland for any length of time as very dim. The army viewed itself as isolated in an effort to hold a mining district that would be of no use if Finland left the war. The army was quite skeptical of the navy and Luftwaffe's ability to secure the sea supply routes around Norway and to keep the enemy from interdicting the ore traffic. The 20th Mountain Army recommended a withdrawal across the Baltic in the event that a situation as depicted in Directive 50 should arise. While the OKW agreed with the 20th Mountain Army's assessment it did not believe that a withdrawal across the Baltic was possible or that Hitler would agree giving up the mines prematurely.

It appeared that some stability was achieved in Finnish–German relations as a result of Jodl's visit. This prompted Hitler to order that Directive 50 should be regarded only as a contingency measure and that no action should be taken for the time being. Several changes in senior German command personnel took place in Finland in late 1943. General Ferdinand Schörner, the commander of the XIX Mountain Corps, departed Finland on October 25 and he was replaced by General der Gebirgstruppe Georg Ritter von Hengl, the commander of the 2nd Mountain Division. General Stumpff, the commander of the 5th Air Fleet, was also given a new assignment on November 2, 1943.

Situation on the Leningrad Front in early 1944
The year 1944 opened with heavy fighting along the entire eastern front. The German armies, bled white in numerous battles in 1943, found themselves withdrawing from one position to the next.

The situation south of Leningrad continued to deteriorate at the end of 1943 and the beginning of 1944. The Soviets made a deep penetration southwest of Velikie Luki at Nevel on November 5, 1943. This deep penetration tore open the front of the 16th German Army. The situation was kept from becoming a total disaster by a lack of follow-up by the Soviets. The slow-moving Soviet military machinery failed to quickly exploit the breakthrough which would have outflanked the new Panther position and might have caused the whole Army Group North's front to collapse.

The German situation in the Leningrad area remained precarious and this led Army Group North, supported by the OKH, to propose an immediate withdrawal to the Panther Line in order to avoid a disaster. Hitler failed to make a timely decision because he worried about the impact of such a withdrawal on the Finns. Nothing happened in the first half of January 1944 to force Hitler's hand since the Soviets were not ready to exploit their earlier success that had created the Nevel salient.

This situation began to change on January 14, 1943, when the Soviets started offensive operations against the 18th Army. They began with strong attacks in the Oranienbaum-Leningrad sectors and against the army's right flank at Novgorod. The hopes that the 18th Army might be able to contain the Soviet offensive vanished by January 17 when the Soviets broke out of the Oranienbaum pocket and began to encircle Novgorod. Field Marshal Küchler gave orders for a withdrawal from the shores of the Gulf of Finland and east of Leningrad on January 18.

The news of the events south and west of Leningrad was received with trepidation in Finland. While the German communiqué admitted heavy defensive fighting in the areas south and west of Leningrad, they maintained that the Soviet offensive had been repulsed. The Soviet broadcasts, on the other hand reported great victories. The Finns soon learned that the Soviet reports were closer to the truth as they had made deep penetrations into the German lines and the 18th Army was in mortal danger. If it continued to hold fast in the center, the two wings would most likely be enveloped and the army would find its lines of communications to the west severed.

Field Marshal Küchler requested permission to make a withdrawal that would shorten his front lines. It involved the line east of Leningrad and the city of Novgorod. This would free up forces that he could use as reserves. Hitler agreed reluctantly but then changed his mind. He was told that it was too late as orders for the withdrawal had already been issued. The army group commander was convinced that he would have to retreat to the Panther Line and that he would not be able to make a stand short of that line. Hitler did not agree despite the fact that Field Marshal Küchler's infantry strength was down to 17,000 troops. Küchler made two trips to Hitler's headquarters to plead his case. Hitler demanded that the withdrawal be limited to the Luga River, a line that basically did not exist and one that the Soviets had already penetrated. Hitler relieved Küchler of his command on January 31, 1943, and placed General Walter Model in command of Army Group North.

Mannerheim doubted that Army Group North would be able to extricate itself and occupy a new defensive line. However, the 18th Army carried out a masterly withdrawal under nearly hopeless conditions without stopping at any intermediate positions. It managed even to bring along all the heavy artillery from the Leningrad area.

OKW's Offer of Help and the Finnish Response

The loss of the territory south of Leningrad left Finnish positions exposed in East Karelia, on the Karelian Isthmus, and along the Svir River. They formed deep salients into Soviet-controlled territories and invited attack. The danger that the German withdrawal posed for the Finns was recognized by the Germans. Consequently, the OKW sent a message to Mannerheim on January 31, 1944, asking him for suggestions on how Germany could help the Finns compensate for the increased Soviet threat they now faced. The message also assured Mannerheim that the 20th Mountain Army would remain in Finland at full strength.

The Finns made a quick response to the German Liaison Staff at Finnish Headquarters on February 1, 1944. The list they presented was long. It included 4,000 M42 machineguns, 200 Soviet 152mm guns, 60 122mm guns, a renewal of the call for artillery for the three brigades being formed, and a request that the 20th Mountain Army take over the Ukhta sector so that the 3rd Finnish Division could be released for other missions. The requirements were sent to OKW on February 3.

General Dietl learned about the Finnish demands and lodged an immediate protest over the request that he take over the Ukhta sector. Dietl had become irritated by previous Finnish protests against the withdrawal of even minor German units from Finland. He felt that it was a waste of manpower to tie down additional German troops on a secondary front and felt that the Finns, who had not accepted the concept of total war, were quite capable of creating reserves from their own resources. Dietl, who was obviously upset, went even further. He questioned the audacity of the Finns in "laying claims on the German Army which is already carrying the entire burden."[15] Instead, Dietl recommended that Mannerheim be requested not to object if the 20th Mountain Army sent all the troops it could spare to Army Group North. The OKW, apparently trying to appease the Finns, rejected Dietl's protests on February 6 and ordered him to effect the relief of the 3rd Finnish Division as quickly as possible.

Negotiations between the Germans and Finns for establishing a new boundary line between the Finnish and German fronts were initiated on February 14, 1944 between General Heinrichs and General Erfurth. The boundary had to be shifted south as a consequence of the Germans taking responsibility for the Ukhta sector. It was not simple to arrive at an acceptable solution, particularly since Dietl was doing so against his will. It took several weeks to settle some of the issues.

After the news of the German reverses south of Leningrad, the Finns called the first half of the 1926 year group to the colors with a reporting date of February 21, 1943. Mannerheim, seeing the need for the country's best-qualified commanders to be at the front, also recalled General Talvela as Finnish representative at OKH and replaced him with Lieutenant General Hugo Viktor Österman. As another precaution, Mannerheim moved the newly formed Finnish armored division from Petrozavodsk to the Viipuri area.

Despite Germany agreeing to virtually everything on the Finnish requirement list of February 3, the Finnish government's worry about the country's future was not alleviated. The withdrawal of Army Group North, the German reverses on other fronts, and increased Soviet bombings of Finnish towns only added to the desire of many to end the war. A heavy air raid on Helsinki on February 6, 1944, caused much damage as did another raid on February 27. The Finns requested German help to protect against Soviet air raids and the Germans responded quickly. German night fighters arrived at Helsinki on February 15, 1944. This was a gracious step when one considers that it was only possible through reducing the air defenses of German cities that were being bombed into rubble.

Diplomatic Negotiations and German Reactions

Efforts to arrange a separate peace between the Soviet Union and Finland had gone on since 1942 and have been touched on at various points in this book. It may be helpful to review them as we approach the decisive events in the summer of 1944.

In his observations of the Finnish political scene Ziemke makes these very accurate observations:

To save what they could of their credit with the democracies, to avoid falling completely under the influence of Germany, and yet to preserve their existence as a nation, the Finns were forced to equivocate, claiming for themselves an exceptional status as cobelligerents and speaking of their German friends as brothers-in-arms rather than allies. These semantic distinctions, which on the surface only created a somewhat ludicrous picture of tiny Finland fighting the Soviet Union and professing itself mildly surprised to find the Germans there too, in fact were evidence of forces which were to influence Finland's entire conduct of war. It must be said to the credit of the Germans that it was mainly their unusual and, for themselves, unprofitable restraint which allowed the Finns to play an independent game to the extent that they did.

Hitler's visit to Finland to pay his respect to Mannerheim on his seventy-fifth birthday on June 4, 1942, had been an unwelcome event for the Finns. While the visit was covered favorably in the Finnish press, it resulted in an immediate deterioration of US–Finnish diplomatic relations. A reduced level of diplomatic relations kept the hope alive that the US would still be a positive influence in Finland's negotiations with the Soviet Union. American–Finnish relations were not helped by Marshal Mannerheim's return visit to Germany in late June where he was accorded the full range of courtesies. The two-day visit ended with Mannerheim flying back to Finland in Hitler's private plane.

This may have been the high point in German–Finnish relations as they deteriorated significantly in the wake of the German failure to achieve a decisive victory in the summer campaign against the Soviet Union. There was a noticeable change in public opinion. This trend accelerated with the news of German defeats in Russia during the winter of 1943 and the troubling reports from North Africa, coming as they did not long after President Roosevelt recalled his ambassador in Helsinki. Only a legation secretary remained to represent the US.

There was an election in Finland in the middle of February 1943. This gave President Ryti, who was re-elected, an opportunity to reshuffle his cabinet in a way that would make the government more acceptable to the Allies. The more pro-German foreign minister Rolf Witting was replaced by Henrik Ramsay who had connections to both the US and Great Britain. This was an unmistakable signal of a change in policy and the US transmitted an offer to establish contact between Finland and the Soviet Union on March 20, 1943.

Ramsay had little experience in diplomacy and naively traveled to Berlin on March 25, 1943 to seek that country's friendly acquiescence in Finland's withdrawal from the war. Ribbentrop quickly dispelled Ramsay's illusions. The Germans were not about to tolerate any flirtations between their "brothers-in-arms" and the Soviets. Instead of acquiescing in Ramsay's request, Ribbentrop demanded that Finland quickly reject the US offer and that the Finns give a written assurance that Finland would not negotiate a separate peace.

The US proposal had not involved any specifics, only an offer to mediate between Finland and the Soviet Union. That part of the German demand was therefore not difficult to deal with; it only involved declining the offer at mediation. Ribbentrop demanded that the text of the Finnish reply to the US be shown to the Germans before it was sent.

This was done before Ramsay departed Germany. The second part of the German demand was the most difficult to meet since it would nullify something Finland had insisted on since the beginning of the war—the status as an independent cobelligerent. The Finns delayed their answer until May 16, 1943 and it took the form of a speech by the prime minister where he stated that the Finns would fight to the end rather than submit itself to the mercy of the Soviet Union. The text of the speech was sent to Berlin with the explanation that it represented the official Finnish attitude. Ribbentrop did not find the answer specific enough and recalled Ambassador Blücher for two months.

Sweden also began to exert pressure on Finland to withdraw from the war. In July 1943 Sweden forwarded an oral offer from the Soviets to discuss peace. The Finns rejected this offer but the same month Ramsay informed the US in a personal message to the Department of State through the Finnish embassy in Portugal that they would not join the Germans in resisting a US invasion of Norway. According to Mannerheim the message went as far as stating that the Finns would not resist even if the US extended its operations into Finland, "an operation which would naturally win my full approval."[16]

In August 1943 three members of the Finnish parliament presented a petition to President Ryti signed by 33 prominent Finns requesting that steps be taken not only to strengthen relations with the US, but to find a way out of the war. We need to put this in the context of the fact that the tide of war had by now turned clearly against Germany. This petition was published in a Swedish newspaper and it touched off a public discussion that showed clear preference among the Finns for a separate peace.

Stalin had promised Churchill and Roosevelt at Teheran in December 1943 to make a peace offer to the Finns that would preserve their national independence. That peace offer was now made through the Soviet ambassador in Stockholm, Alexandra Kollontai. Finland did not dare jeopardize its relationship with the US and dispatched a former prime minister, Dr. Juho K. Paasikivi, to Stockholm to receive the Soviet offer. Paasikivi returned from Stockholm on February 24, 1944, with the Soviet terms. They involved the restoration of the 1940 borders, Finnish internment of the German troops in Finland, war reparations, and the demobilization of the armed forces. The Soviet offer was more stringent than expected and it was rejected by the Finns, particularly the part dealing with the internment of German troops which they considered impossible. However, both the Finns and Soviets indicated willingness for further negotiations and this led to an invitation for a Finnish delegation to come to Moscow. This may have been a genuine action on the part of the Soviets, or they may have hoped for a Finnish rejection which would have allowed them to disregard the promise made by Stalin at Teheran and given them a free hand to deal with the Finns on their own terms. The invitation was accepted and Paasikivi and former Foreign Minister Carl Enckell flew to Moscow on March 26, 1944.

The Finnish delegation returned from Moscow on April 1, 1944. The conditions given the Finns for a peace were no more lenient than those given in Stockholm. They were:

1. Internment or elimination of German troops in Finland, with Russian support if necessary.
2. Restoration of the 1940 peace treaty and Finnish withdrawal to the boundary established by that treaty.
3. Immediate release of Soviet prisoners of war.
4. Demobilization of the Finnish armed forces.
5. Reparations to the amount of $600 million over five years.
6. Surrender of the Pechenga area in return for Hanko.

These conditions were made public on April 3, 1944. The Finnish government was particularly resistant to the requirement for the internment or elimination of the 20th Mountain Army, the demobilization of the armed forces, and the hefty reparations. The parliament endorsed the government's position on April 12, 1944, and the Finnish answer was provided to the Soviets through the Swedish government. The answer left the door open for further negotiations.

The alarm in Finland that had resulted in Paasikivi's visit to Stockholm had subsided by the beginning of March 1944. General Model had brought Army Group North back to the Panther Line and managed to establish a somewhat stable front. The stabilization of this front had a calming effect on the charged political atmosphere in Finland. The German occupation of Hungary in March 1944 also demonstrated the fate that could befall a defector from the German cause.

The Finnish attempt to find a way out of the war came as no surprise to the Germans. The Germans at first adopted a wait-and-see attitude since they did not think the Finns were ready for the expected harsh Soviet terms. However, Hitler began taking steps to bind Finland irrevocably to the fortunes of Germany as soon as General Model managed to stabilize the military situation on the Narva front. The Germans began reducing the flow of weapons to Finland and in early April 1944 he directed Dietl to inform Mannerheim that further German weapons would not be provided until the possibility of them falling into Soviet hands was removed.

The free Finnish press, which had been very supportive of the war in 1941, had now turned hostile towards Germany. Stories condemning the actions of German troops in Estonia and Italy, occupation and repression in Hungary, and the imposition of martial law in Denmark began to circulate in the Finnish media. This infuriated the leadership in Germany. Keitel made it clear to the Finns that these conditions were intolerable for the German troops in Finland. With respect to negotiations with the Soviets, the rather feeble Finnish explanation to Germany was that they were necessary to convince the Finnish people that obtaining acceptable terms from the Soviet Union was impossible.

Military Events in Finland in early 1944

While the fronts in Finland continued quiet in early 1944, by February unmistakable signs appeared of a large Soviet buildup of forces in the sectors of the 20th Mountain Army. In the opinion of both the 20th Mountain Army and the OKW, these signs pointed to a full-scale Soviet offensive. In mid-March the 20th Mountain Army and the Finnish High Command concluded that the new troops which had appeared in front of the 20th Mountain Army were forces withdrawn from the Finnish Maaselkä front. It was estimated that the forces opposing the Germans in the Kestenga and Kandalaksha sectors had grown from about 100,000 to at least 150,000 (possibly 165,000). All intelligence pointed to a large-scale Soviet offensive before the end of the month.

On March 13, 1944 Dietl requested that Mannerheim delay the withdrawal of the 3rd Finnish Division. This division had been withdrawn from the line in the Ukhta sector but had not yet moved out of the area. Dietl wanted the division left behind the boundary of the German and Finnish fronts. Dietl also wanted two Finnish battalions left in the Ukhta sector for the next four weeks. Mannerheim agreed to leave the two battalions in the Ukhta sector and to station the reinforced 11th Infantry Regiment in the Suomussalmi-Kuusamo area but he reiterated his intention to move the rest of the 3rd Division to the Karelian Isthmus.

It appeared to the Germans that the Soviets were continuing to switch forces from the Karelian front to the Kestenga and Kandalaksha area. The Germans viewed this as preparation for striking a severe blow against the 20th Mountain Army at the same time as they were negotiating with the Finns. The greatest threat was in the XXXVI Mountain Corps sector where the Soviets had brought up two new divisions and four brigades. They had also brought up additional artillery and rocket launchers and were in process of extending their right flank northward in an attempt to envelop the German left.

On March 22, 1944 Dietl renewed his appeal to Mannerheim to transfer a Finnish division to central Finland. On the next day Dietl informed his army that Soviet attack preparations were completed and that an attack could be expected at any time. He ordered his troops to hold their well-prepared positions at all costs. His stirring order of the day ended with the ominous words, "There is no road back."[17]

Marshal Mannerheim had now become more accommodating to Dietl's requests. While he could not spare a division as Dietl had requested, he agreed on March 25, 1944, to transfer the reinforced Finnish 3rd Brigade to the Lake Kemi area. The Germans were well prepared for the anticipated Soviet offensive and the victor of Narvik, at the end of his career, may have achieved another spectacular success. However, the Soviet offensive did not materialize. It remains a mystery why the Soviets did not attack. Perhaps they never intended to attack and the whole buildup may have been a successful deceptive maneuver.

In an apparent attempt to influence Finnish attitudes in their negotiations with the Soviets, Field Marshal Keitel sent a message to Mannerheim on April 2, 1944, expressing appreciation for the accommodation of Dietl's request by the transfer of the 3rd Finnish Brigade. He expressed the opinion that this action signaled Finnish intentions to continue the war. He also leveled mild criticism at the Finnish peace movement and the fact that this could possibly lead to a lowering of the fighting spirit of the Finnish Army. In view of the strong Finnish interest in the Narva front he assured Mannerheim that the situation there had stabilized and invited the Finn to judge for himself by sending a delegation of Finnish officers to that front.

Mannerheim accepted Keitel's invitation on April 3, 1944. He respectfully rejected the German notions about the fighting spirit of the Finnish Army. German arrangements for the inspection trip by Colonel Valo Nihtilä, chief of operations of the Finnish General Staff, and his group, in the second week of April, were well planned. The Finns were apparently impressed by German defensive preparations.

General Österman, the Finnish liaison officer at OKW, was ordered to report to the Finnish High Command in early April. He had a meeting with Field Marshal Keitel before his departure on April 4, 1944. Keitel told him that the coverage in the Finnish press about military measures taken by Germany against Hungary had caused much resentment in Germany. General Österman was asked to obtain clear answers from Mannerheim as to future Finnish policy. Keitel's discussion with Österman contained clear warnings of problems if Finland continued down the road it appeared to be taking. Österman was warned that there were already discussions in the OKW about the advisability of continuing arms deliveries to Finland.

In early April 1944 Dietl requested a meeting with Marshal Mannerheim to discuss the military situation. The meeting took place at Mikkeli on April 6. Dietl pointed out to Mannerheim that it appeared that the Soviets were positioning themselves for an envelopment of the German left flank that would threaten the German supply route from Salla. Dietl outlined his plan to disrupt the Soviet attack preparation by an attack of his own. Mannerheim liked the plan and offered to relieve the German security forces at the Kolosjoki nickel mines by moving the Finnish 3rd Brigade to that area. Dietl replied to this offer by pointing out that the German security force at the mines was not suited for offensive missions. It had become obvious to Dietl that Mannerheim was interested in the attack in the Kandalaksha sector, as long as it was performed by German forces. The meeting broke up without a decision.

OKW was also interested in the operation and General Erfurth was requested on April 11, 1944, to try to convince Mannerheim to participate with Finnish troops. Mannerheim rejected the proposal.[18]

Hitler Applies Pressure on Finland

Despite the fact that the Finns rejected the Soviet peace terms for a second time on April 12, 1944, the whole sequence of events resulted in a loss of confidence by the Germans in their "brothers-at-arms." There can be no doubt that Mannerheim and some of the other Finnish military leaders approved of the action of the government, actions they saw as necessary for the survival of the Finnish nation. The difference in the behavior of the Finnish political circles and those of the military leaders had become blurred in the eyes of the Germans and this led to a new reality in German–Finnish relations.

Hitler had become increasingly annoyed and his distrustful nature was deeply offended by the Finns going their own way. He began to exert pressure on the Finns in the military and economic area that was intended to insure that the peace offensive would come to a final end. He ordered grain shipments to Finland stopped on April 13, the day following the Finnish parliament's rejection of the Soviet peace terms. This was followed by an embargo on war matériel on April 18. The incident that Hitler used as a pretext for applying strong pressure on Finland was a critical article in the Finnish press over German action to evacuate the collections and other items from Tartu University in Estonia, ostensibly to keep them from falling into the hands of the Soviets.

The directive from the OKW informed the recipients that the Finns were not to be told about the arms embargo. This placed Dietl and Erfurth in an awkward position since they were sure to be queried by the Finns when planned shipments did not arrive as scheduled. OKW directed that such inquiries be forwarded to them for answers, on a case-by-case basis. Only such equipments as were absolutely necessary for the fighting ability of the Finnish Army would be provided in the future. This meant an end to Finnish hopes for modernizing and expanding their army.

Both Dietl and Erfurth protested the embargo and pointed to the unpleasant consequences that were likely to follow. They explained that the Finns would find it difficult to believe that an article in a newspaper, which most Finns were not familiar with, could cause Germany to take such extreme measures. The OKW refused to modify the directive, probably because it had been drawn up by Hitler. The requirement for secrecy was left standing and this seriously undermined the frankness and honesty that had, for the most part, characterized the dealings between Finnish and German military leaders.

Erfurth writes that the OKW "endeavored to re-strengthen the weakened German–Finnish relations by inviting General Heinrichs, the

Finnish Chief of Staff, to the Führer's headquarters."[19] I believe he is wrong in his assessment of German motives based on the events that transpired during the visit. It is more likely that it was a continuation of the increased pressure Hitler was applying on the Finns.

The OKW invitation was accepted and Heinrichs and Erfurth departed for Salzburg on April 27, 1944. They were billeted at Berchtesgaden. General Kurt Zeitzler, chief of the German General Staff, was staying at the same hotel and Heinrichs paid him a courtesy call on April 28 as Erfurth had a meeting with Keitel and Jodl prior to the visit by Heinrichs.

The meeting between Field Marshal Keitel and General Heinrichs did not go well. Heinrichs had obviously expected to be received as an honored guest as on previous visits to Germany but he was in for an unpleasant awakening. Keitel started out with a condemnation of the peace talks that Finland had held with the Soviets over the past weeks. He pointed out that there was great danger in Finland allowing a political minority to dictate its policies. The reproachful tone of Keitel's remarks surprised Heinrichs who tried to defend the Finnish government's action since they were in accord with the wishes of the Finnish people as expressed by the parliament. Neither Keitel nor Heinrichs fully appreciated how political opposition was handled in the other man's country. Keitel also complained of the unfriendly attitude of the Finnish press and used the Tartu University case as an illustration. Heinrichs claimed he knew nothing about the incident.

After the dressing down by Field Marshal Keitel, General Jodl took over—in a friendlier tone—to brief the guest on the situation on the various fronts. Neither he nor Keitel made any reference to the arms embargo already in effect. Jodl ended his briefing by making two requests:

1. That Heinrichs obtain an authoritative written statement that arms given to Finland by Germany would never be allowed to fall into Soviet hands. This was a prerequisite for continued German military assistance.
2. That Heinrichs use his influence to stop attacks on Germany and the Wehrmacht in the Finnish press.

In a private conversation between Jodl and Erfurth after the meeting, the former promised to use his influence to have Hitler cancel the embargo, provided he received a declaration from Marshal Mannerheim or President Ryti on the points he had raised in his briefing to Heinrichs.

Heinrichs felt that the Keitel's tone had been overbearing, that he did not understand the Finnish situation, and that his statements were reproachful and contained unjustified thinly veiled threats against Finland. The lavish social entertainment in Heinrichs' honor failed to soften the blow of the bad official treatment.

It was a very reflective Heinrichs who headed back to Helsinki. He had now experienced the full range of Finnish–German relations from their birth in 1940/41 to what now looked like the beginning of a rupture. He still knew nothing about the embargo. That news awaited him on his return to Mikkeli. The chief of staff of the Luftwaffe had inadvertently let that information slip out in a discussion with the Finnish air attaché in Berlin.

While the Finns had no prior knowledge about the embargo they obviously knew that something was not right when expected shipments failed to arrive. Both military and food assistance were indispensable for Finland. Grain deliveries ceased at the beginning of May 1944.

Marshal Mannerheim gives a very different account in his memoirs of General Heinrichs' visit to Germany from that of Erfurth.[20] There is, for example, no mention of the conditions laid down for the continuance of military assistance. However, there is no doubt that the Finns had become fully aware of the seriousness of the situation and they tried to find a way to appease Hitler by agreeing to Jodl's suggestions. Two letters from the Finnish High Command were sent to the Führer's Headquarters on May 12, 1944. General Heinrichs prepared one letter to Jodl while Marshal Mannerheim wrote one to Hitler. Mannerheim's letter failed to change the situation since Hitler considered it too noncommittal and full of generalities. Again, Mannerheim makes no mention of these two letters. The German embargo continued.

General Hermann Hölter, the new chief of staff of the 20th Mountain Army, made an introductory call on Marshal Mannerheim on May 16, 1944. He had replaced General Ferdinand Jodl.[21] General Hölter brought several requests from General Dietl. The harder German attitude seems to have brought results since Mannerheim granted the requests. These included leaving the bulk of the 3rd Finnish Brigade in a position behind the front of the XXXVI Corps, but under Finnish control. Mannerheim also agreed to the use of units of the 3rd Brigade on the left flank of the XXXVI Mountain Corps, something he had resisted earlier. The 11th Finnish Infantry Regiment was to be withdrawn from the Kestenga sector and rejoin its division. However, the Finns agreed to replace it with a Finnish construction battalion that could complete the construction of the Sofyanga Position. Two of the four border guard battalions were to remain in the Kestenga sector despite Mannerheim's earlier insistence during negotiations with Dietl in 1943 that these battalions be returned.

The Finns also took token action to satisfy the Germans with respect to their complaints about articles appearing in the Finnish newspapers. The newspaper *Svenska Pressen*, which had displayed an anti-German attitude was closed down for a period of three months on June 8.

Hitler's Letters to Mannerheim and Ryti

A letter from Hitler to Mannerheim arrived at the Finnish High Command on June 1, 1944. It was in answer to Mannerheim's letter of May 12 and added new complications to an already strained relationship. As far as Mannerheim personally was concerned, the letter was written in a polite and friendly manner. However, Hitler was harsh in his condemnation of the independent approach taken by Finland and he warned of serious consequences. He explained the vastness of the German undertakings and that "we feel all the more offended by the way in which one ally [Italy] has broken faith to a large extent, while other allies consider it a matter of course to go their own ways."[22] It was not purely a Finnish matter, Hitler wrote, to enter into peace negotiations with a common enemy.

Hitler wrote that Mannerheim was correct in referring to his requests for armaments from Germany as massive. He pointed out that his responsibility to the German people made it impossible for him to withhold urgently needed weapons from the German armed forces and send them to another front where their employment was in question.

While there is no discussion of Hitler's letter of June 1 in Mannerheim's memoirs, there is no doubt that it caused a crisis situation for the Finnish military and political leadership. Most civilian and military leaders were assembled on June 4, 1944, to observe Mannerheim's seventy-seventh birthday and the situation in which the country found itself was of course the main topic of discussion. They were desperately trying to find a way to appease Hitler without giving up the nation's independence in foreign affairs, something the parliament would not accept.

The discussions about what to do continued for several days without an apparent decision. Mannerheim may have tried to extricate himself from this controversy and leave it to the diplomats. He sent a letter thanking Hitler for his birthday wishes and added a few words thanking Hitler for his June 1 letter! That apparently closed the matter as far as Mannerheim was concerned although he could not escape the fact that the Finnish armed forces would soon find themselves in a desperate situation without German assistance.

NOTES
1. Erfurth, *The Last Finnish War*, p.107.
2. Mannerheim, *Memoirs,* pp.460–462.
3. According to Richard Ernest Dupuy and Trevor N. Dupuy, *The Encyclopedia of Military History*, New York: Harper & Row, 1970, p.1100, the German losses were 70,000 killed or wounded, 3,000 tanks, 1,000 artillery pieces, 5,000 motor vehicles, and 1,400 aircraft. The Soviet losses were probably slightly less.
4. Blucher, *op. cit.*, pp.341–342.
5. Erfurth, *The Last Finnish War*, pp.108–109.
6. A 20th Mountain Army document dated January 14, 1943 as cited in Ziemke, *The German Northern Theater of Operations*, p.243.
7. *Ibid*, p.245.
8. *Ibid*, p.249.
9. Trevor-Roper, *op. cit.*, pp.216–217.
10. Blücher, *op. cit.*, p.342.
11. Mannerheim, *Memoirs*, pp.468–469.
12. *Ibid*, p.469.
13. Blücher, *op. cit.*, pp.342–343.
14. *Ibid*, p.343.
15. Message from the 20th Mountain Army to OKW on February 3, 1944 as cited in Ziemke, *The German Northern Theater of Operations*, p.273.
16. Mannerheim, *Memoirs*, p.467.
17. Erfurth, *The Last Finnish War*, p.133.
18. *Ibid*, pp.135–136.
19. *Ibid*, p.138.
20. Mannerheim, *Memoirs*, pp.474–475.

21. Not to be confused with General Alfred Jodl, the Chief of Operations at OKW, who was Ferdinand's brother.
22. Erfurth, *The Last Finnish War*, p.144.

NINE

SOVIET SUMMER OFFENSIVE— JUNE 9–21, 1944

Soviet Plans

A s seen in previous chapters, the Soviets and Finns had basically left each other alone on the Finnish front since the completion of the Finnish offensives at the end of 1941, except for the Soviet counteroffensive in early 1942. The Finns had resisted all German requests that they cross the Svir River in force or participate in the attack on Leningrad. This soon became apparent to the Soviets who had their hands full dealing with the Germans. It was therefore not in their interest to undertake offensive operations on the Finnish front.

The rather peaceful atmosphere on the fronts in southern and southeastern Finland was about to change. Roosevelt, Churchill, and Stalin had met in Teheran in December 1943 to orchestrate their military plans. The war plans called for the US and Great Britain to land troops in France in June 1944. At the same time the Soviets committed themselves to undertake a major offensive on the eastern front (Operation *Bagration*).

No action was contemplated against Finland unless that country refused to withdraw from the war prior to the offensive in Central Europe and accept a list of Soviet conditions for peace. The Finnish rejection of the Soviet demands accompanying the peace offer in April 1944 caused a hardening of the Soviet attitude. The Allies had agreed to demand unconditional surrender not only from the Germans but also from her allies. After the rejection of the April 1944 peace offer, Finland fell squarely into the unconditional capitulation category.

There were at least two political reasons for the Soviet decision on the timing of the offensive against Finland. Stalin was still skeptical about the planned US and British landings in France. Spending some time after that landing attending to Finland would give him a chance to see how that operation developed before beginning Operation *Bagration* in Byelorussia. Probably more important was his strong desire to have the Finnish question decided early. He was aware that Finland still enjoyed considerable sympathy in the West and that the US had not declared war on that country. Stalin wanted to settle things with Finland so that its fate rested in the hands of the Soviets alone and did not become part of the wider settlement of issues after the war against Germany ended. Stalin is reported to have told Averell Harriman, the US ambassador in Moscow on June 10, 1944 that "They [the Finns] are a serious, stubborn, blunt people and a sense must be hammered into them."[1]

While the above political objectives were overriding, the Soviets also saw some military advantages in dealing with Finland immediately. First, an attack against Finland would draw German attention away from the planned operation in Byelorussia. Second, knocking Finland out of the war could free a significant number of troops for other missions. Finally, forcing a Finnish withdrawal from the war would isolate and neutralize the 20th Mountain Army in central and northern Finland.

The main Russian offensive in 1940 during the Winter War had been delivered in the western part of the Karelian Isthmus area with the city of Viipuri as its objective. It was the shortest distance from the Soviet border into the industrial and population center of Finland. The Finnish front on the Karelian Isthmus was only about 30 kilometers from the northern outskirts of Leningrad. It would not be surprising therefore that they would repeat the same strategy in 1944, particularly since there was a dense communications network in the area of Leningrad, something that was lacking both along the Svir and in Eastern Karelia.

The Soviets had actively planned a summer offensive against Finland ever since Finland had rejected the Soviet peace offer in April 1944. The objective was rather simple. The Finnish Army was to be destroyed forcing Finland to capitulate. To achieve this, Stalin demanded the attack to be exceptionally violent and quick. Like the Finns in 1941, the Soviets decided to stagger their offensive. They planned to start their offensive on the Karelian Isthmus on June 10 with troops from the Leningrad front. The main effort would take place in the western part of the isthmus. The Soviets expected to defeat the Finnish forces on the isthmus and capture the city of Viipuri within 12 days. They would then press on north and west and capture Helsinki by the middle of July. Soviet troops in the eastern part of the Karelian Isthmus were to drive north to trap the Finnish troops in East Karelia. When the Finns began to move forces from the fronts in East Karelia, the Soviets would start their next phase with troops from the Karelian front attacking in Maaselkä and across the Svir River. This was expected to happen around June 20.[2]

General Leonid Aleksandrovich Govorov had command on the Karelian Isthmus and was given two armies—the 21st and 23rd (later also the 59th)—consisting of seven corps. General Kiril Meretskov was responsible for operations in East Karelia and he also had two armies at his disposal—the 32nd and 7th. The front on the Karelian Isthmus was only 70 kilometers wide and in this relatively narrow sector the Soviets committed 270,000 troops, 1,660 pieces of artillery, 620 tanks, and 1,500 aircraft. The resources committed on the 220-kilometer wide Karelian front were also impressive: 184,000 troops, 2,140 pieces of artillery, 363 tanks, and 700 aircraft. Westerlund states that the Soviet quantitative advantages on the Karelian Isthmus were as follows: troops 4:1, armor 5:1, artillery 6:1, and aircraft 15:1.[3]

Some of the troops allocated to the offensive would be needed to support Operation *Bagration* in Byelorussia, an offensive scheduled to begin on June 22, 1944. The Soviet planners felt confident that they could achieve their major objectives in Finland in the period between June 10 and the start of the offensive in Byelorussia. Stalin believed the fighting qualities of the Finnish Army had declined through exhaustion as evidenced by their peace feelers. However, the operation was well prepared and the Soviets intended to use their experience in successful operations against the Germans. The troops trained for their mission for several weeks and detailed reconnaissance was carried out while maintaining the strictest operational secrecy.[4]

Finnish Force Dispositions and Readiness

The total strength of the Finnish Army in June 1944 was about 450,000 men. However, only a part of the army was located along the most likely Soviet avenue of approach on the Karelian Isthmus at the time of the Soviet offensive. Large forces were stationed along the Svir River in

Ladogan Karelia and in the Maaselkä sector north of Lake Ladoga.[5] Two corps faced the Soviets on the Karelian Isthmus. The various sources give a somewhat confusing picture of the order of battle. Both Westerlund and Ziemke write that the Finnish troops on the isthmus consisted of six divisions and two brigades. These forces also included those in Marshal Mannerheim's reserve and were not at the front. For example, the Finnish armored division was located east of Viipuri.

The right sector bordering on the Gulf of Finland was held by IV Corps, commanded by Lieutenant General Taavetti Laatikainen. It consisted of the 10th Division under General Johanns Sihvo and the 2nd Division under Major General Armas-Eino Martola. The left sector on the isthmus was held by III Corps under General Siilasvuo. It consisted of the 18th Division under Major General Paavo Paalu and the 15th Division under Major General Niilo Hersalo.[6] Ziemke writes that the Finns had three divisions in the front line and one brigade in reserve. He also notes that another three divisions were in the VT Line along with a brigade involved in building fortifications.[7] The divisions Ziemke has in the VT Line must include the 3rd and 18th Divisions, and the third division to which he refers must be the armored division. There were 289 field artillery pieces supporting these forces.[8]

The Finnish V and VI Corps held the Svir front while II Corps held the front in East Karelia. The V Corps consisted of the 7th Division, 11th Division, and the 20th Brigade. The 5th and 8th Divisions as well as the 15th Brigade were assigned to VI Corps. II Corps consisted of the 1st Division and 29th Brigade. Furthermore, the 14th Division was in the Rukajärvi area. There were also three large units in a reserve status on the Svir and Maaselkä fronts—4th Division, 17th Division, and 20th Brigade. It is not clear whether these reserves were under corps control or if they were part of Mannerheim's general reserve.

The defense of the Karelian Isthmus was based on three defensive lines. The first represented the front occupied by the Finns on June 9, 1944, and it coincided roughly with the 1939 border. The Valkesaari (Beloostrov) area in the IV Corps zone was considered the most exposed sector of the Finnish front and work on strengthening and expanding on the fortifications in this area had been ongoing for some time.

The second line, referred to as the VT position, was directly behind the front on more defensible terrain, at a distance of 14 to 22 kilometers behind the front. It ran from the town of Vammelsuu on the Gulf of Finland to the village of Taipale (Solovevo) on Lake Ladoga. The third line—referred to as the VKT position—ran from the city of Viipuri to the town of Kuparsaari and then along the Vuoksi River to Taipale. It was located on naturally defensible terrain but construction had only begun six months before the Soviet offensive and was far from complete. There was also a line to the north of the VKT position, representing the 1940 border between Finland and the Soviet Union. This was located in unfavorable terrain for defense and the fortifications had basically been neglected since 1941.

The Finnish forces had spent the period from the end of 1941 in a defensive posture. They prepared new defensive positions in the areas they had captured but it appears that the work was not carried out thoroughly nor with vigor. The lack of urgency may be related to the fact that the Finns felt a sense of security as long as Army Group North was in position in the Leningrad area. The work on the VKT and U positions (north of Lake Ladoga), for example, was not begun until November 1943 when it had become obvious that the Germans might lose their hold on the area to the south and southwest of Leningrad.

This long period in an almost garrison-type setting may have led to a lowering of morale and the loss of the fighting élan that was so evident in the 1941 offensives. The Finnish troops had been in the line for over two and a half years by the early summer of 1944. This resulted in both fatigue and a certain degree of mental burnout. The troops and their leaders appear to have become somewhat complacent as a result of this long period of trench inactivity. This is reflected in the lack of vigorous training, lack of urgency in the construction of fortifications, and a slackening in aggressive gathering of intelligence.[9] The Finns may also have underestimated the Soviets and based their opinions on their own experience in the Winter War and the 1941 offensive, not factoring in the German experience on the eastern front since 1941. The increasing political opposition to the war and rumors of peace feelers probably had their impact on the morale of the soldiers.

There were also several serious deficiencies in armaments. The lighter Finnish antitank weapons were ineffective against the modern Soviet heavy tanks. Those that were effective were so heavy and cumbersome that they were difficult to move around on the battlefield. The modern German infantry antitank weapons were only made available on a rush basis after the start of the Soviet offensive and training in the use of these weapons was virtually nonexistent. The field and antiair-craft artillery had been modernized by weapons received from Germany, but their numbers were inadequate.

As mentioned earlier, the Germans (OKW and 20th Mountain Army) had rated the ability of the Finns to withstand a major Soviet offensive as low in January 1943. General Dietl predicted again in June 1943 that the Finnish Army could not withstand a strong Soviet attack. He concluded that the Finns were superior to the German troops as for-est fighters and war under the severe climate in Finland but that they had a strong preference for avoiding major battles.[10] Ziemke goes on to explain that there was a feeling among the Germans that the Finns had not adapted to the conditions of total war and that they had failed to appreciate the problems faced by the Germans on the eastern front. Most of these observations were confirmed by an OKW officer who vis-ited southern Finland in July 1944.[11]

It is difficult to assign blame to any one individual for the apparent negligent positioning of forces and the less than satisfactory condition of defensive positions. As pointed out by Olli Vehviläinen, this issue is one of the most hotly debated in Finnish military history.[12] It is rather clear that, as in all military operations, the primary responsibility rests with the commander, Marshal Mannerheim and his general staff. It is curious that they did not take immediate and energetic action as soon as it became evident that the Germans would not be able to maintain their grip on Leningrad. Some strengthening of the forces on the Karelian Isthmus had taken place in the spring of 1944 and the con-struction of fortifications was speeded up. However, it was too little and too late.

The Finns also fell short in their evaluation of both the strategic and tactical situations. Mannerheim writes that "it seems, from a military point of view, strange that the Russians attacked Finland at all," since "there could be no doubt that the Finnish question would find its solu-tion in the defeat of German arms." He observes that "It could be taken for granted that Finland, even without being attacked, would accept bearable peace conditions, and it was not reasonable to assume that we could constitute a danger to the Soviet Union in the last phase of the war."[13] In retrospect, he offers the correct reason. The Soviet Union wanted to knock Finland out of the war so that it did not become part of the general settlement after the war. They wanted to ensure that they had a free hand in this area. It seems obvious, however, that he based his actions in early 1944 on the military assumption that the Soviets would leave Finland alone to wither on the vine, an apparent neglect of the fact that wars are fought for political objectives.

It may have been because of his preoccupation with the lack of military justifications for an attack on Finland that Mannerheim continued to keep the bulk of the Finnish Army in East Karelia, possibly hoping that possession of this area would give Finland a bargaining chip in the settlement that would obviously follow a German defeat. The failure of the Finns to request large numbers of infantry antitank weapons from the Germans, knowing that a major Soviet offensive would involve strong armored forces, points in the same direction—a full-scale Soviet offensive was not expected. These weapons had proved very effective on the eastern front and Germany had begun mass production of them in 1942.

The Finns were taken by surprise by the Soviet offensive. Part of this, as explained above, can be traced to how they viewed the geopolitical situation. This outlook may have influenced their faulty interpretation of intelligence warnings—which were not lacking. The Finnish intelligence service repeatedly warned the High Command that a Soviet offensive should be expected, but they were apparently not believed.[14] Mannerheim mentions some of these warnings in his memoirs:

> Since the early spring, enemy reconnaissance and artillery activities on the Karelian Isthmus had increased. In May, reports were received of a change in the composition of the enemy troops, of the appearance of new infantry divisions, artillery, and armoured detachments and an army staff not observed before.[15]

There were also several company-size probing attacks in both the Finnish and German sectors and the Soviets had busied themselves with mine-clearing operations in the Gulf of Finland. On June 1, the Finnish army intelligence service warned the General Staff that a Soviet offensive should be expected within ten days. The Soviets also imposed radio silence on their units four or five days before the offensive, a sure sign that something big was afoot. Even this did not convince the Finnish General Staff.[16]

The military logic of a Soviet offensive taking place on the Karelian Isthmus and all the warning signs should have energized the Finns. There was still time to bring in reinforcements from East Karelia but this was not done until the Soviet attack was well underway. In addition, troops who had been furloughed to participate in agricultural work were not recalled. Finally, settlers had been allowed to enter the recovered territories and they were now about to be caught in the maelstrom. As Vehviläinen correctly notes, the "highly motorized Red Army hungry for victory was met by an army ill-prepared in both morale and equipment for confrontation on the massive scale that was being fought in 1944."[17]

The Soviet Offensive—June 9–10

Most sources give the start of the Soviet summer offensive as June 10, a day that Mannerheim describes as "the black day of our war history."[18] However, preparatory actions began on June 9 with a strong Soviet air offensive on the Karelian Isthmus. According to General Erfurth, over 1,000 Soviet aircraft carried out saturation bombing of the forward Finnish positions between the Gulf of Finland and Lake Lembaloskoye on the border between IV Corps and III Corps.[19] The bombing campaign included the rear area of IV Corps. The Soviet artillery joined in laying down a heavy barrage on the Finnish front lines. Strong infantry probing attacks were also launched against the Finnish positions. Heavy fighting followed, particularly in the area adjacent to the Gulf of Finland, but the Finns were able to repel the attacks and seal the enemy penetrations.

The full offensive began at 0500 hours on June 10. Preparatory fires by Soviet artillery and aircraft were exceedingly violent. The Soviet infantry, supported by heavy tanks, also launched their attack. The main effort was directed at the right flank of the 10th Finnish Division, which was holding the sector along the Gulf of Finland. Several writers report that the artillery and air preparation was the heaviest of the war on the eastern front up to then, surpassed only by the storm of fire unleashed in the Soviet crossing of the Oder–Neisse line in their final drive on Berlin in 1945. It is reported that the Soviets deployed 200–400 pieces of artillery for each kilometer of front.[20] The 13–14-kilometer wide front of the 10th Finnish Division was hit by 220,000 artillery shells within a couple of hours and the 17-kilometer wide front of the

2nd Finnish Division was hit by 60,000 shells.[21]

The main effort of the 21st Soviet Army was directed at the Finnish 10th Division. When the artillery preparation described above and the thousands of tons of bombs are included, the results were predictable. The pulverizing effect of the Soviet fire destroyed the Finnish front line trenches. The avalanche of exploding shells buried soldiers under tons of sand, earth, and debris. The protective minefields and barbed wire entanglements were practically destroyed. Units lost telephone communications with their headquarters as the rain of high explosive shells severed the lines, and radios were virtually impossible to use due to the incredible noise created by the continuous explosions. The noise was so loud and continuous that it rattled windows in the town of Mikkeli, the site of the Finnish General Headquarters. Mannerheim writes that the noise from the battlefield could be heard both in Mikkeli and in Helsinki, located 220 and 260 kilometers from the battlefield respectively.[22]

The counterbattery fire by the Finnish artillery was of little help, and the battery positions were constantly attacked by Soviet aircraft. The hell-on-earth situation in which the Finnish soldiers found themselves had a paralyzing effect. The debris and smoke from the thousands of exploding shells reduced visibility to only a few meters. The losses were heavy and rising. Panic developed in many areas and when the Soviet infantry reached the Finnish trenches they sometimes found them empty except for dead and wounded.[23]

The weight of the Russian attack by three corps (109th, 30th, and 97th) fell on the Finnish 10th Division and particularly on the regiment at Valkesaari, commanded by Colonel Viljanen. The regiment was virtually annihilated in the massive assault by three Soviet divisions. A steady stream of enemy tanks and artillery batteries pushed through the breach. Within seven hours of launching its massive attack, the 21st Soviet Army had broken through the Finnish front and was rapidly approaching the VT Line.

It took hours before the Finnish General Headquarters had some idea of what was happening along the front on the Karelian Isthmus. This was not an unusual situation in a large battle where all means of communications are destroyed and where the enemy air situation is such as to prevent travel on the roads leading into the sector under attack.

The Finnish Cavalry Brigade, located along the Gulf of Finland, tried to stem the Soviet onslaught but was almost immediately forced to withdraw by the oncoming steamroller. It withdrew into the VT Line. The badly mauled 10th Finnish Division was also making a rapid retreat to the second defensive line, having lost most of its artillery. This forced the adjacent 2nd Division, which had so far held its positions, to bend its right wing north in trying to maintain contact with the 10th Division. The Soviets had not yet exerted any strong pressure against the III Finnish Corps on the eastern half of the Karelian Isthmus and it remained in the original front line.

The Soviets relied on the method of attack that had served them well in their battles with the Germans. They had assembled a force of some 24 divisions in the Karelian Isthmus sector to achieve a breakthrough and carry out a pursuit. To achieve this, the Soviets relied almost entirely on their vast superiority in armor, artillery, and aircraft. As they had done so often against the Germans, the Soviet offensive was concentrated on a narrow front to achieve a quick breakthrough and then exploit that breakthrough by several corps operating abreast.

By midnight on the first day the Soviets had expanded their penetration in the IV Finnish Corps sector and widened the salient to a distance of almost 35 kilometers. The IV Corps commander, Lieutenant General Laatikainen, was ordered to recapture the original defensive line. The Finnish General Headquarters still had no clear picture of the magnitude of the Soviet offensive and the critical situation at the front. General Laatikainen tried to carry out his orders but the 30th Soviet Guards Army Corps, leading the advance in the center of the breakthrough, made such a rapid advance that any Finnish offensive operations were out of the question. The lead element of the Soviet corps had reached the Finnish artillery positions either by the end of the first day, or early the next. Before withdrawing, the artillery personnel resorted to using their indirect weapons in a direct-fire role. Some of the artillery fell into enemy hands.

Mannerheim and his staff were now becoming aware of the magnitude of the Soviet offensive and it became obvious that the original front could not be restored through counterattacks. The best that could be hoped for was to seal off the penetration. To achieve this, Mannerheim intended first of all to use whatever forces that were immediately available. These included the armored division east of Viipuri, the 3rd Division in the vicinity of the VT Line, the 200th Estonian Regiment, and a few battalions and batteries from the 2nd and 18th Divisions that were located adjacent to the 10th Division.[24] All personnel on leave were recalled to their units. Reinforcements from outside were also ordered to the Karelian Isthmus. These included the 3rd Brigade in the Salla area of the 20th Mountain Army sector and the 4th Division from the Maaselkä front in East Karelia. Some of the fighter aircraft from the 3rd Air Regiment and 60 bombers from the 4th Air Regiment were ordered to the Karelian Isthmus.[25]

Marshal Mannerheim, having realized that counterattacks would not work to restore the situation, ordered General Laatikainen to withdraw his forces to the VT Line. The problem was that the Soviet troops could reach the VT Line before the Finns could occupy the positions. The lack of artillery and the demoralized state of the troops withdrawing from the front hampered the delaying actions required for an orderly withdrawal.

The Soviet Offensive—June 11 and 12

The 3rd Finnish Division, from Mannerheim's strategic reserve, occupied its part of the VT Line on June 11. The badly mauled 10th Division withdrew to the rear through the 3rd Division. The Cavalry Brigade occupied the VT positions between the 3rd Division and the Gulf of Finland. Those units of the Finnish IV Corps that had not been driven out of their positions on June 10 were driven back to the VT Line on June 11. The 2nd Division took up positions on the east flank of the 3rd Division. The 18th Division was also ordered forward and took up positions to the east of the 2nd Division. In order to avoid the development of a gap in the front the Finnish III Corps continued to bend its right wing northward to maintain contact with IV Corps.

By July 12 the Finns had managed to occupy the VT Line in the IV Corps area and the forces were arranged in the following order from west to east:

1. Cavalry Brigade.
2. The 3rd Division.[26]
3. The 2nd Division.
4. The 18th Division (actually straddling the border between IV and III Corps).

At the rear of the VT Line was the Armored Division, the remnants of the 10th Division, and some other units as part of Mannerheim's reserve. The Finnish High Command also ordered III Corps, which had not been under serious attack, to withdraw to the VT Line. This allowed the front, which had become bent with the withdrawal of IV Corps, to be straightened out and shortened.

Marshal Mannerheim sent General Erfurth, the German liaison officer, a request that the Germans lift their embargo on ammunition. This query was immediately sent to the OKW. The Finnish request on June 11 was followed by a new one on June 12. The first part of the request involved Luftwaffe support. The Finns wanted the Luftwaffe to take over air operations in the southern part of the Karelian Isthmus to disrupt Soviet supply movements into the operational area. The second part of the request involved the immediate delivery of aircraft, assault guns, and anitaircraft artillery that the Finns had ordered earlier but which had been held back in Germany. The initial OKW reply was to announce that the ammunition and grain deliveries that had been halted earlier would resume immediately.

The Soviet 21st Army attacked the VT Line at Vammelsuu and Kivennapa (Pervomajskoje) on the morning of June 12. The Soviets also attacked the Finns east of Kivennapa where the III Corps was in the process of withdrawing to the VT Line. In spite of continuous heavy attacks throughout the day the Finns held out about five kilometers south of the VT Line. The most serious equipment shortcoming in the Finnish Army was the lack of antitank weapons for the infantry. In spite of this, the Finns reportedly managed to destroy 29 Russian tanks in front of the VT Line on June 12.[27]

The most important question now facing the Finnish High Command was whether the VT Line could be held with the forces available. The 3rd Brigade from Salla and the 4th Division from the Maaselkä front were on their way to the Karelian Isthmus but there was no great optimism that these additional units would be able to make the difference.

The Soviet Offensive—June 13–15

General Dietl, the commander of the 20th Mountain Army, met General Erfurth in Helsinki on June 13, 1944. They were both pessimistic about the situation on the Karelian Isthmus, believing that the Finns would not be able to hold the VT Line. Dietl also visited President Ryti who displayed a confident and calm outlook. Dietl was forced to spend the night at Mikkeli because his aircraft slid off the runway when he dropped off General Erfurth. There he met with Defense Minister Walden, Lieutenant General Heinrichs, the chief of the Finnish General Staff, and in the morning of June 14 with Marshal Mannerheim at the latter's country estate at Sairila. As opposed to President Ryti, Mannerheim appeared genuinely concerned about the military situation and believed that the Soviets were striving for a decisive outcome in their offensive.

Heinrichs told Dietl that if the VT Line could not be held the Finns intended to give up the Svir and Maaselkä fronts and pull back to a shorter line northeast of Lake Ladoga, thus making two or three divisions available for the Karelian Isthmus. Since November 1943, when the possibility loomed that Army Group North would be driven from the Leningrad area, the Finns had worked on the so-called U Line. This line ran from Koirinoja on Lake Ladoga to Loymola and then northeast to Tolvajärvi. Dietl urged General Heinrichs to carry out that plan as quickly as possible, but he considered it quite possible that in their reluctance to give up East Karelia, the Finns would procrastinate so long that the withdrawal would be jeopardized. This was the gist of Dietl's report to the OKW upon his return to Rovaniemi. He recommended to Hitler that the Finns be given as much support as possible but that Germany dictate a Finnish course of action that would not so dissipate their energy in holding East Karelia that it would preclude other options. Dietl believed that the Finns could hold out indefinitely in a shorter line and thereby spare the Germans from having to carry out the planned withdrawal to Norway.[28]

Mannerheim ordered the transfer of the 17th Division and the 20th Brigade by rail from the Svir front to the Karelian Isthmus. Even with these reinforcements—on top of the 4th Division and 3rd Brigade—it appeared doubtful that the Finns would be able to hold their own in view of the men and matériel the Soviets had poured into their offensive.

As more and more Finnish units were on their way to or had received orders to move (the 11th and 6th Divisions) to the Karelian Isthmus, Mannerheim found it necessary to make some command changes. Since tactical control of operations on the Karelian Isthmus had become difficult from Mikkeli, Lieutenant General Oesch was ordered from the Lake Onega area to take command of all forces on the Karelian Isthmus except for the strategic reserves. Lieutenant General Talvela assumed command of all Finnish forces on the Svir front and Major General Mäkinen took over the Maaselkä front. Oesch assumed his post on June 15. His staff was inadequate in numbers at the outset.

The Finns expected the Soviets to continue their drive along the shortest line to Viipuri and that the main effort on this drive would be in the vicinity of Kivennapa. They therefore concentrated the 3rd Division and the Armored Division for the defense of this town. The left flank of the 3rd Division was located at the town of Siiranmäki where it tied into the 2nd Division, which was responsible for the protection of the III Corps right flank.

General Govorov paused his drive momentarily in front of the VT Line on June 13 while the lead elements reconnoitered for weak spots in the Finnish defenses. They found that Kivennapa was well defended but that the line appeared weakest to the west, in the vicinity of the town of Kuuterselkä (Lebyazhe), and to the east near Siiranmäki. The Soviets therefore divided their main effort into two attacks. Against Kuuterselkä they committed three infantry divisions, a brigade of armor, one assault regiment, one armor assault regiment, and two assault gun regiments. The 98th Army Corps was committed against Siiranmäki. The 30th Guard Corps took up positions at Kivennapa while the 97th Army Corps constituted the reserve.

The situation grew critical again for the Finns on June 14. The Soviets launched full-scale attacks against the VT Line from Siiranmäki to Vammelsuu. The attack against Vammelsuu was repelled by the Finnish Cavalry Brigade. The Soviets broke into the Finnish line at Sahakylä, northeast of Vammelsuu, but they were driven back in a counterattack. The main attack against Kuuterselkä was preceded by a heavy artillery and air preparation. The attack by two Soviet divisions and an armored brigade fell on a single Finnish battalion and led to a penetration that was sealed off with difficulty by local reserves. Some of the troops that attacked Kuuterselkä turned to the left and struck the Finnish Cavalry Brigade's left flank and rear. The brigade had to make a hasty withdrawal to avoid being encircled.

The IV Corps commander, Lieutenant General Laatikainen, ordered a counterattack by troops from a light infantry brigade and the assault

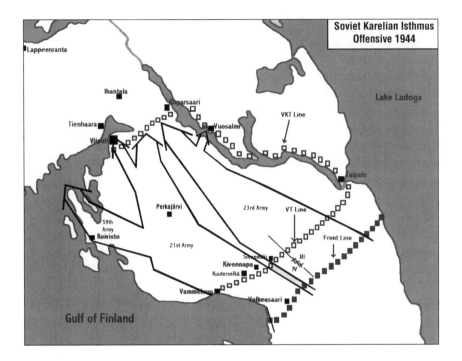

gun battalion from the Armored Division to regain the positions in Kuuterselkä. The counterattack, supported by 20 bombers and artillery, made good progress initially and the lost positions were recaptured. Ten Soviet tanks were destroyed in a violent tank battle that raged throughout the night near the town. However, the counterattack ran out of steam and ammunition. The Finnish losses were heavy, including the assault gun battalion commander, and they were forced to withdraw. The enemy followed the withdrawing Finns and poured through the penetration in the VT Line in increasing numbers and continued in the direction of the town of Perkjärvi (Kirpitshnoje), to the northwest of Kuuerselkä. By the morning of June 16 the penetration was deepened to a distance of 10 kilometers. Heavy enemy artillery fire and air activity prevented the movement of forces to seal the penetration. The 2nd Division further to the east was also subject to heavy attacks.

Since the Finnish infantry was having great difficulty coping with Soviet tanks, the Finnish High Command made an emergency request to the Germans for light antitank weapons. The request was acted on immediately. The first shipment arrived by plane from the 20th Mountain Army in Rovaniemi. A larger amount was brought in by a German torpedo boat.

The OKW was increasingly worried about the Finns' ability to halt the Soviet offensive and sent a Führer directive to the 20th Mountain Army to hasten the construction of rear defensive positions in Lapland. The Finns, who had their hands full with the events on the Karelian Isthmus, were either not aware of the directive or failed to pay it any attention.

It had become obvious to the Finnish High Command by June 15 that they would not be able to hold the VT Line. The reinforcements from East Karelia had not yet arrived. It appears that some thought was given to occupying the old Mannerheim Line from the Winter War rather than withdrawing directly to the VKT Line. Lieutenant General Oesch, who had just taken over command on the Karelian Isthmus, did not think that sufficient time remained for occupying the Mannerheim Line, and he pointed out that it was in poor condition from damage inflicted during the Winter War as well as from mismanagement in the period following. Oesch's recommendation was for a tough fighting withdrawal directly to the VKT Line to allow time for the reinforcements to reach their destinations. His recommendation was accepted.

The Soviets had in the meantime continued their offensive and by June 15 they had torn up the Finnish front over a 13-kilometer stretch between Kuuterselkä and the Viipuri–Leningrad Railroad along the Gulf of Finland. The enemy was obviously heading for Viipuri and the Finns had no forces available to stop them. The greatest Finnish worry was that the Soviets would, for the time being, bypass the city and head for the 27-kilometer isthmus between the Bay of Viipuri and the Vuoksi River. If they carried out this operation, the Soviets had a good chance of reaching that isthmus before the III and IV Corps could be withdrawn. Such an event could be decisive since it would prevent the occupation of the western part of the VKT Line and force the Finns to retreat northward across the Vuoksi. They would probably be forced to abandon their heavy equipment in the process since there was only one bridge across the river.

Under continued heavy attacks Mannerheim ordered a withdrawal to the VKT Line on June 16. The Finns were to conduct a tough fighting withdrawal but not become involved in decisive engagements that would risk their destruction. Some of the early reinforcements from East Karelia were now beginning to arrive. The 4th Division was directed to the lake country between Viipuri and the Vuoksi River. The 20th Brigade was directed to the area southeast of Viipuri.

Eastern Sector of the Karelian Isthmus

According to Soviet plans, Lieutenant General A. Tjerepanov's 23rd Army initially had the mission of binding the Finnish forces in its sector while the 21st and 23rd Armies conducted the main attack further west. Later, it was to attack the Finnish III Corps and cross to the eastern bank of the Vuoksi River. Because of its more limited tasks in the offensive the 23rd Army consisted of only two corps initially. The plans were to add a corps as operations progressed. The 23rd Army was faced with the III Finnish Corps under Lieutenant General Hjalmar Siilasvuo but because its area of responsibility overlapped the sector of the Finnish IV Corps, it also faced significant forces of the Finnish 2nd Division belonging to that corps.

Soviet troops attacked the 2nd Division on June 10 between Kivennapa and Termola. The Finnish defenses held but the situation further west at Kuuterselkä forced the IV Finnish Corps to order a withdrawal. In the evening of June 11 the 2nd Division was established in the VT Line at Siiranmäki and eastward.

On 14 June, the Soviet 97th Army Corps, supported by heavy artillery preparations and tank forces, attacked the reinforced 7th Finnish Infantry Regiment, commanded by Lieutenant Colonel Adolf Ehrnrooth. The attack led to heavy fighting in a seesaw battle that raged for two days. The 97th Corps was relieved by the 98th Corps, but the 7th Infantry Regiment continued the fight without reinforcements. The regimental losses rose to 900 troops and fatigue became an important factor. The Soviet losses were much greater and they lost at least 21 tanks. The 7th Infantry Regiment held its positions but was finally ordered back to the VKT Line at Äyräpää in order to avoid being encircled.

With the expected arrival on the Karelian Isthmus of the 11th and 6th Divisions from East Karelia, the Finns had switched the preponderance of their forces from East Karelia to the Karelian Isthmus. To command the increasing number of Finnish forces on the Karelian Isthmus the commander of the Finnish V Corps, Major General Antero Svensson, and his staff were moved from the Svir front to the Viipuri area. On June 22, General Svensson's V Corps took over the reinforcements assembling in this area, including the 17th Division, 20th Brigade, and a number of smaller units.

Soviet Offensive—16–21 June

Soviet attacks and Finnish retreats continued unabated on June 16 and 17. The strongest Soviet pressure was in the area along the coast near the Gulf of Finland. The Finns slowly retired in the direction of the VKT Line but continued to hold the eastern part of the VT Line from Siiranmäki to the shore of Lake Ladoga. This eastern part of the VT Line was evacuated on orders from the Finnish High Command on June 17.

The Soviets, employing strong armored forces, captured the town of Perkjärvi southeast of Viipuri but it was recaptured in a Finnish counterattack. The Soviets also made an armor-led breakthrough in the Kuolemajärvi area but the Finns were again able to avert a deep penetration and the Soviets reportedly lost 34 heavy tanks. The potential of the newly arrived infantry antitank weapons had been demonstrated.

The main elements of the 4th Division and the 3rd Brigade arrived on June 16. The 17th Division and the 20th Brigade arrived between June 18 and 20. The 20th Brigade was sent to Viipuri. The 17th Division was split. Its 13th Regiment was assigned to the IV Corps and two battalions of that regiment took part in the fighting in the 4th Division sector. The rest of the 17th Division was moved to the Kilpenjoki area as part of the strategic reserve.

The III Finnish corps occupied the long eastern part of the VKT Line, along the eastern bank of the Vuoksi River to Taipale. A small bridgehead was retained on the western bank of the Vuoksi in the Vuosalmi area. This bridgehead was occupied by four battalions.

The VKT Line was the last defensive line on the Karelian Isthmus. The 20th Brigade was responsible for the defense of Viipuri on a five-kilometer wide sector. It tied into the 3rd Brigade in the east, which also held a sector of approximately five kilometers. To its east was the 18th Division, which held a 10-kilometer sector followed by the 3rd Division, which held the sector to the Vuoksi River where it tied into the 2nd Division of III Corps. The reserve consisted of the Armored Division, the 10th Division, the Cavalry Brigade, and the 17th Division minus one regiment. These were all located to the west or southwest of Viipuri. The 10th Division and the Cavalry Brigade had been badly mauled and had lost most of their artillery and heavy equipment. The 6th and 11th Divisions were still on their way to the Karelian Isthmus.

On Lieutenant General Oesch's recommendation it had been decided not to halt and defend the old Mannerheim Line. General Govorov had expected this line to be heavily defended, remembering its tenacious defense in the Winter War. When the Soviet forces reached this line and pushed through it with virtually no opposition, they took it as an indication that the Finnish Army was finally destroyed. General Govorov was quickly promoted to Marshal of the Soviet Union in anticipation of receiving a delegation of Finnish officers who would acknowledge their defeat.

The Soviet advance continued and their troops soon reached Tali to the northeast of Viipuri. Their order of battle was impressive. There were two corps in the vicinity of Viipuri and another six corps to the east of Viipuri. These corps contained 20 infantry divisions, three artillery divisions, four armored brigades, five to seven armored regiments, and seven self-propelled assault gun regiments. It looked discouraging for the Finns who were still trying to establish themselves in the VKT Line. Against these units, the best the Finns could hope for by using all their reserves was a force of 10 divisions and four brigades.

Mannerheim hoped to continue the delaying actions until the last reinforcements from East Karelia arrived. In part of his order of the day on June 19 he exhorted his soldiers:

When the army now takes up the defense in the VKT-positions, it is time to bring the enemy's penetration into the country to an end. . . . I know that the fortifications are nonexistent or unfinished, but I trust the Finnish soldier will, if necessary, use the terrain and his perseverance to create an unwavering defense.[29]

The city of Viipuri fell quickly to the Soviets on June 20 after a short fight, within the scheduled time frame laid down in their plans. The Soviet fixation on the capture of the Karelian capital may have helped the Finns escape what could have been a disaster. The main Soviet effort had been directed against Viipuri. Had they directed their offensive a little further east, against the narrows between Viipuri and Vuloksi, they could have frustrated Finnish efforts to establish themselves in the VKT Line, the general area where they stopped the Soviet advance in 1940.

In the evening of June 21, Lieutenant General Oesch ordered Lieutenant General Laatikainen to send the 17th Division from Juustila, north of Viipuri, to the northern coast of Viipuri Bay at Tienhaara to prevent a Soviet crossing of that bay. Only the 61st Infantry Regiment, a separate battalion, a mortar company, and most of the divisional artillery were available.

The 61st Infantry Regiment, under Lieutenant Colonel Alpo Kullervo Marttinen, arrived at Tienhaara in the afternoon of June 22 and established itself along the shore. German aircraft from Group *Kuhlmey* carried out a bombing attack against the amphibious craft assembled by the Soviets on the other side of the bay. Troops from two Soviet divisions attacked across the bay in the evening of June 22 following a heavy artillery barrage. The attack was repelled but new attempts were made throughout the night.

Marshal Govorov decided that trying to cross the Bay of Viipuri would be too costly and time-consuming. The Soviet troops involved were relieved by other forces and moved to the main operational theater in the Juustila-Ihantala area.

Despite having frustrated Soviet attempts to cross the Bay of Viipuri, things were far from bright for the Finns. The loss of Viipuri was a heavy blow to Finnish morale. Having captured Viipuri the Soviets could direct their offensive both westward along the northern shore of the Gulf of Finland against the harbor city of Hamina and northward to Ihantala and Lake Saimaa from Lappeenranta to Imatra. After reaching these areas the terrain opened up and the possibilities for an armor-led advance were excellent. The Finns knew that the decisive fight was close at hand.

German Assistance and Political Developments

As soon as the magnitude of the Soviet summer offensive became evident, the Finnish military leadership realized that they could avert catastrophe only with help from Germany. The only other alternative was to seek peace with the Soviet Union. Both avenues were tried—simultaneously. The two avenues were actually linked since the Finns had concluded that the only way they could get acceptable terms from the Soviets would be by stabilizing their fronts. In their desperate situation the Finns were prepared to use German aid for purposes that were against the interests of their brothers-in-arms. The Germans may well have realized what the Finns were up to in view of the many flirtations with the West and the Soviet Union over the past two years but there was not much they could do about it except, as we shall see in the next chapter, conditioning their aid on a firm commitment by the Finns to stay in the war at the side of Germany. Not providing the requested aid would only lead to Finland being promptly knocked out of the war.

The Germans responded quickly to Finnish requests for assistance despite their own precarious situation. Hitler lifted the embargo on June 13. German torpedo boats brought in 9,000 Panzerfausts.[30] Mannerheim also requested a large number of Panzerschrecks[31] as well as ground support aircraft. The Finnish request stated that the VKT Line could be held only if these requests were approved and delivery expedited. Five thousand Panzerschrecks were airlifted to Finland on June 22.

The Finns also tried to get military assistance, in the form of arms, from Sweden. A request to that effect was made on June 18. It resulted in a unanimous refusal by the Swedish government.

Lieutenant General Heinrichs asked Erfurth late on June 19 whether the Germans were prepared to provide aid other than weapons. He specifically asked for six divisions to take over the front in East Karelia in order for the Finns to concentrate their efforts on the Karelian Isthmus. The formal request was made by Mannerheim on June 20.

The German answer came quickly. It pointed out that to provide the six divisions Mannerheim requested was impossible but other help was promised. This was a sensible answer in view of Germany's own force requirements. However, setting these aside, it made little military sense to send a large German force to East Karelia. The Germans already had their strongest army tied up in central and northern Finland, contributing virtually nothing to the war effort. It would be folly to send an equally strong force to be isolated in East Karelia where there would be great difficulties keeping it supplied.

The OKW answer on June 20 was based on the verbal request from Heinrichs on June 19. Aside from not being able to provide the requested six divisions, OKW promised significant help as long as they were assured that the Finns were determined to hold the VKT Line. Besides weapons, ammunition, and supplies, the Germans offered the 122nd Infantry Division from Army Group North, and the 303rd Assault Gun Brigade.[32] They also agreed to make available Luftwaffe units. Air Group *Kuhlmey*, consisting of one fighter group and a group plus a squadron of Stuka ground support aircraft were made available. These 70 aircraft came from the 1st and 5th Air Fleets. They were stationed at Imola Airfield outside Helsinki. The air support was immediate and the German aircraft flew 940 support sorties in support of the Finnish Army on June 21.[33]

This was substantial aid considering the desperate situation in which the Germans found themselves. The Western Allies had landed in Normandy while the greatest Soviet offensive of the war was expected any day.

The Finnish political leaders, surprised by the magnitude of the Soviet offensive, were prepared to make peace quickly and on almost any terms. The loss of the VT Line caused a political crisis in Finland. Linkomies and Tanner decided on June 15 that there should be a change in government and that President Ryti had to step down so that a new government acceptable to the Soviet Union could seek peace. They felt that Mannerheim should take over as president. They believed he would be acceptable to the Soviet Union and at the same time his prestige would help keep the country together after the expected harsh conditions.

Ryti was willing to give up the presidency and Mannerheim agreed with a change in government and suing for peace but he refused adamantly to accept the position being offered.[34] Mannerheim was obviously in a pessimistic mood and that is understandable as the VT Line had been lost, his troops were retreating, and reinforcements were not in place. He urged that the proposed steps be undertaken quickly since it was not a matter of days but of hours. He soon had a change of heart, probably because of promised German assistance and the fact that his troops were fighting a successful delaying action that would provide the time needed for reinforcements to arrive. He concluded that it was risky to burn the bridge to Germany by discussing peace terms with the Soviets until the front had been stabilized.[35]

NOTES
1. As quoted in Vehviläinen, *op. cit.*, p.135.
2. Westerlund, *op. cit.*, p.155.
3. *Ibid*, p.154.
4. Vehviläinen, *op. cit.*, p.137 and K. A. Meretskov, *Serving the People* (Moscow: Progress Publishers, 1971), pp.286–301. See also S. M. Shetemenko, *The Last Six Months. Russia's Final Battles with Hitler's Armies in World War II*. Translated by Guy Daniels (Garden City, New York: Doubleday & Company, Inc., 1977), pp.340–359.
5. Raunio, *op. cit.*, p.212.
6. *Ibid*, p. 220 and Westerlund, *op. cit.*, p.156.
7. Ziemke, *The German Northern Theater of Operations*, p.279.
8. Westerlund, *op. cit.*, p.156.
9. Vehviläinen, *op. cit*, p.138.
10. General Erfurth's comments on Part II of Ziemke *The German Northern Theater of Operations*, in June 1957 as cited by Ziemke in that work, p.279.
11. Ziemke, *The German Northern Theater of Operations*, p.279.
12. Vehiläinen, *op. cit.*, p.137.
13. Mannerheim, *Memoirs*, p.487.
14. Vehviläinen, *op. cit.*, pp.137–138 citing inter alia *Jatkosodan historia*, volume IV, pp.280–281.
15. Mannerheim, *Memoirs*, p.475.
16. Comments by General Erfurth to Ziemke, *The German Northern Theater of Operations*, p.279.
17. Vehviläinen, *op. cit.*, p.138.
18. Mannerheim, *Memoirs*, p.476.
19. Erfurth, *The Last Finnish War*, pp.176–177.
20. Ziemke, *The German Northern Theater of Operations*, p.280 and Mannerheim, *Memoirs*, p.476.
21. Westerlund, *op. cit.*, p.163.
22. Mannerheim, *Memoirs*, p.476 and Erfurth, *The Last Finnish War*, p.177.
23. Westerlund, *op. cit.*, p.163 and Vehviläinen, *op. cit.*, p.138.
24. Erfurth, *The Last Finnish War*, p.178. The 200th Estonian Infantry Regiment was formed from Estonians who had fled to Finland.
25. Westerlund, *op. cit.*, p.164.
26. Some sources have the badly mauled 10th Division in the line instead of the 3rd Division, which they place behind the line. I believe that the 10th Division withdrew to the rear of the VT line through the 3rd Division.
27. Erfurth, *The Last Finnish War*, p.178.
28. 20th Mountain Army messages to General Jodl on June 14 and to Hitler on June 16 as cited in Ziemke, *The German Northern Theater of War*, pp.280–281.
29. Translation of quote in Westerlund, *op. cit.*, p.172.
30. The Panzerfaust was a small, disposable pre-loaded tube firing a 6.4lb high-explosive warhead capable of penetrating 7.9 inches of armor. It served as a model

for the Soviet RPG-2 and the later RPG-7.

31. The Panzarschreck was an 88mm reusable antitank rocket launcher similar to the US 2.36-inch rocket launcher (bazooka).

32. The 303rd Assault Gun Brigade was actually a battalion-size unit commanded by Captain Hans-Wilhelm Cardeneo. It was equipped with 22 StuG III Ausf. G., each with a 75mm high velocity assault gun as main armament. The brigade was also equipped with nine StuH 42 assault howitzers.

33. Fighter Detachment (Gefechtsverband) *Kuhlmey* was an ad hoc unit commanded by Lieutenant Colonel Kurt Kuhlmey. It arrived at Immola Airfield in Finland on June 17, 1944. Kurt Kuhlmey was a famous Luftwaffe pilot who was awarded the Knight's Cross of the Iron Cross. After WWII he entered the West German Air Force and retired as a major general. He died in 1993. Detachment *Kuhlmey* flew over 2,700 missions in Finland and is credited with shooting down 150 Soviet aircraft and destroying 200 tanks. It lost 41 aircraft. See Christer Bergström, *Bagration to Berlin: The Final Air Battles in the East 1944–1945* (Buress Hill: Classic Publications, 2008).

34. Vehviläinen, *op. cit.*, p.139.

35. Notes by Tanner, June 19 and 20, 1944 as cited by Vehviläinen, *op. cit.*, p.139.

TEN

SOVIET OFFENSIVE
ENDS—FINLAND LEAVES
THE WAR

East Karelia

In anticipation of Soviet attacks on the Svir and Maaselkä fronts, Mannerheim issued orders on June 16 for a gradual withdrawal to the so-called U Line (from Koirinoja on Ladoga Lake to Loymola). Ziemke reports that at the last minute the OKW intervened unsuccessfully to have Mannerheim reverse his decision.[1] This was a strange turn of events in view of the strong recommendations by General Dietl to both the OKW and Hitler that the withdrawal be speeded up so that the Finns could concentrate their forces in a shorter line where he thought they could hold out indefinitely.

Ziemke offers three reasons for the German change of heart. First, he notes correctly that it had become a virtual obsession of Hitler not to surrender any ground to the enemy. The second reason, which he feels was more important, was that by giving up East Karelia the Finns would lose their most important bargaining chip with the Soviets, and thus their motivation for staying in the war. Finally, with a major offensive pending on the eastern front, the Germans may have surmised that the Soviets would stop short of a decisive effort in Finland. He concludes that "the OKW line of reasoning had much to recommend it—from the German point of view but not from the Finnish."[2]

The reasoning attributed to OKW is not convincing. Dietl had correctly concluded that the Finns could not hold widely separated fronts amounting to 290 kilometers in length against massive Soviet assaults and that they risked having their forces cut off and defeated in detail. He believed that concentrating their forces on a much shorter line would offer the best prospect for keeping Finland in the war. In February 1944, after Army Group North withdrew to the Neva River

294

(see Chapter 8), OKW had offered to provide the Finns with additional military assistance in recognition of newly exposed salients in East Karelia and along the Svir River. OKW was fully aware that Mannerheim had already set in motion a thinning out of forces on the Maaselkä and Svir fronts to bolster his forces on the Karelian Isthmus. These withdrawals left the two fronts even less capable of surviving a Soviet onslaught in their forward positions. Dietl and Mannerheim were right and it would be odd if OKW did not share their views.

It should be kept in mind that at this time the Finns had requested the Germans to provide six divisions (see Chapter 9) to take over the fronts in East Karelia. This request was turned down; even had they wished to do so, no forces were available to send to Finland. In addition, had they any troops to dispatch to East Karelia, they would have been difficult to supply and subject to entrapment. OKW's last-minute intervention was most likely related to the Finnish request and the German refusal and also in line with Hitler's obsession against any withdrawals.

The Maaselkä front between the northern point of Lake Onega and Lake Seg (Seesjärvi) was defended by the Finnish II Corps, under the command of Major General Einar Mäkinen. It had consisted of three divisions, one brigade, and two separate battalions until two divisions were withdrawn and sent to the Karelian Isthmus. After these withdrawals, the II Corps was no longer considered capable of mounting a forward defense against the 32nd Soviet Army of three divisions, one tank regiment, and ample artillery and air support. It was this situation that led Mannerheim to order the II Corps on June 16 to make a fighting withdrawal to the old border along with the forces on the Svir front. The forces from both sectors were placed under the command of Lieutenant General Paavo Talvela.

Major General Mäkinen ordered his troops to hold their positions until the evening of June 21. The Soviets launched their attack on June 21 and the following night II Corps commenced its planned withdrawal. The town of Medvezhyegorsk (Karhumäki) was abandoned on June 24. The withdrawal was conducted over two widely separated routes. The 1st Division withdrew southward from Kontuphoja (Kondopoga) and Munjärvi (Munozero) towards Suojärvi and Loymola. The 21st Brigade withdrew over a route almost 100 kilometers to the north— from Medvezhyegorsk via Porosozero to Ilomantsi. The 21st Brigade's delaying actions in the north had a very important objective. This unit had to ensure that Soviet troops in the north were sufficiently delayed to allow Finnish troops coming north from the Svir along the east shore of Lake Ladoga to arrive at the U Line before their route to the west was cut.

The troops on the Svir front and east of Lake Ladoga were under the VI Corps commanded by Lieutenant General Paavo Talvela. After the movement of the 11th Division to the Karelian Isthmus, the forces consisted of the 5th, 7th, and 8th Divisions and the 15th Brigade. There was also a coastal brigade on the shores of Lake Onega. The number of troops was about 45,000.

Facing these troops was the Soviet 7th Army, commanded by Lieutenant General Alexei Krutikov, of about 150,000 with 1,600 field artillery pieces and rocket launchers, 340 tanks, and 600 aircraft. Soviet forces were organized into eight divisions, three brigades, a tank brigade, and a multiple rocket launcher brigade.

Fortifications behind the Svir front were under construction by the Finns but, as in other places in the country, they had not been completed. The so-called PSS Line north of the Svir River ran from Pisi via Saarimäki to Sammatus. The next defensive line under construction was the U Line. The 7th Army's operational objectives were the cities of Sortavala and Petrozavodsk.

Mannerheim's order was that the troops in the east, when faced with attacks by vastly superior enemy forces, should initiate a fighting withdrawal to the old border. The Finns evacuated the large bridgehead south of the Svir River on June 18 without Soviet interference and established themselves behind the northern bank of the Svir. These troops were issued some 200 German infantry antitank weapons.

The first Soviet attack was a relative minor one. They tried to capture the hydroelectric dam and power station on the Svir. Their attempt was unsuccessful and the Finnish troops blew the sluice gates causing the western part of the river to rise significantly.

The Soviet 7th Army, following a three-hour heavy artillery and air preparation, began its attack on the Finnish troops behind the Svir River on June 21. Over 76,000 shells and 62,000 bombs fell on the Finnish defense line. Soviet troops crossed the river in assault boats and amphibious tanks on both sides of Lodeynoye Pole and quickly established a two-kilometer deep bridgehead on the north bank of the river.

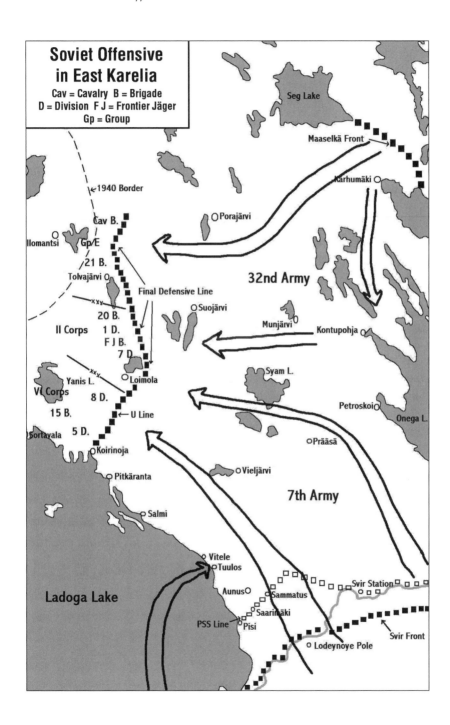

Soviet Offensive
in East Karelia
Cav = Cavalry B = Brigade
D = Division F J = Frontier Jäger
Gp = Group

The Finns made a deliberate withdrawal to the PSS Line and were established there by the evening of June 22.

The 7th Finnish Division on the eastern part of the isthmus withdrew northward along the shore of Lake Onega. The city of Petrozavodsk was abandoned on June 27. The 7th Division's further withdrawal was by train while the coastal brigade joined the withdrawing VI Corps. This withdrawal took on a sense of urgency as Soviet troops from the Maaselkä front threatened to cut the Finnish line of retreat.

In a further attempt to cut off the Finnish line of retreat the Soviets landed a naval infantry brigade in the rear of the VI Corps north of Tuloksa. Finnish attempts to counter this landing were ineffective. The landing took place outside the effective range of the coastal artillery and the Finnish Air Force could not prevent the landing. The naval infantry brigade was able to establish a bridgehead and cut the road leading north to Salmi, which was the line of retreat of the Finnish 5th Division and the 15th Brigade. The Finns counterattacked the bridgehead, but they were unable to eliminate it.

The bulk of the VI Corps was in danger of being encircled. The Finns had begun construction of an interior road to (Vedlozero) Vieljärvi in the spring of 1944 and it appears the Soviets were unaware of this road. While not completed, the Finns used this road to withdraw in a series of delaying actions around the bridgehead in the Tuulos-Vidlitsa (Vitele) area. This kept the line of retreat open for the 7th Division and the coastal brigade. The Soviets expanded their bridgehead at Tuloksa by landing troops at Vidlitsa. It was critical for the Finns to hold open the road north from Vidlitsa so that the other troops could join the VI Corps in the U Line. This was accomplished on July 10 when the 7th Division joined the other troops of VI Corps.[3]

The U Line was relatively well laid out. It actually consisted of three lines, each a short distance behind the other. The Soviet 7th Army was reinforced by a new corps and a tank brigade. These forces succeeded in breaking through the first two lines. The Finns were not certain that they could hold the U Line, and construction was begun on defensive positions between Yanis Lake and Lake Ladoga. The fighting for the U Line lasted over a week, but all Soviet attempts to break through the third line failed. The last attempt was made on July 17.

Lieutenant General Talvela succeeded in establishing a strong defensive front north of Lake Ladoga. After July 17 the front became stabilized and later actions can best be described as positional warfare. The final deployment in this line was as follows: The VI Corps held the southern sector between Koirinoja and Loymola with the 5th Division on the right and the 8th Division on the left. The 15th Brigade was in reserve. Further back, in the vicinity of Sortavala was a coastal brigade. The center was held by II Corps consisting of the 7th Division, a border jäger brigade, the 1st Division, and the 20th Brigade, from south to north in that order. The northern part of the line was held by Group E, consisting of the 21st Brigade and a cavalry brigade.

The 21st Brigade of the II Finnish Corps abandoned the town of Kondopoga on Lake Ladoga on June 27, the same day that the town of Petrozavodsk was abandoned. The 32nd Soviet Army had been reinforced by a new corps and the situation for the Finnish II Corps would have become critical were it not for the fact that VI Corps withdrawing from the Svir managed to hold the lines of retreat open. Major General Mäkinen was therefore able to bring his forces back in good order.

However, a new critical situation had developed to the east of Ilomantsi. There was a real risk that the Soviets would be able to break through the Finnish forces towards this town and thereby penetrate the northern portion of the new defensive line. Major General E. Raappana (commander of the Finnish 14th Division) was brought down from the Rugozero (Rukajärvi) area to take command of the forces northeast of Ilomantsi—the 21st Brigade, the cavalry brigade, and two infantry battalions from the Armored Division. General Raappana commenced operations on July 30 and the Finns were able to encircle the two attacking Soviet divisions—the 176th and 289th. The Soviets brought in reinforcements but these were also encircled. Most of the encircled Soviet troops managed to slip out of the trap but had to abandon much of their equipment. General Erfurth claims that four Soviet regiments were destroyed in this action.[4] The Finns captured 51 artillery pieces, six tanks, and 41 trucks.[5] This successful operation, which ended on August 10, was Finland's last major operation of the war.

General Raappana returned to his own division after the successful conclusion of the operation east of Ilomantsi. The 14th Division was attacked by a Soviet division, but two Soviet battalions were immediately encircled. This ended Soviet activity in this area and General Raappana was able to bring his division back to the old border in good order.

The command arrangements of the forces in East Karelia were

changed on July 18. Lieutenant General Talvela returned to Mikkeli. On July 22 he succeeded General Österman as Finnish military representative at the OKW, a job he had held once before. The two corps in East Karelia were placed directly under Mannerheim.

The Soviets Attack the KTV Line

It was on the Karelian Isthmus that the decisive battle was being fought. Soviet troops had so far kept to the time schedule in their plan. In less than two weeks they had driven the Finnish defenders back almost 100 kilometers. This was a serious loss of terrain in the critical Karelian Isthmus as the Finns now found themselves in the last defensive line before the Soviets could reach the open country north of Viipuri, terrain well suited for tank forces.

The Finnish troops had fought well against overwhelming odds. Their morale had not been broken despite heavy losses—including the ancient city of Viipuri—and continual retreats. Reinforcements had arrived on the Karelian Isthmus from East Karelia and this bolstered their morale. Matti Koskima attributes the loss of ground to lack of operational mobility, inadequate radio communications, and ineffective antitank weapons.[6] He could have added that the failure of the General Staff to properly interpret the many signs of an imminent Soviet offensive and an unfortunate delay in giving up the forward positions in East Karelia had contributed to the loss since reinforcements from there were slow in arriving. However, the tough defensive fighting by the Finnish soldiers bought the time required for reinforcements to arrive from East Karelia and from Germany to stabilize the situation.

Soviet troops were also beginning to show signs of fatigue. They had suffered significant losses, especially in men and tanks. But the Soviets had large reserves, which allowed them time to rest and reorganize their forces. This was especially true for the elite 30th Guards Corps, which had basically rested between June 12 and 24. However, the time was nearing when Soviet troops would be needed in the great offensive against the Germans. Marshal Govorov had received orders to be on a line from Lappeenranta to Imatra no later than June 28. He had a short week to accomplish his task.

The Soviets quickly concentrated their troops in the area to the northeast of Viipuri. The plan was for the 59th Army and the 21st Army to drive north with the 59th Army expected to capture Lappeenranta while the 21st Army turned west, north of Viipuri, in the direction of

Miehikkälä and Hamina. The 23rd Army would strike further to the east with the main force heading for Imatra while part of the army would turn east towards Hiitola.

There was heavy fighting at Tali, east of Viipuri, from June 22 onward. The terrain was particularly suitable for tank operations. A breakthrough here could bring about the collapse of the Finnish front.

The Soviet attack on the isthmus between Viipuri and Kuparsaari was intensive. For example, on a 15-kilometer wide sector they concentrated 14 divisions, three or four tank brigades, and 70 12-gun artillery batteries. There was an artillery piece every five meters in the areas of the main attacks.[7]

These troops attacked in the morning of June 25 with the main effort in the direction of Ihantala. The fire from almost 400 tubes of artillery and rocket batteries was directed at the defenders' front line and as far in the rear as Portinhoikka. The attack by the 30th Guards Corps tore open the Finnish front between Lakes Leitimojärvi and Karstilänjärvi. The Finnish troops in the path of this steamroller were the 48th Infantry Regiment and the 3rd Battalion of the 13th Infantry Regiment. The Soviet infantry that exploited the intensive artillery preparation had only to occupy the Finnish lines, as there were no soldiers left alive to offer any resistance. The Soviets followed the tank spearhead in a deep penetration that by the end of the day had captured Portinhoikka, and from there reached halfway to Ihantala. A Soviet tank unit continued in the direction of Juustilankangas, but was stopped by a unit of heavy Finnish tanks from the armored division. The Soviet tank unit was thrown back and the Finns reoccupied Portinhoikka in the evening.[8]

Over the following four days of heavy fighting the Finns succeeded in sealing the Soviet penetration but not in restoring the front. The Soviets held a dangerous salient near terrain north of Tali that was favorable for mobile warfare.

The Ribbentrop–Ryti Pact

While the Finnish military was seeking German help, the Finnish political leaders were still trying to find a way out of the war. The Foreign Affairs Committee decided to explore again the Soviet attitude on the subject. An unofficial feeler was delivered to the Soviet ambassador in Stockholm, Alexandra Kollontai, on June 22, asking if the Soviet government would agree to receive a peace delegation to discuss peace with a new Finnish government. The feeler resulted in an answer from Moscow the following day. The answer demanded that as a precondition for receiving a Finnish delegation, the Finnish president and foreign minister must sign a declaration to the effect that Finland was ready to surrender.[9] The answer was interpreted by the Finns as a demand for unconditional surrender, something they were not ready to accept.

On June 21, the day before the Finnish government approached the Soviets for peace conditions, Mannerheim sent a message to Hitler thanking him for the aid and stating that Finland was prepared to establish closer ties with Germany.[10] It would appear on the surface that there was a split in Finnish leadership but it is more likely evidence that the Finns were playing a double game, trying to keep doors open to both Germany and the Soviet Union. German military and economic assistance in the present crisis had been provided without any preconditions despite German worries that Finland might seek a separate peace. The Germans now decided that the time was ripe for binding Finland irrevocably to Germany. On June 22, as the Finns were telling the Soviets that they were ready to exit the war and asking for conditions, Hitler sent Foreign Minister Joachim von Ribbentrop to Helsinki. The sudden appearance of Ribbentrop illustrated the importance the Germans attached to this mission.

The Finns were surprised and dismayed by the arrival of the German foreign minister. Ribbentrop basically demanded a political alliance between Germany and Finland where Finland would firmly obligate herself to continue the war at Germany's side in return for continued German aid. Mannerheim should not have been surprised in view of his message to Hitler on June 21, which had basically invited closer relations between the two countries.[11] Even in the absence of this message, it should have come as no surprise to Mannerheim that the Germans, in their own predicament, would demand some form of guarantee that Finland would remain in the war before providing further assistance.

The German demand led to intense discussions within the government. It was recognized that an agreement ratified by the Finnish parliament was not likely in view of the peace sentiments that prevailed in the country. The Germans expressed a willingness to accept a letter signed by President Ryti in lieu of a document ratified by the parliament.[12] The German position was strengthened the following day—

June 23—when the Finns received the Soviet answer, basically demanding unconditional capitulation.[13]

The negotiations were lengthy and intense. In the evening of June 24, President Ryti and Foreign Minister Ramsay met with Mannerheim at his headquarters to discuss the situation. Hitler added pressure by a directive stating plainly that without a public declaration of Finland's attitude, German assistance to Finland would end.

Finland did not have much choice. Its leaders had to accept the Soviet demand for an unconditional surrender, or the German demand for a binding alliance. The government was split. Tanner, leader of the Social Democrats, was adamantly opposed to an understanding with Germany. Prime Minister Linkomies, on the other hand was equally adamant against surrender. Mannerheim made it clear that Finland could not continue the fight without German armament assistance. This was underscored by the news from the fronts where the Soviets were continuing their advances. In his memoirs Mannerheim makes no secret of the fact that his support for the alliance with Germany which resulted from the Ribbentrop visit was not done to "enable the country to continue the war, which had to be regarded as lost, but to stabilize the position and create a basis for peace negotiations."[14] The majority in the government supported the views of the prime minister.

President Ryti initially refused to agree to Germany's demands without the approval of parliament. However, when it became clear that there was no parliamentary majority in favor of the understanding with Germany, Prime Minister Linkomies refused to submit the question under threat of his resignation. It may well have been his intention not to submit the issue to a parliamentary vote since not doing so could afford the Finns a loophole in later abrogating the agreement. This was also the view of Mannerheim who wrote that such an understanding "would not bind the people of Finland" and that under a future president, "Finland would be free to act as the situation demanded."[15] The end result was that President Ryti agreed to sign a letter to Hitler where he stated that neither he nor a government appointed by him would make a separate peace with the Soviet Union. Ryti's letter also assured Hitler that Finland's commitment to Germany would be made public in a speech to the nation. This announcement was made by Prime Minister Linkomies, in a radio broadcast on June 27. The speech stressed Finland's determination not to conclude a separate peace without the agreement of Germany.

Ribbentrop's visit and the German demands placed great stress on political unity in Finland. Within the government the Social Democrats and Progressive Party voted against the understanding with Germany and the Social Democrats even issued a proclamation disavowing the government's policy. The Swedish People's Party withdrew its support for the government. After an acrimonious debate, however, the Social Democrats decided to stay in the government.

There was a price to pay for the new agreement. The US severed diplomatic relations with Finland on June 30. The breaking of relations, however, did not result in a declaration of war. Erfurth writes that this was due to a "masterful political strategy" by the Finns. The Swedes also denounced the German–Finnish alliance in a speech by the Swedish prime minister on July 2 and the Swedish press made references to the Ryti coup and a German dictatorship in Finland.[16]

While Ribbentrop returned to Germany in triumph, he brought with him a Finnish agreement that was unenforceable by Germany. Ribbentrop's high-handed pressure tactics ended up obscuring the generosity that the Germans had shown despite their own predicaments. The Finns concluded they had been subjected to blackmail and it removed some of their own feelings of guilt in what they were about to do.[17]

Tali-Ihantala Battle

While Ribbentrop was applying maximum political pressure on the Finns in Helsinki the decisive battle between the Finnish Army and Soviet forces was raging in the Tali-Ihantala area on the isthmus between Viipuri and the Vuoksi River. Marshal Govorov's simple objective was to defeat the Finnish Army in a final battle and then penetrate the defenseless interior of the country. This time he found his task much more difficult. With the arrival of reinforcements from East Karelia, the Finns had eleven divisions and four brigades on terrain favorable for defensive operations.[18] These divisions were deployed as follows: The 10th and 17th Divisions along with the Cavalry Brigade and the Gulf of Finland Coastal Brigade were located in the area north of the Bay of Viipuri. The 20th Brigade and the Armored Division were located north of Viipuri. The 18th, 4th, and 3rd Divisions were in line from Tali to Kauparsaari in that order from west to east. The 6th and 11th Divisions had just arrived in the area north of Viipuri. The 2nd and 15th Divisions and the 19th Brigade were deployed in that order from north to south along the Vuoksi River. There was also the 3rd Coastal Regiment located along the west shore of Lake Ladoga.[19]

By its tough defensive fighting the 18th Finnish Division under Major General Paavo Paalu had succeeded in stemming the Soviet offensive long enough for reinforcements to arrive in the form of the 6th and 11th Divisions. The 18th Division had been helped immeasurably by counterattacks launched by the Finnish Armored Division. The arriving 11th Division took over some of the sectors for which the 18th Division had been responsible, as in the area of Ventelanselka and Ihantala. The 4th Division took over defensive positions on the 11th Division's left flank. The battalions in the 13th Infantry Regiment, which had been in the thick of fighting, were given a chance to rest and reorganize.

The front line, which had somewhat stabilized over a period of several days of hard fighting, contained several penetrations that had been sealed but not eliminated. For example, north of Repola a substantial wedge had been driven into the Finnish defensive line and the Finns had not been able to eliminate it by counterattacks. Because of the resulting zigzag front, larger forces were needed to man it. General Oesch recommended to Mannerheim that the front be straightened out and his recommendation was accepted.

The Soviets noticed what was going on and began a new series of attacks to frustrate the Finnish plan. The relief of forces could not be carried out as planned and the straightening of the front was only partially successful. The responsibility for defensive operations on the most northerly front against the center of the main Soviet thrust fell to the 6th Division under Major General Einar Vihma.

The 6th Division fought a remarkable defensive battle. The Soviets attacked it repeatedly with tank support but each time they were driven back. German and Finnish aircraft tried repeatedly to interdict the lines of communications of the forward Soviet troops by carrying out bombing attacks against bridges. But Soviet infantry attacks continued with the support of tanks, artillery, and aircraft. A report by the Finnish General Headquarters on July 1 mentions Soviet air formations of up to 200 aircraft and takes note of the destruction of 57 Soviet tanks in the Tali area.[20] The Finns were beginning to reap the benefits of their shortened line of defense. The Soviet penetration of the Finnish front was limited to a depth of seven kilometers and there was no breakthrough.

A Finnish intercept of Soviet radio traffic on July 3 indicated that several elite guard and tank units were preparing a decisive attack in the direction of Ihantala. The Finns concentrated all the artillery they could lay their hands on—about 250 pieces. They fired on the area where the attack formations were assembling just before the attack was to be launched. This heavy artillery attack was followed by attacks by 26 German Stukas from Group *Kuhlmey* and by Finnish aircraft. The mortars also laid down a solid barrage in front of the Finnish position. The terrible fire covered the whole area between the roads that ran from Portinhoikka to Juustila and from Portinhoikka to Ihantala. The planned Soviet attack was completely frustrated.

However, the Soviet attacks did not stop. For almost a week they continued to carry out combined arms attacks against the whole 6th Division sector with air support. Most of these attacks were repelled, primarily through excellent use of artillery and mortar fire. The Finnish losses were also great. Among those who were killed was Major General Einar Vihma, the division commander. Only minor penetrations of the Finnish line took place and the front was restored through counterattacks.

The fighting, which had taken place in the Tali-Ihantala area northeast of Viipuri over a three-week period, is referred to as the largest battle in Nordic history. It ended in a Finnish defensive victory, which undoubtedly had its impact on later political developments. The fighting had been carried out successfully against a vastly superior enemy and the margin between success and failure had often been razor-thin.

Several elements came together to make this defensive victory possible. Reinforcements from East Karelia arrived just in the nick of time to prevent a decisive Soviet breakthrough. Finnish defensive operations had become firm and this must in large measure be attributed to their new technique in the use of artillery. Like the Soviets, the Finns massed their artillery in the threatened sectors and this had a devastating effect on the attackers. The new antitank weapons received from the Germans demonstrated their effectiveness even against the heaviest Soviet tanks. The Finnish Air Force, reinforced by the German Group *Kuhlmey*, also proved its effectiveness. Finally, the toughness of the individual Finnish soldier had been restored.

On July 13 Marshal Govorov was ordered to transfer five fully equipped divisions to Leningrad because they were needed in southern Russia. Govorov ordered his troops to end their attacks in the Ihantala sector. Finnish intelligence noted that although Soviet strength on the Karelian Isthmus had grown to 26 infantry divisions and 12 to 14 tank brigades, some of the best guard units had begun withdrawing and were being replaced by garrison troops. While Soviet attacks ended northeast of Viipuri, operations in the Bay of Viipuri and at Vuosalmi continued.

Soviet Attempt to Cross the Bay of Viipuri

On July 2, the commander of the Soviet 59th Army, Lieutenant General L. Korovnikov, was ordered to cross the Bay of Viipuri with two divisions, one armored brigade, and one naval infantry brigade. The troops numbered about 20,000 and were supported by some 180 pieces of artillery, rail-mounted guns, multiple rocket launchers, amphibious craft, and hundreds of bombers and close-support aircraft. The initial objective of the amphibious operation, after securing a beachhead, was to capture the town of Tienhaara. The obvious goal of the Soviets was to thereby threaten the right flank of the IV Corps.

The Soviets successively captured the small islands in the Gulf of Viipuri. The two islands of Teikarinsaari and Melansaari were defended tenaciously by the 22nd Coastal Artillery Regiment between July 3 and 5, but the Soviets' vast superiority eventually prevailed. The islands were captured on July 5. Some defenders saved themselves by swimming to the mainland.

The 59th Army was now ready to launch the main attack against the northern shore of the bay. The Finnish defenders were reinforced by the arrival of the 122nd German Infantry Division and it was in the sector of this unit that the main attack struck, on a 10-kilometer wide front between Niemenlautta and Harjuniemi. The 122nd Division had just moved up to relieve the Finnish Cavalry Brigade in this sector. The decisive battle in this area was fought in the period July 8 to 10. The Soviet operation was a complete failure as the Germans attacked and repelled the landing force. The Soviets had succeeded in gaining a small foothold in the river delta of the bay where the water was too shallow for Finnish torpedo boats to intervene.[21] The defensive operations by the Finns and Germans in the Bay of Viipuri became a victory when Lieutenant General Korovnikov received orders canceling his attack.

Soviets Cross the Vuoksi River at Äyräpää

The III Finnish Corps withdrew to its sector of the VKT Line without serious interference from the enemy. The 2nd Division had now been transferred from IV Corps to III Corps and it reached its assigned segment of the VKT Line in the Vuosalmi area. Two battalions of this division—belonging to the 7th Infantry Regiment—were left in a small bridgehead on the western bank of the river while the rest of the division went into positions on the eastern bank.

The reason for leaving two battalions on the western bank of the Vuoksi River was related to topography. The western bank was about 20 meters higher in elevation than the eastern side in this sector. The river varied in width between 200 and 600 meters and occupation of the western ridge gave the Finns a good view of the river valley. It was therefore an excellent spot from which to direct artillery fire and it was important that it be held. Soviet forces, particularly armor, were expected to assemble in attack positions west of the river. The small islands in the river presented the Soviets with good intermediate objectives.

The commander of the 23rd Army, Lieutenant General Tjerepanov, deployed his forces so that two divisions had the mission of seizing the ridgeline at Äyräpää. These divisions were supported by almost 60 tanks and 20 artillery batteries. The Finns held the ridgeline initially, but it was just a matter of time before they would have to abandon the bridgehead.

The fighting for the ridgeline on the west bank of Vuoksi River developed into a large battle. The commander of the 23rd Army was replaced by Lieutenant General V. Sjvetsov and the army was reinforced by another corps.

The Soviets started new attacks on July 3 and 4, but it was not until July 9 that the Finns were forced to give up their positions on the west bank of Vuoksi south of Vuosalmi. The eastern bank of the river also came under attack that same day after heavy artillery bombardment and the employment of several hundred aircraft. Under cover of this strong supporting fire the Soviets crossed the river on a two-kilometer front using assault boats. They were able to seize a one-kilometer deep bridgehead on the eastern bank. The Finns lacked the strength to eliminate the bridgehead and could only resort to containment.

Within a short time, however, the Soviets widened the bridgehead to such an extent that they were able to deploy one infantry division supported by tanks. The Jäger Brigade and assault guns from the Finnish Armored Division were moved from the Tali-Ihantala area to reinforce the III Corps. The Soviets were able to expand their bridgehead despite these Finnish reinforcements due to the hasty and incomplete construction of fortifications. The situation was difficult for the Finns because the dominant terrain on the west side of the river was occupied by the Soviets. This made operations to contain or eliminate the bridgehead exceedingly difficult and costly.

Nevertheless, the defenders were eventually able to limit the dangerous penetration and prevent a breakthrough. Finnish artillery continued to dominate the river crossing sites and this prevented a large inflow of Soviet reinforcements and complicated their supply situation. The combat activity lessened and the front took on the aspects of trench warfare.

The Soviets are reported to have lost 15,000 troops in the Vuosalmi area. Finnish losses were also heavy, primarily in the 7th and 49th Infantry Regiments. These two regiments had 2,296 casualties. The fact that 13 men were decorated with the Mannerheim Cross, the highest Finnish military decoration, speaks to the intensity of the combat.

German Military Assistance

The overriding purpose of the negotiations with Ribbentrop as far as the Finns were concerned had been to secure assistance to stop the Soviet offensive in order to stabilize their front and thus perhaps receive acceptable peace terms from the Soviets. To some the Finnish attitude may appear callous—they wanted German assistance in order to break their understanding with Germany. They wanted the help promised by Ribbentrop but had no intention of honoring the condition which called for them not to conclude a separate peace without German acquiescence. However, the prime responsibility of the Finnish government and Mannerheim was the continued survival of their country as an independent nation. This took priority over an agreement that had been virtually forced on them under the most unfavorable circumstances. Clausewitz' dictum that "One country may support another's cause, but will never take it as seriously as it takes its own"[22] applies to the German–Finnish coalition as it does to all coalitions.

For the Germans the primary purpose of the agreement was to keep Finland in the war. While they provided valuable assistance that was instrumental in achieving what the Finns wanted—the stabilization of the fronts—it was less than what Ribbentrop had promised. This is also understandable under the circumstances. The Germans wanted to provide the assistance but they were overwhelmed by military catastrophes in both the east and west. They also eventually made the decision that stabilizing their own fronts took priority over aid to Finland.

The massive Soviet offensive against Army Group Center that began on June 22, Allied breakouts in Normandy, and the offensive in Italy, imposed an overwhelming drain on German resources. Nevertheless, the help provided was effective. The Panzerfaust and Panzerschreck provided by Germany greatly increased the Finnish Army's ability to thwart Soviet armor attacks. They were instrumental in restoring the fighting morale of the Finnish infantrymen who had previously felt helpless against Soviet tank attacks.

Claims that German aid was provided only as a result of the Ryti–Ribbentrop agreement are not true.[23] As we have seen, the deliveries of infantry light antitank weapons by both air and sea were provided before June 22 without preconditions. Over and above the deliveries ordered on June 13 and 15, additional supplies were ordered delivered on June 20. Among these were 500 Panzerschreck and 150,000 hand grenades. Five thousand Panzerschreck were sent by air on 22 June. Seventy aircraft from Group *Kuhlmey* had flown 940 sorties on June 21.

The 303rd Self-propelled Assault Gun Brigade reached Finland by ship on June 23 and was committed on the front to the east of Viipuri on June 27. One-third of the combat elements of the 122nd Infantry Division were ready for shipment at Tallinn on June 23. This division arrived in Finland on June 28, and the OKW approved Finnish plans to commit it to the right flank of the Finnish front north of Viipuri. It moved from Helsinki to the Karelian Isthmus by railroad and relieved the Finnish Cavalry Brigade just in time to thwart the 59th Soviet Army's attempt at an amphibious landing on the north shore of the Bay of Viipuri.

Despite Germany's own precarious position, Hitler ordered that warships be employed to speed up the deliveries of weapons and ammunition. Seven hundred thousand rounds of artillery ammunition, as well as antitank and assault guns were either sent or ready in German ports for shipment.[24] However, no further combat units could be spared. It was intended to send an additional assault gun brigade but it had to be diverted to Army Group Center at the last minute. However, German supplies and weapons, including some tanks, continued to be sent to Finland.[25]

Help from the 20th Mountain Army was out of the question. That army was required to guard a long front and the forces were just sufficient for that task. The greatest service it could provide to the Finns was to remain in position and keep the Soviets from penetrating the waistline of Finland and thus threaten the Karelian Isthmus front from the north. However, the Luftwaffe shifted one fighter and one ground support squadron from the 20th Mountain Army to support the Finns in the south.

On June 27, the same day as Ribbentrop flew back to Germany, two German officers arrived in Finland. One was the new commander in chief of the 20th Mountain Army, General Lothar Rendulic.[26] He came from Croatia where he had commanded the 2nd Panzer Corps. The second officer was Major General Hero Brüsing, commander of the 122nd Infantry Division.

Rendulic's appointment had been kept secret for several days in order to conceal that General Dietl had been killed in a plane crash in the Austrian Alps on June 23 as he was returning from a visit with Hitler. The 20th Mountain Army and Finnish Headquarters learned about Dietl's death and Rendulic's appointment at the same time, on June 27, 1944. It was thought that Dietl's death might adversely affect Ribbentrop's negotiations in Helsinki since the general was very popular in Finland. Mannerheim sent condolences to both Dietl's widow and to Hitler. Dietl was awarded the highest Finnish war decoration, the Grand Cross of the Finnish Cross of Freedom. General Rendulic made a short courtesy visit to Mannerheim and then flew to Rovaniemi and assumed command of the 20th Mountain Army.

The Finnish requests for aid kept coming. On June 30, 1944, Mannerheim asked for another German division as well as one additional assault gun brigade. This was followed on July 3 with an urgent request for the early delivery of rifles and submachine guns. A large amount of small-arms ammunition had been lost in the withdrawals from the original front on the Karelian Isthmus and from the VT Line. The Germans had difficulties filling the ammunition requests for the Finnish rifles and it was suggested to OKW that Germany undertake to arm the Finnish infantry and artillery with German weapons for the sake of uniformity.

Mannerheim's request for another German division came at a time when the central German front in Russia had collapsed. OKW answered on July 5 that it was not possible to accommodate Mannerheim's request in view of the situation on the eastern front. However, the OKW agreed to give help in other areas of Finnish shortage by providing heavy weapons and by bringing the 122nd Division's assault-gun battalion up to brigade strength. Mannerheim protested and reminded OKW that he had recommended acceptance of the German proposal during the Ribbentrop visit based on German promises of help. If that help was withheld, the military situation would deteriorate and his prestige in Finland damaged. Hitler thereupon promised two more assault-gun brigades, tanks, artillery, and assault guns. The two self-propelled assault-gun brigades ended up being sent to the eastern front, one on July 17 and the second on July 18.[27]

In the period June 18–20, 1944 the Finns received information that confirmed that the Soviets were withdrawing forces from the Karelian Isthmus and transferring them to the Narva front. Some of the forces were replaced with new infantry divisions and fortress units. However comforting this news was to the Finns, they had to keep in mind that the Soviets continued to be superior in numbers and smaller-scale offensives could be expected. The Finns estimated that the Soviet forces confronting them now consisted of the following: 29 light infantry divisions, two light infantry brigades, ten armored brigades, and a number of fortress units. These forces were certainly capable of carrying out further offensive operations.

While the Finns had managed to stabilize their fronts by the second half of July, the situation for the Germans on the eastern front had grown desperate. Army Group Center had been decimated and driven back into Poland. Army Group North was about to be isolated in the Baltic States unless it withdrew behind the Dvina River. Hitler placed General Schörner in command of Army Group North with orders to hold the line between Narva and Pskov. The loss of this line was also critical to the Finns since with the Baltic coast under Soviet control their supply route from Germany for both military assistance and food would be jeopardized. The Germans recalled Air Group *Kuhlmey* and returned it to the 1st Air Fleet supporting Army Group North on July 21. The fall of Pskov on July 23 and Narva on July 27 was bad news for the Finns. The Finns had been promised that an additional assault-gun battalion (1122nd) would be added to the 122nd Infantry Division. The Finns were informed on July 22 that this battalion would not be coming. Finnish alarm was increased on July 29 when Hitler ordered the 122nd Division back to Army Group North. The OKW explained that the quiet situation in Finland was the deciding factor in the division's withdrawal and that the Germans would come to Finland's aid in the future if they were needed. The sector held by the 122nd Division was taken over by the Finnish 10th Division. Mannerheim requested that the German division leave from Hanko rather than Helsinki to avoid alarming the Finnish public.

Aside from German assistance, the gravest problem facing the Finnish Army at the end of June 1944 was the lack of manpower. And this concern was growing daily. It was difficult to replace the large losses suffered since June 9. By the end of June, Finnish losses in the Soviet offensive had reached 18,000. Only 12,000 of these were replaced. The losses continued to rise at an alarming rate, reaching 32,000 by July 11 and 44,000 by July 18.[28]

The Finnish solution to compensate for the loss in manpower was to redraft older members of the reserves. However, these numbers were small. The losses were mostly in the infantry but there were only about 9,000 infantrymen in the 1907 and 1908 year groups and the number was the same for the 1905 and 1906 year groups. The untrained reserve numbered about 10,000–12,000 men. The last resort was to call to active duty the infantrymen from the 1902–1904 year groups but even these numbered not more than 15,000 and they were definitely old for the rigors of infantry service. The 1926 year group was at training camps but these 17-year-olds were not sent to the front. A total of 31,700 reservists were called up and brought to the front as replacements for the 44,000 who had been lost.[29]

Political Developments—Mannerheim Becomes President
Excerpts of President Ryti's letter to Hitler on June 26 were leaked to the Western press shortly after. The Stockholm correspondent of the British newspaper *The Observer* provided the story. It has not been established who leaked the story and many parties are candidates as culprits. Since the story goes into some background and mentions that the

letter was extracted from a weak Finnish government under pressure from Germany, it is not likely that Germany was behind the leak. It mentioned that Ribbentrop's visit coincided with the readiness of a Finnish delegation going to Moscow to terminate the war. It is therefore most likely a Finnish leak, probably by circles opposed to making the commitment to Germany.

Peace sentiments in Finland were increasing day by day and the internal political crisis brought on by the Ryti–Ribbentrop agreement were reflected in the press. The sentiments of many, including the Finnish labor unions, were that the war was lost. The political opposition increased in strength and urged that peace be concluded even under harsh conditions and that the interests of Germany were irrelevant.

Tanner, the leader of the Social Democrats, was searching for a solution and he returned to his earlier proposal of a change in government and president. This proposal contained the implied threat that the Social Democrats would leave the government coalition if it were not accepted. It also appears that Mannerheim had concluded that Finland had to detach itself from Germany. The Ryti–Ribbentrop agreement had served Mannerheim's purposes by obtaining the aid needed from Germany to stabilize the fronts.[30] By the end of July the fronts were quiet and Germany was withdrawing the reinforcements it had sent to Finland. Tanner and Ryti held a secret meeting with Mannerheim at his country estate at Sairila on July 28. Ryti announced his intention to resign and both he and Tanner urged Mannerheim to accept the presidency.

Ryti's resignation was submitted to the parliament on July 31. The parliament had to quickly draft a new law that would allow Mannerheim to become president without an election. The law was passed by unanimous vote on August 4. The stage was now set for a reversal of Finnish policy. This had to start with a repudiation of the agreement it had made with Germany six weeks earlier, followed by a petition to the Soviet Union for peace.

The new prime minister was a conservative from the National Coalition Party, Antti Hackzell. He had been a former ambassador to Moscow and foreign minister in the 1930s. The foreign minister post went to Carl Enckell who had been part of Paasikivi's delegation to Moscow in March. The rest of the cabinet was made up, as had the previous administration, of members from the two prominent parties—National Coalition Party and the Social Democrats.[31]

The Germans appear to have been caught offguard by Ryti's resignation. They were not sure what the changes in the Finnish political landscape meant. Mannerheim had the prestige to rally the nation to continued resistance and his staunch opposition to communism over many years gave the Germans some hope. However, most concluded that the change was not advantageous to Germany.[32] Nevertheless, they had no power to influence the direction of the new government.

The Finns had directed a general inquiry to the Germans about the situation in the Baltic area and this inquiry was used as a reason for the OKW to send General Schörner, the commander of Army Group North, to make a personal report to Mannerheim, on August 3. The trip appears to have been arranged between General Talvela and the German Attaché Branch.

Mannerheim was surprised at the rather sudden appearance of Schörner, whose instructions seemed to be limited to briefing Mannerheim on the situation of his army group. It took an eternal optimist like Schörner to paint the situation in Army Group North as encouraging. After the fall of Narva and Pskov, most of the Narva–Peipus line had remained in German hands but at the end of July the Soviets had broken through to the Baltic Sea, thus isolating Army Group North. As a result, telephone communications were broken between Germany and Finland, and Lufthansa suspended its flights into Finland. This may have been what caused the Finns to enquire about the situation in the Baltic states.

General Schörner was undaunted by the catastrophic situation of his army group. He promised Mannerheim that the Baltic area would be held, that his troops would be supplied by air and sea, and that armored forces from East Prussia would break the encirclement. Mannerheim probably did not believe these promises. However, Schörner through his determination—fully supported by Hitler—kept his promise. Holding the Baltic states was of direct benefit to Finland. It did not convince Mannerheim to remain in the war but it gave him the time needed to negotiate an end before Finland was completely isolated.[33]

The military situation in Finland had returned to positional warfare and the Soviets continued to withdraw forces from the fronts. The Soviet forces on the Karelian Isthmus were reduced to 10 infantry divisions and five tank brigades by mid-August. The military situation looked more promising than even the most optimistic observer could have predicted only four to six weeks earlier.

Marshal Keitel, chief of the OKW, was sent to Helsinki by Hitler on August 17. He brought an oak leaf cluster for Mannerheim and a Knight's Cross of the Iron Cross for General Heinrichs.[34] The German military situation at the time of Keitel's visit could not give the Finns any confidence. The Allies had broken out of Normandy, and had also landed in southern France, the liberation of Paris was imminent, and the Germans had been driven back to the Gothic Line in Italy. The Soviets were on the outskirts of Warsaw. Few observers would have guessed that the war would last almost nine more months.

Keitel's mission was to reassure the Finns that Germany would continue to provide both military and economic aid. Mannerheim, now both head of state and military commander in chief, used the opportunity of Keitel's visit to abrogate the Ryti–Ribbentrop agreement. While the military situation had stabilized, Finland could not endure a second bloodletting. The pact between Ryti and Ribbentrop had been made under dire circumstances and Finland felt that Ryti's resignation invalidated the agreement and that Finland would only fight as long as it served its interest to do so.[35] Keitel was surprised by this blunt announcement. While he rejected the premise, he pointed out that he was not authorized to concern himself with political matters. The official notification that Finland had abrogated the Ryti–Ribbentrop Pact was not provided to Germany until August 26, 1944.

Armistice

Vehviläinen writes that Mannerheim "prevaricated for three weeks before taking the crucial step" of opening negotiations with the Soviets.[36] It was no doubt painful for the old soldier to seek peace with the country he had faced in war three times in 26 years but he was well aware that the Finnish Army would not be able to repel another full-scale Soviet attack.

However, there were practical considerations. Finland was totally dependent on Germany for food aid and this would cease once relations were broken. Negotiations with Sweden to fill the needs after a breach with Germany were initiated, and Sweden undertook to provide grain and other foods needed by the Finns for a period of six months.[37] Furthermore, the Finns were not sure what the reactions of Germany would be to a Finnish withdrawal from the war. Steps to counter any

German military moves were undertaken, such as strengthening the defense of the Åland Islands. Finally, the possibility existed that portions of the army and public would refuse to accept a peace and would continue to support the Germans. Over the summer the Germans had toyed with various ideas to keep Finnish resistance going but none went beyond the discussion stage.[38]

The deteriorating German military situation may have hastened the eventual decision. The announcement of an armistice between the USSR and Romania on August 24, 1944 also increased the pressure for Finland's withdrawal from the war. Vehviläinen writes that the Finns had received a communication from the Soviet Union via Stockholm that they should act speedily, that the terms would be reasonable, and that it was not the goal of the Soviet Union to terminate Finland's independence.[39] The decision to sue for peace was made on August 24 and on the following day a message was sent to Alexandra Kollontai, the Soviet ambassador in Stockholm, asking if the Soviet Union would receive a Finnish peace delegation. The Soviets were also told that Finland had repudiated the Ryti–Ribbentrop Pact, although Germany was not informed until the following day.

On August 29, 1944 the Soviet Union sent its conditions for accepting a peace delegation. First, Finland had to make an immediate public declaration that it was breaking diplomatic relations with Germany. Secondly, Finland had to demand publicly that Germany withdraw its troops from Finland by September 15, 1944. Any German troops remaining in the country after September 15 would be disarmed and handed over to the Soviets as prisoners. In order to prevent any Finnish procrastination, the message stated that the terms were also made on behalf of Great Britain, and with the approval of the US.[40]

While these preliminary terms did not demand unconditional surrender as had been demanded in the terms of June 23, Finland was required to break with Germany without knowing what the final terms would be. The Soviet answer required that Finland reply within four days—not later than September 2, 1944. The Finnish government convened a special session of parliament and recommended acceptance of the Soviet demands. The vote in the parliament on September 2 was 113 to 43 for accepting the Soviet terms. Those who voted against it were from the National Coalition Party, the Agrarian League, and the Patriotic People's Movement. A recommendation to sever diplomatic relations with Germany was also approved and the Finnish foreign minister notified Ambassador Blücher that evening that Germany had to remove its troops from Finland by September 15.

The Germans knew about the negotiations that had been underway but had hoped that, as in the past, the Soviet demands would be unacceptable to the Finns. They were therefore surprised by the Finnish acceptance and the announcement of a cease-fire. In a last-minute effort on September 2, General Rendulic called on Mannerheim and warned that the Soviet demands could bring on a conflict between German and Finnish troops. Such a conflict would result in heavy losses on both sides since the best troops in Europe would be pitted against each other.[41]

Having accepted the Soviet demands, the Finns sent an armistice delegation headed by Prime Minister Hackzell to Moscow. The delegation also included General Walden, the minister of defense, and General Heinrichs, Mannerheim's chief of staff. It was also authorized to negotiate a peace settlement. Mannerheim proposed to Stalin that a cease-fire take effect at 0700 hours on September 4, 1944. Through a misunderstanding, or possibly to underscore their victory, the Soviets did not cease fire until 24 hours later.[42]

On September 2, 1944, Mannerheim's adjutant handed General Erfurth a long personal letter from the marshal to Hitler. It read in part:

> In this hour of hard decisions I am impelled to inform you that I have arrived at the conviction that the salvation of my nation makes it my duty to find a means of ending the war. . . . The Russians' great assaults in June exhausted our reserves. We cannot expose ourselves to another such bloodletting without the whole future of the small Finnish nation being jeopardized.
>
> I wish especially to emphasize that Germany will live on even if fate should not crown your arms with victory. Nobody could give such an assurance regarding Finland. If that nation of barely four millions be militarily defeated, there can be little doubt that it will be driven into exile or exterminated. I cannot expose my people to such fate.
>
> Even though I can hardly hope that my opinions and reasons will be accepted by you, I wish to send you these lines before the hour of decision. . . .

I regard it as my duty to lead my people out of the war. The arms which you have generously given us I will never of my own accord turn against Germans. I cherish the hope that, even though you may take exception to my letter, you will share my wish and the wish of all Finns, that the change in our relations may not give rise to animosity.[43]

The Finnish delegation reached Moscow on September 7 but a week passed before it was given the Soviet armistice terms. These included the restoration of the 1940 borders. They also included the entire Pechenga region thus depriving the Finns of a northern outlet to the ocean. The Soviets did not insist on the retention of Hanko or Salla, but in return they demanded a 50-year lease on Porkkala in the Gulf of Finland, which was within artillery range of Helsinki. The demand for reparations was cut in half to $300,000,000 to be paid in the form of goods over the next five years. The Finnish Army was required to withdraw to the 1940 border within five days and be reduced to peacetime strength within 10 weeks. The Soviets demanded the right to use Finnish ports, airfields, and merchant shipping for the duration of the war against Germany and a Soviet commission was established to supervise the armistice.[44] After some wrangling in the Finnish cabinet, the armistice was signed before noon on September 19, 1944.

<hr />

NOTES
1. OKW War Diary (Kriegstagesbuch), *Report, The Northern Theater of War, January 4–December 31, 1944*, pp.29–30 as cited in Ziemke, *The German Northern Theater of War*, pp.284–285.
2. *Ibid*, p.285.
3. Vehviläinen, *op. cit.*, p.138 and Shtemenko, *op. cit.*, pp.360–361.
4. Erfurth, *The Last Finnish War*, p.194.
5. Westerlund, *op. cit.*, p.203.
6. Matti Koskimaa, *Veitsen terällä: vetäytyminen Länsi-Kannakselta ja Talin-Ihantalan suurtaistelu kesällä 1944* (Porvoo: W. Söderström, 1993), p.70 as cited in Westerlund, *op. cit.*, p.181.
7. Westerlund, *op. cit.*, pp.182–184.
8. *Ibid*, p.184.
9. Vehviläinen, *op. cit.*, p.139.
10. Earl F. Ziemke. *Stalingrad to Berlin: The German Defeat in the East* (Army

Historical Series. Original publication date 1968. New York: Barnes & Nobles, 1996), p.300.
11. Waldemar Erfurth writes that he had "some evidence of a possible Finnish decision to bind themselves closer to the Reich." Erfurth, *The Last Finnish War*, p.186.
12. Blücher, *op. cit.*, p.371.
13. Mannerheim, *Memoirs*, p.482.
14. *Loc. cit.*
15. *Loc. cit.*
16. Erfurth, *The Last Finnish War*, pp.186–187 and Vehviläinen, *op. cit.*, p.142.
17. Ziemke, *op. cit.*, p.283.
18. Vehviläinen, *op. cit.*, pp.142–143.
19. Raunio, *op. cit.*, pp.252–253. The discrepancy in the numbers given by Vehviläinen and those units listed by Raunio is probably due to the former counting the 122nd German Infantry Division and not counting the 3rd Coastal Regiment along the shore of Lake Ladoga.
20. Westerlund, *op. cit.*, p.194.
21. Erfurth, *The Last Finnish War*, p.190.
22. Clausewitz, *On War*, VIII: 6, p.603.
23. Ziemke, *Stalingrad to Berlin*, pp.300–301.
24. Erfurth, *The Last Finnish War*, p.189.
25. Ziemke, *The German Northern Theater of Operations*, p.284.
26. General Rendulic was one of several officers who rose to high position in the German Army in the closing months of World War II. Another who also came from the Finnish theater of war was Ferdinand Schörner. They were valued by Hitler for their unquestioned loyalty and harshness bordering on brutality. In his book *Stalingrad to Berlin* (pp.432–433) Ziemke writes "Rendulic, in the few months left in the war, was setting out to carve for himself a niche in history next to Schörner. One characteristic remarked on by all of his former superiors had been his absolute nervelessness. . . . In one order he made the battalion and regimental commanders responsible for every 'foot of ground' voluntarily given up and appended the example of a captain he had ordered shot the day before for taking his battalion back a mile after it had been broken through. In another, he ordered 'flying courts-martial' created to scour the rear areas. Every soldier not wounded, picked up outside his unit area, was to be tried and shot on the spot."
27. Ziemke, *The German Northern Theater of Operations*, p.286.
28. Erfurth, *The Last Finnish War*, pp.188, 192, 193.
29. *Ibid*, p.194.
30. Vehviläinen, *op. cit.*, p.143 citing Tanner's notes from July 22, 1944.
31. Mannerheim, *Memoirs*, p.492.
32. Ziemke, *Stalingrad to Berlin*, p.387.
33. *Ibid*, p.388.
34. According to General Erfurth, *The Last Finnish War*, p.201, the idea of the visit originated with General Rendulic, the commander in chief of the 20th Mountain Army. Rendulic had reported to Hitler that the quick turn in the political situation

in Finland was caused by a message from Roosevelt to Ryti, discussions with British representatives in Lisbon, and the withdrawal of the 122nd Division. He recommended that the 122nd Division be left in Finland.

35. Mannerheim, *Memoirs*, pp.492–493; Blücher, *op. cit.*, pp.395–396; Erfurth, *The Last Finnish War*, p.206; and Vehviläinen, *op. cit.*, p.144.
36. Vehviläinen, *op. cit.*, p.145.
37. Mannerheim, *Memoirs*, p.493.
38. Blücher, *op. cit.*, p.369, Ziemke, *The German Northern Theater of Operations*, p.290.
39. Vehviläinen, *op. cit.*, p.145.
40. Mannerheim, *Memoirs*, p. 493.
41. Lothar Rendulic, *Gekämpft, Gesiegt, Geschlagen* (Wels: Verlag Welsermühl, 1952), p.283–284, and Mannerheim, *Memoirs*, pp.495–496.
42. Mannerheim, *Memoirs*, pp.497–498.
43. *Ibid*, pp.494–495.
44. *Ibid*, pp.499–500.

ELEVEN
FROM FRICTION
TO FIGHTING

German Plans and Preparations after Directive 50

The prospect of a Finnish defection became obvious to the Germans in February 1944. Military planning was immediately revived which had been called for in Directive 50 of September 28, 1943, but postponed when the situation began to improve later that year. Part of the planning now expedited related to German control of the Gulf of Finland and the Baltic Sea. If Finland defected, this would become problematic. The Soviet Baltic Fleet had been bottled up in the Bay of Kronstadt and was for all practical purposes neutralized. The situation began to change with the lifting of the siege of Leningrad and was expected to change further if the Germans were unable to hold the Panther Line.

Increased efforts by the Soviets to clear mines in the Gulf of Finland provided evidence that they expected to put their fleet back into operation. The Soviet fleet had to be kept bottled up—otherwise German naval control of the Baltic would be jeopardized.

Suursaari Island—located in the middle of the inner Gulf of Finland, southwest of Viipuri—served to block the exit of the Soviet Baltic Fleet as long as Finland remained an ally and the same was true for the Åland Islands, at the southern end of the Gulf of Bothnia, with respect to the German iron ore shipments from Luleå in Sweden. The occupation of Suursaari would prevent or hamper the exit of the Soviet Baltic Fleet. The occupation of the Åland Islands would help secure the sea–lanes to the northern ports in that Gulf. The loss of these islands would threaten the sea supply route for the 20th Mountain Army and the flow of iron and nickel to Germany.

To prevent this from happening Hitler ordered on February 16,

322

1944, that both the Åland Islands and Suursaari be occupied immediately in case Finland defected. The planned operation against Suursaari was given the code name *Tanne Ost* (Fir East) and the occupation of the Åland Islands was code-named *Tanne West*. Army Group North was initially given the responsibility for providing troops for the occupation of Suursaari. This was later changed to a naval operation but one SS parachute battalion was also held in readiness.

One infantry division and the 6th Parachute Regiment were earmarked for the Åland operation. In addition, the Army of Norway would provide coastal artillery. The navy had completed its preparations for *Tanne West* by the end of March 1944. OKW retained overall control of these operations.

The major part of the contingency planning involved the withdrawal of the 20th Mountain Army—given the code name *Birke* (Birch). It was a monumental operation. The 20th Mountain Army, of over 200,000 men,[1] had to pivot and withdraw its 600-kilometer front from one facing east to one facing both east and south at a distance of 500 kilometers from its right wing. Its lines of withdrawal were limited and poor and could become unusable with the onset of winter. General Hermann Hölter, chief of staff of the 20th Mountain Army, describes the ambitious idea and goal of *Birke* succinctly: "While holding on to the Murmansk front, disengage from the enemy at Loukhi and Kandalaksha, withdraw to the north via Rovaniemi, and build up a new defensive front facing east from south of Kautokeino to south of Ivalo."[2]

The Germans planned to conduct this complicated operation, under possible strong pressure, in two phases. The first phase of the operation involved the withdrawal of the XXXVI and the XVIII Mountain Corps from the Kandalaksha, Luokhi, and Ukhta sectors to Rovaniemi. A strong covering force between Kemijärvi and Autinkylä (east of Rovaniemi) would screen this operation until the main German forces had passed through Rovaniemi on their way north towards Ivalo. The second phase involved the movements of the two corps from Rovaniemi to their new defense positions. The XXXVI Mountain Corps would move along the Arctic Ocean Highway into positions south of Ivalo and tie into the right flank of the XIX Mountain Corps. The XVIII Mountain Corps route was via the road from Rovaniemi to Skibotten in Norway. It would take up defensive positions in the vicinity of

Karesuando near the Swedish border.

The plan for the second phase of the withdrawal was based on it being executed in summer since the road to be taken by the XVIII Mountain Corps was impassable in winter. In case of a winter withdrawal, both mountain corps would withdraw via the Arctic Ocean Highway. After reaching the area south of Ivalo, the XVIII Mountain Corps would continue its withdrawal into Norway. The XXXVI would occupy the same positions as it would in the summer but would also provide forces to man the line near Karesuando.

The Army of Norway was tasked to reconnoiter and prepare fall-back positions for the German withdrawal between the Swedish border and Lyngenfjord. These positions were to be located so that Bardufoss Airfield and the town of Tromsø were within the German lines. The Army of Norway also assisted the 20th Mountain Army in the preparation of supply bases in northern Finland and construction on the road from Muonio to Skibotten.

The preparation of supply bases in northern Norway to support *Birke* was well on its way as was the establishment of a supply base in Ivalo. The 20th Mountain Army had begun moving some of the stores from central Finland to the new depots at Ivalo. Work to improve the road from Rovaniemi to Skibotten was underway. Most of the construction of roads and supply depots was carried out by the Todt Organization, augmented by construction troops from the Army of Norway. However, much of the work did not get underway until May 1944 because of the snow and frost.

Over 3,300 laborers were employed on the Ivalo positions starting on July 1, 1944, and another 1,800 men were employed in the Karesuando position beginning on August 1. Work was also undertaken to improve the main roads, and bridges were strengthened to the point where they could support heavy military traffic. The movement of large stocks of supplies to the areas at Ivalo and Pechenga was also begun. It was a monumental task to move about 180,000 tons of military supplies, fuel, and foodstuffs from central Finland to the new depots in a timely manner.

The 20th Mountain Army questioned the wisdom of proceeding with construction of the defensive positions near Ivalo and Pechenga, behind the Murmansk front. The army's point was that such construction would reveal German intentions to carry out long-term defensive operations on Finnish territory. The 20th Mountain Army proposed that their activities be limited to a reconnaissance of the new positions. The OKW did not go along with the recommendation of the 20th Mountain Army but ordered General Erfurth to make the Finns aware that the Germans intended to construct fortifications in Lapland but that these positions would not be occupied voluntarily. Erfurth informed the Finns on June 14, 1944, but they had their hands full with the Soviet offensive and apparently did not attach much importance to the information.[3]

The 20th Mountain Army had raised strong objections to Directive 50 on various grounds when it was issued in September 1943. These objections were still valid. The main problem, as seen by the 20th Mountain Army, was that the sea route along the Norwegian coast and in the Baltic would certainly be cut by the enemy, leaving the army without the possibility of replenishing supplies. Should that happen, the 20th Mountain Army would be able to hold out for only a few months. The withdrawal would be channeled via two routes—possibly just one in winter—that would be subjected to continual air attacks in summer. The attitude of Sweden was uncertain and the possibility that transit for Soviet troops would be granted threatened Narvik and the withdrawal route of the 20th Mountain Army and the other German units in Norway's two northernmost provinces. As the nickel and iron ore mines would lose their importance once their ores could no longer be sent to Germany, the 20th Mountain Army viewed the occupation of new defensive positions under highly unfavorable conditions as a waste of precious resources.

The 20th Mountain Army had voiced these arguments after Directive 50 was issued without receiving any satisfactory answers. General Dietl, who understood the gravity of these problems better than anyone else, visited Hitler at the Führer Headquarters on June 22, 1944 and again voiced his objection, unsuccessfully. As fate would have it, Dietl never returned from this visit. He was killed on June 23 when the aircraft bringing him back to Finland crashed in the Austrian Alps. General Lothar Rendulic assumed command of the 20th Mountain Army on June 28, 1944.

Anticipated Overland Withdrawal Problems
The planning for *Birke* had been very tentative because the military

situation at the time of its execution could not be predicted in advance. Much depended on the attitude of the Finns and the time of year at which a withdrawal would take place. It must have come as a great relief to the German planners in Rovaniemi when it appeared that the Finns would do their best to cooperate with the Germans in their withdrawal, at least until the time imposed in the armistice agreement for expulsion or internment of the German troops—September 15, 1944.

The Germans could not, however, base their plans on a rosy scenario that would most likely prove false. It was fully realized that the 20th Mountain Army would find itself in an untenable and perilous position when Finland withdrew from the war. Along the front it was in contact with three Soviet armies of the Karelian Front under General K. A. Meretskov: the 14th Army in the Murmansk area under Lieutenant General V. I. Shcherbakov, the 19th Army in the Kandalaksha sector under Lieutenant General G. K. Kozlov, and the 26th Army in the Kestenga sector under the command of Major General L. S. Skvirsky.[4]

Most serious of all was the fact that both the 20th Mountain Army's right flank and rear were wide open. While the Germans were only aware of the broad outlines of the armistice agreement announced by the Soviets on September 19, they had to assume that the 26th Soviet Army would penetrate into Finland south of the German right flank without opposition from the Finns. The Germans may not have been aware that the armistice provisions called for the Soviets to cross the Finnish 1940 border only if they were asked to do so by the Finns. Even had they known, it would not have been wise to put too much credence in such a provision.

It appears that the Soviets interpreted the armistice agreement in such a way that they should stop at the border if confronted by Finnish units but felt free to cross into Finland in areas where they confronted German troops. For example, General Kozlov's 19th Army facing the Germans in the Kandalaksha sector was given the mission of advancing as far as Rovaniemi. The Soviets realized that a gap had developed between the withdrawing Germans and the advancing Finns and that if they pursued the Germans towards Rovaniemi, the 19th Army could find itself caught between the Finns coming from the south and the withdrawing Germans. The Soviet decision was to let the 19th Army move to the border and upon reaching it on September 17/18 the army halted, allowing the Finnish forces to move north in front of it.[5]

The Germans also had to assume that the bulk of the Finnish Army could be turned against its open flank in order to satisfy Soviet demands for internment or expulsion of the German forces. They had to keep in mind what had happened in Romania when that country capitulated on August 23, 1944. Two Romanian armies allied themselves with the Soviets, trapping and destroying most of the German 6th Army and 8th Army. Hitler probably had the disaster in Romania in mind when he issued orders on September 3, 1944, directing that relations with the Finns should be handled in a friendly and compromising manner.[6] He also ordered that the detention of Finnish ships, held in German harbors in retaliation for a decision by the Finns not to allow German ships to leave from southern Finnish harbors, be discontinued.

The question of what would happen after the two corps of the 20th Mountain Army in central Finland disengaged was one on which there was total disagreement between the Finns and Germans. The Finns told the Germans that the Soviets would not advance across the 1940 border and that once the Germans had disengaged from the front the withdrawal would become a purely technical matter involving the movement of troops, equipment, and supplies. General Rendulic, the commander in chief of the 20th Mountain Army, believed that the Finns were living in a fantasy world or were intentionally dishonest in what they told their former brothers-in-arms. The Finns had to take military action against any Germans left in Finland as of September 15 and the Finns had calculated that it would take the Germans at least three months to remove their troops and equipment.[7] General Rendulic considered it extremely unlikely that the Soviets would respect the border and instead he believed that their intention was to occupy all of Lapland. This was the only logical conclusion the Germans could draw. The German withdrawal had, therefore, to be conducted as a tactical operation in unfriendly territory.[8]

It was not only the southern flank of the forces in contact that was in jeopardy, the whole rear area of the 20th Mountain Army was wide open, to include the ports on the Gulf of Bothnia. This area was over 300 kilometers wide from east to west and over 600 kilometers long from south to north. The road network in this area was poor and the only railway line ran from Salla to Rovaniemi.

At the same time, the tasks that Hitler had spelled out in Directive

50 were still in force. This included maintaining control over the Pechenga area and the nickel mines. Finally, winter was drawing perilously close in the arctic. Despite the planning that had taken place since the fall of 1943, the Germans were indecisive, primarily because all courses of action appeared to be nothing more than invitations to disaster.

The 20th Mountain Army had no assurance that it would succeed in establishing a new defensive line about 400 kilometers north of Rovaniemi that would hold as required by Directive 50. The new defensive line was planned to run from just south of Ivalo westward to Karesuando, located at the southern end of a sliver of Finnish territory extending into Norway south of Lyngenfjord.

The first leg of the German withdrawal from Finland would be perhaps the most difficult and perilous. With few exceptions, the troops were not motorized. While the XIX Corps continued its defensive mission on the Murmansk sector, the XXXVI Corps would disengage and withdraw to the Ivalo position via Rovaniemi while the XVIII Corps planned to withdraw directly to the Norwegian border.

There were only three routes available for the withdrawal and the onset of winter could prevent the use of large stretches of these routes. The first route, the one to be used by the XIX Corps when it eventually withdrew, ran from the front to Kirkenes where it linked up with the main north–south road in Norway, Route 50. The XXXVI Corps was expected to use the road from Alakurtti to Rovaniemi and Ivalo and when that position was vacated the route of withdrawal continued through Ivalo via Inari across the Norwegian border at Karasjok to where the road intersected with Route 50 at Lakselv. The roads the XIX Corps and XXXVI Corps were expected to use had been constructed or improved during the war by the Todt Organization. The XVIII Corps was expected to withdraw to Rovaniemi and then continue by way of Muonio to Skibotten in Norway.

The task given to the 20th Mountain Army was enormous and it would take a virtual miracle for it to succeed. Cut off from its supply line to Germany, it had to disengage its forces along a 600-kilometer front while facing a vastly numerically superior enemy. In addition, Mannerheim was sending forces north to honor the obligation of the armistice agreement to capture or expel all German forces still in the country on September 15, 1944.

Operation Tanne

The German Navy had responsibility for Operation *Tanne West* and its preparations were completed by the end of March 1944. The Germans expected the Åland Islands to be defended by between 3,000 and 4,000 Finns, supported by coastal batteries. The Germans earmarked the 416th Infantry Division in Denmark and the 6th Parachute Light Infantry Regiment for this operation. Coastal artillery batteries for the defense of the islands were to be brought in from Norway.

The OKW also had made an effort to gain a foothold in the Åland Islands through peaceful means. The German Navy was ordered on April 24, 1944, to discuss the stationing of German naval forces on the islands with the Finns. The reason to be given for this request was to protect against the possibility of a sortie by the Soviet Baltic Fleet from Kronstadt and its future operations from Estonian ports. Apparently, the Naval Staff elected to handle the request through the German liaison staff at Mannerheim's headquarters. The request was provided to the Finns on May 10. It placed the Finns in an awkward position since the stationing of foreign military forces on the islands would be a violation of the 1921 treaty. It appears they elected to ignore the request, hoping that the issue would go away.

The planned operation against the Åland Islands was controversial in Germany and in the end presented more problems than advantages. Sweden was a co-guarantor of the status of the Åland Islands by the 1921 treaty. German occupation of these islands would undoubtedly elicit a strong reaction from the Swedes and put in jeopardy the flow of iron ore and ball bearings from that country.

In addition to these political objections, there were also problems in providing the necessary forces. The 416th Infantry Division was needed in Denmark as Allied amphibious operations against this area were considered possible. The 50th Infantry Division was slated to replace the 416th, but had to be moved to the eastern front. About 14,000 men on leave in Germany from the 20th Mountain Army had been held back in Danzig despite General Dietl's objections. These troops were considered for use in Operation *Tanne* and were therefore placed at the disposal of the OKW. However, it was quickly decided that this mixed force lacked unit organization and they were transferred as individual replacements to the eastern front. It was also difficult to come up with sea transportation. Finally, the German Naval Staff had serious objections since the navy needed all its forces to block the Gulf of Finland. Because of the serious ramifications the occupation of the Åland Islands would have on German–Swedish relations, Hitler reserved the final decision for himself. Apparently, the lack of forces, and danger to the flow of raw materials and finished products from Sweden caused Hitler to cancel *Tanne West* on September 3, 1944.

The *Tanne Ost* (Suursaari Island) operation was to be carried out by Army Group North under the direction of OKH. The objective of the planned operation was to block the Gulf of Finland. The OKW had considered whether Hanko or another point on the southern coast of Finland should be occupied instead of Suursaari but had concluded that the island was the most suitable location. A change in the planning occurred on July 4, 1944, when Hitler ordered that the navy should carry out the operation instead of Army Group North. The stabilization of the Finnish front led to a postponement of the operation on July 9.

The armistice between the Soviet Union and Finland revived the operation. Although the navy reported on September 3 that the operation could not be carried out due to a lack of trained troops, the OKW issued a warning order for the operation in the evening of September 4.[9]

The operation remained in limbo for another week. The carrying out of the operation was given impetus by a report from the German naval liaison officer on Suursaari on September 11: the Finnish commander on the island had told him that he would never fire on German troops, even if ordered to do so.[10] At the urging of the navy, which now apparently did not believe the quality of their troops important since no opposition was expected, Hitler ordered preparations for the occupation of Suursaari speeded up. On September 13 the time for the attack was set for 0200 hours on September 15.

The German Navy embarked a mixed force of naval and army personnel in Reval. Ziemke reports the size of the force as approximately that of a regiment. It was likely somewhat larger since the first wave comprised 1,400 men. A Finnish source gives the size of the landing force as 2,500.[11] The landing commenced at the specified time.

The defense of Suursaari was the responsibility of the 16th Coast Artillery Regiment, part of the East Gulf of Finland Coastal Brigade. It had approximately 1,600 troops on the island.[12]

The Germans landed their first wave directly in the harbor and demanded a Finnish surrender. The Finnish commander refused the

German demand in accordance with his instructions, and hostilities commenced. The Germans were only able to occupy a part of the northern half of the island. The Soviets intervened with heavy air strikes after daylight and the second wave, consisting mostly of naval personnel, was prevented from landing. The fighting continued the whole day but the Germans eventually gave up and withdrew as many personnel as they could from the island.[13]

The Suursaari operation was a total fiasco for the Germans. They suffered 153 killed and the Finns took 1,231 prisoners, 175 of which were wounded. The Finnish 16th Coastal Artillery Regiment had 36 killed, 67 wounded, and eight missing.[14] The German prisoners were turned over to the Soviets in accordance with the terms of the armistice agreement.

The repercussions from the operation were equally detrimental to German interests. The Finns immediately ordered all Finnish ships in the Baltic to Finnish or Swedish ports. This order also applied to the Finnish ships that the Germans had leased to carry equipment and supplies back to Germany. Mannerheim also demanded on September 15, 1944, that General Rendulic immediately vacate the area south of a line running from Oulu to Suomussalmi and the entire Bothnian coastline to the Swedish border. Since much of this area had already been evacuated, the 20th Mountain Army replied that it would abide by the Finnish request.[15] However, the Germans were slow in complying and this soon led to serious consequences.

Finnish relations with the Soviet Union benefited from the fighting on Suursaari. The action demonstrated to the Soviets, at a time when sensitive negotiations were taking place in Moscow that the Finns were prepared to use force against their former brothers-in-arms.

Evacuations from Baltic Ports

The Germans began withdrawing staff, nonessential personnel, troops destined for the eastern front, and supplies from Finland shortly after the Finnish–Soviet armistice became effective. These evacuations were carried out by sea from ports in the Gulf of Finland and Gulf of Bothnia. The 303rd Self-Propelled Assault Gun Brigade, which had been at the Finnish front, was loaded on ships and sailed from Finland on September 6, despite a request from the 20th Mountain Army on 24 August to have that unit come under its command. All Germans in southern Finland, including diplomatic and military staff, had left Finland by September 13.

The 20th Mountain Army evacuated 4,049 nonessential troops, 3,336 wounded soldiers, 332 political refugees, and 42,144 tons of supplies from the ports of Oulu, Kemi, and Tornio on the Gulf of Bothnia. A number of the ships used in the evacuation were leased from the Finns. Some of these ships failed to sail to Germany but put in at southern Finnish ports or in Sweden. A total of 13,064 of the 42,144 tons of supplies evacuated were thus lost. There was not enough shipping for most of the supplies and 106,000 tons were destroyed to keep them from falling into enemy hands. The Germans evacuated the port of Oulu on September 15 and the last ship left the port of Kemi on September 21. The German Navy evacuated their base at Uno on September 15. The 20th Mountain Army shifted its evacuation from the ports to the road leading to Skibotten in Norway on September 18.[16]

Disengagement of XVIII Corps

The Germans planned to start the disengagement with the XVIII Corps, commanded by General Friedrich Hochbaum, in the Kestenga-Ukhta sector. This corps had to cover the longest distance. The movement of this corps would also address two chief concerns of the 20th Mountain Army, the army's open rear area stretching all the way to the Gulf of Bothnia and the unprotected right flank of the XVIII Corps.

The Germans learned that the Finns were moving two divisions north for the stated purpose of preventing a vacuum to develop between the Finnish Army in the south and the 20th Mountain Army. It was feared by both Finns and Germans that the Soviets might exploit such a vacuum. In case the Finnish motives for the move were not as stated, General Rendulic hastily assembled a force to screen the withdrawal against interference from the south and a possible Finnish attempt to move behind the 20th Mountain Army. It consisted of the army reserve—a motorized regiment commanded by Major General Hans Steets—reinforced by units withdrawn from the Loukhi and Kandalaksha sectors. These forces, divided into Battle Group East and Battle Group West, moved southward to set up screening positions along a line extending eastward along a chain of lakes from Oulujärvi. These two battle groups were concentrated in the Oulu and Hyrynsalmi areas, behind the flanks of the agreed demarcation line. Their mission was to guard against any threatening advance by the Finnish Army against Rovaniemi. The screening forces were to retire northward gradually while protecting the lines of communication of XVIII Corps. They were to destroy lines of communication behind them sufficiently to hamper a pursuit by motorized forces.[17]

The German concerns for the right flank of the XVIII Corps were somewhat alleviated when the front in the Kestenga sector was pulled back to new defensive positions at Sofyanga, and by the promise of the Finnish 14th Division, on the Finns' left flank, to maintain contact with the Germans until they had withdrawn west of the Finnish border.[18]

The first part of the withdrawal was to pull the XVIII Mountain Corps back from its forward positions east of Kestenga to rearward positions at Sofyanga, which had been under construction for several months. The corps consisted of the 6th SS Mountain Division and Divisional Group Kräutler east of Kestenga. This group consisted of the 139th Mountain Regiment, formerly part of the 3rd Mountain Division, two ski battalions, and a regiment of artillery. The 7th Mountain Division in the Ukhta sector was also part of the XVIII Corps.

It had been planned to occupy the Sofyanga position even if Finland remained in the war. This position, anchored on two lakes, was shorter and allowed the formation of a corps reserve.

The OKW had approved the move to the Sofyanga position, pending its completion, on June 9, 1944. However, Hitler reserved to himself the decision as to the timing of the move. The approval for the move was given on August 24, and was expected to take place within a few days. The move got underway on September 6. The 6th SS Mountain Division and Division Group Kräutler were securely established in the Sofyanga position on September 10 and the 7th Mountain Division had begun its withdrawal from the Ukhta sector.

The withdrawal of the XVIII Corps from the Sofyanga position began in the middle of September 1944. The first serious clash between Soviet and German forces in this area took place on September 16 and 17. The Germans repelled the Soviet attacks and thereafter the evacuation of the XVIII Corps proceeded smoothly since, to the surprise of the Germans, the four Soviet divisions stopped their pursuit at the Finnish border. The Finns moved in to fill the vacuum left by the XVIII Corps. The Germans maintained contact with the Finnish units on the right flank until September 18.

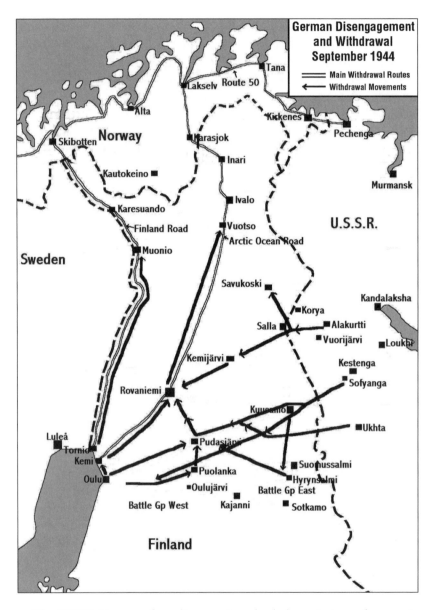

The XVIII Corps, after disengaging, had the mission of screening the withdrawal of XXXVI Corps from the Kandalaksha sector and covering its withdrawal to Ivalo via Rovaniemi. Having carried out this mission the XVIII Corps would commence its slow withdrawal through

Rovaniemi and on to Norway via Muonio. To carry out its mission after disengaging, the XVIII Corps spread out across central Finland with the 7th Mountain Division in the east while Divisional Group Kräutler moved west to screen the coastal sector between Tornio and Oulu. From these locations the Germans would give ground gradually and form a bridgehead southeast of Kemi in the first week of October. Battle Group East, located near Oulu, was to fall back to Pudasjärvi to converge with the 7th Mountain Division. This position was to be held until the first week of October when a slow withdrawal to Rovaniemi was to commence. The 6th SS Mountain Division executed a more direct withdrawal via Kuusamo to Rovaniemi, which its advance elements reached on September 22.

By the middle of September Mannerheim had deployed or was in the process of deploying the bulk of the Finnish Army against the Germans in the area to the south of XVIII Corps. The Finnish 6th Division had been moved into the Kajaani area. The Border Jäger Brigade was also moved into the area south of Hyrynsalmi. The main concentration took place in the west along the coast of the Gulf of Bothnia. The 15th Brigade, 3rd Division, the Armored Division, and the 11th Division were moved into this area. Lieutenant General Hjalmar Siilasvuo, designated as commanding general of the Finnish forces in Lapland, established his headquarters in Oulu. Siilasvuo arrived in Oulu on September 26 and immediately severed all contacts with the 20th Mountain Army Headquarters in Rovaniemi. The designation of Siilasvuo as commander was probably not accidental. In addition to being an excellent commander he had not exactly demonstrated a friendly attitude towards the Germans ever since his III Corps had been attached to Mountain Army Norway in 1941.

The Finnish 6th Division began its advance from the Hyrynsalmi-Kajaani area on September 19. This unit encountered Soviet troops which had crossed the Finnish border near Suomussalmi, but there were no incidents. The 6th Division reached Puolanka north of Oulujärvi on September 24. Lieutenant General Siilasvuo placed the Finnish troops west of Oulujärvi under the commander of the Armored Division, Major General Lagus, on September 19. The 15th Brigade was ordered to advance towards Kemi on September 21 and the Armored Division was given the town of Pudasjärvi as its objective. The advance began on September 24.

Disengagement of XXXVI Corps

While the disengagement of XVIII Corps had proceeded rather smoothly, the disengagement of the XXXVI Corps from the Kandalaksha sector resulted in bitter fighting. The XXXVI Corps, under the command of General Emil Vogel, consisted of the 163rd and 169th Infantry Divisions. In Chapter 8, it was noted that the Soviets had undertaken to extend their right flank northward in the Kandalaksha sector in an attempt to envelop the German left flank. General Dietl, who recognized the danger, proposed an attack to disrupt the Soviet plans. He traveled to see Marshal Mannerheim in March 1944 and asked for Finnish troops to support the attack. Mannerheim declined to participate in the operation and it therefore never came about.

The northward and westward extension of the Soviet right flank had continued and it was evident that they intended to trap and destroy the XXXVI Mountain Corps. While General Vogel was aware of the danger to his corps, his timetable for withdrawal was also dictated by activity in other areas of the theater. Foremost was the requirement to time his withdrawal in such a manner that the XVIII Mountain Corps could pass through Rovaniemi behind his troops.

Although the Germans were aware of Soviet efforts to outflank the Kandalaksha sector, they were taken by surprise when Soviet troops captured Korya, northwest of Salla, on September 7, 1944. The Soviets managed to cut the road from Korya to Salla, an important supply route for the Germans. They had also managed to bring in tanks over terrain that had been considered impassable even for infantry. The use of the tanks did not prove very productive for the Soviets since, although they had succeeded in bringing them forward, the terrain was such that they could not be adequately supported. Nevertheless, within days, the Soviets had brought in a tank brigade and a reindeer brigade and were threatening the town of Salla and the line of retreat of the entire corps. The appearance of Soviet tanks in the rear area of an infantry corps had serious psychological effects and made commanders view the threat as greater than it actually was.

The XXXVI Mountain Corps began evacuating the Verman Lake line in the evening of September 9 because the corps' rear was endangered. The order of withdrawal was the 169th Infantry Division, followed by the 163rd Infantry Division. The Soviet attack into the corps' rear area had split the German forces into two groups. The 169th

Division took up an all-around perimeter defense in the Salla area but was unable to prevent Soviet forces from moving south from Korya to cut the road from Salla to Alakurtti between Salla and the Kayrala Lake narrows on September 11. This cut the main withdrawal route of the 163rd Infantry Division. The Germans had built an alternate road that ran south from Alakurtti via Vuorijärvi and Mikkola back to the main road west of Kayrala. The Soviets were apparently unaware of this road and traffic was able to proceed over it without interruption, although its capacity was limited. The 163rd Division had to attack towards the west in order to clear the main route and this was accomplished after bitter fighting on September 13, 1944, when the two German divisions again linked up.

The rear elements of the XXXVI Mountain Corps passed through Alakurtti on September 14 and although the Soviets mounted a second attack against the southern flank in the direction of Vuorijärvi, the Germans escaped what was intended to be a Soviet trap. The statement by Mannerheim that the German corps in the south disengaged "without the Russians making the slightest attempt to hold them"[19] is hard to square with what actually happened on the ground.

In view of the weight of the Soviet attacks in the XXXVI Mountain Corps sector, the Germans changed their route of withdrawal. There was a danger that the Arctic Ocean Highway would be cut by the Soviets between Rovaniemi and Ivalo. Therefore, instead of withdrawing all its troops from Salla and Kemijärvi to Rovaniemi, the XXXVI Corps sent two-thirds of the 169th Division northwest to Savukoski to block a Soviet drive against the highway between Rovaniemi and Ivalo.

Salla had to be held until the XVIII Mountain Corps had withdrawn sufficiently in the direction of Rovaniemi to be out of harm's way. This necessitated the XXXVI Corps holding positions in the vicinity of Korya and Kayrala for another ten days. The Germans withdrew from their bridgehead at Kayrala on September 24 and continued quickly westward through Salla to Kemijärvi and Savuloski. The Soviet forces did not pursue into Finnish territory. The XXXVI remained in this area until October 3. The withdrawal was then continued after the destruction of the very large railroad bridge across Kemi Lake.

Onset of German–Finnish Hostilities

The Finns wanted to spare their country from devastation and the

Germans also wished to avoid hostilities with their former "brothers-in-arms." They therefore had a mutual interest in seeing that the German withdrawal proceeded as smoothly as possible. However, given that they fully expected the Soviets to intervene or otherwise pressure the Finns to become more active, the Germans would have been derelict in their duty had they left the road network behind them intact.

Ollie Vehviläinen writes that this mutual interest between the Germans and Finns "resulted in a secret agreement between the Finnish and German military authorities in which the Germans agreed to limit the devastation of the country and the Finns to facilitate the Germans' withdrawal even after 15 September."[20] Also, Westerlund refers to the Lapland War as the "Sham War" (Skenkrig). These contentions don't paint an altogether accurate picture of the situation.

Relations between the Finns and Germans were as good as could be expected until September 15, the end of the grace period for a German voluntary withdrawal from Finland. Finnish liaison officers continued to perform their functions at various German headquarters and the 20th Mountain Army instructed the Germans to behave in a friendly manner towards the Finns. Ziemke notes, as an example of the loyal cooperation, that the Finns told the 20th Mountain Army on September 13 that they had moved all railroad rolling stock between Salla and Rovaniemi to the west of Rovianiemi but would not prevent the Germans from seizing this stock.[21] This is true but not of much consequence for the northward withdrawal since there were no railroad lines north of Rovaniemi. It did assist some in the movement of supplies from the Salla area and from Rovaniemi to the ports on the Gulf of Bothnia.

A primary purpose of the railroad stock in the Rovianiemi area was to facilitate the evacuation of Finnish civilians from Lapland to the coast and to Sweden. Cooperation between the Finns and Germans in this area resulted in 133,000 refugees being moved from Lapland (particularly the Salla and Pechanga areas) to southern Finland and Sweden. A total of 77,000 were moved across the temporary demarcation line between German and Finnish forces to the southern part of the country while 56,000 were moved through Tornio to Sweden.[22]

By September 15, the 20th Mountain Army and the Finnish Army had worked out an agreement governing the behavior of both sides.[23] The agreement was designed to avoid clashes between the Germans and Finns, while allowing the Finns to report steady progress to the Soviets in their task to expel the Germans. The fact that liaison officers were withdrawn as of September 15 made its smooth execution more difficult. The agreement involved the Germans providing the Finns with phase lines for the withdrawal and tentative boundaries between the two armies were established based on these phase lines. The initial demarcation line ran from Oulu along the Oulu River to the town of Sotkamo. The Germans were to give the Finns a two-day notice before moving from one location to the next. The Finns, in return, agreed to German destruction of roads, railroads, and bridges and promised not to rebuild railroad bridges and to make the rebuilding of road bridges so light that they would not support heavy military traffic. The destruction of the roads and bridges also gave the Finns an excuse to the Soviets for their slow northward advance. This arrangement appeared to have worked relatively well even after the Germans tried to seize Suursaari on September 15.

Erfurth paints a less rosy picture of the cooperation. He notes that "frictions and even serious clashes occurred soon after the departure of the German diplomatic and military representatives from Helsinki and Mikkeli."[24] Without assigning guilt, he tells about Finnish coastal batteries firing on German ships, Finnish liaison officers at some headquarters subordinate to the 20th Mountain Army being disarmed by the Germans, and the baggage of German units being detained and confiscated.

Nevertheless, the agreement worked out between the Finns and Germans generally held for ten days. The Finns followed the German forces from phase line to phase line without undue pressure. German troops were destroying all bridges and roads as they passed, sometimes within view of Finnish troops. The troops who watched the destruction and the newspapers reporters who reported on it were not aware that it was something their government had agreed to.

General Erfurth also argues persuasively against the notion that the conflict in Lapland was a "sham war." In describing the incidents during the withdrawal he writes "These engagements were by no means sham fights in order to make the Russians believe that the Finns had fulfilled their obligations, but the fighting was real according to German and Finnish standards."[25] His conclusion is fully supported by what Emil Schuler and Roland Kaltenegger write about the 7th Mountain Division.[26] The fighting was hard and the casualties high. M. Kräutler writes that "The Finnish attack on Kemi and Tornio in conjunction with their advance on Rovaniemi unfortunately cost much German and Finnish blood."[27]

That conflicts should occur is not difficult to understand. Finnish soldiers were witnessing German destruction of the country's infrastructure and the withdrawal was slow. The shock of the Finnish secession from the war caused the feelings of many German soldiers to change from one of trust and confidence in the Finns to one of distrust and bitterness. Many Finns attributed the destruction to German revenge for Finland's withdrawal from the war. Repeated clashes took place between German and Finnish troops during the second half of September. Most of the clashes were minor and generally involved the possession of bridges. Later, as destruction became more widespread, incidents between Germans and Finns increased.

The Germans resorted to a scorched-earth policy similar to that used in north Norway at the conclusion of the withdrawal. While the writings of most Germans who participated deny any wanton destruction, there is little doubt that in many places the devastation was more widespread and thorough than what is permitted under the 1907 Hague Convention in such circumstances.[28] According to Finnish sources, of the 113,531 buildings in Lapland 41,306 were destroyed by the withdrawing Germans.[29]

An incident on the German southern wing occurred on September 28, 1944, that led to a short exchange of fire between German and Finnish forces. After fire was opened, a Finnish battalion commander demanded that the 7th German Mountain Division evacuate the town of Pudasjärvi before nightfall. The 20th Mountain Army at first dismissed the incident as the action of an overzealous Finnish officer. Later, when it became obvious that the Finns refused to negotiate, General Rendulic gave the 7th Mountain Division permission to return fire if that should become necessary. He also sent a message to General Siilasvuo, the Finnish commander in Lapland, asking him to affirm that the Finns would continue to observe the agreement they had made with the Germans or accept the consequences of open hostilities. Incidents in Pudasjärvi continued for the next two days, resulting in the capture of a German platoon on September 30. Incidents were also taking place at Tornio and Kemi between Finnish and German troops. These incidents appear to have resulted from Soviet pressure on the Finns for their lack of determination in enforcing the terms of the armistice. To reinforce their demands, Soviet troops crossed into Finland at Suomussalmi and Kuusamo.

General Rendulic sent a note to the Finnish Military Headquarters on October 1 announcing that he would be forced to take counter-action if the Finns did not live up to previous agreements. The Finnish answer on October 4 refuted the German complaints in an indignant tone and Rendulic reported to OKW that relations with the Finns were continuing to deteriorate.

The Germans sincerely believed that the Soviets would advance deeply into Finland with motorized forces and intercept the non-motor-ized German units in their withdrawal, bringing about their destruction. It was therefore militarily imperative for the Germans to impede Soviet progress as much as possible. They believed themselves justified accord-ing to the rules of war to deprive the enemy of the means of trans-portation and billeting, so important in arctic warfare. Furthermore, a sense of bitterness towards their former allies who had now turned against them had set in among the German soldiers. They were aware of the events in Romania and Bulgaria and felt betrayed when the same pattern began to unfold in Finland.

OKW Assessment

When looking at the directions and decisions of the OKW pertaining to Finland in the wake of that country's withdrawal from the war, one is struck with the impression of uncertainty and inconsistency. This is not strange in view of the position in which the German military leadership found itself. Faced since June 1944 with devastating offensives in both the west and east, Finland had basically become a footnote in this great struggle. Nevertheless, halfway measures and a reactive posture in regard to Finland were not in Germany's interests. The continued insis-tence on hanging on to the Pechenga nickel mines is difficult to under-stand once the shipment route of nickel to Germany was severed. A quick withdrawal to Norway before winter with minimum losses was the logical course of action. Any delay posed serious danger to German forces in both Finland and north Norway.

In late September 1944 the OKW made some significant revisions to their earlier plans for the 20th Mountain Army. The OKW was mak-ing an overall strategic assessment of the situation in Scandinavia and the revised outlook by the OKW was caused to a large extent by this assessment.

The loss of the submarine bases on the French coast was an important element in the assessment. The loss of these bases had caused an immense increase in the importance of naval bases in Norway. The German Navy planned to resume large-scale submarine warfare with new types of submarines equipped with snorkels and hydrogen peroxide engines.[30] The OKW expected the Allies to do all they could to eliminate this threat and they also expected that the British wanted to prevent the Soviets from gaining a foothold in northern Scandinavia. A move by the Western Allies in this direction would place the supply route from Germany to Norway and along the Norwegian coast to north Norway, completely under their domination.

It was finally decided that the nickel from Pechenga had lost its importance. Albert Speer, in charge of war production, stated that there were sufficient quantities of nickel on hand in Germany to cover their needs. The OKW therefore believed that there was no further need to hold the *Birke* position in the Murmansk sector.

The OKW concluded that the 20th Mountain Army had to be withdrawn from Finland before the expected action by the Western Allies against Norway. Not to do so could result in its loss since the 20th Mountain Army depended entirely on sea transportation for supplies. The Anglo-Americans would be able to dominate this supply line even without landing troops in Norway. A withdrawal of the 20th Mountain Army would relieve the pressure on coastal shipping. Such a withdrawal would also strengthen the defenses of Norway both against the threat from the Western Allies and against the possibility that Sweden would intervene on the side of the Allies. In short, a withdrawal of the 20th Mountain Army would alleviate most of the problems facing the Germans if they remained in Finland.

The conclusions of the OKW were given impetus by receipt of 20th Mountain Army plans on September 28, 1944. These plans outlined how the army intended to conduct operations in the Rovaniemi position as well in the next two positions: the Ivalo–Karesuando line and the Lyngenfjord–Swedish frontier line. Both the OKW and 20th Mountain Army planners concluded that every day of delay would make the withdrawal to the Lyngenfjord position in Norway more perilous.

The lateness of the season made the 20th Mountain Army's suc-

cessful withdrawal to the Lyngenfjord position in Norway very problematic. This raised the unpleasant possibility that, due to the onset of
winter, the operation could not be accomplished until June 1945.
Nevertheless, General Rendulic was told to prepare for the possibility
that the withdrawal would have to be executed during the winter.

The issues and recommendations in the OKW assessment were left
unresolved until Hitler was briefed on September 30. He approved the
withdrawal to the Lyngenfjord position on October 3 and the OKW
issued the necessary warning orders on October 4 and 5. The operation
was given the code-name *Nordlicht*, not to be confused with the earlier
operation against Leningrad with the same code name.

The Fighting at Tornio

At dawn on October 1 the Finns landed a regiment from the 3rd
Division behind the German lines at Tornio. The troops had been
embarked on transports at Oulu on September 30 and covered the
approximately 100 kilometers in the Gulf of Bothnia during the night.
A smaller Finnish force of about 300 troops had taken preparatory
measures at Tornio, paving the way for the landing.

Erfurth writes in 1977 that "The details and motives of this regrettable incident, which largely influenced German–Finnish relations, have
not yet so shaped up as to form a clear picture for historians."[31] He goes
on to speculate that it may have been the action of local Finnish commanders and not in accordance with the intentions of the highest
Finnish military leadership. He also suggests that it may have taken
place as a pre-emptive move by the Finns to keep the bridge over the
Tornio River to Sweden from being destroyed. Lundin writes that the
landing in the rear of the Germans at Tornio was intended to hasten the
German withdrawal "so that they would not have time to destroy anything on their way."[32]

Vehviläinen writes that "The phony war that the Finns were conducting in the north was glaringly at odds with the terms of the
armistice agreement, and it placed the whole country in jeopardy."[33]
The Soviet Control Commission had arrived in Finland at the end of
September and it had begun to apply pressure on the Finns to take effective measures to honor their commitment under the armistice agreement
to expel or intern the German troops. The Finns were given what
amounted to an ultimatum by the Soviet head of the Control Com-

mission, Lieutenant General Savenenko, on September 30. This ultimatum, according to Vehviläinen, caused Mannerheim to order General
Siilasvuo "to do something spectacular enough to satisfy the
Russians."[34] According to Vehviläinen, General Siilasvuo thereupon
ordered an amphibious landing at Kemi, later changed to Tornio.

The sequence of events within the time frame suggested by
Vehviläinen does not hold up to scrutiny. An amphibious operation of
this type, even a makeshift one, requires planning, assembly of forces
and shipping, and briefings before it can be launched. To suggest that
all this and the transport to the objective took place within about 12
hours defies logic. The planning and execution of the operation probably took several days. It may have taken place at the initiative of
General Siilasvuo (or Mannerheim and Siilasvuo), but it could not have
been in response to an ultimatum issued by General Savenenko on
September 30. Mannerheim himself writes that the troops were ready to
sail on September 29 (the day before the ultimatum) but a storm forced
a postponement.[35] The fact that a number of foreign journalists were
brought along by the Finns to witness the fighting at Kemi and Tornio
illustrates that it was a well planned operation intended to influence foreign opinion and disprove Soviet accusations that the Finns were not living up to their agreement.

The Germans did not have many troops at Tornio. Divisional
Group Kräutler, with one infantry battalion, two battalions of artillery,
and some supply troops, was responsible for Tornio, Kemi, and about
100 kilometers of coastline. The German troops in Tornio were apparently taken by surprise by the landing and initially did not offer resistance. This soon changed and heavy fighting broke out between
German and Finnish troops in and around the town as Divisional
Group Kräutler rushed troops into the area. The Finns, who had also
carried out a landing on the islands outside Kemi harbor, brought in the
rest of the 3rd Division under Major General Aaro Pajari and later also
the 11th Division under Major General Kalle Heiskanen. The Luftwaffe
sank two ships carrying troops from the 11th Division.[36] Erfurth relates
that Finnish troops entered the German hospital in Tornio and allegedly carried out violence against staff and patients. They also attacked and
captured the German fuel depot north of Tornio.[37]

General Rendulic took steps to regain control of the situation in the
Kemi-Tornio area. The regimental-size Battle Group West, which had

joined the 7th Mountain Division as it withdrew through Pudasjärvi, was ordered to join Divisional Group Kräutler. Another two infantry battalions and the Machinegun Ski Brigade were also ordered into the sector of Divisional Group Kräutler on October 2.[38] The Machinegun Ski Brigade had been the largest unit in Battle Group East. It was formed in the summer of 1944 as a reserve for the 20th Mountain Army when Hitler blocked the return of personnel on leave in Germany. It consisted of three machinegun ski battalions and some infantry.

It was important for the 20th Mountain Army not to let events in Tornio and Kemi interfere with the withdrawal. The army's quartermaster reported on October 2 that all supplies at Rovaniemi had been evacuated. It was therefore only necessary to hold Rovaniemi, the Lapland capital, long enough for the XXXVI Mountain Corps and the 6th SS Mountain Division from XVIII Corps to pass through. The 7th Mountain Division from XVIII Corps was ordered to hold Pudasjärvi until 6th SS Mountain Division and the 163rd Infantry Division from XXXVI Corps had passed through Rovaniemi. General Rendulic did not consider it necessary to retake either Kemi or Tornio, only to keep the Finns bottled up in those areas so they would not be able to interfere with the withdrawal. Those were the orders he gave to Divisional Group Kräutler.

However, the fighting around Kemi and Tornio was heavy. Hölter notes that "the losses on both sides were high."[39] Divisional Group Kräutler made some progress in its attack against the Finnish beachhead at Tornio on October 3 but the Finns were bringing in heavy reinforcements. The Germans were not able to push into Tornio or to recapture the important fuel depot. The Germans east of Kemi were also forced back on October 4, and with pressures in the Kemi area building, the 20th Mountain Army ordered a withdrawal to begin on October 7. All German troops had departed the Tornio-Kemi region by October 10.

Part of Group Kräutler was ordered to withdraw along the Swedish frontier to Muonio while the rest were told to engage in delaying action along the road from Kemi to Rovaniemi. The next day, the Finns, resorting to "*motti*" (shallow encirclement) tactics, encircled a German force north of Tornio. The withdrawal had to be postponed for twenty-four hours while the encirclement was broken after heavy fighting.

The combat in the Kemi-Tornio area, which lasted for several days, resulted in heavy losses for both sides. The Finns reported that they had

1,700 casualties, including 189 killed. They also claimed to have captured 1,000 German troops. The majority of these appear to have been support troops. The captured soldiers were later turned over to the Soviets.

The protest that General Rendulic had lodged as a result of the incident at Pudasjärvi on September 28 was finally answered by Siilasvuo late on October 2. Siilasvuo rejected Rendulic's ultimatum. He stated that no agreement had ever been made that was contrary to the terms of the armistice entered into with the Soviets. Siilasvuo stated that the Finnish military leadership would not be bound by arrangements made by local commanders.

On October 3 General Rendulic announced that the German troops would from now on operate against the Finns without restraint. He abandoned the policy of limiting destruction to lines of communication. The Germans viewed the Finnish action at Kemi and Tornio as treachery and Rendulic ordered that "all cover, installations, and objects of use to the enemy are to be destroyed."[40] The taking of hostages was also begun on a large scale but halted within a few days by orders from OKW.[41] This OKW action was apparently taken in order not to cause an open breach with Sweden.

At the same time as the operations against Kemi and Tornio were underway, Major General Lagus began an advance further to the east, in a northerly direction from Pudasjärvi. The Finnish forces there consisted of the Armored Division, the 6th Division and elements of the Border Jäger Brigade.

The Jäger Brigade of the Armored Division, under Colonel Valter Nordgren, met stiff resistance south of Rovaniemi. After fighting that lasted four days, the Germans abandoned the town of Rovaniemi on October 16 and the 7th Mountain Division and elements of Group Kräutler withdrew northward through Lapland. The town of Rovaniemi was utterly destroyed by the Germans.[42] The Germans admit that it far exceeded that permitted by the exigencies of war but Rendulic points out that some of that destruction was caused by the detonation of an ammunition train carrying 400 tons of explosives standing at the Rovaniemi railway station. Before this mishap, according to Rendulic, only a few buildings had been destroyed and he notes that "We sincerely regretted the fate of this city."[43] The Finnish troops continued their pursuit but did not seriously hamper the German withdrawal.

The Finnish troops pursuing towards Muonio consisted of the 3rd and 11th Divisions and the 15th Brigade. These units had to cope with tough German delaying actions in their area of main effort along the Swedish frontier and at Vuotso, south of Ivalo.

The Germans succeeded in keeping the withdrawal routes open for the troops withdrawing from Rovaniemi. Several attempts at encirclement failed as the Germans managed to avoid the traps.[44] This was commented on by the Soviet Control Commission and led Mannerheim to admonish Siilasvuo to use stronger forces for encirclements.[45]

NOTES

1. The number of men drawing rations in the middle of August was 204,064. Erfurth, *The Last Finnish War*, p.221.
2. Hölter, *op. cit.*, p.37.
3. Erfurth, *The Last Finnish War*, p.221.
4. Shtemenko, *op. cit.*, p.347.
5. *Ibid*, pp.369–371.
6. Vehvilainen, *op. cit.*, p.149 and Erfurth, *The Last Finnish War*, p.224.
7. Vehvilainen, *op. cit.*, p.149.
8. 20th Mountain Army War Diary scattered entries September 1–December 18, 1944, as referenced in Ziemke, *The German Northern Theater of Operations*, p.293. See also Rendulic, *op. cit.*, pp.286–287.
9. Ziemke, *The German Northern Theater of Operations*, p.292 and Erfurth, *The Last Finnish War*, p.224.
10. Ziemke, *The German Northern Theater of Operations*, p.296.
11. Mikkola, *op. cit.*, p.30.
12. Westerlund, *op. cit.*, p.212.
13. Erfurth, *The Last Finnish War*, p.226 reports that the fighting lasted two days. This is not supported by Finnish sources.
14. Raunio, *op. cit.*, p.187. Earl F. Ziemke, *Stalingrad to Berlin*, p.394, writes that the Finns reported the capture of 700 prisoners based on a German Naval War Diary entry.
15. Ziemke, *Stalingrad to Berlin*, p.394, reports that Rendulic initially refused but that a compromise was worked out with the Finns.
16. Erfurth, *The Last Finnish War*, pp.225–226 and Ziemke, *The German Northern Theater of Operations*, p.295.
17. Hölter, *op. cit.*, pp.38–39.
18. *Ibid*, p.43.
19. Mannerheim, *Memoirs*, p.503.
20. Vehviläinen, *op. cit.*, p.150.

348   FINLAND'S WAR OF CHOICE

21. Ziemke, *Stalingrad to Berlin,* p.394.
22. Westerlund, *op. cit.,* p.213.
23. Ziemke, *Stalingrad to Berlin,* pp.394–395.
24. Erfurth, *The Last Finnish War,* p.227.
25. *Ibid,* p.229.
26. Emil Schuler, *Mit dem Bergschuh im Russland und Finnland,* München: Eigenverlag Emil Schuler, 1959, pp.152–197 and Roland Kaltenegger, *Schicksalsweg und Kampf der "Bergschuh" Division* (Graz: Leopold Stocker Verlag, 1985), pp.287–331.
27. Kräutler and Springenschmidt, *op. cit.,* p.385.
28. Hölter, according to Lundin, *op. cit.,* p.242, denies the destruction of villages. This is in sharp contrast to his frank admission of the thorough destruction carried out in the Province of Finland in Norway a few months later—Hölter, *op. cit.,* p.71.
29. Lundin, *op. cit.,* p.245.
30. Ziemke, *The German Northern Theater of Operations,* p.301.
31. Erfurth, *The Last Finnish War,* p.235.
32. Lundin, *op. cit.,* p.243.
33. Vehviläinen, *op. cit.,* p.150.
34. *Loc. cit.*
35. Mannerheim, *Memoirs,* p.504.
36. Westerlund, *op. cit.,* p.214.
37. Erfurth, *The Last Finnish War,* p.235.
38. Hölter, *op. cit.,* p.51.
39. *Loc. cit.*
40. 20th Mountain Army War Diary entries of October 2 and 3, 1944, as cited in Ziemke, *The German Northern Theater of Operations,* pp.299–300.
41. It should be noted that General Rendulic was tried as a war criminal by the Military Tribunal in Nuremberg. The charges dealt with his activities in Yugoslavia and Finland. He was found guilty on the charges related to treatment of civilians in Yugoslavia but the charges concerning the scorched-earth policy in Lapland were dropped. On the Yugoslav charges he was sentenced to 20 years in prison. The sentence was later reduced to 10 years and he was released from prison on February 1, 1951.
42. Westerlund, *op. cit.,* p.214.
43. Rendulic, *op. cit.,* p.306.
44. Hölter, *op. cit.,* pp.52–53.
45. Westerlund, *op. cit.,* p.214.

TWELVE
THE 20TH MOUNTAIN
ARMY'S *KATABASIS*[1]

Operation Nordlicht

Hitler approved the withdrawal of the 20th Mountain Army to the Lyngenfjord defense line in Norway after the OKW assessment was presented to him on October 3, 1944, but no date was set for the withdrawal of the XIX Mountain Corps on the Murmansk front. That Corps had to remain in position until the units withdrawing from central Finland were out of harm's way. The OKW issued warning orders for the withdrawal of the 20th Mountain Army on October 4 and 5. The operation was code-named *Nordlicht* (Northern Lights) on October 6.

Operation *Nordlicht*, which is actually an extension of Operation *Birke*, has no parallel in military history. It involved the withdrawal, under pressure, of over 250,000 men and their equipment and supplies during winter in the arctic. The distances from Ivalo and Kirkenes to Narvik, respectively, were 1,100 kilometers and 1,000 kilometers. It was realized by all that the planned withdrawal could succeed only with great good luck and adherence to a strict timetable and centralized command.

The XXXVI was the most fortunate of the German corps in that it had an all-weather road for its withdrawal from Rovaniemi via Ivalo and Inari to Karasjok and Lakselv in Norway. It was planned to move the following units along this road: XXXVI Corps Headquarters, 169th Infantry Division, 163rd Infantry Division, and Group Steets.

The XVIII Mountain Corps was to withdraw over the so-called Finland Road from Tornio via Muonio to Skibotten in Norway. The road from Tornio in the south was unimproved to Muonio. Between Muonio and Skibotten it was only half completed and had a low carry-

349

ing capacity. The motorized units of the 6th SS Mountain Division were to withdraw from Rovaniemi to Muonio and lead the withdrawal from there to Norway. The infantry elements of the division would follow and the withdrawal of the division could not be complete at its destination until their arrival. Other strong units sent on the road to Skibotten included the 7th Mountain Division, Division Group Kräutler, all the horse-drawn heavy artillery units, and XVIII Corps Headquarters.

The 6th SS Mountain Division was given movement priority to the Bjørnefell area east of Narvik to protect against possible Swedish intervention in conjunction with the landing of Norwegian forces from England. A radio announcement by the Norwegian king on October 26, 1944 that Norwegian forces would soon intervene in north Norway at the side of the Soviets strengthened the fear of Swedish intervention. This fear was also given as one of the reasons for the German decision to evacuate the civilian population and adopt a scorched-earth policy in Finnmark Province—so as to prevent the enemy from gaining a foothold in the area vacated by the Germans.

The XIX Corps would use the Pechenga–Kirkenes road in the initial phase of its withdrawal. Thereafter it would use Route 50 via Lakselv to Lyngenfjord. The units expected to use this route included the corps headquarters, 6th Mountain Division, 2nd Mountain Division, Division Group van der Hoop, and the 210th Infantry Division. It was planned for units of the XIX Mountain Corps to arrive west of Lakselv (Salmon River) by November 15 at the latest. Route 50 between Lakselv and Kirkenes was usually impassable because of snow between October 1 and late spring. The autumn of 1944 was unusually mild but that was not expected to last. A mobile rear guard from XIX Mountain Corps would cover the withdrawal.

The Lyngenfjord defensive line and the Narvik area were to be manned by units from LXXI Corps stationed in Norway. In addition, units from the withdrawing forces were also earmarked for this defensive line. These included the XIX Corps Headquarters, the 6th and 7th Mountain Divisions, the 210th Infantry Division, the Bicycle Reconnaissance Brigade Norway, and the Machinegun Brigade Finland. The 20th Mountain Army was informed that it had to rely on its own fuel stocks until April 1945.

There were numerous unknown problems and unanswered questions facing the Germans in this history-making withdrawal. Would the mild autumn weather continue or would the normal October gales set in with heavy snowfall which would make the withdrawal routes impassable? Would the Finns, following the two corps withdrawing from central Finland, launch offensives with superior forces? While the Soviets were expected to launch an offensive against the XIX Mountain Corps their objectives could not be anticipated. Would they turn south-westward against the XXXVI Corps at Ivalo or would they follow both the XXXVI Corps and the XIX Corps into Norway?

Other possibilities also had to be considered. Would the Soviets or the Western Allies cut off the whole 20th Mountain Army by attacking Narvik or the long and narrow coastal area between Narvik and Trondheim? As is true of all prudent military planners, the Germans had to assume that the Soviets would continue their pursuit at least as far as the Lyngenfjord defense line. Route 50, interrupted by many ferry crossings, paralleled the coast for long stretches and it was therefore vulnerable to both sea and air power. Sweden's attitude towards Germany had become increasingly hostile, and as pointed out above, an intervention could not be ruled out. Sweden had already abrogated its trade agreement with Germany. The withdrawal route of the XVIII Mountain Corps took it very close to the Swedish border for several hundred miles and any minor incident could develop into open hostilities.

German Situation on the Murmansk Front

The withdrawal of the XIX Mountain Corps was forced by a Soviet offensive that began on October 7, the same day that General Rendulic ordered the withdrawal from Kemi and Tornio in the southwestern part of his area of operation, and more than a week before the Germans evacuated Rovaniemi. The 20th Mountain Army was still scattered over an area of 200,000 square kilometers.

The XIX Mountain Corps consisted of 2nd and 6th Mountain Divisions, the 210th Infantry Division, Division Group van der Hoop, and the Bicycle Reconnaissance Brigade Norway. It had no armored units assigned. The strength of the XIX Mountain Corps, commanded by General Ferdinand Jodl, was approximately 56,000. This number and the fact that the corps consisted of four divisions is by itself very misleading since the number involved large units of static and support troops and two of the combat units were small in comparison to divisions.

The 210th Infantry Division, of five fortress battalions, was a static division and had only approximately 5,900 men assigned. The designation of van der Hoop's outfit as a division group is also misleading. It was composed of two infantry regiments (193rd and 503rd) and had only about 4,000 men assigned. Colonel Adrian Freiherr van der Hoop had assumed command of this group on June 25, 1944, when its former commander, Major General Rossi, was killed in the same plane crash as General Dietl. When General Rossi had commanded the group it was known as Division Group Rossi. The Bicycle Reconnaissance Brigade Norway had an authorized strength of 2,130, but the actual strength is unknown. This unit had been brought in from Norway. General Rendulic had also planned to send the Machinegun Ski Brigade into the XIX Corps area but it was diverted to the Kemi-Tornio region. The 2nd Mountain Division had an assigned strength of about 16,000, and the 6th Mountain Division, with the 388th Infantry Regiment attached, had an assigned strength of about 18,000.[2]

The 210th Infantry Division was scattered in static positions from Alta to Kirkenes in Norway. Division Group van der Hoop was deployed from Pechenga Bay in the west to the mouth of Titovka River and thus included the neck of the Rybachiy Peninsula. The 6th Mountain Division held the main Litsa front from the Titovka River mouth south to Lake Chapr. It covered the main front and this was the reason it was reinforced with the 388th Infantry Regiment. The 2nd Mountain Division, with two regiments, held a strongpoint line along the Titovka River south and southwest of the 6th Mountain Division. The Germans had worked on their elaborate defensive positions on the Murmansk front since the summer of 1941.The German defenses along the Litsa and Titovka Rivers were based on lines of strongpoints *(stutzpunktlinie)* built over the past three years. The first line in this interlocking belt was occupied while the remaining two were ready for occupation. The strongpoints were built on dominating terrain and consisted of steel and concrete bunkers with all-around fields of fire. The bunkers were surrounded by barbed wire and minefields.

Major James Gebhardt gives a good description of one of these bunker complexes:

In the 2nd Mountain Division sector, for example Strongpoint Zucherhutl was manned by a company of mountain infantry, a

reinforced engineer platoon, and an artillery observation section. This force was armed with thirteen light machine guns
(145,000 rounds), four heavy machine guns, two 80mm mortars (2,100 rounds), two light infantry guns (1,600 rounds), and
two 37-mm antitank guns (770 rounds). In the entire division
sector, there were ten reinforced company-size strongpoints and
several smaller positions occupied by a platoon or less. . . .
Direct and indirect fires, engineer obstacles, minefields, and
patrol covered the low ground between strongpoints, which
varied in width to as much as two to four kilometers. Realizing
that these gaps constituted a major weakness in the defensive
system, the 2nd Mountain Division units constructed or
improved additional intermediate positions in the week before
the Soviet offensive began.[3]

A second defensive line was located 10–12 kilometers behind the
front, along the west bank of the Titovka River. The final defensive line
ran along the west bank of the Pechenga River, some 20–25 kilometers
behind the second line. This line was strongest in the approaches to the
towns of Pechenga and Luostari. In addition, there were defensive
works covering the mining area at Nikel and the ports.

The Germans were aware of Soviet build-up and offensive preparations on the Murmansk front since the first half of September 1944. It
was not possible to conceal these preparations in the open tundra.
Construction of roads into the operational area and a trench system
approaching the initial defensive line had been going on for many
weeks.

The XIX Corps had brought these ominous signs of an impending
offensive to the attention of the 20th Mountain Army and stressed the
need for an early withdrawal. The 20th Mountain Army was therefore
well aware of the danger of a major Soviet offensive in the Murmansk
sector. But General Rendulic was in a dilemma. While he knew that he
could not count on the mild weather continuing, he could not withdraw
the XIX Mountain Corps from their well-prepared defensive lines
because a Soviet push either to the northwest or southwest would
imperil the withdrawal of all corps.

Some of the problems were caused by OKW insistence on evacuating large stores of supplies and equipment from the south over bad

roads with limited means of transportation. Nevertheless, a sense of urgency was not evident since two weeks passed after the quartermaster reported that all stores in Rovaniemi had been evacuated before the town was vacated. This apparent lack of urgency may have been due to the belief that the XIX Corps' well-constructed defensive front would halt any Soviet offensive and the belief at OKW that a withdrawal of the XIX Corps could be carried out in November. This last OKW opinion proved to be true as the mild weather continued into December but it should not have been the basis for planning since it was contrary to all past experience.

It was also important to delay the withdrawal for another reason. This involved the evacuation of the many facilities along the Arctic Ocean. German army facilities in Finnmark also had to be evacuated. The same was true for the Luftwaffe and its ground personnel. The Navy had to evacuate its bases in Finnmark. All this required time

Erfurth, however, maintains that the main reason for the delay can be traced back to Hitler.[4] He was still obsessed with the need to hold the nickel mines despite Albert Speer's statement minimizing their importance. Hitler's preoccupation with the nickel mines was undoubtedly a reason for delay before October 3—when he was briefed by the OKW— but not subsequently. The delay to order the execution of *Nordlicht* in the XIX Corps area was probably more connected to the evacuation of supplies and the slow northward progress of the other two corps. Hitler, like others in the OKW, may well have been more worried about the effects of giving up well-prepared positions and thereby starting a process that could unravel the whole withdrawal. Even the XIX Mountain Corps appeared to have believed that the defenses on the Murmansk front would hold.[5]

Soviet Offensive Plans and Preparations

General Kirill A. Meretskov commanded the Karelian Front. This was a position he had held since February 1944, when planning for the offensive against the XIX Corps had begun. War games of the plans were conducted in April and May at all echelons from regiment to front.

The 14th Soviet Army had defended the approaches to Murmansk since the beginning of the war in 1941. The 14th Army was still there and commanded by Lieutenant General V. I. Shcherbakov, who had taken command in early 1942. Reinforcements for the 14th Army had flowed into the Murmansk sector since August. Forces available to General Shcherbakov at the onset of the offensive included:

1. Two light infantry corps (126th and 127th). These units were formed in early 1944 from naval infantry brigades and separate ski units. The 126th Light Infantry Corps, composed of two brigades, was commanded by Colonel V. N. Solovev. Major General G. A. Zhukov commanded the 127th Light Infantry Corps, also composed of two brigades. Major Gebhardt points out that with an authorized strength of 4,334 men in each brigade, a light infantry corps was slightly smaller than a full-strength Soviet division.[6]
2. Three regular infantry corps—31st, 99th, and 131st. The 31st Infantry Corps, composed of two infantry divisions (83rd and 367th), was commanded by Major General M. A. Absaliamov. The 99th Infantry Corps was commanded by Lieutenant General S. P. Mikulskii and was composed of three infantry divisions (65th, 114th, and 368th). The 131st Infantry Corps, commanded by Major General Z. N. Alekseev, had two infantry divisions (10th and 14th). The three corps were at 60–65 percent of authorized strength.
3. A corps group named Pigarevich after its commander Lieutenant General B. A. Pigarevich, which was a composite unit consisting of one infantry division (45th) and two infantry brigades.

General Meretskov had concluded that the area of the 2nd Mountain Division was the key in the German defensive system. If that division were to be defeated, the routes to Pechenga, Luostari, and Nikel would be opened. He decided to launch his main attack on a very narrow front against the 2nd Mountain Division sector south of Lake Chapr.

Meretskov decided to use his two light infantry corps to turn the southern German flank where it dwindled away in the hinterland along the Finnish border. One of these corps, the 127th, was given the additional mission of advancing to the lake region at Salmijärvi about 55 kilometers west of the German right wing, so as to cut the Arctic Ocean Highway. His main forces would turn north to roll up the German defenses along the Titovka River. Group Pigarevich, which had been on the defensive during the breakthrough operations, would now go over to the offensive in a frontal attack on the German defensive line.[7]

Shtemenko writes that the density of artillery and mortars in the breakthrough sector was 160–170 per kilometer.[8] Other sources generally agree. In addition to the organic artillery and mortar units, seven mortar regiments and seventeen artillery regiments were brought in from the other two armies of the Karelian Front, the 7th and 32nd. General Shcherbakov was also given three regiments and two brigades of the dreaded Katyusha Multiple Rocket Launchers (MRL), a total of 120 systems.[9] The Soviets also enjoyed air superiority, bordering on air dominance. The Karelian Front had a total of 747 aircraft of all types and the Northern Fleet had another 275.[10]

The 14th Army did not have any organic armored units since all armored forces belonged to the Karelian Front. General Meretskov brought in three tank units for the attack on the German defenses in the area east of Pechenga—a total of about 70 T-34 tanks. Two self-propelled artillery units were also brought forward. Meretskov also asked the Supreme Soviet High Command (STAVKA) for a regiment of heavy KV tanks. His request was granted after some initial reluctance since the General Staff felt that the T-34s were more suitable.[11] Twenty-one KV-85 tanks were attached to his command. This unit of heavy tanks was paired with one of the heavy self-propelled artillery regiments and attached to the 131st Infantry Corps. The 7th Tank Brigade (T-34s) was paired with another heavy artillery regiment and attached to the 99th Infantry Corps.

The Soviets also employed about 35 engineer battalions. Two special-purpose motorized battalions, each with 94 American-built amphibious vehicles, were attached to the 99th and 131st Corps. In addition there was ample river crossing equipment and much of this was attached to the attacking divisions.[12]

General Meretskov submitted his plans to STAVKA for approval. STAVKA made several modifications, some dealing with the relations between the 14th Army and the Soviet Northern fleet under Admiral Golovko. The Northern Fleet was in position to land sizable forces on the Rybachiy Peninsula and at various points along the coast to the west. STAVKA wanted this capability utilized and Admiral Golovko was ordered to have the naval infantry brigade already on the Rybachiy

Peninsula break through the German defenses of Group van der Hoop. Another naval infantry brigade was to be landed on the mainland west of Rybachiy Peninsula and advance into the rear of the German defenses along the Titovka River.

STAVKA felt that this would eliminate the need for Meretskov's forces to turn north along the Titovka River. Its order was clear: "Do not scatter your forces for a thrust to the northeast along the Titovka River."[13] Instead, STAVKA wanted the main forces to advance on Pechenga as quickly as possible. Finally, STAVKA put a break on the southern envelopment. It did not want the 127th Light Infantry Corps to advance as far as the Salmijärvi region, where it could risk being isolated. Instead, Meretskov was ordered to echelon that corps along the left flank of the Soviet attack.

The 99th and 131st Infantry Corps were assembled east of the breakthrough area south of Lake Chapr in early October and all required supplies were brought forward.

The Soviet Attack

The Soviet offensive, launched in the morning of October 7, 1944, was preceded by an artillery preparation that started at 0800 hours and lasted two hours and thirty-five minutes. Over 140,000 rounds for artillery and mortars were allocated for the preparation. In addition, about 8,500 MRL rockets were fired on each square kilometer against selected strongpoints.[14]

The Soviet infantry launched their attack when the supporting fire was shifted to targets behind the German front line positions. About four divisions from the 99th and 131st Corps made a massed attack on a very narrow front against the 2nd Mountain Division positions immediately south of Lake Chapr, near that division's boundary with the 6th Mountain Division. The devastating attack quickly swept over several strongpoints and Soviet troops were closing on the Titovka River by noon.

The 2nd Mountain Division was thoroughly stunned by the inferno of artillery and mortar fire and the massed Soviet infantry attack. The Bicycle Reconnaissance Brigade Norway, which had been in reserve, was ordered to establish defensive positions along the Division's supply road (named Lanweg—Lan Road—by the Germans), which intersects the Arctic Ocean Highway at Luostari.

On October 8, the 2nd Mountain Division fell back on the positions along the Lan Road. The 20th Mountain Army ordered that the Soviets had to be prevented, at all costs, from cutting the Arctic Ocean Highway. It gave the XIX Corps permission to pull the 6th Mountain Division back from the Litsa front in order to shorten the line and create reserves.

The Soviet main effort was switched to the south on October 9 with the 126th Light Infantry Corps moving around the right flank of the 2nd Mountain Division along the Lan Road and proceeding towards the Arctic Ocean Highway. At the same time the Soviets launched heavy attacks against the right flank of the 2nd Mountain Division, driving it back and creating a gap between the left flank of the 2nd Mountain Division and the right flank of the 6th Mountain Division. To prevent a collapse of the XIX Mountain Corps' front, the 20th Mountain Army ordered a regiment from the 163rd Division, a machinegun battalion, and a SS battalion into the XIX Mountain Corps area. However, these units were still some distance from the XIX Corps area.

October 10 brought the XIX Mountain Corps a series of crisis situations. First, Soviet naval infantry landed on the mainland west of Rybachiy Peninsula. This force was able to turn the flank of Group van der Hoop, forcing it to give up its positions at the neck of the peninsula. Secondly, the 99th Infantry Corps sent two regiments north through a gap that had developed between the 2nd and 6th Mountain Divisions. Their objective was to cut the Russian Road, the 6th Division's line of retreat to Pechenga.

Units of the 126th Light Infantry Corps pushed past the right flank of the 2nd Mountain Division and cut the Arctic Ocean Highway for a distance of eight kilometers west of Luostari. The 31st Infantry Brigade from the 126th Light Infantry Corps dug in astride the Arctic Ocean Highway facing west to hinder German reinforcements. The 72nd Naval Infantry Brigade from the same corps dug in astride the same highway facing east to block the German withdrawal route. The Soviet troops were beginning to show signs of exhaustion and supplies were running short. Several tons of ammunition and supplies were parachuted to the 126th Light Infantry Corps on the night of October 11–12. While units of the 2nd Mountain Division still held the road junction at Luostari, the Soviets held about eight kilometers of the Arctic Ocean Highway to the east.

The coherence of the 20th Mountain Army was beginning to unravel and the 2nd and 6th Mountain Divisions faced immediate danger of encirclement. If the Soviets were able to push south as far as Ivalo, the withdrawal route for the XXXVI Corps through Karasjok would be unusable. This had to be prevented at all costs. Units of the XXXVI Corps, under the command of Major General Karl Rübel, the commander of the 163rd Infantry Division, which had already withdrawn past Kemi River on the Salla–Rovaniemi road, were turned north and ordered to move into the sector of the XIX Corps at top speed. Part of Group Rübel—one regiment and three battalions—arrived in the area northwest of Luostari on October 11 and established a screen to prevent the Soviets from advancing toward Ivalo. The arrival of the 163rd Infantry Division on the battlefield is described by the division's operations officer:

> After a motorized march of more than 400 kilometers, the 307th Regiment literally detrucked on the battlefield. Soldiers almost frozen stiff had to be committed in battle immediately after leaving their vehicles because the enemy had already penetrated westward beyond the road fork. . . . The bulk of the 307th Regiment arrived by the afternoon of 12 October and received orders to attack in the evening, to drive back the enemy, and to occupy the road fork as its first objective.[15]

The 20th Army reserve under Major General Steets was also sent north to link up with Rübel's forces. Rübel remained in command of his makeshift unit and while it is variously referred to as Battle Group Rübel or as Corps Group Rübel, I shall simply refer to it as Group Rübel.

The 127th Light Infantry Corps was meanwhile advancing across the trackless terrain to the south and crossed the Pechenga River in the morning of October 10. In the north, the 6th Mountain Division was ordered to attack westward and clear the Russian Road, cut by troops from the 131st Infantry Corps. Then the 6th Mountain Division and Group van der Hoop were to fall back to a line from Pechenga to Luostari. Preparations for the destruction of the nickel works were finalized.

The 6th Mountain Division managed to clear the Russian Road in the morning of October 11 but the Soviets cut it for a second time on October 12 after a bitter all-night battle with heavy casualties on both sides.[16] The 6th Mountain Division and Division Group van der Hoop fell back to positions east of Pechenga by October 13.

The Soviet 99th Infantry Corps was meanwhile attacking to the south of the 131st Infantry Corps. Heavily supported by KV-85 and T-34 tanks as well as self-propelled artillery, the lead elements of the corps crossed the Titovka River on the night of October 10–11. The crossing of numerous mechanized and motorized vehicles, which could only be deployed on the road because the terrain was too rugged, caused a major traffic jam west of the river on October 11.

The Soviets captured Luostari on October 12 in a multi-directional attack, and on October 13 they reached the Pechenga River. Landings of Soviet naval infantry from speedboats were also made in the Bay of Pechenga. Shtemenko describes the fighting as exceedingly bitter but claims that the Soviets shot down 66 German planes.[17] This is undoubtedly an exaggeration since the Soviets' own estimate of total German air strength in the region was only 160.

Group Rübel and dispersed units of the 2nd Mountain Division that had come under its command attempted to clear the Soviets from the Arctic Ocean Highway. They were not successful. To make matters worse, the Soviet 72nd Naval Infantry Brigade, from the Soviet 126th Light Infantry Corps, drove north behind the 2nd Mountain Division and cut the Tårnet Road, the German line of retreat from Pechenga to Kirkenes. The XIX Corps was now isolated and some unpleasant decisions had to be made in an attempt to save the situation.

The high hopes that the OKW had entertained about German ability to hold the Pechenga region were shredded. The elaborate defensive installations constructed by the Germans over three years had been swept aside in less than a week. The OKW appears to have labored under the impression that the tundra terrain east of Pechenga was totally unsuitable to support large-unit operations. This false premise was probably shared by the 20th Mountain Army and the XIX Mountain Corps. It may also explain why the Germans had no armored forces in the XIX Mountain Corps area of operations.

Ziemke takes a slightly different view of things. While recognizing that the Germans had miscalculated when it came to Soviet ability to move and support large formations, including tanks and self-propelled

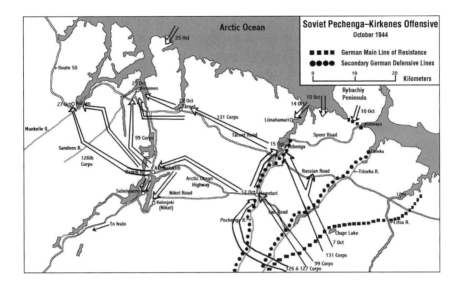

artillery, he holds that the rapid collapse of the 2nd Mountain Division demonstrates that three years of inactivity had produced complacency and a decline in combat readiness on the part of the Germans. With regard to the German assumption that the terrain presented a serious obstacle to the employment of large formations he has this to say:

> Nevertheless, their original assumption was only partially dis-
> proved, since the Russians employing a vastly superior force of
> specially trained troops with skillful and daring leadership
> against an opponent whose chief desire was to avoid a decisive
> engagement, failed—just as the Mountain Corps Norway had in
> 1941—to achieve their main objective, to trap and destroy the
> XIX Mountain Corps.[18]

Some of Ziemke's conclusions are supported by Soviet writers. Gebhardt, using primarily Soviet sources, writes that the absence of usable roads seriously affected the battle since combat units could not replace their dwindling ammunition stocks or reposition their artillery. The lead elements of the 99th and 131st Infantry Corps had already advanced past the range of supporting artillery on October 9. The lack of artillery support was somewhat compensated for on that day by the Soviet Air Force, which flew over 1,000 sorties.[19]

German Withdrawal from the Pechenga Area

Despite the disastrous events in the XIX Mountain Corps area, the OKW and Hitler appeared to cling to the idea of temporarily halting the XIX Mountain Corps along a line running from the mining area along the Arctic Ocean Highway. The reason for this puzzling decision was that large amounts of supplies were stockpiled in the area. Most of these stockpiles had not been removed and 40 ships were in the process of positioning themselves in north Norwegian harbors for their evacuation. The OKW failed to appreciate the effects of the oncoming winter, the magnitude of the Soviet offensive, and the serious reduction in fighting power of the XIX Corps after the thrashing it had been subjected to in the past week. Trying to maintain a forward defense line for the purpose of evacuating supplies and equipment was a recipe for catastrophe.

Erfurth maintains that it was an officer with particular experience in the arctic region who was instrumental in having the policy changed.[20] General der Gebirgstruppe Georg Ritter von Hengl had commanded a regiment in the 2nd Mountain Division during the invasion of Norway, moved up to command the division in Finland, and eventually took over as corps commander on the Murmansk front. He served in that capacity until 1944 when he was posted to OKH as head of the National Socialist Leadership Staff. Hengl was worried about the developments in the arctic. His new position included excellent connections to the OKW; consequently he was able to convince General Alfred Jodl that an immediate evacuation was necessary. This was also the argument made by the 20th Mountain Army. Hitler finally agreed.

General Hengl was ordered to fly to north Finland and, according to General Erfurth, was given authority to issue the necessary instructions to General Rendulic if the situation on the ground warranted.[21] The objective was now switched from priority to save matériel, to one where saving the men took priority.

Hengl left Berlin on October 14 and arrived at the XIX Corps Headquarters the following day where he immediately attended a conference with General Rendulic, General Ferdinand Jodl, and the XIX Corps' division commanders. After a situation briefing he exercised his authority and called for an immediate evacuation.

Ziemke takes note of General Hengl's visit but downplays its importance in the scheme of things.[22] He relates that General Rendulic was so surprised by the turnaround in the thinking of OKW related by Hengl that the 20th Mountain Army's chief of staff, General Hölter, placed two calls to General Alfred Jodl to make sure that General Hengl had his story straight.

On October 15, the same day as General von Hengl met with the senior officers of 20th Mountain Army and the XIX Mountain Corps, Soviet assault elements crossed the Pechenga River and captured the town of Pechenga. Simultaneously, Soviet naval infantry that had landed in the Bay of Pechenga seized the port of Liinahamari to the north.

The XIX Mountain Corps, no longer capable of attacking eastward, requested a new directive from the 20th Mountain Army that would allow the corps to attack westward to reopen Tårnet Road, its only route of withdrawal, which had been cut by Soviet naval infantry on the night of October 12–13. The Germans had meanwhile decided that after reopening Tårnet Road, the badly mauled 2nd Mountain Division was to withdraw behind Group Rübel to rest and reorganize. The rest of the XIX Mountain Corps would screen the area between Pechenga and Kirkenes until priority supplies were evacuated. On October 17, the 20th Mountain Army ordered that the Kolosjoki and Kirkenes area be held for the time being.

Group Rübel, now approaching the size of two divisions, was ordered to hold a line northeast of Kolosjoki to give time for the defenses to be established further back to cover the town of Kirkenes in Norway. Holding this line would allow high-priority supplies to be evacuated and would prevent the Soviets from moving southwest against Ivalo. In fact, the units in this group held the fate of much of the 20th Mountain Army in its hands.

German troops were able to eliminate the Soviet forces blocking Tårnet Road west of Pechenga in heavy fighting by October 14. This allowed the 6th Mountain Division and Division Group van der Hoop to withdraw westward into Norway. In its operational summary at 0700 on October 16, the Karelian Front reported that "The remnants of the enemy's battered units in the Petsamo region are retreating along a road running northwest toward Norwegian territory. . . ."[23]

The 14th Soviet Army had advanced 35–60 kilometers in heavy fighting over difficult terrain following its breakthrough on October 7.

The troops were exhausted and units had run out of supplies since the road network was inadequate. To allow the troops a chance to rest and allow the logistic system to bring up supplies, Lieutenant General Shcherbakov ordered a three-day halt to rest, reorganize, and resupply his forces.

The pause in Soviet offensive operations also gave the Germans a much-needed respite. On October 18, the 20th Mountain Army authorized the separation of XIX Mountain Corps and Group Rübel. Group Rübel was ordered to execute a retirement to Salmijärvi within three days.

The Germans realized early in the offensive that they were not going to be able to save much of their immense stores of supplies in the Pechenga area. Evacuation of supplies was prioritized, with fuel at or near the top of the list. Only 30,000 tons were removed through the port of Kirkenes and only 10,000 were evacuated from the Ivalo-Inari area to Porsangerfjord.

This does not include what was pre-positioned in supply points along the withdrawal routes. For that part of the XIX Mountain Corps' withdrawal in the direction of Kirkenes, and then Lakselv, supply points had been established along Tårnet Road and Route 50. Supply points had also been established along the Arctic Ocean Highway as far as Ivalo. The XXXVI Corps, now consisting of the 2nd Mountain Division, 169th Infantry Division, and the 163rd Infantry Division, had supply points along the road from Ivalo as far as Lakselv. The pre-positioned supply points for the XVIII Mountain Corps, consisting of the 7th Mountain Division, 6th SS Mountain Division, and Division Group Kräutler, were located along the road leading to Skibotten and as far as Karesuando. The large stores at Muonio were evacuated successfully but it took a considerable period of time due to the atrocious state of the road.[24] The supplies left in the Pechenga area fell into Soviet hands.

The Withdrawal into Norway

In a conference with his subordinate commanders on October 15, General Rendulic ordered the 6th Mountain Division to defend the Kirkenes area as long as possible to allow for the evacuation of supplies. The rest of the XIX Mountain Corps (except for the 210th Infantry Division already located in Norway) was to withdraw in the direction of Ivalo. Group Rübel was ordered to defend the road network east of

Akhmalakhti and Nikel for as long as possible. The 2nd Mountain Division was ordered assembled at Salmijärvi, and to support Group Rübel. The Germans expected the Soviets to resume their offensive on October 18.

The Ivalo defensive position was occupied in the night of October 18. It had to be held until all forces from the Murmansk front had passed through. The Germans destroyed the roads and bridges as they withdrew and the Luftwaffe provided valuable help in completing the destruction behind the withdrawing ground troops.

On approaching the Norwegian frontier, General Meretskov requested permission from Stalin on October 18 to pursue the Germans into Norwegian territory. Merentskov had expected a long answer with all kinds of political instructions. To his surprise, Stalin's answer was short and without any political guidance: "That'll be good."[25]

Since the Germans had split their forces for the withdrawal with one group moving towards Kirkenes and the other towards Ivalo, the Soviets did likewise. When the Soviet offensive was resumed on October 19, they directed their main effort against the forces withdrawing towards Ivalo with a strong secondary effort against Kirkenes. In the direction of Kirkenes the Soviets employed the 131st Corps with three infantry divisions and a guard tank brigade. The corps was also equipped with more than 90 American-built 2½-ton amphibious vehicles for river-crossing operations.

The main Soviet effort was directed towards Akhmalakhti, just north of Salmijärvi. By securing Akhmalakhti the Soviets would be at the Pasvik River, which marked the Norwegian border. The 99th Infantry Corps, with three infantry divisions, a guard heavy tank regiment, and a heavy self-propelled artillery regiment, had the mission of advancing on Akhmalakhti. The 126th Light Infantry Corps was ordered to support the 99th Infantry Corps by advancing to the Pasvik River on the north flank of the 99th.

The 31st Infantry Corps, with two divisions, attacked along the south flank of the 99th Corps toward the Nikel settlement southeast of Salmijärvi. The corps was reinforced with three artillery regiments, two MRL regiments, and a tank regiment. The 127th Light Infantry Corps was to make a cross-country advance in support of the 31st Infantry Corps by severing the road leading south from Nikel, thus isolating the German troops north and east of that town. Nikel, and Nautsi further south, comprised the center of the Finnish mining areas.

The main Soviet attack was directed against Group Rübel but it withdrew west along the Arctic Ocean Highway and thus escaped the full force of the 99th Corps' assault. However, Group Rübel's situation became dangerous on October 20 when the 127th drove around its southern flank and threatened to cut the Arctic Ocean Highway behind it. Rübel averted the danger by withdrawing his troops during the next two days to the lake and river narrows in the south. The Soviet pressure thereupon lessened and Group Rübel was able to make a rapid withdrawal to Ivalo.

On October 21, the nickel plants (Kolosjoki) and the Nikel settlement were evacuated by the Germans after thorough destruction. The Soviets captured Nikel the following day and soon thereafter they secured Nautsi further to the south, just south of the corner of Norwegian territory extending into Finland.

The 126th Light Infantry Corps crossed the Pasvik River at Akhmalakhti on October 24 and continued its drive northwestward in the direction of the Norwegian town of Neiden, which it reached on October 27, thereby cutting Route 50. The 6th Mountain Division and other German forces had already withdrawn through the town toward the west. The Germans withdrawing along Route 50 benefited from a double stroke of good fortune—the tough defensive fighting of Group Rübel which slowed the Soviet advance towards Neiden and the decision by the 20th Mountain Army—approved by OKW—not to fight for Kirkenes. If either of these had gone the other way the German forces east of Neiden would have been trapped.

At the same time as the main attack was carried out against Group Rübel, the 131st Infantry Corps advanced against the 6th Mountain Division defending Kirkenes. There was no way the 6th Mountain Division could stop the Soviet advance since the Soviets held a 3:1 superiority. The ground attack was accompanied with naval infantry landings on the arctic coast northeast of Tårnet. Tårnet was the location of the hydroelectric plants supplying power to Kirkenes. The cutting of electrical power meant that the ships in Kirkenes could no longer be supplied with water for their boilers. The 20th Mountain Army therefore requested permission from OKW on October 22 to stop the evacuation from Kirkenes. Permission was granted.

The Germans withdrew rapidly northwest along Route 50, and only minor rear-guard actions preceded the Soviet capture of Kirkenes on October 25. The evacuation of the Varanger Peninsula, including the town of Vardø, began on October 26.

The Soviet pursuit ended at Tanafjord while the Germans continued their withdrawal to Lakselv. Of the stores in Kirkenes, 45,000 tons were saved while about 90,000 tons were destroyed to keep them from falling into Soviet hands. Heavy losses were suffered at Kirkenes during the last two days of embarkation of supplies due to Russian air attacks over 24 hours. Evacuation of supplies and equipment from the large area between Porsangerfjord and Lyngenfjord proceeded according to plans after the Soviets ended their pursuit.

Operation Nordlicht *Ends*

The German evacuation of their forces from Ivalo and along the Swedish border went according to plan, with little interference from the enemy. The 169th Infantry Division of the XXXVI Mountain Corps occupied defensive positions south of Ivalo from the middle of October. The XXXVI Corps also established a protective screen in the direction of Lutto and Ristikent to the east. The Lutto position was abandoned on October 30 after the last units of Group Rübel had passed through Ivalo on their way to Lakselv. The Germans began abandoning their defensive positions south of Ivalo on October 31, and had cleared the area by November 3 when the last elements of the 169th Division's rear guard left. The 2nd Mountain Division, which marched to Norway on the Arctic Ocean Highway under some joint pressure from the Finns and the Soviets, reached Route 50 at Lakselv on November 2. Here it joined the main forces of the XIX and XXXVI Mountain Corps for the final stage of the withdrawal to Lyngenfjord.

The XVIII Mountain Corps held Muonio until the large ammunition depot located there had been evacuated. The withdrawal from Muonio began on October 29. The 7th Mountain Division established a covering position west of Karesuando that had been constructed for Operation *Birke*. Occupation of this narrow strip of Finland between Norway and Sweden served to protect the flank of the Lyngen position and the German forces withdrawing along Route 50. The 139th Regiment was stationed at the Norwegian settlement of Kautokeino, off the left flank of the 7th Mountain Division.

Two divisions of the LXXI Corps in Norway were attached to the

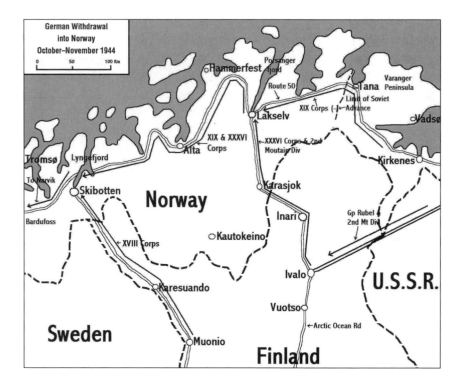

XIX Mountain Corps in October 1944 and provided security along Route 50 for the withdrawing German forces in the area between Lakselv and Skibotten. The Germans withdrew westward along Route 50 from Lakselv without enemy pressure. Only four mobile infantry battalions on skis were left behind as well as small detachments at Hammerfest and Alta.

The rear guards of the 20th Mountain Army withdrew past Billefjord on December 18. This was the signal for the 139th Regiment to begin its withdrawal from Kautokeino. The last German troops left this area on December 19. The 7th Mountain Division held its covering position at Karesuando without any Finnish pressure until January 12, 1945, when it withdrew through the Lyngen position held by the 6th Mountain Division. Over 50,000 German soldiers and 6,030 vehicles were ferried across Lyngenfjord during November.[26]

Operation *Nordlicht* terminated at the end of January but the name continued to be used until the end of the war for the movement of units of the 20th Mountain Army back to Germany. The large Finnmark Province was practically empty of German troops. There was a small German detachment at Hammerfest and another one at Alta. These continued to evacuate supplies until February 1945 when they were withdrawn. By the middle of November, the Germans occupied only a few square kilometers of Finnish territory in the northwest part of the country, part of the Lyngen defensive position. It was not until April 28, 1945, that Lieutenant General Siilasvuo could report to Marshal Mannerheim that the last German soldier had left Finland at 1330 hours on April 27. Since then, April 27 has been celebrated as Finland's Veterans Day.[27]

Scorched Earth

Hitler was intent on preventing the Russians or the Norwegian government in England from gaining a foothold in the areas in north Norway from which the Germans were withdrawing. Therefore, he ordered that a scorched-earth policy be carried out east of Lyngenfjord. A systematic destruction of roads and structures was carried out after the withdrawing Germans had passed. Route 50 was destroyed to such an extent north and east of Lyngenfjord that no major movements were possible.

As part of the scorched-earth policy employed in the Finnmark Province of Norway, Hitler had issued orders on October 28 that the whole Norwegian population east of Lyngenfjord was to be evacuated. This evacuation was mostly carried out in small boats in order to keep Route 50 clear for military traffic. While the evacuation began as a voluntary measure, force was soon used against those who declined to participate.

The Wehrmacht played a large role in this evacuation and there can be no doubt that General Rendulic wanted to use the same scorched-earth strategy in Norway as he had used in Finland to secure a safe retreat. Norwegian representatives from Nasjonal Samling (NS—Quisling's party) also participated. The measures resorted to in the absence of an active pursuit exceeded those which may be considered necessary in military operations. Even subordinate officers complained in writing to Rendulic and some local commanders, at great personal risk, allowed some families, homes, and food supplies to remain in the evacuated areas.[28]

Hitler's order was nevertheless carried out in most places with typical German thoroughness. An area much larger than Denmark was completely devastated. Over 10,400 homes were destroyed along with 115 schools and 27 churches. About 43,000–45,000 individuals were driven out of Finnmark Province by the Germans or NS representatives.

General Rendulic claimed that only about 200 escaped the evacuation, and he promised to hunt them down.[29] Despite the thoroughness of the evacuation it appears that between 20,000 and 25,000 managed to avoid the exodus. This included at least 10,000 from Kirkenes and Varanger Peninsula who could not be evacuated because of the tactical situation and 8,500 nomadic Laps who were exempt. The actual number who avoided the forced exodus was therefore considerably larger than Rendulic admitted.

Norwegian Forces Appear in Finnmark

The Norwegian government in exile had maintained a military liaison mission in Moscow headed by Colonel Arne D. Dahl, a former battalion commander in the 6th Norwegian Division during its operations against the Germans in 1940.[30] In anticipation of an end to the war, the US, USSR, and UK had entered into an agreement with the Norwegian government in exile on March 17, 1944, on civil administration on Norwegian territory that might be occupied by one of the signatories. This agreement invested Allied commanders with supreme authority for civil administration in time of hostilities. The USSR used this agreement, as well as the address by the Norwegian king and a message from the Norwegian government, as authority for the 14th Soviet Army to begin the initial work of establishing a functioning civil administration following the departure of the Germans and pending the arrival of Norwegian forces from the UK.[31]

Despite worries by the Norwegian government and the Western Allies, most Soviet forces withdrew rather quickly from Norwegian territory. Only a detachment in Kirkenes was left at the end of the war and this was withdrawn in August–September 1945. Despite the rapid German withdrawal to the Lyngen position, the conquest of the northeast corner of Finnmark Province had not been a "walk in the park" for the Soviets. This is demonstrated by the fact that almost 2,900 Soviet soldiers lost their lives on Norwegian soil.[32]

A token force of Norwegians was sent to Finnmark but it did not arrive until January 1945. It consisted of the 2nd Mountain Company from the Norwegian brigade in Scotland, staff, and civilian administrators—a total of about 300. The force was under the command of Colonel Dahl and was soon reinforced (including by Norwegian military police troops from Sweden) and eventually grew to about 3,000. These Norwegian troops remained under Soviet command until February 6, 1945.

While relations between the Soviets and Norwegian civilians were good, this was apparently not true of initial relations between civilians in Finnmark and the Norwegian troops who were referred to as "Londoners." Provisions for the devastated population that remained in Finnmark were exceedingly slow in arriving. Civilians were criticized by the new arrivals for lack of patriotism and the custom of shaving the heads of women who had fraternized with Germans was particularly resented. Colonel Dahl saw to it that this practice was quickly discontinued.[33]

Some Reasons for the Success of Operation Birke

Operation *Birke* and its extension—Operation *Nordlicht*—had begun with minimal hopes of success. All German options looked like invitations to disaster. It turned out to be a surprising success with an outstanding display of skill and endurance on the part of the troops and leaders of the 20th Mountain Army in one of the most inhospitable areas of the world for military operations in winter.

However, luck also played a big part in the successful extrication of the army. The anticipated dangers and threats did not materialize. The Soviets started their offensive on the Murmansk front late. An earlier start would almost certainly have caused the Germans serious problems. Closely associated with this is the fact that the Soviets failed to pursue aggressively and showed a reluctance to cross the Norwegian frontier other than in the Kirkenes area. When it became obvious that the Soviets were not going to advance west from Tana and the Finns were not moving against Porsangerfjord, the Germans could continue the withdrawal at a leisurely pace.

The Soviet decision not to pursue was undoubtedly based primarily on military considerations with political overtones. *Nordlicht* took place when the resources of the Soviets and the Western Allies were strained to their limits on the main fronts in Europe. The Russian efforts in Finland were therefore relatively modest, and after having captured Kirkenes, units were quickly moved to the main theater of operations in the south. The Western Allies made no appearance in north Norway. Their offensive in the west had come to a temporary halt while they waited for their supply situation to be sorted out.

The dreaded winter in north Norway showed up late, letting much of the German withdrawal take place during one of the mildest autumns on record. When the snowfall and temperatures of minus 30 Celsius finally made their appearance, the most difficult part of the withdrawal was over.

The main achievement was that no units were cut off or destroyed, so that the Mountain Army remained fully intact except for battle losses. While the 22,236 casualties were almost the same as the losses in the German offensive in Finland in 1941, they were small compared to what was happening to other German armies.

The Fate of the 20th Mountain Army

The Army of Norway had passed 1944, as it had the previous two years, waiting for an invasion that never came. In the middle of the year its strength was 372,000 but by the time the withdrawal from Finland began 80,000 of these had been removed for use on the eastern front or in France. When the threatening attitude of Sweden forced the army to deploy units to the border east of Trondheim and Oslo, the army experienced a shortage of personnel for the first time in the war.

The arrival of the 20th Mountain Army in Norway brought the strength in that country back up to between 450,000 and 500,000. However, the continual demand for troops on the continent caused this number to decline rapidly. Many of the troops that came back were transferred to other fronts but even that transfer involved difficulties. The troops had to march not only to the Lyngen position but from that position southward, in most cases as far as Mo in Nordland Province and in certain cases as far as Trondheim. This was done in order to relieve traffic on the low-capacity Mo–Oslo line. Upon arrival in Oslo they were transported to Denmark and then on to other fronts. The movements were not only difficult and exhausting because of the distances involved in the inclement season, but dangerous because enemy air and surface attacks at sea caused considerable casualties.

As many units as could be spared were sent to Germany during the winter. The 6th SS Mountain Division embarked in Oslo in mid-November and between November 1944 and April 1945, the 2nd Mountain Division and the 163rd, 169th, and 199th Infantry Divisions were sent south. The lack of coal for the railroad brought the transfer program to a crawl in March 1945 and the next division scheduled to be sent to Germany—the 7th Mountain Division—became bogged down in Trondheim at the end of April.

The arrival of the 20th Mountain Army in Norway also ushered in a period of major organizational and personnel changes. The LXXI Corps became part of the 20th Mountain Army in October and the army assumed responsibility for the Narvik area. General Falkenhorst, who had been commander in Norway since he led the invasion in 1940, returned to Germany and General Rendulic became armed forces commander in Norway. The Army of Norway and the 20th Mountain Army were joined into one organization named the 20th Mountain Army. A new organization, Armeeabteilung Narvik (Army Detachment Narvik) took over the Lyngenfjord-Narvik area and was composed of the XIX Mountain Corps and the LXXI Corps under the command of Headquarters, XIX Mountain Corps. Headquarters, XXXVI Mountain Corps, assumed command of the troops stationed on the Swedish border.

Warfare in the north for the remainder of the war was limited to air and sea operations. The British continued to raid the ports and coastal shipping while German submarines kept up their activities with increasing losses. Bergen and Trondheim had become the main German submarine bases after the loss of the Atlantic ports and the British gave them special attention.

The 20th Mountain Army in Norway watched helplessly as German armies on the continent were torn to pieces. In January 1945 General Rendulic was transferred to the eastern front to take command of Army Group North. General Franz Böhme took over as armed forces commander in Norway.

Except for increased resistance activity, Norway was one of the most peaceful places in Europe. The 20th Mountain Army was nevertheless a source of worry for the Allied Supreme Command. They considered it possible that it might become an area for a last desperate stand by the Nazis.

The 20th Mountain Army had no plans for a last stand or for disobeying orders from the OKW. Böhme even refused a Swedish offer, at the prodding of Himmler's representative Walter Schellenberg, to have the 20th Mountain Army and all German military personnel in Norway interned in Sweden. On May 8, the day after Germany's unconditional surrender, Böhme was told that doing anything contrary to the surrender terms would have dire consequences for the German people.

In announcing the surrender to his troops Böhme described the 20th Mountain Army as undefeated, and one that only accepted the dictates of the enemy for the greater national interest. In a message to OKW on May 10 complaining about the severity of the surrender terms, he concluded with "Woe to the vanquished."[34]

NOTES

1. *Anabasis* was Xenophon's history of the Greek retreat from Persia around 400 B.C. The word *anabasis* refers to an expedition from a coastline up into the interior of a country. *Katabasis*, on the other hand, describes a trip from the interior down to the coastline and is therefore more appropriate in describing the journey of the 20th Mountain Army.
2. Major James F. Gebhardt, *The Petsamo-Kirkenes Operation: Soviet Breakthrough and Pursuit in the Arctic, October 1944.* Leavenworth Papers Number 17 (Fort Leavenworth, Kansas: Combat Studies Institute, U.S. Army Command and General Staff College, 1989), pp.6–8.
3. *Ibid*, p.8.
4. Erfurth, *The Last Finnish War*, p.237.
5. Gebhardt, *op. cit.*, pp.10–11.
6. *Ibid*, p.14.
7. Meretskov, *op. cit.*, pp.317–319.
8. Shtemenko, *op. cit.*, p.372.
9. Gebhardt, *op. cit.*, p.17.
10. *Ibid*, pp.24–25.
11. Meretskov, *op. cit.*, p.320.
12. Gebhardt, *op. cit.*, p.21.
13. Shtemenko, *op. cit.*, p.373.
14. Gebhardt, *op. cit.*, p.19.
15. *Ibid*, p.43 quoting from Semen Petrovich Mikulskii and Minzakir Absaliamov, *Nastupatel'nyee boi* (Moscow: 1959), p.28.
16. *Ibid*, pp.40–41.
17. Shtemenko, *op. cit.*, p.373.
18. Ziemke, *The German Northern Theater of Operations*, p.306.
19. Gebhardt, *op. cit.*, pp.35–36.

20. Erfurth, *The Last Finnish War*, pp.239–240.
21. *Ibid*, p.240.
22. Ziemke, *The German Northern Theater of Operations*, p.307.
23. Shtemenko, *op. cit.*, p.374.
24. Erfurth, *The Last Finnish War*, p.242.
25. Meretskov, *op. cit.*, p.324.
26. Erfurth, *The Last Finnish War*, p.245.
27. Westerlund, *op. cit.*, p.215.
28. Stein Ugelvik Larsen, *Norsk Krigslexikon*, part of *NorgesLexi*, directed and edited by Stein Ugelvik Larsen at the University of Bergen, *Tvangsevakueringen i Finnmark*.
29. Report by Headquarters, Army of Norway, dated December 15, 1944 titled *Bericht über Evakuierung Nordnorwegens* as cited in Ziemke, *The German Northern Theater of Operations*, p.308.
30. Colonel Dahl (later Lieutenant General) was the only Norwegian officer in the Narvik campaign with previous combat experience. He had fought as a young lieutenant in a British unit in the Battle of Somme in 1916. He was also the first Norwegian officer to attend the US Command and General Staff College in 1941.
31. Shtemenko, *op. cit.*, p.377.
32. *Ibid*, p.378.
33. Larsen, *op. cit.*, *Frigjøringen av Finnmark*.
34. Message from the Army of Norway to OKW dated May 19, 1945 cited in Ziemke, *The German Northern Theater of Operations*, p.314.

EPILOGUE

Germany and Scandinavia in World War II

The war in Finland cannot be considered as an isolated event, but must be viewed in relation to German goals in Scandinavia as a whole. The northern theater of war presented Germany with four major strategic advantages:

1. Access to mineral resources—Swedish iron and Finnish nickel.
2. Expansion of its base for naval operations against the Allies.
3. Control of the Baltic and Baltic approaches.
4. Interdiction of the Murmansk supply route after the German attack on the Soviet Union.

Ziemke claims that the Germans, for a variety of reasons, did not accomplish their objectives and that the German presence in Scandinavia was not enough to discourage its enemies from focusing their activities in other directions.[1]

These observations neglect important points by concentrating on specific strategic considerations. It is in the general realm of German interests that we have to look for answers to the question of what Germany perceived as its advantages in Scandinavia. Walter Hubatsch claims that the flow of high-grade Swedish ore made the great battles of 1942–44 possible for the Germans and a similar claim can undoubtedly be made for Finnish nickel as well as the supply of finished products from Sweden, such as ball bearings.[2]

We have to place ourselves in the position of the German planners and ask what the situation would have been for the Germans if they had not moved into Scandinavia. By failing to do so, the Allies could have exerted pressure on Sweden and Finland and may well have succeeded in eliminating Swedish export of iron ore and Finnish export of nickel to Germany. An Allied presence in Scandinavia would probably have kept Finland from joining Germany in its attack on the Soviet Union and Stalin would not have had to worry about an arctic front or a threat to his supply lines from the west. A further advantage in the minds of German planners was the protection of Germany's northern flank, and this they ranked quite high. Allied air power from Scandinavia would have been very effective in the Baltic and over German ports on the southern shores of that sea.

Whether the German preoccupation with Scandinavia was an unnecessary drain on its resources is debatable. Hitler's exaggerated concern for an invasion of the north must be ranked as a major error. The enormous resources that Germany poured into this theater drained them away from other areas. It took a reinforced army and vast expenditures in resources to defend Norway. Another army was tied down in Finland from 1941. These armies were trapped into defensive missions that had virtually no influence on the outcome of the war.

Finland's Decisions

The debate over whether Finland's decision to side with Germany in its attack on the Soviet Union in June 1941 was made out of necessity, or simply reflected a conscious choice, has continued unabated for nearly 65 years and there is no unanimity. Wuorinen's book in 1948—actually written by Professor Arvi Korhonen—states that "Finland had been drawn into the war—against her will—. . ."[3] In another place he describes the start of hostilities in 1941 as "Finland, having fallen victim to an unprovoked attack, could in the beginning have no other 'war aims' than to repel the attack. . . ."[4]

Fifty-four years later Vehviläinen writes that "there was no way that Finland could have avoided becoming involved in a new war" and that at the beginning of their contacts with the Germans in 1940 "Finland's aims were to get security guarantees from Germany."[5] He goes on to state that "Without realizing the real nature of National Socialism and Hitler's war aims, the Finns fought to preserve their way of life and to ensure security from what they considered an eternal threat from the east."[6]

A few comments on what has been written by these authors—and others—are in order. The opening of hostilities by the Soviets was provoked and Mannerheim and other leaders admitted as much in a conversation (between Mannerheim, Tanner, Linkomies, General Walden, and General Heinrichs) on August 9, 1943—as I quote in Chapter 2. There were several German divisions in the country with the rather obvious intention to initiate ground operations and the Finns had ordered a general mobilization several days earlier. The first air attacks against Soviet targets were carried out by German aircraft operating from Finnish bases or through Finnish airspace. The German and Finnish navies had already begun laying mines in the Gulf of Finland.

Vehviläinen's claims that the Finns were unaware of the real nature of National Socialism or Germany's war aims are likewise absurd. What were they doing while Germany swallowed up Czechoslovakia, invaded Poland, overran their fellow Scandinavians in Denmark and Norway, and invaded the Netherlands, Belgium, Luxembourg, France, and the Balkans. While the details of the persecution of the Jews and others may not have been known, enough was known about the conditions in Germany for them to make up their minds about the nature of National Socialism.

As far as Germany's war aims are concerned, they were well known to some Finnish leaders. See, for example, General Heinrichs' pro memoria of June 3, 1941, and the verbal comments he made at that time which I quote from in Chapter 1.

Finland's initial aim may well have been to obtain security guarantees from Germany after it became isolated. They should have known that such guarantees would carry a costly price tag. The aim of security guarantees quickly gave way to the recapture of lost territories and the conquest of East Karelia. Wuorinen writes that "Finland's military objectives were strictly limited: her own defense and security. At no time during the war did the country want to go, or go, any further than these objectives."[7] I believe that this erroneous explanation is put to rest in this book.

The notion that Finland fought a separate war is also absurd to an outsider although many Finns undoubtedly believed it. The notion that a small nation such as Finland launched an attack on the Soviet Union and surprisingly found itself at the side of Germany is hard to swallow. Nevertheless, the fact that they did not have a formal alliance with

Germany eventually served Finland well and gave them a special status among the nations that fought at Germany's side.

There are no doubts that the Soviets followed a policy that made Finland fear for its safety. This short-sighted policy helped propel isolated Finland into the arms of Germany. For example, at the time of the Moscow Peace in March 1940, Finland approached Sweden and Norway about a defensive alliance. Things looked promising until the Soviet Union vetoed the idea. Such an alliance may have worked to the great advantage of the Soviets by causing the Germans to have second thoughts about their planned attack on Denmark and Norway.

In October 1940, after Norway was removed from the calculations by the German invasion, Sweden agreed to a defensive alliance and political union with Finland provided the latter agreed not to wage a war of revenge against the Soviet Union. Finland agreed. The idea was again resisted by the Soviet Union and this time also by Germany (see Chapter 1).

Proceeding with this military/political union even against the wishes of the Soviet Union and Germany presented the Finns with an option that might have proved viable. It is unlikely that the Soviet Union would have attacked both Finland and Sweden since it would have threatened vital German interests and may have seriously affected their relations with both the UK and the US. Germany is also unlikely to have resorted to military measures in view of the potential loss of Swedish iron and Finnish nickel at a time when these were sorely needed by the German armament industry.

Later, the Soviets had second thoughts as Finland drew closer to Germany. A Finland tied to a neutral Sweden no longer looked like a bad option. They told Finland that they were prepared to re-evaluate their earlier opposition to a Swedish/Finnish defensive alliance and political union. This was in May 1941, too late to change Finland's new orientation to Germany.[8]

Finland, unlike many of Germany's allies, retained its independence after the war and the terms of peace could well have been harsher. The reason was probably not any sense of magnanimity on the part of the Soviet Union. Credit must be given to the fighting quality of the Finnish soldiers and the Soviets may have concluded that it was not worth another costly offensive to impose harder terms. Credit must also be given to the fact that the Finns still enjoyed considerable sympathy in

the western democracies, especially in the US. This may have served as
a brake on Soviet policy.

German Mistakes in 1940–41

Germany's association with Finland is a classic study in how not to
enter into a military coalition. Since Germany had decided to bring
Finland into the war on its side in July 1940, sufficient time existed to
iron out issues presented in coalition warfare. These include war aims,
allotment of tasks, campaign plans, and command relationships.

As demonstrated in this book, there were no operational agreements
between Germany and Finland much past the opening salvoes in the
war. That Finland made no effort to have these issues discussed and
resolved prior to the outbreak of hostilities is understandable. Their aim
was to maintain maximum flexibility in their coalition with Germany,
and leaving things rather vague fit in well with this aim. It is much more
difficult to understand why the German military planners did not insist
on nailing down these issues. The most likely answer is that all were
caught up in the rosy scenario of a quick campaign that would destroy
the military potential of the Soviet Union. Therefore, the notion that no
elaborate arrangements or understandings were necessary was a major
miscalculation that caused friction within the coalition almost from the
very beginning.

If Finland had recoiled at making such arrangements, it would have
been infinitely better for the Germans to learn that as early as possible.
That would have allowed them to adopt the plan for Operation
Barbarossa along the lines of the one prepared by General Erich Marcks
at OKH, discussed in Chapter 2. His plan recommended postponing
Finnish participation since the weight of the German attack would be in
the south and center without a major drive to Leningrad. The anticipated benefits from Finnish participation along with the desire to control the Baltic Sea may have led to the dissipation of effort involved in
three major drives into the Soviet Union.

The Germans had a very important lever that they could have used
in the planning stages to get Finland to agree to support their two major
goals of advances against the Murmansk Railroad and Leningrad. The
Finns were eager to recover their lost territory, but would probably not
have been able to do that while also defending the 500-kilometer long

front in the arctic and in Lapland. This problem had become abundantly clear during the Winter War. With Germany taking over these fronts the Finns had sufficient forces to undertake the recovery of lost territories and the conquest of East Karelia. When leverage exists and is not used at the appropriate time, it is lost. The last time it could have been used was in 1942, to get the Finns to undertake operations against the Murmansk Railroad while German armies were making spectacular advances on all fronts. A German threat to withdraw from central Finland unless the Finns were more cooperative might have energized them.

It is a long-standing principle that each partner in a coalition must benefit from its membership. This was not the case in Finland. Finland benefited hugely in 1941 because of the German presence in their country, as described above. They benefited equally from the advance of Army Group North as it drew forces away from the Finnish fronts.

The Germans, on the other hand, reaped virtually no benefits from the coalition after the Finns recovered their lost territories and conquered East Karelia. The Finns refused to help the Germans against Leningrad and effectively did the same with respect to interdicting the Murmansk Railroad. The end result was that the Germans were left to dance to the Finnish fiddler. Their army in Lapland and the arctic was trapped both geographically and operationally. It did not have the strength to cut the Murmansk Railroad alone. That army could have served the German war cause better on other fronts. For Germany, Finland was a blind alley.

The Human Cost of the War

The war in Finland was a costly experience in lives and resources for the Soviet Union, Finland, and Germany. Finnish losses amounted to 52,500 killed, 7,300 missing, and 148,000 wounded. This includes 800 killed and 3,000 wounded in engagements against the Germans in Lapland. To these must be added the losses in civilian lives. The German losses are placed at 84,000. About 16,400 of these were killed, 60,400 wounded, and 6,800 missing. Again, this includes the losses in their fights with the Finns in Lapland. The Soviet losses, as estimated by the official Finnish history of the war, were 270,000 killed and 550,000 wounded.[9]

Military Lessons

The problems of coalition warfare, without a proper foundation, were glaringly apparent throughout the war in Finland. The failure to agree on war aims, lack of agreement on each nation's contribution to a common strategy, and the failure to achieve unity of command were age-old principles that were violated from the outset. This was a recipe for failure.

The Germans also failed to assign adequate forces to the theater of operations so as to quickly accomplish the all-important task of seizing Murmansk or interdicting the Murmansk Railroad. This may have been the result of an underestimation of Soviet capabilities and the problems caused by terrain and weather. However, the fact that Germany's military was overextended was obvious at the start and became worse as the war progressed.

The Germans grappled with the problem of establishing and maintaining a clear-cut main effort from the very beginning. They conducted offensive operations from three areas with no definitive focus. The problems of adequate lines of communication made the support of large-scale operations difficult in all areas, but the best road network was in the Kandalaksha sector where there was also a railroad on both sides of the border. This is where the main effort with adequate forces should have been made, leaving forces in other sectors just sufficient to tie the Soviets down by presenting them with potential threats.

The problems caused by lack of lines of communication within Finland were exacerbated by long and inadequate routes for reinforcements and supplies. One gets the impression that these problems were not adequately addressed or solved in the planning process.

The war in Finland established a historical precedent. It was the first time—except for the campaigns around Narvik and in the Nordland Province of Norway in 1940—that major troop formations conducted prolonged operations in an arctic wilderness. The Germans found that mobility was severely restricted, that sweeping encirclements were not possible, and that momentum was difficult to regain once lost.

War in the arctic cannot be successfully conducted with troops who do not have specialized training and equipment. The human element predominates in warfare under the conditions found in the arctic. The Finns, native to the area, proved superior to the Germans in the kind of terrain and weather encountered in Finland.

While the effectiveness of machines and equipment is greatly reduced in arctic warfare, the Soviets proved in 1944 that it is possible to maneuver large units, including armor. There are no ideal periods for offensive military operations—climate and terrain always pose obstacles. From the standpoint of mobility, winter is often the best period for action but troops are confronted with the practical and psychological problem of severe cold and total darkness. Specially trained and equipped troops are required. The thaw invariably presents insurmountable problems for military operations in spring and early summer. One or two good lines of communication—such as the Murmansk Railroad—can prove decisive.

Long Term Effects

Their experiences in World War II led the Scandinavian countries to take different paths in their foreign and defense policies. Sweden, which had successfully maintained its security through a flexible policy of armed neutrality, has continued that policy. Although it joined the European Union (EU) it has not joined the North Atlantic Treaty Organization (NATO). For Denmark and Norway there was no return to the policy of neutrality. They both embraced collective security and became charter members of NATO. Denmark also joined the EU while Norway, showing its independent streak, twice turned down membership through plebiscites. It remains one of only a few countries in western and central Europe that has not joined or petitioned to join that organization. Finland has also joined the EU but has continued a neutrality-oriented security policy by not joining NATO.

NOTES
1. Ziemke, *The German Northern Theater of Operations*, p.315.
2. Lunde, *op. cit.*, p.550.
3. Wuorinen, *op. cit.*, p.184.
4. *Ibid*, p.123.
5. Vehviläinen, *op. cit.*, p.171.
6. *Loc. cit.*
7. Wuorinen, *op. cit.*, p.114.
8. Frietsch, *op. cit.*, pp.241–242 and Lundin, *op. cit.*, pp.83–84.
9. These figures are from *Jatkosodan historia*, volume 6, pp.277, 388ff, 478 and Westerlund, *op. cit.*, pp.234–235.

Appendix I
COMPARATIVE GENERAL OFFICER RANKS[1]

GERMAN	FINNISH	US
Reichsmarshall[2]	Suomen Marsalkka[3]	None
Generalfeldmarshall	Sotamarsalkka[4]	General of the Army
Generaloberst	Kenraalieversti[5]	General
General der Infanterie, der Artillerie, etc	Jalkavaenkenraali	Lieutenant General
Generalleutnant	Kenraaliluutnantti	Major General
Generalmajor	Kenraalimajuri	Brigadier General

The German Waffen SS had its own general officer rank structure. Below are the four ranks and their equivalent in the German Army:

SS	GERMAN ARMY
Oberstgruppenführer	Generaloberst
Obergruppenführer	General der Infanterie, der Artillerie, etc
Gruppenführer	Generalleutnant
Brigadeführer	Generalmajor

NOTES
1. Based on table in Ziemke, *The German Northern Theater of Operations*, p.318.
2. Held only by Göring.
3. Rank given to Mannerheim in 1942 on his 75th birthday and held only by him.
4. Held only by Mannerheim.
5. No Finnish officer held this rank in World War II.

Appendix II
OPERATIONAL CODE NAMES

Bagration	Soviet summer offensive in Byelorussia in 1944.
Barbarossa	German invasion of the Soviet Union on June 22, 1941.
Birke	German plan for the 20th Mountain Army to North Finland in 1944.
Blaufuchs 1 & 2	Movement of XXXVI Corps forces from Germany and Norway to Finland in June 1941.
Claymore	British/Norwegian operation in the Lofoten Islands in March 1941.
Harpune Nord & Sud	German deception operations staged to divert attention from Operation *Barbarossa* from May to August 1941.
Jupiter	Planned British operation against Pechenga and Banak in 1942–43.
Klabautermann	German boat operations on Lake Ladoga to interdict Soviet supply and evacuation operations for Leningrad in the summer of 1942.

Lachsfang   Proposed German-Finnish operations against the Murmansk Railroad at Kandalaksha and Belomorsk in the summer and fall of 1942.

Nordlicht   Planned German operations against Leningrad in the fall of 1942.

Nordlicht   Withdrawal of the 20th Mountain Army from Finland to Norway, October 1944–January 1945.

Panther Line   Narva River–Lake Peipus line of German field fortifications constructed in the fall of 1943.

Parkplatz   Proposed German operations against Leningrad in the spring of 1943.

Platinfuchs   Operations by Mountain Corps Norway in 1941.

Polarfuchs   Operations of German XXXVI Corps in 1941

Renntier   German plan for the occupation of Pechenga, June 1941.

Silberfuchs   Operations of Army of Norway (including Finnish III Corps) out of Finland in 1941.

Tanne Ost   German plan for the occupation of Suursaari Island in 1944.

Tanne West   German plan to occupy the Åland Islands in 1944.

Wiesengrund   Proposed German occupation of the Rybachiy Peninsula in the summer of 1942.

Zittadelle   German operation against the Kursk salient in southern Russia in July 1943.

Appendix III
FINNISH AND RUSSIAN
GEOGRAPHIC NAMES

A problem encountered in writing this book was dealing with the names of places in territories now under Russian rule. In most cases the names have changed. Finnish references, including their military atlases, understandably use the former Finnish names while modern atlases give the Russian names. This created a problem because not all the names used in Finnish references can be located on an atlas and furthermore, one cannot be absolutely sure that one is dealing with the same place. Also, some of the places mentioned have apparently been depopulated and do not appear on maps.

With the help of the Finnish Embassy in Washington, D.C., and Jukka Juutinen in Finland, I have been able to come up with a list of Finnish names and their Russian equivalent for some of the places in question. The list is far from complete.

FINNISH	RUSSIAN
Ääninen	Onezhskoye Ozero (Onega in English)
Ahvenanmaa	Åland (Swedish)
Antrea	Kamennogorsk
Aunus	Olonets
Enso	Svetogorsk
Hatsina	Gatchina
Heinjoki	Veshtshevo
Jääski	Lesogorsky
Jänisjärvi	Yanisyarvi (or English Yanis Lake)
Johannes	Sovetsky
Kaarlahti	Kuznechnoye

FINNISH	RUSSIAN
Käkisalmi	
(Kexholm in Swedish)	Priozersk/Kegsgolm
Kantalahti	Kandalaksha
Karhumäki	Medvezhyegorsk
Kemi (on the White Sea)	Kem
Kilpola	Kilpolansaari
Kistinki	Kestenga
Kivennapa	Pervomajskoje
Koivisto	Primorsk
Kolosjoki	Nikel
Kontupohja	Kondopoga
Korja	Korya
Korpiselkä	Korpiselkya
Kostamus	Kostomuksha
Koutero	Kovdor
Kontupohja	Kondopoga
Kuokkala	Repino
Kuolajärvi	Kuoloyarvi
Kuuterselkä	Lebyazhe
Laatokka	Ladozhskoye Ozero (Ladoga in English)
Lahdenpohja	Lakhdenpokhya
Lieksarjärvi	Leksozero
Loimola	Loymola
Lotinapelto	Lodeynoye Pole
Louhi	Loukhi
Munjärvi	Munozero
Parajärvi	Lendery
Perkjärvi	Kirpitshnoje
Petroskoi	Petrozavodsk
Petsamo	Pechenga
Pitkäranta	Pitkjaranta
Porajärvi	Porosozero
Porlampi	Sveklovichnoye
Poventsa	Povents

FINNISH	RUSSIAN
Prääsä	Prjazha
Pummanki	Zemyanoye
Puutoinen	Pudozh
Raivola	Roshchino
Rajajoki	Sestra
Repola	Reboly
Riustseppälä	Zhitkovo
Rukajärvi	Rugozero
Saarimäki	Sarmjagi
Sammatus	Sambatuksa
Seesjärvi	Seg Lake
Sekee	Segezha
Seuloskoi	Vsevolozhsk
Sierattala	Sertolov
Siestarjoki	Sestoetsk
Sorokka	Belomorsk
Suojärvi	Suojarvi
Suursaari	Gogland
Säämäjärvi	Syamozero
Syväri	Svir
Taipale	Sulovevo
Terijoki	Zelenogorsk
Tolvajärvi	Tolvayarvi
Tuulos	Tuloksa
Tytärsaari	Bolshoi Tyuters
Uhtua	Ukhta
Uuras	Vysotsk
Uustia	Sosnovyi Bor
Valkeasaari	Beloostrov
Värtsilä	Vyartsilya
Vieljärvi	Vedlozero
Viipuri	Vyborg
Vitele	Vidlitsa
Vuorijärvi	Vuoriyarvi

BIBLIOGRAPHY

Beaumont, Joan. *Comrades in Arms: British Aid to Russia 1941–45* (London: Davis Poynter, 1980)

Bellamy, Chris. *Absolute War. Soviet Russia in the Second World War* (New York: Alfred A. Knopf, 2007)

Beranek, August von. *Mannerheim* (Berlin: Luken & Luken, 1942)

Bergström, Christer. *Bagration to Berlin: The Final Air Battles in the East 1944–1945* (Buress Hill: Classic Publications, 2008)

Blau, George. E. *The German Campaign in Russia: Planning and Operations, 1940–1942* (Department of Army Pamphlet No. 20-261a. Washington, D.C.: Department of Army, 1955)

Blücher, Wipert von. *Gesandter zwischen Diktatur und Demokratie* (Wiesbaden: Limes Verlag, 1951)

Born, Ernst von. *Levnadsminnen* (Helsingfors: Sönderström, 1954)

Buchner, Alex. *Gebirgsjäger an allen Fronten* (Hannover: A. Sponholtz, 1954)

Carell, Paul. *Hitler Moves East 1941–1943.* Translated from the German by Ewald Osers (New York: Bantam Books, 1966)

Carell, Paul. *Scorched Earth. The Russian-German War 1943–1944.* Translated from the German by Ewald Osers (New York: Ballantine Books, 1971)

Churchill, Winston S. *The Second World War.* Six volumes (Boston: Houghton Mifflin Company, 1948–1953)

Clark, Alan. *Barbarossa. The Russian-German Conflict 1941–45* (New York: The New American Library, Inc, 1966)

Clausewitz, Karl von. *On War.* Translated from the German by O. J. Matthijs Jolles (Washington, D.C.: Combat Forces Press, 1953)

Clausewitz, Karl von. *On War.* Edited and translated by Michael

Howard and Peter Paret (Princeton, New Jersey: Princeton University Press, 1976)

Condon, Richard W. *The Winter War. Russia against Finland* (New York: Ballantine Books, 1972)

Das Deutsche Reich und der Zweite Weltkrieg (Stuttgart: Militargeschichtliches Forschungsamt, 1983–1984)

Deutsch, Harold C. Presidential address presented on December 27, 1946, at the 25th Anniversary meeting of Phi Alpha Theta, held in New York jointly with the meeting of the American Historical Association

Devins, Joseph H. Jr. *The Vaagso Raid* (Philadelphia: Chilton Book Company, 1968)

Dietl, Gerda-Luise and Hermann, Kurt. *General Dietl* (München: Münchner Buchverlag, 1951)

Dupuy, Richard Ernest and Dupuy, Trevor N. *The Encyclopedia of Military History from 3500 B.C. to the Present* (New York: Harper & Row, 1970)

Ellinger, Tage. *Den Forunderlige Krig* (Oslo: Gyldendal Norsk Forlag, 1960)

Erfurth, Waldemar. *Der Finnische Krieg 1941–1944* (Wiesbaden: Limes Verlag, 1950)

Erfurth, Waldemar. *Problemet Murmanbanan under Finlands senaste Krig.* Translated by Axel Öhman (Helsingfors: Söderström & Co Förlagsaktiebolag, 1952)

Erfurth, Waldemar. *Surprise.* Translated by Dr. Stefan T. Possony and Daniel Vilfroy (Harrisburg, Pennsylvania: Military Service Publishing Company, 1943)

Erfurth, Waldemar. *The Last Finnish War* (Written under the auspices of the Foreign Military Studies Branch of the Historical Division, Headquarters, European Command. Washington, D.C.: University Publications of America, Inc. 1979)

Finland, Ministry of Foreign Affairs. *The Development of Finnish-Soviet Relations During the Autumn of 1939 in the Light of Official Documents* (Helsinki: FMU, 1940)

Frietsch, Carl Olof. *Finlands Ödesår 1939–1943* (Helsingfors: Sönderström 1945)

Gebhardt, James F. *The Petsamo-Kirkenes Operation: Soviet Breakthrough and Pursuit in the Arctic, October 1944.* Leavenworth

Papers Number 17 (Fort Leavenworth, Kansas: Combat Studies Institute, U.S. Army Command and General Staff College, 1989)

Germany, Auswärtiges Amt. Documents on German foreign policy, 1918–1945 (Washington: US Government Printing Office, 1954)

Germany, Kriegsmarine. Fuehrer Conferences Dealing with the German Navy (Washington, D.C.: Office of Naval Intelligence, Navy Department, 1947) volumes for 1941–1944.

Germany. Oberkommando der Wehrmacht (Wehrmactfürungsstab). Kriegstagebuch des Oberkommando der Wehrmacht 1940–1945/ geführt von Helmuth Greiner und Percy Ernst Schramm; im Auftrag des Arbeitskreises für Wehrforschung herausgeben von Percy Ernst Schramm (München: Bernard & Graefe, 1982. Four volumes in eight. Originally published: Frankfurt am Main: Bernard & Graefe, 1961–1965)

Germany. Seekriegsleitung. War Diary of the German Naval Staff (Operations Division) (Washington, D.C.: Office of Naval Intelligence, 1948–1955)

Görlitz, Walter. History of the German General Staff 1657–1945. Translated by Brian Battershaw (New York: Praeger, Inc., 1957)

Goltz, Rüdiger von der. Als politischer General im Osten (Leipzig: K. F. Koehler, 1936)

Gotaas, Birger. Fra 9. april til 7. juni. Episoder og opplevelser fra krigen i Norge. (Oslo: J. Dybwad, 1945)

Greiner, Helmuth. Die Oberste Wehrmachtführung 1939–1943 (Wiesbaden: Limes Verlag, 1951)

Halder, Franz. Kriegstagebuch. Tägliche Aufzeichnungen des Chefs des Generalstabes des Heeres, 1939–1945. Generaloberst Halder. Three volumes (Hereausgeben vom Arbeitskreis für Wehrforschung, Stuttgart: W. Kohlhammer, 1962–1964).

Halder, Franz. The Halder War Diary 1939–1942. Edited by Charles Burdick and Hans-Adolf Jacobsen (Novato, CA: Presidio Press, 1988)

Hassel, von. The Von Hassel Diaries 1938–1944 (New York: Doubleday and Company, Inc. 1947)

Hess, Wilhelm. Eismeerfront 1941 (Heidelberg: Kurt Vowinkel Verlag, 1956)

Hitler, Adolf. Hitler's Secret Conversations 1941–1944. Translated by

Norman Cameron and R. H. Stevens (New York: Farrar, Strauss and Young, 1953)

Hölter, Hermann. *Armee in der Arktis. Die Operationen der deutschen Lapland-Armee* (Bad Nauheim: H. H. Podzun, 1953)

Hölter, Hermann. *Armee in der Arktis. Die Operationen der deutschen Lapland-Armee.* Second Edition (München: Schild Verlag, 1977)

International Military Tribunal. *Trials of the Major War Criminals.* (Nuremberg, 1947)

Jacobsen, Alf R. *Nikkel, jern og blod. Krigen i nord 1939–1945* (Oslo: Aschehoug, 2006)

Jatkosodan historia (Porvoo: WSOY, 1988–1994)

Jensen, Erling and Ulstein, Ragnar. *Kompani Linge* (Oslo: Gyldendal Norsk Forlag, 1962)

Jokipii, M. *Jatkosodan synty. Tutkimuksia Saksari ja Suomen sottlaallisesta yheitsyöstä 1940–41* (Keuruu: Otava, 1987)

Jones, Michael. *Leningrad. State of Siege* (New York: Basic Books, 2008)

Juutilainen, Antti and Leskinen, Jari (editors). *Jatkosodan pikkujättiläinen* (WSOY, 2005)

Kaltenegger, Roland. *Schicksalsweg und Kampf der "Bergschuh"–Division. Die Kriegschronik der 7. Gebirgs-Division, vormals 99. leichte Infanterie-Division* (Graz: Leopold Stocker Verlag, 1985)

Kemp, Paul. Convoy. *Drama in Arctic Waters* (London: Arms and Armour, 1993)

Kershaw, Ian. *Fateful Choices. Ten Decisions that Changed the World, 1940–1941* (New York: The Penguin Press, 2007)

Khrushchev, Nikita S. *Khruschev Remembers.* With an introduction, commentary and notes by Edward Crankshaw. Translated and edited by Strobe Talbott (New York: Bantam Books, Inc., 1971)

Koskimaa, Matti. *Veitsen terällä: vetäytyminen Länsi-Kannakselta ja Talin-Ihantalan suurtaistelu kesällä 1944* (Porvoo: W. Sönderström, 1993)

Kräutler, M. and Springenschmidt, Karl. *Es war ein Edelweiss. Schicksal und Weg der zweiten Gebirgsdivision* (Graz: Leopold Stocker Verlag, 1962)

Krosby, H. Peter. *Finland, Germany and the Soviet Union 1940–1941. The Petsamo Dispute* (Madison: University of Wisconsin Press, 1968)

Kurowski, Franz. *Generaloberst Dietl. Deutscher Heerführer am Polarkreis* (Berg am Starnberger See: Verlagsgemeinschaft Berg, 1990)

Langer, William L. and Gleason, S. Everett. *The Undeclared War 1940–1941* (New York: Harper, 1953)

Larsen, Stein Ugelvik, editor. *Norsk Krigslexikon* (Oslo, 1995)

Lewin, Ronald. *Hitler's Mistakes.* (New York: William Morrow, 1986)

Liddell Hart, B. H. *History of the Second World War* (New York: G. P. Putnam's Sons, 1971)

Lossberg, Bernhard von. *Im Wehrmachtführungsstab. Dericht eines Generalstabsoffiziers* (Hamburg: H. H. Nölke, 1949)

Lunde, Henrik O. *Hitler's Pre-emptive War. The Battle for Norway, 1940* (Drexel Hill: Casemate, 2008)

Lundin, C. Leonard. *Finland in the Second World War* (Bloomington: Indiana University Press, 1957)

Mann, Chris and Jörgensen, Christer. *Hitler's Arctic War* (New York: Thomas Dunne Books, St. Martin's Press, 2002)

Mannerheim, Carl Gustaf von. *The Memoirs of Marshal Mannerheim.* Translated by Count Eric Lewenhaupt (New York: E. P. Dutton & Company, Inc., 1954)

Mannerheim, Carl Gustaf von. *Minnen.* Two volumes (Stockholm, Norstedt, 1952)

Manninen, Ohto. *Molotovin cocktail-Hitlerin sateenvarjo* (Painatuskesus Oy, 1994)

Maynard, Sir Charles. *The Murmansk Venture* (London: Hodder and Stoughton, Ltd., 1928)

Meissner, Otto. *Staatssekretär undter Ebert-Hindenburg-Hitler* (Hamburg: Hoffmann und Campe Verlag, 1950)

Meretskov, Krill A. *Serving the People.* Translated from the Russian by David Fidlon (Moscow: Progress Publishers, 1971)

Mikola, K. J. *Finland's Wars During World War II (1939–1945)* (A 32-page undated pamphlet)

Mikulskii, Semen Petrovich and Absaliamov, Minzakir. *Nastupatel'nyee boi* (Moscow, 1959)

Olson, Alma Luise. *The Background for Neutrality* (New York: J.B. Lippincott Company, 1940)

Procopé, Hjalmar J. Editor. *Fällande dom som friar* (Stockholm: Fahlcrantz & Gumælius, 1946)

Raunio, Ari. *Sotatoimet. Suomen sotien 1939–45 kulku kartoin*

(Kustantaja: GHenimap Oy, 2004)

Rendulic, Lothar. *Gekämpft Gesiegt Geschlagen* (Wels: Verlag Welsermühl, 1952)

Reynolds, David. *In Command of History* (New York: Random House, 2005)

Roskill, Stephen Wentworth. *The War at Sea 1939–1945* (London: HMSO, 1954)

Salisbury, Harrison E. *The 900 Days. The Siege of Leningrad* (New York: Avon Books, 1970)

Sandvik, Trygve. *Operasjonene til lands i Nord-Norge 1940.* 2 volumes (Oslo: Forsvarets Krigshistoriske Avdeling, 1965)

Schmidt, Paul. *Hitler's Interpreter* (New York: Macmillan, 1951)

Schmidt, Paul. *Statist auf diplomatischer Bühne, 1923–45* (Bonn: Athenäum Verlag, 1949)

Schramm, Percy Ernst. *Hitler: the man and the military leader.* Translated, edited, and with an introduction by Donald S. Detwiler (Chicago: Quadrangle Books, 1971)

Schuler, Emil. *Mit dem Berschuh im Russland und Finland* (München: Eigenverlag Emil Schuler, 1959)

Shearman, Hugh. *Finland. The Adventures of a Small Power* (London: Stevens and Sons Limited, 1950)

Shirer, William L. *The Challenge of Scandinavia* (Boston: Little, Brown and Company, 1955)

Shirer, William L. *The Rise and Fall of the Third Reich. A History of Nazi Germany* (New York: Simon and Schuster, 1960)

Shtemenko, S. H. *The Last Six Months. Russia's Final Battles with Hitler's Armies in World War II.* Translated by Guy Daniels (Garden City, New York: Doubleday & Company, Inc., 1977)

Sontag, Raymond James and Beddie, James Stuart, editors. *Nazi-Soviet Relations 1939–1941* (German Foreign Office Documents released by the US Department of State. New York: Didier, 1948)

Speer, Albert. *Erinnerungen* (Berlin: Propyläen Verlag, 1969)

Stenman, Kari and Keskinen, Kalevi. *Luftwaffe Over Finland* (Mechanicsburg, PA: Stackpole Books, 2001)

Tanner, Väinö. *Finlands Vag 1939–1940* (Stockholm: Albert Bonniers Forlag, 1950)

Tanner, Väinö. *Suyomen tie rauhaan 1943–1944* (Helsinki: Kustannusosakayeyhtiö Tammi, 1952)

Tippelskirch, Kurt von. *Geschichte des Zweiten Weltkriges* (Bonn: Athenaeum, 1956)

Trevor-Roper, H. R., editor. *Hitler's Wartime Directives 1939–1945* (London: Pan Books Ltd., 1966)

Upton, Anthony F. *Finland in Crisis, 1940–1941 (A Study in Small-Power Politics* (Ithaca, N.Y.: Cornell University Press, 1965)

Vehviläinen, Olli. *Finland in the Second World War. Between Germany and Russia*. Translated by Gerard McAlester (New York: Palgrave Publishers Ltd, 2002)

Warlimont, Walter. *Inside Hitler's Headquarters 1939–45*. Translated from the German by R. H. Barry (Novato, California: Presidio Press, 1964)

Warner, Oliver. *Marshall Mannerheim and the Finns* (London: Weidenfeld & Nicolson, 1957)

Wegner, Brnd. *From Peace to War: Germany, Soviet Russia, and the World 1939–1941* (Providence, RI: Berghahn Books, 1997)

Westerlund, Göran. *Finland överlevde. Finlands Krig 1939–1945 i ord och bild* (Helsingfors: Schildts Förlags Ab, 2007)

Woodman, Richard. *Arctic Convoys* (London: John Murray Publishers Ltd., 1994)

Wuorinen, John H. *Finland and World War II, 1939–1940* (New York: The Ronald Press Company, 1948)

Ziemke, Earl F. *Stalingrad to Berlin: The German Defeat in the East* (Army Historical Series. New York: Barnes & Noble Books, 1996 [Original publication date 1968])

Ziemke, Earl F. *The German Northern Theater of Operations 1940–1945* (Washington, D.C.: Department of the Army (Pamphlet No. 20-271), 1959)

INDEX